WARFARE IN HISTORY

Women, Crusading and the Holy Land in Historical Narrative

WARFARE IN HISTORY

ISSN 1358-779X

Series editors
Matthew Bennett, Royal Military Academy, Sandhurst, UK
Anne Curry, University of Southampton, UK
Stephen Morillo, Wabash College, Crawfordsville, USA

This series aims to provide a wide-ranging and scholarly approach to military history, offering both individual studies of topics or wars, and volumes giving a selection of contemporary and later accounts of particular battles; its scope ranges from the early medieval to the early modern period.

New proposals for the series are welcomed; they should be sent to the publisher at the address below.

Boydell and Brewer Limited, PO Box 9, Woodbridge, Suffolk, IP12 3DF

Previously published titles in this series are listed at the back of this volume

Women, Crusading and the Holy Land in Historical Narrative

Natasha R. Hodgson

THE BOYDELL PRESS

First published 2007
The Boydell Press, Woodbridge
Paperback edition 2017

ISBN 978 1 84383 332 1 hardback
ISBN 978 1 78327 270 9 paperback

The Boydell Press is an imprint of Boydell & Brewer Ltd
PO Box 9, Woodbridge, Suffolk IP12 3DF, UK
and of Boydell & Brewer Inc.
668 Mt Hope Avenue, Rochester, NY 14620–2731, USA
website: www.boydellandbrewer.com

The publisher has no responsibility for the continued existence or accuracy
of URLs for external or third-party internet websites referred to in this book,
and does not guarantee that any content on such websites is,
or will remain, accurate or appropriate

A CIP catalogue record for this book is available
from the British Library

This publication is printed on acid-free paper

Contents

In memoriam Paul Ivison, a fellow enthusiast

General Editor's Preface

Crusading, like other kinds of warfare, might seem a 'boy's game', fit for play only between consenting males from a warrior culture. The role for a woman, at best, was surely restricted to shouting encouragement from the sidelines, much as they did at contemporary tournaments. While it is true that, in all but a tiny minority of cases, women did not get involved in actual fighting, save perhaps as victims, there were many opportunities for certain female individuals to influence events in ways not previously much considered by historians. In part this was because crusading was an activity engaged in by Latin Christian societies as a whole; so that young and old, male and female, secular and celibate, could all fulfil useful roles in the 'great project' of the capture and retention of the Holy Land, its associated territories and many lands far distant from the original destination of Jerusalem.

What Dr Hodgson makes clear in this volume is that women played a crucial role in the propagation of crusader ideas and in their practical support through the provision of finance and often direct military aid to operations. In the Kingdom of Jerusalem itself, from 1186–1228 (effectively covering the period of the loss of the city until its recovery by Emperor Frederick II) four queens dominated the politics of the time. It was inevitable that rulers and aristocratic women in general would play the greatest part in directing activities concerning crusading, although some of lesser rank could also be influential. Those who accompanied their husbands on crusade (and to a surprising degree those who went unaccompanied) were making the same statement as their men-folk about the need to find salvation through pilgrimage. Of course, they rarely if ever bore arms, that defining statement of the holy warrior, yet their presence was felt everywhere.

Despite their assumed *fragilitas sexus*, the female could be represented as powerful in many ways. Drawing strength from the image of the Virgin Mary as Queen of Heaven, women could, in their roles as mothers, daughters, wives and widows, demonstrate influence and command authority in supporting crusader activities. In the following pages there is a host of examples of women behaving in ways described by contemporary sources with both approbation and derogation, but they are never ignored. There was certainly misogyny in the era, and clerical authors can tend to attribute sexual motives for what in men might be seen as acts of policy. Eleanor of Aquitaine's alleged liaison with her uncle at Antioch is a famous (but not sole) example. The fear of sexual pollution was a continual strand throughout contemporary commentators' identification of why things went wrong with crusading plans or campaigns. Also, women who fell into enemy hands were assumed to have been defiled, and lost social value as a result.

On the whole, though, what leaps out of this study is the strength of character, determination and all-round effectiveness of many of the female characters studied. Marguerite of Provence, queen to Louis ix of France, actually gave birth to a son in Egypt while her husband was a prisoner of the Muslims, but still had the presence of mind to prevent his Italian auxiliaries from fleeing the city of Damietta in which she and they were besieged. Or consider Constance of Antioch, whose response to a domineering mother and an exploitative first husband was to choose a dashing young household knight – Reynald de Chatillon – when the chance arose. Then there was Countess Ida of Louvain who joined the crusade of 1101 in order to search for her husband who had gone missing in Asia Minor. Her own fate was an unhappy one, as she probably died in a Turkish ambush, although legend has it that she survived in the harem of her captor and bore the great Muslim leader Zengi.

This last example makes an important point about the nature of the sources, to which Dr Hodgson pays careful attention, valuing both *historia* and *fabula* for what they can tell us about perceptions as much as 'the truth' of events. Both had a didactic purpose, and neither should be read in entirely the same way as modern evidence-based history. Careful *Quellenkritik* helps us to understand the subtleties that often lie behind some seemingly obvious plot lines, yet does not hamper the narrative drive of the rattling good stories that entertain and educate as well as inform the reader. This work is a valuable contribution to crusader studies and should expand the outlook of anyone seeking to understand women and crusading.

MATTHEW BENNETT
Royal Military Academy Sandhurst

Acknowledgements

Tʜɪs study developed from my PhD thesis for the University of Hull in 2005, and I am deeply indebted to a large number of people for its completion. In particular I must thank Dr Julian Haseldine for stepping into the breach as supervisor and advising on Latin translations, and Professor John Palmer, who was very understanding as I balanced PhD completion with work as a research assistant on the Hull electronic Domesday project. I am indebted to my examiners, Professor Bernard Hamilton and Professor David Crouch, for their cogent advice and encouragement. Heads of Department John Bernasconi and Professor Glenn Burgess, as well as Dr Les Price, Dr Peter Grieder, Dr John Walker, Dr David Omissi, Professor Brian Levy, Alison Price and others, lent guidance and helped to provide me with enough teaching to keep the wolf from the door. In terms of my scholarship, I am deeply indebted to Dr Susan B. Edgington, who was kind enough to allow me to use her translation of Albert of Aachen before its publication and has provided guidance on many issues, including Kerbogha's mother. I have Kate Arnold to thank for her advice on Old French translations, and Dr Amanda Capern for suggesting useful reading lists and applying her expertise in early modern gender history to the parameters of this study.

I would like to thank others working in the field who have shared or inspired ideas during the course of this project, including Dr Tom Asbridge, Professor Marcus Bull, Dr Alan V. Murray, Professor Peter M. Holt, Sarah Lambert, and Dr Conor Kostick. Matthew Bennett's comments as series editor are much appreciated, as are the patience and support of Caroline Palmer, Vanda Andrews, Helen Barber and Anna Morton at Boydell. Many thanks also to Dr David Roberts for his efficiency in typesetting, and to cartographer Phillip Judge for the maps.

Colleagues in the History department at Royal Holloway, University of London have provided advice and a friendly ear during my postgraduate studies, including Professor Nigel Saul, Professor Justin Champion and Professor Caroline Barron. I am grateful to all the administrative staff in the History departments at Hull and Royal Holloway for their efficiency and organisation. I would also like to thank my students on the 'Women, Crusades and Frontier Societies' course that runs as part of the Crusader Studies MA at the University of London, and undergraduates on the part-time BA in Arts and Humanities at the University of Hull. Some of the latter had never even studied History before, but gave up their Wednesday evenings to learn about the

Crusades. Such people have continued to provide me with fresh perspectives on the source material and helped to hone my enthusiasm for the subject.

My family and friends, especially my mother and sisters, have rallied round on numerous occasions to aid with proof-reading and particularly thorny translations, or simply provided moral support, for which I am truly grateful. My greatest debt, however, lies with Professor Jonathan Phillips, whose excellent approach to teaching first captured my interest in this field, and who has supported me unstintingly throughout my academic career: initially in his official capacity as a supervisor at Royal Holloway, and later as a colleague and a friend. Without his guidance in collating source material and decisive approach to editing I would have been unable to render this study into its present form.

Abbreviations

AA	Albert of Aachen, *Historia Ierosolimitana*, ed. and trans. Susan B. Edgington (Oxford, 2007).
AA SS	*Acta Sanctorum quotquot toto orbe coluntur*, ed. Johannes Bollandus and G. Henschenius (Antwerp, 1643–); *Acta Sanctorum: Editio novissima*, ed. Joanne Carnandet *et al.* (Paris, 1863–).
Ambroise	*The History of the Holy War: Ambroise's Estoire de la Guerre Sainte*, ed. and trans. Marianne Ailes and Malcolm Barber, 2 vols (Woodbridge, 2003).
ATF	Alberic of Trois Fontaines, *Chronicon*, ed. Paul Scheffer-Boichorst, MGH SS 23 (1874), 631–950.
BB	Baudri of Bourgueil, *Historia Jerosolimitana*, in RHC *Occ.* 4 (Paris, 1879), 1–111.
CCCM	*Corpus Christianorum Continuatio Mediaevalis.*
DEL	*De expugnatione Lyxbonensi*, ed. and trans. Charles Wendell David (New York, 2001). 2nd edition with new foreword by Jonathan Phillips.
Eracles	*La Continuation de Guillaume de Tyr 1184–1197*, ed. Margaret R. Morgan (Paris, 1982).
Ernoul	*La Chronique d'Ernoul et de Bernard le Trésorier*, ed. Louis de Mas Latrie (Paris, 1871).
FC	Fulcher of Chartres, *Historia Hierosolymitana (1095–1127)*, ed. Heinrich Hagenmeyer (Heidelberg, 1913).
GF	*Anonymi Gesta Francorum*, ed. Heinrich Hagenmeyer (Heidelberg, 1890).
GN	Guibert of Nogent, *Dei Gesta Per Francos et cinq autres textes*, ed. Robert B. C. Huygens, CCCM 127A (Turnhout, 1996).
GP	Gunther of Pairis, *Hystoria Constantinopolitana*, ed. Peter Orth (Hildesheim, 1994).
GT	Ralph of Caen, *Gesta Tancredi*, in RHC *Occ.* 3 (Paris, 1866), 603–716.
GW 'De Principis'	Gerald of Wales, 'De Principis Instructione Liber', in John S. Brewer, James F. Dimock and George F. Warner eds. *Giraldi Cambrensis Opera*, 8 vols, RS 21, (1861–91), 8.1–139.
GW 'Itinerarium'	Gerald of Wales, 'Itinerarium Kambriae', in *Giraldi Cambrensis Opera*, 6.1–152.
Itinerarium	'Itinerarium Peregrinorum et Gesta Regis Ricardi', in William Stubbs ed. *Chronicles and Memorials of the Reign of Richard I*, 2 vols, RS 38 (London, 1864), vol. 1.
JMH	*Journal of Medieval History*
Joinville	John of Joinville, *Histoire de Saint Louis, Credo et lettre a Louis X*, ed. and trans. Natalis de Wailly (Paris, 1874).
Kinnamos	John Kinnamos, *The Deeds of John and Manuel Comnenus*, trans. Charles M. Brand (New York, 1976).
MGH *Scr. Rer. Ger.*	*Monumenta Germaniae Historica Scriptores Rerum Germanicarum* (Hanover, 1871–).

MGH SS   *Monumenta Germaniae Historica Scriptores* (Hanover, 1826–).

MP   Matthew Paris, *Chronica Majora*, ed. Henry Richard Luard, RS 57, 7 vols (London, 1872–83).

OD   Odo of Deuil, *De Profectione Ludovici VII in Orientem*, ed. and trans. Virginia Gingerick Berry (New York, 1948).

OV   Orderic Vitalis, *The Ecclesiastical History of Orderic Vitalis*, ed. and trans. Marjorie Chibnall, 6 vols (Oxford, 1969–80).

PT   Peter Tudebode, *Historia De Hierosolymitano Itinere*, ed. John Hugh and Laurita L. Hill (Paris, 1977).

RA   *Le Liber de Raymond D'Aguilers*, ed. John Hugh and Laurita L. Hill (Paris, 1969).

RC   Robert of Clari, *La Conquête de Constantinople*, ed. Philippe Lauer (Paris, 1924).

RHC   *Recueil des Historiens des Croisades.*

— Arm.   *Documents Armeniens*, 2 vols (Paris, 1906).

— Lois   *Assises de Jérusalem*, 2 vols (Paris, 1841–3).

— Occ.   *Occidentaux*, 5 vols (Paris, 1841–95).

— Or.   *Orientaux*, 5 vols (Paris, 1872–96).

RHGF   *Recueil des Historiens des Gaules et de la France*, 24 vols (Paris, 1869–1904).

Rothelin   *Continuation de Guillaume de Tyr de 1229 à 1261, dite du manuscript de Rothelin*, in RHC *Occ.* 2 (1859), 489–639.

RR   Robert of Rheims, *Historia Hierosolymitana*, in RHC *Occ.* 3 (Paris, 1864), 717–882.

RS   Rolls Series (London, 1858–91).

St Ambrose   St Ambrose, *De Viduis*, in Jacques-Paul Migne ed. *Patrologia Latina* 16 (Paris, 1880), cols 185–278.

SBO   *Sancti Bernardi Opera*, ed. Jean Leclercq and Henri Marie Rochais, 8 vols (Rome, 1955–77).

TF   Thomas of Froidmont, *Hodoeporicon et pericula Margarite Iherosolimitane*, in Paul Gerhard Schmidt, '"Peregrinatio Periculosa." Thomas von Friedmont über die Jerusalemfahrten seiner Schwester Margareta', 472–85, in Justus Stache, Wolfgang Maaz and Fritz Wagner eds *Kontinuität und Wandel. Lateinische Poesie von Naevius bis Baudelaire. Franco Munari zum 65. Geburtstag* (Hildesheim, 1986), 461–85.

Villehardouin   Geoffrey of Villehardouin, *La Conquête de Constantinople*, ed. and trans. Edmond Faral, 2 vols (Paris, 1938)

WC   Walter the Chancellor, *Bella Antiochena*, ed. Heinrich Hagenmeyer (Innsbruck, 1896).

WM   William of Malmesbury, *Gesta Regum Anglorum*, ed. and trans. Roger A. B. Mynors, completed by Rodney M. Thompson and Michael Winterbottom, 2 vols (Oxford, 1998–9).

WN   William of Newburgh, 'Historia Rerum Anglicarum', in Richard Howlett ed. *Chronicles of the reigns of Stephen, Henry II and Richard I*, 4 vols, RS 82 (London, 1884), vols 1–2.

WT   William of Tyre, *Chronicon*, ed. Robert B. C. Huygens, 2 vols (Turnhout, 1986).

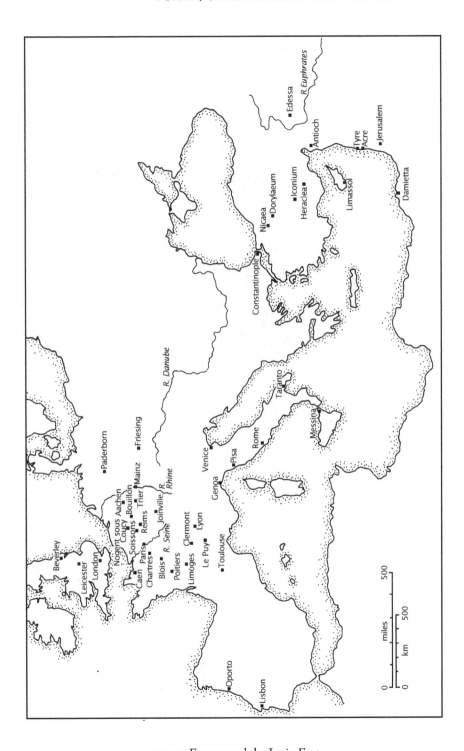

MAP I Europe and the Latin East

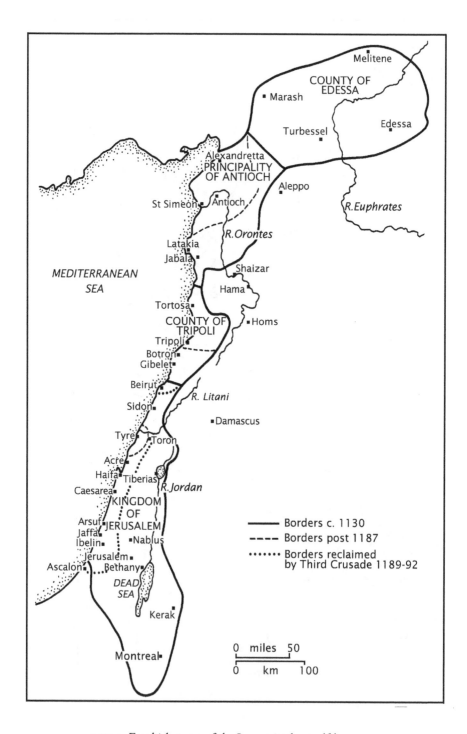

MAP 2 Frankish states of the Levant in the twelfth century

TABLE I Relationships between named female participants of the early crusades and settlers up to *c.* 1120

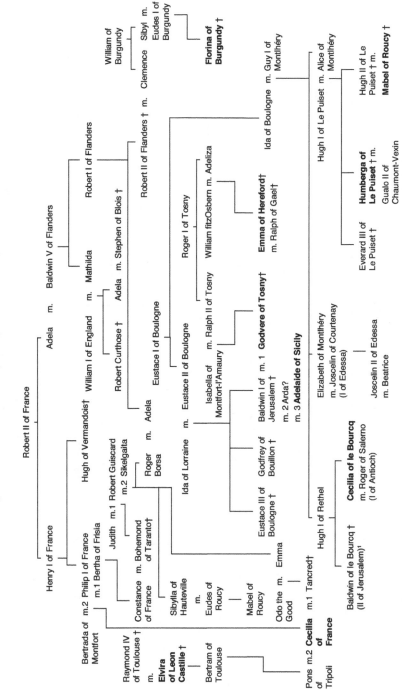

This is not a table of all named early female crusaders, but shows the close kinship networks between some of their families. Persons marked † were recorded as having taken part in a major expedition. **Bold type** indicates named women, including those known to have settled in the East, without taking part in a major expedition. Two female First Crusaders missing from this table are Hadvide of Chiny, and Emeline of Bouillon.

TABLE 2 Rulers of Jerusalem and the settler states, 1118–1205 (Rulers of the kingdom of Jerusalem are shown in **bold**.)

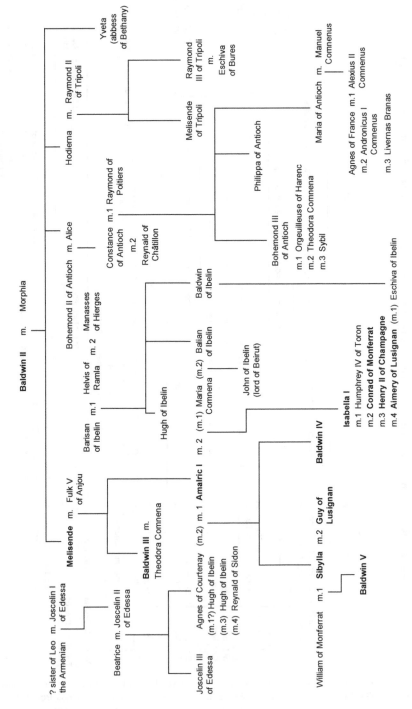

TABLE 3 Rulers of Jerusalem and the settler states, 1205–91 (Rulers of the kingdom of Jerusalem are shown in **bold**.)

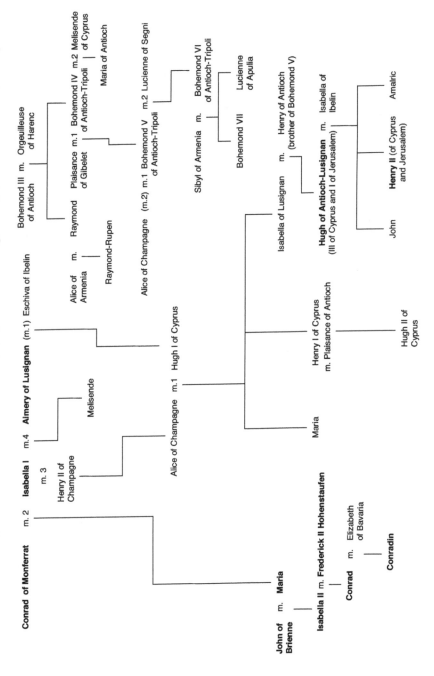

Introduction

IN the spring of 1188, Gerald of Wales accompanied Archbishop Baldwin of Canterbury on a preaching tour to promote the Third Crusade. At Abergavenny, Baldwin encountered a nobleman called Arthenus, who, wavering over his decision to take the cross, wished to consult his friends first. The archbishop asked if he wanted the guidance of his wife as well. Arthenus, shamed, took up the cross immediately, saying: 'This is man's work we are undertaking, the advice of a woman is not required.'[1]

The perception of crusading as 'man's work' has lingered in historical tradition. Throughout successive generations of scholarly interest, the crusades have stayed firmly entrenched within the confines of military and religious history – areas that were dominated by men for the majority of recorded memory. Later historians were largely content to emulate their medieval counterparts by giving negligible attention to the role that women played in the crusade movement.[2] In the second half of the twentieth century, however, scholarship began to shift away from the military exploits of crusaders and the politics of Holy War to an increasingly panoramic view of the impact that crusading had on medieval society.[3] This has paved the way for new studies about the roles played by women on specific crusades, and those who lived in settler

---

[1] GW 'Itinerarium', 48–9. Edbury asserts that Baldwin's motive in asking the question may have been genuine, but Gerald's approval of Arthenus' response is apparent. See Peter W. Edbury, 'Preaching the Crusade in Wales', in A. Haverkamp and H. Vollrath eds *England and Germany in the High Middle Ages* (Oxford, 1996), 227–8.

[2] The first book to focus exclusively on women and crusading appeared in the mid-nineteenth century, Celestina Angenette Bloss, *Heroines of the Crusades* (Iowa, 1853), and was undoubtedly a product of its time. She wrote about high-profile noblewomen of the period: Adela of Blois, Eleanor of Aquitaine, Berengaria of Navarre, Isabella of Angoulême, Violante (Isabella II) of Jerusalem and Eleanor of Castille. Bloss interspersed their life-stories with narratives of eight major crusade expeditions. The work combines highly romanticised fictional episodes and fairly tortuous descriptive scenes with flowery dialogue. It is a testament to current interest in the subject that her work has recently been reprinted by the Michigan Historical Reprint Series (2005). My thanks to Deborah Gerish for bringing this work to my attention (see below, n. 7).

[3] For detailed assessments of the shifts in historical approaches to crusading, see Giles Constable, 'The Historiography of the Crusades', in Angeliki E. Laiou and Roy Parvitz Mottahedeh eds *The Crusades from the Perspective of Byzantium and the Muslim World* (Washington, 2001), 1–22; Christopher Tyerman, *The Invention of the Crusades* (London, 1998), 99–126; Jonathan Riley-Smith, 'The Crusading Movement and Historians', in idem ed. *The Oxford Illustrated History of the Crusades* (Oxford, 1995), 1–12. For an assessment of crusade historiography from the eighteenth to the early

societies of the Latin East, Iberia or the Baltic.[4] Riley-Smith has established the importance of certain noblewomen in recruitment and finance for the early crusades, and has explored the impact that these expeditions had on their lives.[5] Canonical views on women, crusading and the regulation of sexuality have been investigated by Purcell and Brundage.[6] More recent contributions include a collection of essays entitled *Gendering the Crusades*, and historiographical overviews of women, gender and the crusade movement from Maier and Gerish.[7]

twentieth century see Elizabeth Siberry, *The New Crusaders: Images of the Crusades in the Nineteenth and Early Twentieth Centuries* (Aldershot, 2000), 1–38.

[4] Articles about women's activities on specific crusade expeditions include Walter Porges, 'The Clergy, the Poor and the Non-combatants on the First Crusade', *Speculum* 21 (1946), 1–23; James A. Brundage, 'Prostitution, Miscegenation and Sexual Purity in the First Crusade', in Peter Edbury ed. *Crusade and Settlement* (Cardiff, 1985), 57–65; Conor Kostick, 'Women and the First Crusade', in C. Meek and C. Lawless eds *Studies on Medieval and Early Modern Women*, vol. 3 (Dublin, 2005), 57–68; Helen Nicholson, 'Women on the Third Crusade', *JMH* 23 (1997), 335–49; James M. Powell, 'The Role of Women on the Fifth Crusade', in Benjamin Z. Kedar ed. *The Horns of Hattin* (Jerusalem, 1992), 294–301; and B. Z. Kedar, 'The Passenger List of a Crusader Ship, 1250: Towards the Popular Element on the Seventh Crusade', *Studi Medievali*, Series 3 (1972), 269–79. For general surveys of noblewomen in the Latin East, see Bernard Hamilton, 'Women in the Crusader States: The Queens of Jerusalem (1100–1190)', in Derek Baker ed. *Medieval Women* (Oxford, 1978), 143–74. See also Sarah Lambert, 'Queen or Consort: Rulership and Politics in the Latin East 1118–1228', in Anne Duggan ed. *Queens and Queenship in Medieval Europe* (Woodbridge, 1997), 153–69. For Iberia, see Heath Dillard, *Daughters of the Reconquest* (Cambridge, 1989), and for the Baltic, see Rasa Mazeika, '"Nowhere was the Fragility of their Sex Apparent": Women Warriors in the Baltic Crusade Chronicles', in Alan V. Murray ed. *From Clermont to Jerusalem: The Crusades and Crusader Societies 1095–1500* (Turnhout, 1998), 229–48, and Megan McLaughlin, 'The Woman Warrior; Gender, Warfare and Society in Medieval Europe', *Women's Studies* 17 (1990), 193–209.

[5] Jonathan Riley-Smith, *The First Crusaders 1095–1131* (Cambridge, 1997); 'Families, Crusades and Settlement in the Latin East 1102–1131', in Hans E. Mayer ed. *Die Kreuzfahrerstaaten als multikulturel Gesellschaft* (Munich, 1997), 1–12, and 'Family Traditions and Participation in the Second Crusade', in Michael Gervers ed. *The Second Crusade and the Cistercians* (New York, 1992), 101–8.

[6] Maureen Purcell, 'Women Crusaders, a Temporary Canonical Aberration?', in Leighton O. Frappell ed. *Principalities, Power and Estates: Studies in Medieval and Early Modern Government and Society* (Adelaide, 1979), 57–67. James A. Brundage, 'The Crusader's Wife; a Canonistic Quandary', *Studia Gratiana* 12 (1967), 425–41; 'The Crusader's Wife Revisited', *Studia Gratiana* 14 (1967), 243–51; 'Marriage Law in the Latin Kingdom of Jerusalem', in Benjamin Z. Kedar, Hans E. Mayer and Raymond C. Smail eds *Outremer: Studies in the History of the Crusading Kingdom of Jerusalem Presented to Joshua Prawer* (Jerusalem, 1982), 258–71, and 'Prostitution, Miscegenation and Sexual Purity', 57–65.

[7] Susan B. Edgington and Sarah Lambert eds *Gendering the Crusades* (Cardiff, 2001) is a collection of essays on gender-related themes. Maier's article focuses on Margaret of Beverley and Catherine of Siena. Christoph T. Maier, 'The Roles of Women in the Crusade Movement: A Survey', *JMH* 30 (2004), 61–82. Gerish's article gives an

After years of such piecemeal treatment, two monographs on the subject of women and crusading, *Frauen auf Kreuzzügen* and *Deus et virum suum diligens*, were published in Germany in 2003.[8] These studies hail from a more traditional school of 'women's history' than my own, focusing on cataloguing and defining female crusaders and their activities while on crusade.[9] However, a comprehensive assessment of attitudes towards women in the context of historical writing about crusading and the Latin East has not yet been attempted – a *lacuna* that this study seeks to fill.

During the period in which crusading was at its height, writing was dominated by a predominantly male and ecclesiastical hierarchy that reflected the views of a patriarchal social system. Accordingly, perceptions of women in medieval histories were shaped by gendered stereotypes, but these could encompass both moderate and extreme views. Crusade narratives in particular have been criticised for their negative attitude towards the female sex. Riley-Smith has observed that 'one of the most clear and straightforward messages of the sources for crusading' was that 'women were inhibitors', although he agrees that in practice some women probably encouraged the crusade effort.[10] The logistical problems posed by non-combatants on crusade were a major concern, and women became the specific focus of misogynistic fears about sexual activity and

excellent outline of how gender theory can be applied to crusader studies, and a useful bibliography. Deborah Gerish, 'Gender Theory', in Helen Nicholson ed. *Palgrave Advances in the Crusades* (Basingstoke, 2005), 130–47.

8   Sabine Geldsetzer, *Frauen auf Kreuzzügen* (Darmstadt, 2003); Christine Dernbecher, '*Deus et virum suum diligens.*' *Zur rolle und Bedeutung der Frau im Umfeld der Kreuzzüge* (St Ingbert, 2003).

9   These works were published several years after I embarked upon this course of study, but fortunately they overlap only a little with my own approach, especially as neither deals specifically with women in the settler society of the Latin East. Both focus on traditional, but important, questions, such as motivation, activities on crusade and canonical views about women's participation, and retain a somewhat 'pioneering' approach. As the first monographs to be published on this subject, they are understandably governed by the desire to prove that women were present and performed important roles in relation to crusading. Perhaps this explains Dernbecher's rather uncritical approach to the sources, although she also demonstrates gaps in some of the recent historiography. Her study begins by outlining the tradition of pilgrimage to the Holy Land, and the role of women who stayed at home, before going on to question the role of women in crusade armies, women warriors, problems associated with sexual activity and women in captivity. Geldsetzer's work takes a more clearly defined scholarly approach, incorporating a wide range of sources. She discusses the definition of female crusaders in detail and focuses on the practicalities of their crusade journeys. She also provides a particularly well-researched and useful referenced appendix containing brief biographies of women linked to crusading and pilgrimage to the East, including those who fulfilled or commuted vows, or whose status as crusaders was uncertain.

10   Giles Constable, 'The Financing of the Crusades in the Twelfth Century', in Kedar *et al.*, *Outremer*, 82; Riley-Smith, *First Crusaders*, 97–8.

the spiritual purity of crusaders. Other stories about women contained within crusade histories are often consigned to the realm of the fictional: treated as 'camp gossip' and 'comic episodes' included for decoration, amusement or admonition about the consequences of sin, but without serious historical value. This study contends, however, that while authors displayed inevitable prejudices based on gender and reflected some of the canonical concerns about women and crusading, their perceptions of women were not consistently negative. In fact they espoused a wide spectrum of views influenced by factors other than sex. Crusading may have been viewed as an unequivocally masculine enterprise, but certain female crusaders and women in settler societies received praise for their character and activities – some even exemplified the crusading ideal – a contradiction that merits scholarly attention.

To a large extent, perceptions about women were governed by the symbiotic relationship between authorship and audience in the world of medieval literary patronage. Crusading and events in the Latin East exerted a strong attraction over ecclesiastical authors and patrons, some of whom exhibited ascetic or puritanical tendencies, but histories were also written for, about, and in some cases by, the lay nobility who were the driving force behind crusading armies. Narratives about crusading and the Latin East were circulated in the courts to encourage nobles and knights to take the cross, providing didactic examples for prospective *crucesignati* and influencing opinions about the activities and morality of both crusaders and settlers. Women also formed a part of this audience, and where female characters appeared in narratives, they too represented a spectrum of models for behaviour according to gender, social status and character. To present a consistently negative portrayal of women was impossible because of the number of important aristocratic women who took the cross, supported crusaders financially, cemented political marriage alliances central to crusading diplomacy, and provided literary patronage. It is the complex links between crusade narratives and the nobility – crusade as a noble pursuit – which help to explain discrepancies between 'traditional' canonical views about women and crusading, and the range of views found in narrative histories.[11]

This argument cannot be sufficiently addressed by recreating the experience of women's participation (or non-participation) in crusading and settlement. In the first place, the task of defining, cataloguing, and describing the activities of recorded female crusaders has already been undertaken with great efficiency by Geldsetzer.[12] In the second, other types of source material such as crusade charters and legal documents can yield profoundly useful evidence to the historian of women, but they tend to focus on arrangements for the families of crusaders that remained in the West or the commutation of vows,

---

[11] See Natasha Hodgson, 'Nobility, Women and Historical Narratives of the Crusades and the Latin East', *Al-Masaq: Islam and the Medieval Mediterranean* 17 (2005), 61–85.

[12] Geldsetzer, *Frauen*.

compounding perceptions of crusading as a male activity.[13] In addition, such sources did not enjoy the same circulation and influence as the histories which helped to shape and define ideas about women's roles in crusading and settlement. A definitive study on women in the Latin East has yet to be produced,[14] but as the majority of named individuals only featured as dynastic linchpins in the historical explanation of political relationships, many examples yield but scant evidence of attitudes towards them beyond emphasising their family role. This study will focus instead on *perceptions* of women in historical narratives in order to use these sources to their best advantage. Such an approach allows stories about women which have been dismissed as largely fictional to produce significant historical evidence, as well as those which can be corroborated with other types of source. In this respect, narratives of crusading and the settler society of the Latin East have not yet been exploited to their full potential as a source for medieval women.

Part I of this study will establish how the history of crusading developed within the context of contemporary literature, and how changing perceptions about gender, nobility and morality were reflected in written histories. The first chapter provides a survey of traditional and contemporary influences on the writing of history, the role of gender and family relationships in medieval texts, the cultural impact of crusading, and its development as a theme within a variety of medieval literary genres. The second chapter gives an overview of authorship and how this may have affected perceptions of women. The third assesses the particular problems posed by women to the historians of crusading and the Latin East, taking into account the role of women as audience, ideas about family and social status, and their role as crusaders and settlers. Part II presents the main body of research in four further chapters focusing on the portrayal of women as daughters, wives, mothers and widows, 'life-cycle stages'

---

[13] There is undoubtedly a great deal of work to be done on charters from the West in examining the impact of crusading on women in western society, but this would be beyond the scope of the current study. Several charters even pertain to women who did accompany their husbands on crusade, such as the charter of returned crusaders Dodo of Cons-la-Grandville and his wife, Hadvide of Chiny – see 112 below. For general overviews on charters as a source for crusading, see Giles Constable, 'Medieval Charters as a Source for the History of the Crusades', in *Crusade and Settlement*, 73–89, and Corliss Konwiser Slack, *Crusade Charters 1138–1270* (Tempe, 2001).

[14] The majority of current scholarship focuses on high-profile women, such as the work of Hamilton and Lambert on the queens of Jerusalem cited above (n. 4). For articles on specific individuals, see Hans E. Mayer, 'Studies in the History of Queen Melisende of Jerusalem', *Dumbarton Oaks Papers* 26 (1972), 93–182; Bernard Hamilton, 'The Titular Nobility of the Latin East: The Case of Agnes of Courtenay', *Crusade and Settlement*, 197–203; and Thomas S. Asbridge, 'Alice of Antioch: A Case Study of Female Power in the Twelfth Century', in Marcus Bull and Norman Housley eds *The Experience of Crusading: Western Approaches* (Cambridge, 2003), 1.29–47.

that represented the focal positions held by women in the family.[15] After identifying key attributes and social responsibilities associated with each role, the
narrative source material has been analysed in the context of crusading and settlement, establishing how crusade historians employed contemporary perceptions about women to inform, instruct, motivate, and relate to their audiences.

[15] See 12–15 below.

· Part I ·

◆ 1 ◆

Literary Context

THIS study is based upon historical narratives of the crusades and the Latin East and therefore it is necessary to provide a 'working definition' of what these entail. As well as narratives, a wide variety of relevant charters, letters and legal records survive from Europe and the Levant. Ecclesiastical records, Greek, Syriac, Hebrew and Arabic sources, and considerable architectural and archaeological data are also available to the historian of crusade and settlement. These forms of evidence provide a great wealth of historical data, but narratives provide a 'precise framework' which is perhaps better suited to 'types of history which are less event-centred, such as the study of social change, thought, and cultural patterns'.[1] It would be hard to postulate any coherent picture of the social and cultural impact of crusading without those authors who chose to interpret the events of crusade and settlement in a narrative format for posterity. The umbrella term 'crusade narratives', however, encompasses texts with divergent political, geographical and literary influences which varied considerably over the 200-year period in which crusading was at its height. Allowing for generic overlap and the pitfalls of categorisation, they can be roughly divided into chronicles, *gesta*, *historiae*, genealogies, annals and hagiographical works. Histories were also written in epistolary form in order to impart news of crusading events, such as the Lisbon Letter, *De expugnatione Lyxbonensi*, or the letters of Stephen of Blois to his wife, Adela.[2]

Not all crusade narratives are of sufficient length to provide detailed information on women, and this study is predominantly based on narratives in Latin and Old French that stand apart as specific *gestae* or *historiae*, often limited to specific expeditions.[3] Monastic chronicles, which usually had a wider or 'universal' historical focus, are included where they provide original material. These sources also circulated information about settler society in the Levant, but by far the most detailed in this respect were William of Tyre and his continuators.

---

[1] Marcus Bull, *The Miracles of Our Lady of Rocamadour* (Woodbridge, 1999), 22.

[2] For a discussion and translation of the Lisbon Letter, see Susan B. Edgington, 'Albert of Aachen, St. Bernard and the Second Crusade', in Jonathan Phillips and Martin Hoch eds *The Second Crusade: Scope and Consequences* (Manchester, 2001), 54–70. Recent scholarship suggests DEL was 'more than a simple report'. DEL, xx–xi. For Stephen's letters, see Heinrich Hagenmeyer, *Die Kreuzzugsbriefe aus den Jahren 1088– 1100* (Innsbruck, 1901), 138–40 and 149–52.

[3] As Rubenstein points out, these were a relatively new phenomenon which owed much to the novelty of the First Crusade as an 'historic' event. Jay Rubenstein, 'What is the *Gesta Francorum*, and who was Peter Tudebode?', *Revue Mabillon* 16 (2005), 180–1.

Essentially, histories written from a Latin Christian perspective form the basis of this study, in order to offer a balanced comparison. Narratives by Christians of Greek or Syrian origin provide additional historical evidence, but cultural, political and doctrinal differences, as well as alternative literary models, dictate that their views on women may depart too significantly from a Latin viewpoint to be of benefit.[4] This is also the case for Muslim sources. Although work by Dillard and Mazeika has shown that there is future scope for a comparison with Iberia and the Baltic, this study has been largely confined to crusading and settlement in the Latin East.[5] In terms of chronological restraints, the sources roughly correspond to the period in which Latin society survived in that area.

I am aware of the chronological and geographical restrictions of such an approach: reviewers have, in recent years, criticised the failure of studies on women to diversify from the traditional time-limits and source material associated with crusading to the Latin East.[6] There is undoubtedly scope for future scholarship outside these boundaries, but for the purposes of this study I would refute such a criticism on the following grounds. First, the theoretical approach employed has yielded considerable amounts of information from the study of traditional sources about crusading to the Holy Land: far more, in fact, than I initially expected. As Gerish herself asserts, 'little has been done in the area of gender studies, nor has gender theory made much of an impact', and with a broader definition of crusade studies, research topics 'grow exponentially in number and shape'.[7] However, I cannot lay claim to a complete 'gendering' of these sources – such a task would involve addressing the subject of masculinity and crusading, on which there is sufficient evidence for another monograph at least. A limitation to twelfth- and thirteenth-century narratives may be 'self-imposed', but they provide the most comprehensive range of perceptions about the theory and practice of crusading from both lay and ecclesiastical perspectives. As a *corpus* of texts they have not been treated satisfactorily so far, and it is not sufficient to talk in terms of 'positive' and 'negative' attitudes towards 'women' as a group, when so many other categories of description need to be investigated. Similarly the chronological restraints of this study are governed by its focus on the image of crusaders and settlers of the Levant as they were

4   Unfortunately this means that the only female historian to provide a perspective on the crusades, Anna Comnena, cannot be given detailed consideration in this study.

5   See Introduction, n. 3.

6   Marcus Bull's review of *Gendering the Crusades* in the *English Historical Review* (2004) underlined the need for further studies outside the twelfth and thirteenth centuries. Maier's criticisms of the same study, *Crusades* 3 (2003), and the work of Geldsetzer and Dernbecher, *Crusades* 5 (2006), are also based on chronological constraints and focus on crusading to the Holy Land. Additionally, Gerish criticises these limits. Gerish, 'Gender Theory', 138.

7   Gerish, 'Gender Theory', 138, 140.

disseminated into western European culture. Histories of crusading continued to enjoy popularity after this period, but without the focus provided by a Latin presence in the Holy Land they were subsumed into family histories and popular literature, or moulded to fit the political and social situation *du jour*. Finally, it is these very narratives which have continued to shape the opinions of historians; thus a 'back to basics' approach, incorporating a re-reading of the most influential texts, must be adopted before the study of gender and crusading can progress further.

Authority and Tradition in Historical Writing

A DISCUSSION of 'truth' in historical narrative may help to define the *corpus* of texts used in this study, and to explain my focus on perceptions rather than the reality of women's experience. The desire to record the exploits of crusaders was not confined to historical writing alone; legends sprang up about the heroes of crusade, engendering *chansons de geste* and romances that blurred the line between *historia* and *fabula*. The authors of medieval historical narratives often tried to set themselves apart from these other literary traditions, distinguishing themselves as imparting the 'truth' of events. However, the nature of narrative in itself demands that historians select evidence according to personal interest, recounting stories and anecdotes, and embellishing their text with descriptive detail in order to appeal to their audience. It is often within these anecdotes, descriptions and dialogue, reconstructed by the imaginative skills of the medieval historian, that women are given greater characterisation.

Historical narrative, in a variety of forms, has dominated traditions whereby one generation passes on knowledge to the next throughout human experience. Its pitfalls as a vehicle for accurate historical explanation are well known. In the first half of the twentieth century the *Annales* school mistrusted narrative as empiricist or 'reconstructionist', and began to apply more general sociological laws and theories to historical evidence in areas such as class and race. Postmodernists addressed the inadequacies of narrative and language itself as a medium for conveying historical 'truth'; thus the skill of the historian lay in surmising what probably happened, complementing narrative sources (which were seen to be polluted by contemporary and ideological language) with statistical information where possible.[8] Others have questioned whether historical narrative is entirely the creation of the historian, or whether events themselves are the driving force behind the historian's emplotment, with narrative filling in the gaps.[9]

---

[8] See Gabrielle Spiegel, *The Past as Text* (London, 1997), 3–28.

[9] For two different views, see Hayden White, *The Content of the Form: Narrative Discourse and Historical Representation* (Baltimore, 1987), 67–8, and David Carr, 'Narrative and the Real World: An Argument for Continuity', *History and Theory* 25 (1986), 117–31.

It is not my intention to embark on a lengthy discussion of the metaphysical intricacies of knowable reality, but it is necessary to consider the tools available for studying women in narrative history. A post-structuralist approach towards individual texts can be used to assess gendered language, and to examine an author's conscious or unconscious use of narrative to impart opinions, but this can also have a negative impact on the study of women. Hoff argues that post-structuralism 'casts into doubt stable meanings and sees language as so slippery that it compromises historians' ability to identify facts and chronological narratives', reducing the experience of women to subjective stories.[10] Mosher Stuard lauds the early historians of medieval women who were 'more at home with digging for the rich truffles of solid scholarship than airy parachuting after theory', but recognises that new theoretical approaches were and still are necessary to meet the 'challenge' of women's history.[11] This study is based on a group of texts which vary in terms of perspective, but are linked by historical events relating to crusading and the Latin East; thus contextual analysis is essential. To an extent, the historian can read from what is 'unseen' or 'unheard', but must at the same time consider what is deliberately intended. Military successes and failures, ecclesiastical and secular politics, and even external factors such as natural disasters were crucial in stimulating and shaping the course of historical narratives, and women had a limited role in such historical events. Medieval authors also perceived History to be essentially didactic in purpose. These factors suggest a more deliberate intervention by the historian when women were included in their narratives, but such interventions were invariably governed by contemporary conventions about sex, status and family.

To the medieval author, the guidelines for producing reliable history were set down by Isidore of Seville in his *Etymologiae*. It was truth, *veritas*, that was the ultimate element distinguishing *historia* from *fabula*, and the eyewitness source was unimpeachable when it came to providing historical truth in the narration of events.[12] Authors also drew authority and inspiration from classical sources, which were acceptable despite their pagan origins as long as they purported to be historical (and preferably eyewitness-based). The Bible and historical works of early Church Fathers such as Eusebius of Caesarea, Isidore and St Augustine were considered to be respectable models. Classical poetry was corrupt and to be avoided,[13] but poets such as Horace, Virgil

---

[10] Joan Hoff, 'Gender as a Post-modern Category of Paralysis', *Women's Historical Review* 3 (1994), 150.

[11] Susan Mosher Stuard, 'The Chase after Theory: Considering Medieval Women', *Gender and History* 4 (1992), 143.

[12] Jeanette M. A. Beer, *Narrative Conventions of Truth in the Middle Ages* (Geneva, 1981), 10–11. See also Peter Damien-Grint, *The New Historians of the Twelfth Century Renaissance* (Woodbridge, 1999), 68–72. See Chapter 2, *passim*.

[13] Beer, *Narrative Conventions*, 10–11.

and Ovid influenced many medieval historians, especially in their portrayal of women.[14]

The unquestioning acceptance of traditional Christian sources and eye-witness authority by medieval historians has led to accusations that they were credulous and plagiarist, but this was not necessarily the case: they were writing within a tradition which held its own criteria for judging the value of historical sources. Plagiarism is a modern concept and was an accepted part of medieval historical writing.[15] The proliferation of anonymous histories and continuations of other works demonstrates that events, and the *veritas* provided by eyewitness evidence, were usually considered more significant than the author's perspective or opinion. The purpose of history was fundamentally didactic, and the focus lay upon the lessons that it could impart, rather than the credentials of the teacher. William of Malmesbury asserted that History 'adds flavour to moral instruction by imparting a pleasurable knowledge of past events, spurring the reader by the accumulation of examples to follow the good and shun the bad'.[16] Perceptions of women in medieval histories were usually governed by classical and religious imagery, but these could be employed in a multiplicity of ways. As Stafford writes, the 'palette of images' available to describe women was mostly biblical and ranged from Mary to Jezebel, but their meanings could be 'contradictory and ambiguous' and 'powerful women became images in themselves, dynastic saints – and sinners'.[17]

Gender, Medieval Sources and 'Life-Cycle Stages'

MEDIEVAL gender history has expanded rapidly in recent years, and is far removed from the few essays devoted to medieval women that were produced by Eileen Power in the early twentieth century.[18] Initially historians of medieval women focused on high-profile figures: the queens, noblewomen, abbesses and religious women considered important enough to feature in chronicles, charters and saints' lives. Where possible, they referred to works of female authors, but these are scant indeed for the period in which crusading was at its height. During the twelfth century, the elusive lay author Marie of

---

[14] For examples, see 146–7 and 231 below.

[15] Helen J. Nicholson, *Chronicle of the Third Crusade: A Translation of the Itinerarium Peregrinorum et Gesta Regis Ricardi* (Aldershot, 1997), 13.

[16] WM, I.151. William's significance as a historian of the crusades has recently been revised in the new edition of Rodney Thompson, *William of Malmesbury* (Woodbridge, 2003), 178–89.

[17] Pauline Stafford, 'The Portrayal of Royal Women in England, Mid-Tenth to Mid-Twelfth Centuries', in John Carmi Parsons ed. *Medieval Queenship* (Stroud, 1994), 144.

[18] See Eileen Power, *Medieval Women*, ed. Michael M. Postan (Cambridge, 1975).

France wrote her celebrated *fabliaux* and *lais*,[19] but evidence of historical writing in western Europe is limited to the tenth-century *Gesta Ottonis* by Hrotsvit of Gandesheim.[20] Some personal letters survive, but the correspondence of women was less often preserved than that of the men with whom they communicated. Of several letters that Baudri of Bourgueil wrote to women at the convent of Le Ronceray at Angers, only one reply survives.[21] Where evidence permits, recent works have developed interdisciplinary approaches and broadened their field of research to explore a combination of legal records, patronage, coins and seals, for significant data about women.[22] Within the temporal scope of this study, written examples from a female perspective are simply too few to assess the social construct of gender effectively, and male-authored works must still supply the majority of the information.

Historical chronicles have often been mistrusted as a source for women. Jewell asserts that they 'were mainly the product of religious houses, and of authors who had little personal experience of women and much exposure to anti-feminist texts'.[23] For this reason, scholarship on the social construct of gender has often focused upon the role of women in fictional works, usually the vernacular prose and poetry that developed around the noble courts. The assumption is that such works provide insight into more genuine 'secular' attitudes, bypassing the 'misogyny' of the ecclesiastics.[24] However, the pro-masculine ideology of the nobility combined with the all-pervading moral influence of medieval Christianity to infiltrate both ecclesiastical and lay literature. Both provided guidelines for the 'good' and 'bad' behaviour of men and women that were inter-related, and sometimes complementary. Crusade narratives were particularly representative of this overlap between spiritual and lay values, as they espoused both ecclesiastical and chivalric ideals: to an extent, they can be used to interlink the literary circles of church and court.

I use the term 'interlink' because crusade histories came in a broad range

---

19 Marie de France, *Fables*, ed. and trans. Harriet Spiegel (Toronto, 1987), and Marie de France, *Lais*, ed. Alfred Ewert (Oxford, 1944).

20 She also wrote saints lives, plays and poetry. See *Hrotsvithae Opera*, ed. Helene Homeyer (Paderborn, 1970).

21 *Les œuvres poétiques de Baudri de Bourgueil*, ed. Phyllis Abrahams (Paris, 1926), 344–9. See Peter Dronke, *Medieval Latin and the Rise of the European Love Lyric*, 2 vols (Oxford, 1968), 1.217.

22 For example, Susan M. Johns, *Noblewomen, Aristocracy and Power in the Twelfth Century Anglo-Norman Realm* (Manchester, 2003).

23 Helen Jewell, *Women in Medieval England* (Manchester, 1996), 130.

24 For example, Penny Schine Gold bases her assessment of 'secular image' almost entirely on the portrayal of women in *chansons de geste* and romances, although she expresses some useful methodological concerns about using such literature for historical purposes. Penny Schine Gold, *The Lady and the Virgin: Image, Attitude and Experience in Twelfth Century France* (Chicago, 1985), 1–42.

of narrative forms and cannot be separated easily into their own 'genre'; nor did their authors as a group hold tangibly different views about women compared to other medieval writers. In modern terms all could be seen to display 'misogynistic' attitudes, but such strong definitions are unhelpful when trying to extract material from a medieval source.[25] It is important to differentiate between those authors who expressly vilified women, and those who made common assumptions based on gender stereotypes, but showed compassion, awareness of feminine concerns, and sometimes even admiration: those whom Blamires calls 'profeminine'.[26] Pope Urban's appeal for the First Crusade came at the heels of eleventh-century reform, coinciding with McNamara's 'Herrenfrage', when 'the newly celibate clerical hierarchy reshaped the gender system to ensure male domination of the new public sphere'.[27] This may have promoted an increase in misogynistic literature during the period in which crusading was at its height, but 'profeminine' literature developed in parallel, engendering a polarisation of views rather than resulting in the increasing debasement of women in medieval writing.[28]

Furthermore, gender was not the only category of analysis for women in medieval thought. Both men and women were perceived to act in accordance with the physical and psychological traits associated with their gender, but social status, lineage, wealth, and the comparative virtues of noble birth and noble character were also fundamental to the image of both sexes. For women, sexual status was of key importance: legitimate wives and chaste women stood in stark contrast to prostitutes and concubines. Most often, women were described in relation to men: as daughters, wives, mothers, widows, aunts, sisters, and even more distant kin, in a manner consistent with male-oriented History. In patriarchal society, the husband–wife link was supposed to take precedence over the parental bond, though in practice the families of both partners retained a shared interest in their marriage. Accordingly many women were described as wives, but their own lineage was often mentioned in place of a name; thus 'x married the daughter of y' where x and y are both men was a common literary formula. The importance of family roles in understanding the power and activity of medieval women was first outlined by McNamara and Wemple

---

[25] R. Howard Bloch, *Medieval Misogyny and the Invention of Western Romantic Love* (Chicago, 1991), 6.

[26] Alcuin Blamires, *The Case for Women in Medieval Culture* (Oxford, 1997), 12.

[27] Jo Ann McNamara, 'The *Herrenfrage*: The Restructuring of the Gender System, 1050–1150', in Clare A. Lees, with Thelma Fenster and Jo Ann McNamara, eds *Medieval Masculinities: Regarding Men in the Middle Ages* (Minneapolis, 1994), 5, 11.

[28] Blamires, *The Case for Women*, 9, 17–18. For a useful collection of contemporary sources illustrating this polarisation, see also Alcuin Blamires, Karen Pratt, and C. William Marx eds *Woman Defamed and Woman Defended: An Anthology of Medieval Texts* (Oxford, 1992).

in the early 1970s.[29] The attributes of these family roles often crossed social boundaries in terms of wealth or nobility, and incorporated marital status with terms such as wife and widow. They even transcended gender, on those occasions when women had to assume a 'manly' role as head of the household.

Age was also used to describe women. The appellation of youth could be applied to an unmarried daughter, a wife, or widow, presumably to imply physical attractiveness and that they were still capable of bearing children. Old age was usually associated with mothers, widows and women past childbearing age. Both old and young could be criticised for acting in a manner inappropriate to their age. The concept of 'middle age' was less distinguishable: the term *matrona*, used to describe a respectable married woman, was perhaps the closest equivalent.

A major difficulty in categorising women's lives by their role in the family is that they were neither mutually exclusive, nor denoted by specific boundaries of age. A woman could be a combination of daughter, wife, mother and even widow all at once. A widow who was young enough might remarry and begin the cycle again. In historical sources a woman was often described differently in comparison to the family member that the author deemed most important, regardless of her own age or current situation. In order to combat some of these difficulties, this study will approach women in terms of 'life-cycle stages', focusing on their roles as daughters, wives, mothers and widows. All forms of social categorisation have their pitfalls, as individuals by nature consistently defy proposed societal 'norms', but the idea of life-cycle stages as a way of categorising the human experience has persisted since classical times with the concept of 'ages of man'.[30] Such an approach enables a discussion of the major criteria that affected perceptions of women, especially their legal status and authority, while at the same time retaining the terminology used by medieval authors.[31]

Crusade Narratives and their Audiences

THE advent of the crusade movement and the subsequent recording of these expeditions coincided with a change in perceptions about the past. This was engendered at least in part by the 'twelfth-century Renaissance', a movement characterised by the establishment of universities and new monasticism,

[29] Jo Ann McNamara and Suzanne Wemple, 'The Power of Women through the Family in Medieval Europe, 500–1100', *Feminist Studies* 1 (1973), 126–41. Reprinted in Mary Erler and Maryanne Kowaleski eds *Women and Power in the Middle Ages* (Athens, GA, 1988), 83–101. For a later revision see Jo Ann McNamara, 'Women and Power through the Family Revisited', in Mary Erler and Maryanne Kowaleski eds *Gendering the Master Narrative: Women and Power in the Middle Ages* (London, 2003), 17–30.

[30] See Michael E. Goodich, *From Birth to Old Age: The Human Life-Cycle in Medieval Thought 1250–1350* (London, 1989).

[31] See Stafford, 'Portrayal of Royal Women', 143–8.

and by a growing culture of literacy amongst the laity.[32] A new interest in writ-ten histories developed parallel to 'courtly' literature, both Latin and vernacu-lar, but History as a discipline was not particularly influenced by a revival of classical models at this time; Classen suggests that only the Italian annalists (including Caffaro of Genoa) can be considered truly 'renaissance' in charac-ter.[33] Hollister describes 'a new interest in the naturalistic cause and effect' in historical writing, influenced by the philosophy of Abelard, which encouraged historians to place 'less emphasis on divine intervention and more on natu-ral explanations'.[34] In contrast, narratives about crusading and the settlement of the Holy Land were based on the fundamental premise that these events were proof of current divine intervention in human affairs: new 'events' worthy of record. Even the most pioneering historians of the twelfth-century Renais-sance who wrote about crusading were unlikely to interpret the movement as resulting from anything other than divine providence. Classical models influ-enced crusade narratives in a traditional rather than innovative sense, but the twelfth-century Renaissance did increase education and the production of written history, bringing classical *topoi* to a wider audience.[35]

Emphasis on the development of vernacular literature during the twelfth-century Renaissance has often focused on fictional *chansons* and romances in identifying the beginnings of a secular literary culture. However, this did not preclude lay interest in the forms of historical writing considered to be more credible: the number of family histories and genealogies grew rapidly during this period.[36] Lay literacy was on the increase, widening the potential audience for crusade narratives. However, a noble could be a patron without being a scholar. Prince Raymond of Antioch was hailed as a patron, even though he had but slight education.[37] King Baldwin III of Jerusalem was said to enjoy reading. His brother Amalric was less scholarly, but he showed a preference for

---

[32] See Robert N. L. Swanson, *The Twelfth Century Renaissance* (Manchester, 1999).

[33] Peter Classen, 'Res Gestae, Universal History, Apocalypse; Visions of Past and Future', in Robert N. L. Benson and Giles Constable eds *Renaissance and Renewal in the Twelfth Century* (Oxford, 1982), 415.

[34] Charles Warren Hollister, 'Anglo-Norman Political Culture and the Twelfth Century Renaissance', in Charles Warren Hollister ed. *Anglo-Norman Political Culture and the Twelfth Century Renaissance: Proceedings of the Borchard Conference on Anglo-Norman History 1995* (Woodbridge, 1997), 9–10.

[35] See 23 below.

[36] Gabrielle M. Spiegel, *Romancing the Past: The Rise of Vernacular Prose Historiography in Thirteenth Century France* (Berkeley, 1993), 11–54; Jean Dunbabin, 'Discovering a Past for the French Aristocracy', in Paul Magdalino ed. *The Perception of the Past in Twelfth Century Europe* (London, 1992), 1–14. See also Maurice Keen, *Chivalry* (New Haven, 1984), 32.

[37] WT, 659. He is known to have had a role in commissioning the original version of the *Chanson des Chétifs*. See Linda M. Paterson, 'Occitan Literature and the Holy Land', in

listening to histories, having a keen memory for what he was told.[38] Crusading itself has been seen as a stimulus to writing histories in the vernacular, but Damien-Grint dismisses this idea, as none of the early examples mention the First Crusade. He asserts that crusading initially inspired vernacular *chansons de geste* instead – most historical narratives continued to be written in Latin throughout the twelfth century.[39] If we are to believe the Limousin chronicler Geoffrey of Vigeois, Geoffrey of Bechada – a knight with some Latin learning – produced a vernacular poem to celebrate the deeds of Gouffier of Lastours on the First Crusade during the early twelfth century, a poem which only survives in a fragment reworked into Occitan, known as the *Canso d'Antioca*.[40] When a group of lords in northern France decided to commemorate their own deeds on the First Crusade, it was a vernacular poem that they commissioned – the *Chanson d'Antioche*.[41]

Events themselves could result in a larger audience for histories. The conquest of Jerusalem in 1099 was interpreted as a miraculous feat that required recording for posterity. Crusading provided a unique combination of both temporal and spiritual values which proved attractive to both a lay and an ecclesiastical audience. It has been argued that crusades demonstrated most fully the difference between twelfth-century history and the traditions of Antiquity, opening the way for 'new dimensions in *gesta*, in war, and in adventures undertaken for a holy cause'.[42] As Ralph of Caen wrote, 'in reading old things and writing new, antiquity may be able to satisfy our needs and we may be able to nourish to the fullest the requirements of our posterity'.[43] Crusading themes were also 'popularised' by preachers and troubadours such as Marcabru, and the large numbers of common folk who swelled the ranks of crusading armies attested to the successful dissemination of that

Marcus Bull and Catherine Léglu eds *The World of Eleanor of Aquitaine: Literature and Society in Southern France between the Eleventh and Thirteenth Centuries* (Woodbridge, 2005).

38   WT, 715, 865.

39   Damien-Grint, *New Historians*, 10–11.

40   *The Canso d'Antioca: An Occitan Epic Chronicle of the First Crusade*, ed. Linda M. Paterson and Caroline E. Sweetenham (Aldershot, 2003), 5–7.

41   Lambert of Ardes asserts that Arnold II of Guines was left out by the 'Antiochene *commendator cantilene*' because he did not pay as others did. Lambert of Ardes, *Historia Comitum Ghisnensium*, MGH Scriptores 24 (Hanover, 1879), 626. DuParc Quioc identifies this as the earlier author of the *Chanson d'Antioche*. Suzanne DuParc Quioc, *La Chanson d'Antioche*, 2 vols [DHRC] (Paris, 1978), 2.92.

42   Classen, 'Res Gestae', 414.

43   GT, 603; translated in *The Gesta Tancredi of Ralph of Caen: A History of the Normans on the First Crusade*, ed. and trans. Bernard S. Bachrach and David S. Bachrach (Aldershot, 2005), 19.

message.[44] However, historical narratives on the subject of crusading were usually aimed at a target audience – the nobility. The crusade was portrayed as a noble and knightly pursuit, and its continued popularity demonstrated that the Church had become proficient in appealing to the nobility. As a social group, their values were increasingly based on a blend of military and Christian ideals; some historians even identify the birth of chivalry as a moral code with the Peace of God movement.[45] Although chivalric codes of behaviour were heavily influenced by the martial nature of social bonds amongst the aristocracy, attempts by the Church to control violence in God's name determined morally acceptable conduct for knights, and crusading found a natural niche in this process. Accounts of Urban II's speech at Clermont echoed this desire to reform the unruly knighthood, entreating warriors to cease fighting amongst themselves and take up the cross.[46] The sermons of James of Vitry specifically addressed the sins of knights, and with the development of the Military Orders, Bernard of Clairvaux's *De laude novae militiae* demonstrated that the Church could incorporate knightly violence in a way that did not undermine spiritual purity.[47] Even the most polemical religious literature in favour of crusading had to reflect the values of lay knights and nobles in order to achieve its aim. The authors of such sermons and texts reflected the need for restraints on the knighthood, but the enthusiastic response to the opportunities offered by the crusade message indicates that they were tuning in to genuine spiritual concerns held by the laity. Thus Ralph of Caen wrote of Tancred's moral struggle with the demands of a secular military life: 'his soul was at a crossroads. Which of the two paths should he follow: the Gospels or the world?'[48]

It is not easy to ascertain how far historical narratives formed part of active crusade propaganda for a target audience of potential *crucesignati*. Menache asserts that 'the crusades contribute the most spectacular example of medieval political communication in actual practice'.[49] The majority of scholarship on crusading propaganda has focused on evidence for preaching (sermons and

---

[44] See Simon Gaunt, Ruth Harvey and Linda Paterson, *Marcabru: A Critical Edition* (Cambridge, 2000); Michael Routledge, 'Songs', in Jonathan Riley-Smith ed. *The Oxford Illustrated History of the Crusades* (Oxford, 1995), 91–111. For a useful overview, see Jack Lindsay, *The Troubadours and their World of the Twelfth and Thirteenth Centuries* (London, 1976).

[45] David Carlson, 'Religious Writers and Church Councils', in Howell Chickering and Thomas H. Seiler eds *The Study of Chivalry: Resources and Approaches* (Kalamazoo, 1988), 143.

[46] FC, 136–7; GN, 113; RR, 728; BB, 14.

[47] St Bernard, 'Liber ad milites Templi de laude novae militiae', SBO, 3.213–39.

[48] GT, 606; trans. Bachrach and Bachrach, 22.

[49] Sophia Menache, *The Vox Dei: Communication in the Middle Ages* (Oxford, 1990), 123.

encyclicals), letters and popular songs,[50] but the specific role of narratives in disseminating crusading ideas is rather more ambiguous. Krey has suggested that the histories of Robert of Rheims, Guibert of Nogent, Baudri of Bourgueil and possibly Peter Tudebode were influenced by a deliberate propaganda drive surrounding Bohemond of Taranto's visit to France in 1106.[51] Sweetenham has argued that Robert intended to justify the First Crusade and actively 'presented a platform for future action'.[52] The manuscript tradition of Albert of Aachen's *Historia* suggests that some reproductions may have been linked to St Bernard's preaching tour of 1146–7.[53] Powell has explored the way in which the success of the First Crusade in particular was disseminated into popular culture and used to encourage others to crusade.[54] Fulcher of Chartres explicitly stated in his prologue that he wished to inspire people to leave their wives and families and take the cross, or to provide alms and prayers for their crusading forebears. This was his aim whether the history was read or recited from memory, suggesting that he was targeting a lay audience.[55] Bishop Oliver of Paderborn, who wrote the *Historia Damiatina*, preached the crusade both before and after the expedition in which he took part.[56] All of these authors firmly adhered to the fundamental principles behind the crusade movement, whether justifying the successes or failures of a specific expedition.[57] The medieval perception of history as a didactic tool meant that many authors could use narratives not only to encourage others to take the cross, but also to provide a variety of models for good and bad behaviour on crusade which were crucial to ensuring the successful outcome of a divinely ordained expedition.

In terms of their ability to connect with an aristocratic audience, it should be pointed out that the authors of narratives of crusading were usually from noble backgrounds. Of the sources used in this study, only John of Salisbury

---

[50] Ibid., 98–123; Penny Cole, *The Preaching of the Crusades to the Holy Land, 1095–1270* (Cambridge, MA, 1991); Christoph T. Maier, *Crusade Propaganda and Ideology* (Cambridge, 2000).

[51] August C. Krey, 'A Neglected Passage in the *Gesta* and its Bearing on the Literature of the First Crusade', in Louis J. Paetow ed. *The Crusades and Other Historical Essays Presented to Dana C. Munro* (New York, 1928), 70–5.

[52] *Robert the Monk's History of the First Crusade: Historia Iherosolimitana*, trans. Carol Sweetenham (Aldershot, 2005), 6–7.

[53] Edgington, 'Albert of Aachen, St. Bernard and the Second Crusade', 54–70.

[54] James M. Powell, 'Myth, Legend, Propaganda, History: The First Crusade, 1140–ca. 1300', in Michel Balard ed. *Autour de la Première Croisade*, 127–41 (Paris, 1996). For a literary perspective, see David A. Trotter, *Medieval French Literature and the Crusades, 1100–1300* (Geneva, 1988).

[55] FC, 115.

[56] See introduction, Oliver of Paderborn, *The Capture of Damietta*, trans. John J. Gavigan (London, 1948), 3, 9, 10.

[57] There were some objections to crusading on pacifist grounds, but these were few and far between. E. Siberry, *Criticism of Crusading 1095–1274* (Oxford, 1985), 208–16.

and William of Tyre are thought to have originated from non-noble stock.[58] In William's case, far from providing a 'common' perspective, he was a champion of royal authority in the East. Lay authors such as Villehardouin and Joinville were noble and wealthy enough to have been educated. Monastic writers such as Guibert of Nogent were known to have come from a noble background. Otto of Friesing, who wrote the *Deeds of Frederick Barbarossa*, was half-brother to King Conrad III of Germany and a participant in the Second Crusade.[59] Even where evidence for the social status of authors does not exist, the close links between the nobility, local churches, and monastic houses in the machinery of medieval government and patronage meant that ecclesiastical authors were familiar with courtly culture. Several of the ecclesiastics who wrote about crusade expeditions took part in them, and show considerable understanding of the martial world of the knight through their experience with crusading armies. Raymond of Aguilers, who went on crusade as a canon of Le Puy with Bishop Adhémar, was also chaplain to Count Raymond IV of Toulouse. His history was ostensibly written for the bishop of Viviers, but he states that he undertook the writing of it jointly with a knight, Pons of Balazun, who died at 'Arqah.[60] His history of the First Crusade placed particular emphasis on the spiritual importance of visions and portents, but he was also concerned to authenticate the Holy Lance and support his lord Raymond against Bohemond of Taranto during the power-struggle at Antioch.[61] Raymond's account showed that even with the strongest religious overtones, crusade narratives could demonstrate lay concerns. His patron, Adhémar, reputedly had a military background and was sufficiently warlike that when Tancred sent him seventy Turkish heads taken in a raid outside Antioch, he was overjoyed, rewarding Bohemond's nephew with a mark for each.[62] Raymond neglects to mention this story, but this was not a result of squeamish sensibilities about portraying Adhémar as a military man – he records the activities of Adhémar's troops at Nicaea and Antioch, and posthumous visions of the bishop leading troops at the siege of Jerusalem.

[58] See *Regesta Regni Hierosolymitani* (1097–1291) ed. R. Röhricht, 2 vols (Innsbruck, 1893), 1.142, no. 531. See also Peter W. Edbury and John Gordon Rowe, *William of Tyre, Historian of the Latin East* (Cambridge, 1988), 14. John of Salisbury was reticent about his background; Brooke suggests that he may have been the son of a married canon of Old Salisbury. See Christopher Brooke, 'John of Salisbury and his World', in Michael Wilks ed. *The World of John of Salisbury* (London, 1984), 3.

[59] See Otto of Freising and Rahewin, *Gesta Friderici Imperatoris*, ed. Georg Waitz, 2 vols; MGH *Scr. Rer. Ger.* 46 (1912).

[60] RA, 35–6.

[61] See Colin Morris, 'Policy and Visions. The Case of the Holy Lance at Antioch', in John Gillingham and James C. Holt eds *War and Government in the Middle Ages: Essays in Honour of J. O. Prestwich* (Cambridge, 1984), 33–45.

[62] GT, 644. France asserts that Adhémar was probably a noble from the Valentinois family and may have been involved in their conflicts. He was known to be a skilled horseman. John France, *Victory in the East* (Cambridge, 1994), 45.

Raymond's omission was probably influenced by the fact that Tancred, despite being given 5,000 *solidi* and two Arabian horses by the count of Toulouse, defected to Godfrey of Bouillon's contingent during the march to Jerusalem.[63] Some clergy were even involved in the fighting, despite the restrictions on clerical violence imposed by eleventh-century reformers. The priest Raol, who Livermore convincingly argues is the author of *De expugnatione Lxybonensi*, related in a charter that 'I ... expelled the infidels with my own bow'.[64]

The secular aspects of crusade narratives did not preclude their appreciation by a monastic audience either. As well as ties of class and patronage, local institutions were often involved in raising money to finance crusading. A number of accounts were ostensibly written for ecclesiastical patrons. Guibert's history was dedicated to Bishop Lysiard of Soissons.[65] Orderic Vitalis records that his *Ecclesiastical History* was prompted by Abbot Roger of Le Sap and was later encouraged by Abbot Warin of Saint-Évroul.[66] Chibnall suggests he intended it for 'monks of knightly class familiar with warfare and *chansons de geste*', but also for secular knights 'in the hope of moderating their brutality and directing their swords to the service of God'.[67] Unfortunately, the lack of a 'common' perspective from the lower levels of society dictates that surviving sources give a distorted reflection of the cultural impact of crusading by focusing so heavily on the nobility. However, the well-attested popularity of crusading amongst rich and poor alike suggests that both social groups found the subject appealing.

Crusade Narratives and Chivalric Literature

I⊤ has been established that ecclesiastical authors shared social roots with their audiences, but they also shared literary influences, to a degree. Several wrote, influenced and borrowed from chivalric literature, which has encouraged questions as to the value of some texts as truly 'secular' sources for lay culture. Barber asserted that if the authors of poems were clerics, due allowance should be made for 'clerical attitudes', but if they were jongleurs, 'the poems are more valuable to us as witnesses of knightly society and its ethics'.[68] Such a division fails to recognise the close relationships of literary influence that extended between church and laity, especially in the discipline of History which relied on political figures (including important ecclesiastics) for its subject matter. Many

---

[63] RA, 112.

[64] Harold Livermore, 'The Conquest of Lisbon and its Author', *Portuguese Studies* 6 (1990), 4.

[65] GN, 77–8. For financial aspects of relationships between crusades and monasteries, see Riley-Smith, *First Crusaders*, 113–29.

[66] OV, 1.38.

[67] *Ibid.*

[68] Richard Barber, *The Knight and Chivalry* (Ipswich, 1974), 54.

fictional texts including *chansons* were written by clergy, and such works were 'intended for popular consumption and reflected popular tastes.'[69] Of the First Crusade historians, at least two are known to have composed poetry for the courts, Guibert of Nogent and Baudri of Bourgueil.[70] It was to a canon of St Peter's at Antioch that Raymond of Poitiers turned for the official composition of the original *Chanson de Chétifs*, a verse narrative built around three 'fantastical episodes' which claimed to be based on proven truth.[71] Nor can lay and ecclesiastical influence be divided on mere stylistic grounds such as poetry and prose. Historical narrative had been cast in epic verse since classical times, and several ostensibly factual accounts of crusade expeditions were written in verse, such as that of Gilo of Paris, or Ambroise. Guibert of Nogent openly discussed his deliberations over whether to cast his *Dei Gesta Francorum* in verse or prose,[72] and Fourth Crusade historian Gunther of Pairis produced a version of Robert of Rheims' *Historia Iherosolimitana* as an epic poem called *Solinarus* in 1186.[73] It was Bishop Eustorge of Limoges who commissioned the *Canso d'Antioca* in the early twelfth century.[74] Even when sources were written in prose, some drew from poetic narratives, or interspersed their histories with lines of poetry, as did Ralph of Caen, amongst others. Robert of Rheims and Gilo of Paris are thought to have shared a further lost source, a history written in Latin hexameters, and Sweetenham asserts that the *chansons de geste* were 'by far the dominant literary influence' in Robert's work.[75] There were complex relationships between crusade narratives and specific *chansons*, for example the strong links between Albert of Aachen and the *Chanson d'Antioche*.[76] Ambroise the poet is credited as being the main source for the IP2 text of the *Itinerarium*, even though both are thought to have been eyewitnesses to the Third Crusade.[77] There was a certain degree of 'snobbery' about the use of 'popular metre',

[69] Jonathan Riley-Smith, *The First Crusade and the Idea of Crusading* (London, 1986), 9.

[70] Guibert admits a brief flirtation with poetry in his *Monodiae*. See Guibert of Nogent, *Autobiographie*, ed. and trans. Edmond-René Labande (Paris, 1981), 134. For Baudri's poetry see *Les œuvres poétiques de Baudri de Bourgueil*, ed. Phyllis Abrahams (Paris, 1926).

[71] Paterson, 'Occitan Literature', 85–7. The *Chétifs* asserts that Raymond liked the story and had the song composed.

[72] GN, 79–84.

[73] See introduction, Gunther of Pairis, *The Capture of Constantinople*, trans. Alfred J. Andrea (Philadelphia, 1997), 7–8.

[74] *Canso d'Antioca*, 6–7.

[75] Gilo of Paris, *The Historia Vie Hierosolimitane*, ed. and trans. Christoper W. Grocock and Elizabeth Siberry (Oxford, 1997), lx. Sweetenham, *Robert*, 61.

[76] See Edgington, 'Albert', 23–37.

[77] *Das Itinerarium peregrinorum: Eine zeitgenössische englische Chronik zum dritten Kreuzzug in ursprünglicher Gestalt*, ed. Hans E. Mayer, Schriften der Monumenta Germaniae historica 18 (Stuttgart, 1962), 62. Mayer divided the text into two sections,

especially in the vernacular, but the impact of crusading on the literary community was such that authors often wanted to reach the widest possible audience.[78] The use of verse in historical narrative does suggest that it was written for performance, possibly at court, and was therefore accessible to those nobles who were less likely to be literate, including women.

Bearing in mind the wide variety of narrative form in which the history of crusading appeared, it is impossible to say that *chansons* and romances were more representative of lay values, even when it came to perceptions of women. Considering the wide-reaching popularity of the movement, it was inevitable that participants, especially the leaders of the First Crusade, would find their way into more 'fictional' literature as legendary heroes. Godfrey of Bouillon was said to be descended from a swan, and this story, along with *chansons* about the capture of Antioch and Jerusalem, was amalgamated into what has become known as 'the epic cycle of the crusades', comprising two different cycles from the twelfth to the mid-fourteenth century.[79] These *chansons* demonstrate a close association with historical narratives, but their portrayal of women has generally been banished to the realm of the 'fictional'.[80] Romances developed in the later twelfth century, although it is unlikely that they 'replaced' *chansons de geste* as the favoured literature at court; both continued to be popular during the thirteenth century.[81] In any case, History was a common component of both. The *roman breton* and the *roman d'antiquité* in particular desired to impart both classical and recent history to an audience unfamiliar with Latin sources, entertaining them at the same time.[82]

Women did feature more prominently in romance texts than the martial *chansons*; thus *amour courtois* may have had a more pronounced effect on perceptions of women in later crusade narratives. Obviously one could not expect to see the same extensive love allegory as in some of the late twelfth and thirteenth

IPI and IP2. The longer IP2 was believed to be a compilation of Ambroise and the author's own eyewitness account. Mayer produced a new edition of the IPI text, which ends with the death of the archbishop of Canterbury in 1190. See Nicholson, *Chronicle*, 6–15. Ambroise, 2.12–13.

[78] Geoffrey of Vigeois upheld Geoffrey of Bechada's decision to write a vernacular poem in order to reach a wider audience, and to reinforce its worth he emphasised that he was commissioned by a bishop, had a Norman adviser, and researched his material for twelve years. See *Canso d'Antioca*, 6.

[79] See Alfred Foulet, 'The Epic Cycle of the Crusades', in Kenneth M. Setton ed. *A History of the Crusades*, 6 vols (Madison, 1969–89), 6.98–115. See also Trotter, *French Literature and the Crusades*, 107–25.

[80] Susan B. Edgington, "'Sont çou ore les fems que jo voi la venir?" Women in the *Chanson d'Antioche*', in Edgington and Lambert, *Gendering the Crusades*, 154–62.

[81] See introduction, Sarah Kay, *The Chansons de Geste in the Age of Romance: Political Fictions* (Oxford, 1995), 1–21.

[82] Peter Ainsworth, 'Legendary History: *Historia* and *Fabula*', in Deborah Mauskopf Deliyannis ed. *Historiography in the Middle Ages* (Leiden, 2003), 401–2.

century texts, but 'as the material of crusade history proved itself so eminently suitable for a romance-reading audience, so too its style and techniques became more akin to those of romance'.[83] It has been argued that the Rothelin continuation of William of Tyre enjoyed more popularity in Old French compilations simply because it supplied a 'more readable narrative': compilers were aware of the need to entertain, as well as teach, their audiences. According to Morgan,

> ... the nature of their work, compared with that of their predecessors, suggests that their readers were not taking the crusades as seriously as an earlier generation had done. What had formerly been an aspect of current events was now a literary topos, a central thread around which to weave multicoloured patterns.[84]

A brief example of the crossover of contemporary feminine *topoi* between history and romance is evidenced by Rothelin's mention of the Amazons' home country as *Femenie*, a place which also featured in a twelfth-century historical romance linked to Eleanor of Aquitaine, the *Roman de Troie* of Benoît de Sainte-Maure.[85] Translations and revisions of William of Tyre and his various continuators meant that they were increasingly seen as a collection of stories.[86] The blend of literary styles can also be seen in the 'miracle stories' given by Ambroise and the *Itinerarium*, and perhaps even earlier with Orderic Vitalis' inclusion of the story of Melaz, daughter of Malik-Ghazi.[87] Spiegel asserts that by 1200, *chansons* and romances, while still popular for entertainment, no longer satisfied the lay appetite for history and were gradually being replaced by vernacular prose as 'the preferred form of history'.[88] This is supported by the increase in vernacular prose histories of crusading in the thirteenth century, written by lay participants or continuators of William of Tyre. Like the use of verse, vernacular prose suggests that authors intended to reach a wider audience. However, a stylistic change to prose did little to differentiate perceptions about women in narrative history from those in romances and *chansons*, as the example of the *Estoire d'Eracles* shows.

[83]   Margaret R. Morgan, 'The Rothelin Continuation of William of Tyre', in Kedar *et al.*, *Outremer*, 255.

[84]   *Ibid.*, 252–4.

[85]   Joan M. Ferrante, *To the Glory of Her Sex: Women's Roles in the Composition of Medieval Texts* (Indianapolis, 1997), 116–18; Rothelin, 503. For a recent assessment of Acre manuscripts portraying Amazons and their identification with crusader ideology in the Levant, see Anne Derbes and Mark Sandona, 'Amazons and Crusaders: The *Histoire Universelle* in Flanders and the Holy Land', in Daniel H. Weiss and Lisa Mahoney ed. *France and the Holy Land: Frankish Culture at the End of the Crusades* (Baltimore, 2004), 187–229.

[86]   Morgan, 'Rothelin Continuation', 255.

[87]   See 68–70 below.

[88]   Spiegel, *Past as Text*, 179.

In fact, prose became the popular style for romances from the early thirteenth century.[89]

Separating any medieval narratives into those displaying 'lay' ideals of the nobility and 'religious' ones is misleading. The didactic messages of proper knightly behaviour in crusade narratives are no more restrictive than those found in chivalric literature. *Raoul de Cambrai*, for example, is a warning against the dangers of excessive violence, pride and, most crucially, abusing the feudal bond between lord and vassal.[90] It could be said that both types of literature were important for imposing moral restraints on the most dangerous element in society, the warriors. While crusade narratives predominantly featured examples of knighthood approved by the Church, *chansons de geste* and romances also focused on proper social behaviour. They could even form an active part in the propaganda for crusading. The author of the *Itinerarium* records how crusaders celebrated the arrival of King Richard at Acre, by 'singing popular songs', or reciting 'epic tales of ancient heroes' deeds', as an incitement to modern people to imitate them – a testament to the didactic power of these genres.[91] Conversely, criticism of crusaders in historical narrative, whether they were accused of going for wealth or glory, betraying fellow Christians or consorting with prostitutes, also represented the social 'reality' of lay participation in crusades. There is no definitive idea of what constitutes 'chivalric literature', but if it can be said to consist of texts which represented knightly views and concerns, there is a strong case for including narratives about crusading within it.

---

[89] Ainsworth, 'Legendary History', 415.

[90] See *Raoul de Cambrai* ed. and trans. Sarah Kay (Oxford, 1992).

[91] *Itinerarium* 202.

Authorship

IT is impossible to generalise about the authorship of crusade narratives. To some extent authors shared social and literary influences, but as well as geographical and chronological diversity, each had unique perspectives or personal agendas in terms of patronage, opinion, justification or propaganda. The widespread practice of plagiarism during the medieval period meant that some authors simply compiled crusade texts, including additional evidence where they had access to it. All of these factors may have influenced opinion of women in crusade narratives. Unfortunately there is not space within the scope of this book to give detailed background information for each author. Instead this chapter will provide an overview of issues such as textual interdependence and authorship in terms of patronage, education, and access to material, in order to show that the authors of histories of crusading and the Latin East cannot be universally described as more misogynistic than their contemporaries.

Textual Interdependence

THE propensity of medieval authors for borrowing extensively from other sources often makes it difficult to assess individual agendas. If a text influenced the development and spread of the crusade idea it might also have influenced attitudes to women's involvement. In these circumstances, a careful comparison of texts can be of benefit. Deletion of information suggested that it was considered inconsequential or incorrect, whereas its inclusion verbatim implied tacit approval. Additions indicated personal knowledge, opinion, or access to external sources. Nicholson views this kind of plagiarism as 'evidence … of how the crusaders themselves saw crusade and how they developed the account of the crusade which they would have eventually retold in Europe.'[1] The intricate details of the relationships between each text cannot be given full consideration within this study, but the most influential should be given at least cursory attention.

From the time of the First Crusade, medieval historians often relied heavily on the limited eyewitness accounts available. The primacy of anonymous *Gesta Francorum* as the earliest and most influential narrative for the First Crusade continues to be a focus of considerable debate, not least because of the presence of other eyewitness accounts, and the close textual relationship between early crusade histories. France thinks it unlikely that there was some kind of

---

[1] Nicholson, *Chronicle*, 14.

'Ur-Gesta' as the Hills suggest.[2] He acknowledges that the Gesta 'cannot be proved to depend on any other written source' but asserts that those authors who drew from the Gesta should not subsequently be undervalued.[3] Similarly, Bull warns against assuming that the Gesta was 'a piece of raw and reliable reportage', on the grounds of literary style and lay authorship, as on closer examination it is not necessarily more valuable than other contemporary histories.[4] Rubenstein has recently entered the fray, breathing new life into the theory of a previous source, a collection of sermons or stories he refers to as the 'Jerusalem History'. He claims that this text existed in a variety of versions and was compiled by subsequent historians, rather than originating with the anonymous author of the Gesta.[5] Harari has recently questioned whether the Gesta was written by an eyewitness at all.[6] Sources continued to be used at second or third hand, causing further complications. Baudri of Bourgueil based his First Crusade history on the Gesta tradition and it enjoyed some popularity, with seven or eight manuscripts surviving from the twelfth and thirteenth centuries. It was to him, rather than the Gesta, that Orderic Vitalis turned for an account of the First Crusade.[7] The reinterpretation of a text could also become more popular than its source – Robert of Rheims' Historia was predominantly based on the Gesta, but manuscript tradition suggests that his history had by far the widest circulation of First Crusade narratives. Hiestand gives a total of ninety-four manuscripts, thirty-nine dating from the twelfth century.[8]

The second group of texts which had a profound influence on western perceptions of crusading and the Latin East were those attributed to William of Tyre and his continuators. William's Chronicle was the fullest and most

---

[2] John and Laurita Hill suggest that the 'libellus' seen by Ekkehard of Aura in Jerusalem in 1101 was not in fact the Gesta, but may have been an earlier common source used by the Gesta, Raymond and Fulcher. See PT, 22–3, and Ekkehard of Aura, RHC Occ. 5.21.

[3] See GF, 39–92, for Hagenmeyer's argument in favour of the Gesta's influence. See also John France, 'The Anonymous Gesta Francorum and the Historia Francorum qui ceperunt Iherusalem of Raymond of Aguilers and the Historia de Hierosolymitano itinere of Peter Tudebode: An Analysis of the Textual Relationship between Primary Sources for the First Crusade', in France and Zajac, The Crusades and their Sources, 59; and 'The Use of the Anonymous Gesta Francorum in the Early Twelfth Century Sources for the First Crusade', in Murray, From Clermont to Jerusalem, 29–30.

[4] Bull, Miracles of Our Lady, 5. Beer uses the Gesta Francorum as an example of the triumph of the authority of the eyewitness over stylistic content. Beer, Narrative Conventions, 23–34. France, 'Use of the Anonymous Gesta', 29–30.

[5] Rubenstein, 'What is the Gesta Francorum', 179–204.

[6] Yuval Noah Harari, 'Eyewitnessing in Accounts of the First Crusade: The Gesta Francorum and Other Contemporary Narratives', Crusades 3 (2004), 77–99.

[7] OV, 5.xiii.

[8] Rudolph Hiestand, 'Il Cronista Medievale e il suo pubblico: Alcune osservazione in margine alla storiographia delle crociate', Annali della Facoltà di lettere e filosophia dell'università di Napoli 27 (1984–5), 227.

influential account of events in the Levant during the twelfth century. Born in the Levant but educated in Europe, William wrote with both an eastern and western audience in mind, creating a didactic history to generate sympathy and support for the Holy Land.[9] The number of extant manuscripts attests to William's popularity – Colin Morris asserts that both William and his continuators were being read by the 'higher aristocracy' in the thirteenth century.[10] William wanted to encourage successful military aid for the Holy Land, which in his opinion relied upon the morality of its lay participants and of the settler society in the East. This work was so successful that it was translated for a French audience and had several continuators, both in Latin and Old French. Davies, however, was pessimistic about the possibility that much of William's initial aim survived in these popularised texts. He asserts that his western audience was probably attracted more by the 'chinoiserie' of William's history – 'he would have been horrified to find that his book was treated as escapist literature'.[11]

Of the French continuations, the most well known groups of manuscripts are published as the *Estoire d'Eracles*, the *Chronique d'Ernoul et de Bernard le Trésorier*, the *Estoires d'Oultremer et de la Naissance Salehadin*, and a further series of manuscripts with continuations after 1232, including the Rothelin continuation.[12] There is a further Latin continuation written in approximately 1220

---

[9]   See Edbury and Rowe, *William of Tyre*, 25, 107–8, 171–3.

[10]   For a list of extant manuscripts, see J. Folda, 'Manuscripts of the *History of Outremer* by William of Tyre: A Handlist', *Scriptorium* 27 (1973), 90–5. A comprehensive edition of the *Eracles* based on the large number of extant manuscripts has yet to be published. The majority of references to the *Eracles* continuation throughout this study will be to the Lyon Manuscript, published as *La Continuation de Guillaume de Tyr 1184–1197*, ed. Margaret R. Morgan (Paris, 1982). This is not only the most recently edited text of the continuation, it gives a more detailed account for the period of 1184–7 than other *abrégés* of Ernoul, although Edbury disagrees with Morgan's assertion that the Lyon manuscript was closest to the original work of Ernoul. It has also recently been translated as *The Conquest of Jerusalem and the Third Crusade*, trans. Peter W. Edbury (Aldershot, 1996). References to the Eracles translation of William of Tyre are from *Guillaume de Tyr et ses continuateurs: texte français du XIIIᵉ siècle, revu et annoté*, ed. Paulin Paris (Paris, 1879–80). The most recent edition of Ernoul is *La Chronique d'Ernoul et de Bernard le Trésorier*, ed. Louis de Mas Latrie (Paris, 1871). See also *Estoires d'Outremer et de la Naissance Salehadin*, ed. Margaret A. Jubb (London, 1990). References to the Rothelin continuation and Acre continuation are both to be found in RHC Occ. 2 (Paris, 1859), and translated in *Crusader Syria in the Thirteenth Century: The Rothelin Continuation of William of Tyre with Part of the Eracles or Acre Text*, trans. Janet Shirley (Aldershot, 1999). Colin Morris, 'Picturing the Crusades: The Uses of Visual Propaganda, c. 1095–1250', in France and Zajac, *The Crusades and their Sources*, 196.

[11]   Ralph H. C. Davies, 'William of Tyre', in Derek Baker ed. *Relations between East and West in the Middle Ages* (Edinburgh, 1973), 74.

[12]   For a discussion of the relationship between these manuscripts, see Margaret R. Morgan, *The Chronicle of Ernoul and the Continuations of William of Tyre* (Oxford, 1973).

which demonstrates the influence of the *Itinerarium* and Roger of Howden, but also contains some original material.[13] These continuations are largely anonymous, and are often compilations of composite authors in differing manuscripts, but some differences in their outlook and agendas can be ascertained.

The *Chronique d'Ernoul* commenced with the foundation of the Latin states in the East and was apparently independent of William of Tyre, although highly condensed by comparison for the period in which they overlap – it is often referred to as the *abrégé*. The author may have been a squire of Balian of Ibelin, and is the main narrative source for the kingdom of Jerusalem after William ended his history in 1184 until 1187: Ernoul's influence over the chronicle after this date has been questioned.[14] Between those dates the *Estoire d'Eracles* is very similar in content to those manuscripts attributed to Ernoul, but additional material in the *Eracles* is independent of both the Ernoul continuation and the *Estoires d'Oultremer*, and was probably derived from oral sources.[15] A close examination of the text by Pryor and his colleagues has revealed that the *Eracles* author also made individual contributions to his translation of William of Tyre. They established that the *Eracles* author was 'far less religiously and morally oriented', making changes to suit a noble audience – he removed many of the classical, biblical and patristic references – and simplifying William's narrative and dating system.[16] Although more secular in tone, the text did not lack ecclesiastical influence: the author was 'almost certainly' a western cleric who had visited the Latin East some time after 1180.[17]

If the *Eracles* account lacked the emotive and moral tone of William's history, this could be explained to an extent by their differing temporal perspective. It is uncertain exactly when the *Eracles* author undertook his translation and revision of William's history; it was probably between 1205 and 1234. Even if only twenty years had elapsed between the authorship of the two texts, extremely significant events such as the Battle of Hattin, the Third Crusade and the conquest of Constantinople had propelled crusading into a new era. William began writing his history in the reign of King Amalric I of Jerusalem to celebrate the

[13] Published as *Die Lateinische Forsetzung Wilhelms von Tyrus*, ed. Marianne Salloch (Leipzig, 1934).

[14] Peter W. Edbury, 'The Lyon *Eracles* and the Old French Continuations of William of Tyre', in Benjamin Z. Kedar, Jonathan Riley-Smith and Rudolph Hiestand eds *Montjoie: Studies in Crusade History in Honour of Hans Eberhard Mayer* (Aldershot, 1997), 143. See also John Gillingham, 'Roger of Howden on Crusade', in his *Richard Cœur de Lion: Kingship, Chivalry and War in the Twelfth Century* (London, 1994), 147.

[15] Bernard Hamilton, 'The Old French Translation of William of Tyre as an Historical Source', in Peter Edbury and Jonathan Phillips eds *The Experience of Crusading: Defining the Crusader Kingdom* (Cambridge, 2003), 2.110–12.

[16] John Pryor, 'The *Eracles* and William of Tyre: An Interim Report', in Kedar, *Horns of Hattin*, 272–7.

[17] Pryor, 'The *Eracles* and William of Tyre', 277–83.

success of a dynasty which had established a firm hold over the Holy Land, but as he continued his work he viewed with increasing pessimism the political developments around him to the extent that he almost considered abandoning his work shortly before his death.[18] In comparison, the *Eracles* author wrote with hindsight of the loss of Jerusalem and two further crusade expeditions that had failed to redeem it. His work may have lacked the urgency of William's call for aid, but in rendering his history into a style more reminiscent of 'a prose version of a *chanson de geste*', he was evidently hopeful that the nobility of his day might be encouraged to emulate the glorious deeds of noble forefathers.[19] The *Eracles* account was particularly well known in the aristocratic courts of northern Europe in the thirteenth century, and may have influenced future leaders of crusade expeditions such as Richard, earl of Cornwall, and Louis ix of France.[20]

In contrast, other sources were less widely circulated, and therefore less likely to have influenced ideas about women and crusading. Odo of Deuil's narrative only exists in one manuscript, as does *De expugnatione Lxybonensi* and the history of Robert of Clari. Odo's narrative seems almost unique – it seems that the failure of the Second Crusade in the Latin East made contemporaries less inclined to write about it in any detail, although crusades in Iberia and against the Wends enjoyed more success.[21] The controversial Fourth Crusade also drew criticism, despite its military success. McNeal has suggested that Robert of Clari's account only survived 'by accident', as it was saved from obscurity when a monk from Corbie copied it into a volume comprising other Old French texts.[22] In a society where information was still predominantly transmitted orally, the number of extant texts can never be a truly accurate gauge of the influence of a manuscript,[23] but it can be tentatively suggested that an exceptionally high number indicates how attuned to contemporary values and tastes certain crusade narratives were.

Ecclesiastics, 'Veritas' and 'Auctoritas'

It might be expected that the cloister affected the writing of monastic authors in a number of ways, especially with regard to gender. As educated men they had a wide frame of literary reference, *auctoritas*, and as celibates they may

---

[18] WT, 1062–3.

[19] Pryor, 'The *Eracles* and William of Tyre', 273.

[20] Hamilton, 'Old French Translation', 112.

[21] See Otto of Freising, *Gesta Friderici*, 65. For a more detailed assessment see Giles Constable, 'The Second Crusade as Seen by Contemporaries', *Traditio* 9 (1953), 213–79.

[22] Robert of Clari, *The Conquest of Constantinople*, trans. Edgar Holmes McNeal (Toronto, 1996; first published 1936), 7–8.

[23] See Leah Shopkow, *History and Community: Norman Historical Writing in the Eleventh and Twelfth Centuries* (Washington DC, 1997), especially 246–75.

have been more inclined to idealise or vilify women, resulting either from lack of personal contact or the extensive literary *topoi* that they had access to. Education was not exclusive to the monasteries, however – Raymond of Aguilers demonstrated a high standard of learning and was well versed in church liturgy.[24] One of the main problems for those authors who remained within the cloister was *veritas* – how to create authoritative history according to Isidore's guidelines on eyewitness testimony. Authors who had participated in crusades regularly asserted their presence in order to uphold the legitimacy of their version of events. Ambroise's repeated claims of being an eyewitness have led to him being considered his own source.[25] Similarly, Robert of Clari ended his history by asserting his truthfulness and reliability as an eyewitness, 'as he bears witness who was there and saw it and heard it'.[26] Those historians who were not eyewitnesses to events had to justify their authority to write in terms of literary skill. Guibert of Nogent asserted that God would place within him the truth of events. He justified his re-working of the *Gesta Francorum* by emphasising the religious import of crusading:

> Just as the style of orators plainly ought to be adapted to the import of the events, so martial facts should be related with a harshness of speech, [and] that which pertains to the divine should be brought forth at a more temperate pace.[27]

He also expressed concern that scholars would not value his history because he was not an eyewitness, and therefore emphasised his use of the *Gesta* and of other sources to cross-reference its veracity.[28] Other authors took care to cite sources, both written and oral, to justify their presentation of evidence as reality, showing awareness of the pitfalls in their approach. William of Malmesbury wrote:

> I guarantee the truth of nothing in past time except the sequence of events; the credit of my narrative must rest with my authorities. But whatsoever I have added out of recent history, I have either seen myself or heard from men who can be trusted.[29]

William is known to have sought additional information from others – another means for cloistered historians to add original material to their chronicles.[30] Crusaders travelled from all over Europe and often relied on monastic support

---

24 RA, 13–20.

25 Ambroise, 1.1.

26 RC, 109; trans. McNeal, 128.

27 GN, 80.

28 *Ibid.*, 80, 166.

29 WM, 1.17.

30 Thompson, *William of Malmesbury*, 72–5.

for shelter or raising funds; thus cloistered authors could still have personal experience of crusaders. Historians known to have conversed with returning crusaders include Ralph of Coggeshall and Matthew Paris.[31] Monks could also travel for information. Orderic Vitalis appears to have visited several monasteries, including Cluny in 1132, and he is known to have consulted the cathedral library in Rouen.[32] Even monastic vows were not a bar to eyewitness evidence. Like women, religious clergy were discouraged from taking the cross, but several took part in crusades and wrote their own accounts. Some monks were also ordained priests: Bishop Otto of Friesing had been a Cistercian abbot at Morimond before taking up his more celebrated position, and he was severely criticised by Ralph Niger for participating in the Second Crusade.[33] Ekkehard of Aura was a monk from Corvey who took part in the 1101 crusade, returning to his monastery in Italy in 1102.[34] Odo of Deuil was a monk and later abbot of St Denis, but accompanied King Louis VII of France on crusade as royal chaplain.[35] It seems likely that this was a common pattern for monks who went on crusade; some were given special dispensation to take part in pilgrimages, but most returned to their monasteries.

It might also be expected that historians working from a monastery had to rely more heavily upon sources authored by crusaders, but as we have seen, 'plagiarism' was not confined to the cloister. Even eyewitnesses borrowed from other accounts, and this did not necessarily preclude originality. Ecclesiastics who did not take part in crusading could still provide relevant eyewitness material of their own. Baudri of Bourgueil and Robert of Rheims were at the Council of Clermont; Gerald of Wales aided the recruitment of the Third Crusade and might have participated in the expedition had it not been for the death of Henry II in 1189.[36] John of Salisbury was at the papal curia both during and after the time of the Second Crusade, but this enabled him to witness the return from the Holy Land to Italy of the king and queen of France in 1149.

Contact with women was undoubtedly restricted, especially for monastic authors, but this did not prevent social connections with women from

---

[31]   Ralph of Coggeshall, *Chronicon Anglicanum*, ed. Joseph Stevenson, RS 66 (1875), xiii–xiv. Matthew's contacts included the crusader Richard, earl of Cornwall, the Scottish master of the Temple and the bishop of Beirut. See Richard Vaughan, *Matthew Paris* (Cambridge, 1958), 13–17.

[32]   OV, I.27.

[33]   Ralph Niger, *De Re Militari et triplici peregrinationis Ierosolimitanae*, ed. Ludwig Schmugge (Berlin, 1977), 79–80.

[34]   RHC *Occ*. 5. ii–v.

[35]   For a recent assessment see Jonathan Phillips, 'Odo of Deuil's *De Profectione Ludovici VII in Orientem* as a source for the Second Crusade', in Marcus Bull, Norman Housley, Jonathan Phillips and Peter W. Edbury eds *The Experience of Crusading: Western Approaches* (Cambridge, 2003), I.80–95.

[36]   Edbury, 'Preaching the Crusade in Wales', 232.

influencing their perception of gender, evidenced by Guibert of Nogent's account of his relationship with his mother.[37] The cloister was seemingly no boundary to Baudri of Bourgueil, who wrote 'surprisingly passionate' verse, and is known to have corresponded with several young women at the convent of Le Ronceray at Angers where he taught them composition and urged them to write to him in verse.[38] Ecclesiastical authors of crusade narratives had much in common with their lay counterparts; all demonstrated established Christian viewpoints and were either born into, or wrote for, the noble class whose inter-ests they upheld. Although the moral and didactic purpose of ecclesiastical his-tory dictated that people were exemplified as heroes and villains, the popularity of historical themes in courtly literature suggests that conventions about the relatively peripheral matter of gender would be recognised and accepted by the audience at which it was aimed: the nobility.

Lay Authorship

THE effects that lay authorship may have had on perceptions of women in crusade narratives must also be considered. Would it be possible to expect a more wide-ranging, less biblical, or perhaps a different frame of liter-ary reference? Were lay-authored accounts of crusading considered to be less credible? Contemporary historians certainly criticised the literary style of the *Gesta Francorum* – Guibert of Nogent, Robert of Rheims and Baudri of Bour-gueil cite this as the ostensible reason for producing their own histories of the First Crusade – but they could not challenge its authority as an eyewitness source.[39] This very fact has, alongside other evidence, induced historians such as Hagenmeyer to consider the anonymous *Gesta* to be the work of a layman.[40] Morris and now Rubenstein have argued that it was composed or compiled by a cleric hailing from a different academic tradition, but this idea has not been universally accepted.[41] There is, however, scope to suggest that the *Gesta* is in fact a far more complex, and indeed well-designed, piece of literature than at first suspected. Wolf asserts that 'there is nothing unsophisticated about the way in which the author transformed a complex body of historical data about

---

37 See Chapter 6, *passim*.

38 RHC *Occ.* 4.iii, Ferrante, *Glory of her Sex*, 31–5.

39 Guibert of Nogent states that he took up the project with a vow to correct a previous work in his introduction; GN, 80. Robert of Rheims asserted that he was writing his history because his abbot had asked him to improve the style of an existing history, and because he had been an eyewitness to the Council of Clermont. RR, 721. Both are thought to have been referring to the *Gesta*.

40 GF, 6–7.

41 Colin Morris, 'The *Gesta Francorum* as narrative history', *Reading Medieval Studies* 19 (1993), 55–71. For criticism of this argument, see France, 'Use of the Anonymous *Gesta*', 30. See also Rubenstein, 'What is the *Gesta Francorum*', 187–8.

an unusual military expedition into a highly coherent and consistent narrative about a pilgrimage to the Holy Land.[42] Whether the author wrote or compiled this text, it suggests that his depiction of women may also be more sophisticated than appears at first glance, especially in the case of Kerbogha's mother.[43]

Lay authors had more regular contact with women than monks, but they were still subject to ecclesiastical influence in their writing, whether in terms of their own education, or their own personal piety, as they were usually sufficiently motivated to become crusaders themselves. Church control over literary education meant that if aristocratic children destined for a role in lay society were educated, it was usually under ecclesiastical guidance, often alongside brothers or sisters who were intended for a religious life. It is probable that most lay authors dictated their histories rather than putting pen to parchment themselves. Beer suggests that Villehardouin's continued use of the term 'sachiez' to reinforce the truth of his argument is 'consistent with the narrative tradition he inherited and possible evidence that he dictated the history'.[44] However, it is possible that this was something of a tradition in vernacular historiography, as authors could not rely on the inherent *gravitas* associated with a Latin text.[45] Standards of scholarship could vary widely between lay historians; McNeal asserts that Robert of Clari's language suited the dictation of an unlettered knight, pointing out that he had an inferior vocabulary to Villehardouin.[46] Even so, as Clanchy emphasised, the modern historian must be wary of equating literacy with civilisation, and whether they were dictated or not, the texts of lay authors still demonstrated a degree of education and enthusiasm for History amongst the aristocracy.[47]

Like ecclesiastical narratives, whether personally inspired or writing to enhance the reputation of individuals or places, each lay author had his own agenda. Caffaro was glorifying the Genoese; Villehardouin was defending the actions of the Fourth Crusaders; and Joinville was writing a semi-hagiographical history of the newly canonised Louis IX. Robert of Clari is credited with providing a genuine perspective on the Fourth Crusade as a member of the lower aristocracy who wished to record his crusading experience for posterity. According to Noble, the character of the work, while not always strictly factually correct, provides a 'less calculated or calculating' account than some of the other 'drier' or more politically motivated chronicles of the Fourth

[42] Kenneth Baxter Wolf, 'Crusade and Narrative: Bohemond and the *Gesta Francorum*', *JMH* 17 (1991), 208.

[43] See 190–6 below.

[44] Beer, *Narrative Conventions*, 45.

[45] See *Canso d'Antioca*, 127.

[46] McNeal, *Conquest*, 12.

[47] Michael T. Clanchy, *From Memory to Written Record*, 2nd edition (Oxford, 1993), 7.

Crusade.[48] Relying on stylistic features can be misleading, however. The poet Ambroise was believed to be a professional jongleur, largely because he demonstrated extensive knowledge of contemporary French poetry rather than Latin literature. It has recently been argued, however, that he must have been an educated cleric, in minor orders at least, who made a conscious decision to use sources suitable for appealing to a noble audience.[49] The work is written in 'a brisk, simple style with a relatively small vocabulary, suitable for recitation'.[50] The *Itinerarium*, in the course of converting Ambroise into a Latin prose chronicle, included more traditional and classical references which also influenced its portrayal of women.[51] The two may therefore be separated on stylistic grounds as well as form and language, but ultimately their interpretation of events and the didactic purpose for which they wrote remained markedly similar.

[48] Peter Noble, 'Villehardouin, Robert de Clari and Henri de Valenciennes: Their Different Approaches to the Fourth Crusade', in Erik Kooper, ed. *The Medieval Chronicle: Proceedings of the 1st International Conference on the Medieval Chronicle* (Amsterdam, 1999), 209.

[49] *L'Estoire de la Guerre Sainte par Ambroise*, ed. and trans. Gaston Paris (Paris, 1897), vi–xii. Ambroise, 2.2.

[50] Nicholson, *Chronicle*, 15.

[51] *Ibid.*, 14–15.

+ 3 +

Women in the History of
Crusading and the Latin East

Women as Audience

HAVING demonstrated that crusade narratives reflected both ecclesiastical and noble values and interests, the next step must be to consider whether the women portrayed in crusade narratives were deliberately intended to provide guidance for a female audience. Would women have had access to such histories through oral transmission, or even have been able to read them? Evidence about literacy amongst women is limited before the late medieval period, but some of the high-profile figures who featured in crusade narratives were associated with education, such as Queen Mathilda of England, Mathilda of Tuscany, Ida of Lorraine, Queen Melisende of Jerusalem, Adela of Blois and Eleanor of Aquitaine. Key indicators of women's literacy were the patronage and ownership of books,[1] but as already established, commissioning literature was not definitive proof of the ability to read and write. Arguments about women's literacy are also governed by the division between traditional Latin literacy and the vernacular literature flourishing at the courts; however, some female aristocrats of the twelfth century were known to be literate in Latin.[2] Queen Mathilda was educated at the convent of Romsey and composed Latin letters to Archbishop Anselm of Canterbury; and both Melisende of Jerusalem and crusader Margaret of Beverley are thought to have owned Latin Psalters.[3] Baudri of Bourgueil composed verse for Adela of Blois which praised her patronage and her skill at composition, but she was interested in the historical past as well. Some of the tapestries hanging on the walls of her chamber depicted events from

---

[1] See Susan Groag Bell, 'Medieval Women Book Owners: Arbiters of Lay Piety and Ambassadors of Culture', in Erler and Kowaleski, *Women and Power in the Middle Ages*, 149–87.

[2] Duby has even claimed that women's involvement in courtly learned culture was 'more precocious, more extensive, than that of males in the secular aristocracy'. Georges Duby, 'The Culture of the Knightly Class: Audience and Patronage', in Benson and Constable, *Renaissance and Renewal*, 258.

[3] See Lina Eckenstein, *Women under Monasticism: Chapters on Saint-Lore and Convent Life Between A.D. 500 and A.D. 1500* (New York, 1963); and Lois L. Huneycutt, "Proclaiming her dignity abroad": The Literary and Artistic Network of Mathilda of Scotland, Queen of England, 1100–1118', in June Hall McCash ed. *The Cultural Patronage of Medieval Women* (Athens, GA, 1996), 155–74. For Melisende Psalter, see 65 below. For Margaret of Beverley, see TF, 481.

the ancient world, and Hugh of Fleury dedicated a Latin history, the *Historia ecclesiastica*, to her.[4] Ferrante asserts that when men wrote for women in power they were more likely to emphasise other women in authority for didactic purposes, 'accepting them as a normal, indeed essential part of History'.[5] Queens held a prominent role in Joinville's history, which was possibly influenced by the fact that Jeanne, Queen of France and Navarre, commissioned it. Joinville told how the queen 'begged me most earnestly to have a book written for her containing the pious sayings and good deeds of our King, Saint Louis,'[6] but she died in 1305, fours years before its completion. The author's dedication was addressed instead to Louis, son of Jeanne and King Philip IV of France, and underlined the didactic purpose of his work:

> … I send it to you, so that you and your brothers – and whoever else may hear it read – may take some good examples from it, and put them into practice, thus winning yourselves favour in the sight of God.[7]

Queen Mathilda was the patron of William of Malmesbury's *Gesta Regum Anglorum*, but like Jeanne she did not live to see its completion, dying in 1118. Copies were sent to three recipients accompanied by different letters of dedication.[8] One of these went to her daughter, the Empress Mathilda, and explicitly stated that the chronicle followed a tradition of didactic historical writing for both kings and queens:

> … in order to provide them with a sort of pattern for their own lives, from which they could learn to follow some men's successes, while avoiding the misfortunes of others, to imitate the wisdom of some and look down on the foolishness of others.[9]

The letter went on to claim that the inception of the history derived from Queen Mathilda's desire for knowledge about her kinsman St Aldhelm and his lineage, as well as to make the kings of England better known, to 'bring her credit', and 'to be both useful and honourable to our foundation'.[10] William's history therefore epitomised the traditional conventions of twelfth-century historical narrative: glorification of a particular person, a dynasty,

---

4 See *Les œuvres poétiques*, 198–200; and Jean Mabillon, *Annales ordinis S. Benedicti*, 6 vols (Paris, 1703–39), 5, 544.

5 Ferrante, *Glory of Her Sex*, 106. Although she focuses on a slightly earlier period (*circa* eighth to mid-twelfth centuries), see chapter 3, 'Women and the Writing of History', for a useful survey of women's patronage of narrative history (68–106).

6 Joinville, 2; trans. Shaw, 163.

7 Joinville, 10; trans. Shaw, 165.

8 WM, 2.6.

9 *Ibid.*, 1.6–9.

10 *Ibid.*, 1.8–9.

and the religious house associated with it. In no way do such letters of dedication suggest that it might be unusual for a woman to be interested in History.

The courtly literature linked to women also contained strong historical elements. As Ferrante asserts:

> The taste for historical narrative with more than a touch of the exotic carries into the romances; indeed, the romances seem to reflect influences from almost all the early histories in French and from some of the Latin histories composed for women as well.[11]

Eleanor of Aquitaine has often been associated with the patronage of courtly culture, following on from a tradition at the Poitevin court begun by her grandfather William IX. In terms of historical romances, she has been linked to the *Roman de Brut* and the *Roman de Rou*, and the more classical *Eneas*, the *Roman de Thèbes* and the *Roman de Troie*, although her role as an active patron has been challenged.[12] Eleanor's controversial relationships with her two powerful husbands meant that she developed a relatively poor image in contemporary histories which focused on the activities of male royalty, although most truly scathing accounts were written after her lifetime.[13] She may have promoted herself through patronage of art and courtly literature because it was not possible for a woman to glorify herself at the expense of male kin within the confines of an 'official' historical narrative.

Limited female patronage may account in part for the lack of feminine role models in historical narratives of crusading and the Latin East, but this did not prevent women's appearance in such sources. For the most part, generalised 'departure scenes' or warnings about the consequences of sexual sin were directed at men, but there is evidence to suggest that some authors, at least, expected a female audience. It is likely that aristocratic women, whose social status relied on lineage, were keen to hear glorified accounts of the deeds of their relatives in the Holy Land.[14]

---

[11]   Ferrante, *Glory of Her Sex*, 111.

[12]   *Ibid.*, 112–18. See Karen Broadhurst, 'Henry II of England and Eleanor of Aquitaine: Patrons of Literature in French?', *Viator* 27 (1996), 53–84. For recent assessments of her role in literary culture, see Bull and Léglu, *The World of Eleanor of Aquitaine*, and Jean Flori, *Aliénor d'Aquitaine: La Reine Insoumise* (Paris, 2004), 337–82.

[13]   See 132–3 below.

[14]   This also ties in with the accepted role of women in 'approving' male prowess. See 46–7 below.

Women's Involvement in the Crusade Movement[15]

CRUSADING affected women's lives whether they stayed in Europe, took the cross, or lived in settler populations. In comparison to men, there is relatively meagre evidence about individual women who took part in the crusades, but as a group they are widely recorded as being present from the very first expedition.[16] Purcell asserts that it is inaccurate to talk of women as crusaders in the twelfth century, as no women were granted legal status as *crucesignatae* until the following century.[17] It has been argued, however, that there was no specific crusade terminology even for male crusaders until the thirteenth century,[18] and there are several accounts of women taking the cross alongside men in public ceremonies.[19] As well as women who took the cross in the narrow sense, Geldsetzer defines women's involvement in terms of three other groups: women associated with crusades to the Holy Land from 1100 to 1300, potential crusaders whose intention to crusade went unfulfilled, and women who do not fall into clear categories. In this final group she includes women who took vows but whose participation cannot be ascertained, travellers to the Near East during the time of the crusades and those with uncertain crusader status, women with male crusaders, and probable pilgrims.[20] With these latter categories it is particularly difficult to surmise the motives of individual women, but there is no reason to suggest that women who did take the cross and endured the penitential hardships of pilgrimage to Jerusalem alongside men considered themselves any less entitled to the spiritual benefits on offer.

In accordance with historical conventions, individual female crusaders who were named in crusade sources were predominantly noble. Of fifteen women listed by Geldsetzer as taking part in crusades between 1095 and 1101, eleven noblewomen have been identified from narratives or charters, the name of the

---

[15] This section was published in an abbreviated version as Natasha Hodgson, 'Women and Crusade', in Alan V. Murray ed. *The Crusades: An Encyclopaedia*, 4 vols (Santa Barbara, 2006), vol. 4, 1285–1290.

[16] The only account devoted solely to a single woman's crusading experience is Thomas of Froidmont's *Hodoeporicon*. First Crusade narratives which emphasised large numbers of female participants include Ekkehard of Aura, *Hierosolymita, de oppresione, liberatione et restauratione Jerosolymitanae ecclesiae*, in RHC Occ. 5 (Paris, 1895), 18; GN, 330; AA, 4–5.

[17] Purcell, 'Women Crusaders', 57.

[18] James Brundage, *Medieval Canon Law and the Crusader* (Madison, 1969), 10.

[19] Eleanor of Aquitaine took the cross directly after her husband at Vézelay according to the *Historia Gloriosi Regis Ludovici VII*, in RHGF, 12.126. Count Baldwin IX of Flanders took the cross with his wife Marie – see 118 below. Eleanor, countess of Montfort, and Beatrice of Flanders are also known to have taken the cross in public ceremonies. Tyerman, *Invention of the Crusades*, 75.

[20] Geldsetzer, *Frauen*, 21.

wife of Ivo of Grandmesnil is unknown, and the other three *anonymae* were a woman who followed her goose on crusade because she believed it was filled with the Holy Spirit, a 'companion' of Adalbero of Metz and a nun from Trier.[21] Women often accompanied male relatives – usually husbands[22] – as stipulated by the Church, although some appear to have travelled without a designated guardian. Two of the nine women known to have joined the Fifth Crusade may have travelled without family.[23] Thomas of Froidmont's account of the adventures of his sister Margaret of Beverley in the Holy Land makes no mention of a male companion.[24] A passenger list surviving from the *Saint Viktor*, a crusade ship of 1250, records that forty-two of the 342 common people *en route* to the Holy Land were women. As many as twenty-two of these had no male chaperone.[25] It should also be noted, however, that some women had to put aside their crusading ambitions, often because a male crusader upon whom they were relying for protection was unable to fulfil his vow.[26] Thus while kinship ties with male crusaders had a strong influence over the crusading activities of women from a variety of social backgrounds, the motivation and initiative of individual female participants cannot be ruled out.

Spiritual rewards such as the remission of sins were attractive to all Christians, and piety was fundamental in the decision to take the cross. The goal of Jerusalem and the dual nature of the crusade as an armed pilgrimage gave women a 'canonical loophole' to take part, despite the military rationale behind these expeditions.[27] Throughout the medieval period, women and men travelled to shrines all over Europe, such as Rome, Compostela and Jerusalem, to ask for advice, healing, and forgiveness for sins.[28] Such journeys were open to all sinners who wished to show their contrition. Jerusalem was the paramount

---

[21] Guibert of Nogent described the mistress of the goose as a poor woman, and was critical of her credulous followers, as was Ekkehard of Aura. GN, 331; Ekkehard, *Hierosolimita*, RHC *Occ.* 5.19. For the other two women, see 96–7, 152 below.

[22] See 39 above.

[23] Powell, 'Women on the Fifth Crusade', 299.

[24] TF, 472–85.

[25] See *Historia Diplomatica Friderici Secundi*, ed. Jean L. A. Huillard-Bréhols (Paris, 1861), 6.784–8; Kedar, 'Passenger List', 272 and Geldsetzer, *Frauen*, 196–8. Geldsetzer lists only twenty-one without male chaperones. Women described by family role consist of fifteen wives (ten unnamed), two named sisters and one named daughter. The remainder include Florina, 'friend' of Ogerius, Avilla Talosana (associated with another passenger, Bavillo Talosano) and Petronilla Porreten (associated with Bernar Porret).

[26] See Geldsetzer, *Frauen*, 182–4.

[27] Constance M. Rousseau, 'Home Front and Battlefield: The Gendering of Papal Crusading Policy (1095–1221)', in Edgington and Lambert, *Gendering the Crusades*, 32–3.

[28] For a useful overview see Diana Webb, *Medieval European Pilgrimage 700–1500* (Basingstoke, 2002), 89–98.

pilgrimage centre through its association with Christ, and because the rigours of the journey were so exacting. Precedents of female pilgrimage to the East appear from as early as 326 when the Empress Helena, mother of the Emperor Constantine the Great, travelled to the Holy Land.[29]

Securing an appropriate escort was one of the main problems facing female pilgrims.[30] Sometimes large groups of widows travelled together, but it was traditional for women to accompany parents, husbands, or sons.[31] Even with a male presence they were vulnerable because pilgrims were not supposed to carry arms. With the innovation of crusading, however, large numbers of armed and unarmed pilgrims could travel to the Holy Land together, as an army sanctioned to fight by the Pope, and considered to be destined by God to succeed. It is possible that the prospect of such an armed escort encouraged many pilgrims, women included, who might not otherwise have travelled to Jerusalem. Following the success of the First Crusade, a continued Latin presence in the Holy Land also made the pilgrimage more achievable. A settler population provided ties of kinship with the West, and organisations such as the Templars were founded with the intention of protecting pilgrims. Although not associated with a major crusade expedition, Ermengarde, countess of Brittany, went on a three-year pilgrimage to Jerusalem with a group of women. She had acted as regent for her husband, Alan IV, both during the First Crusade, and when he subsequently joined a monastery in 1112. She took the veil in Dijon in 1130, but around 1132 her half-brother King Fulk of Jerusalem invited her to visit the Holy Land. In her mid-sixties she took the opportunity to travel to the East, spending some time in Nablus and at the nunnery of St Anne's in Jerusalem,[32] and returning to Brittany before 1135.[33]

As non-combatants, women, along with the old, the infirm and children, were often criticised for causing logistical problems, using up supplies and slowing the pace of crusading armies, but they also fulfilled practical functions. They helped with manual tasks such as clearing rubble and filling in ditches.[34] Women were praised by the author of the *Gesta* for bringing refreshments and encouragement to First Crusaders at the battle of Dorylaeum.[35] Ambroise recounted that women brought water for the

[29] See 167 below. For a fourth-century account of the travels in the Holy Land of a female pilgrim thought to have been a Spanish nun, see M. L. McClure and Charles L. Feltoe, *The Pilgrimage of Etheria* (New York, 1919). For a brief account of traditions of female pilgrimage to the Holy Land before 1096, see Dernbecher, *Deum et Virum*, 13–26.

[30] Webb, *Medieval European Pilgrimage*, 92.

[31] *Ibid.*, 93.

[32] See 142 below.

[33] Hans E. Mayer, 'Angevins *versus* Normans: The New Men of King Fulk of Jerusalem', *American Philosophical Society* 133 (1989), 8. Geldsetzer, *Frauen*, 211.

[34] GN, 264; *Itinerarium*, 101–2. See also 119, below.

[35] GF, 200.

crusade host as they marched by, weeping and praying for the safety of the army.[36] Albert of Aachen relates how, at the siege of Jerusalem in 1099, women and other non-combatants helped to transport materials to weave the panels of a siege engine, presumably an activity at which they were skilled.[37] Prostitution evidently took place on crusade and was heavily criticised,[38] but other activities for women ranged from washing clothes to lice picking.[39] On the Fourth Crusade, women in the army were entitled to a share of the booty, demonstrating that their contribution to the expeditions was recognised.[40] Fifth Crusade statutes also maintained women's right to booty, and both Christian and Muslim women were employed grinding corn, while the women of the camp maintained markets for fish and vegetables, and probably tended to the wounded and sick.[41] One Parisian woman tended Louis IX when he was extremely ill from dysentery after his defeat at Mansurah in 1250: Geldsetzer has identified her as Hersenda, a woman who appears in two records practising medicine in later twelfth-century Paris, which means that she may have been taken on crusade specifically for this purpose.[42]

In narratives of crusading, like most martial histories, women were most often described as the victims of warfare: they were associated with booty and military success or failure. It is possible that this was something of a literary *topos*. Friedman has explored variations on the phrase 'all the men were killed and the women and children taken captive', which frequently appears in crusade narratives. Based on Prawer's comparison of the *Assises de la cour de Bourgeois* and the Provençal *Lo Codi*, Friedman notes that in the Latin kingdom, heirs to property were beholden to ransom parents and children of either sex, rather than just a son or father.[43] She interprets this as supporting the notion that women were more likely to be taken captive than men, but demonstrates awareness that the phrase was also a *topos* following biblical style.[44] On the other hand, there was probably a discouraging amount of historical 'truth' behind such accounts. Enslaving women often made more economic sense

---

[36] Ambroise, 1.7, lns 386–406. While the curiosity and support of locals in bringing water is mentioned in the *Itinerarium*, he does not specify that they were women. *Itinerarium*, 150–1.

[37] AA, 408–9.

[38] See 135–9 below.

[39] Ambroise, 1.92, lns 5688–91.

[40] RC, 96.

[41] Powell, 'Women on the Fifth Crusade', 300.

[42] Joinville, 170; Geldsetzer, *Frauen*, 193–4.

[43] Yvonne Friedman, *Encounter Between Enemies: Captivity and Ransom in the Latin Kingdom of Jerusalem* (Leiden, 2002), 166. See *Assises de la cour de Bourgeois*, RHC Lois 2.170, and Joshua Prawer, *Crusader Institutions* (Oxford, 1980), 445, 449.

[44] Friedman, *Encounter Between Enemies*, 162–86.

than holding them for ransom, as they commanded a lesser sum than their male counterparts and were further 'devalued' by the sexual slur that captivity entailed. In Balian of Ibelin's negotiations with Saladin on the surrender of Jerusalem, a woman was valued at a third, and then half the price of a man.[45] In Europe, the practice of hostage-taking for diplomatic or economic purposes had been customary for some time, where it came to be closely associated with ideals of knighthood and the proper conduct of warfare. In any form of medieval warfare the personal safety of female hostages could never be assured, but with the added dimension of religious conflict, their position was even more precarious.[46] Both male and female captives could be subject to physical torture, and women were often assumed to have been raped as a result of captivity. Women might survive capture through their economic value for ransom or slavery rather than through any chivalrous ideal; men represented a military threat, and were, unless they were particularly valuable, more likely to be killed.

Amongst the new Latin aristocracy of the Levant, the survival rate of women, compared to that of men, dictated that power was often transferred through widows and heiresses. Hamilton suggests that they 'provided continuity to the society of Outremer' by intermarriage with crusaders from the West, which is undoubtedly true of the high nobility.[47] The importance of aristocratic marriages to the settler society cannot be over-estimated; they were crucial in cementing political alliances between Latins from the West and the Levant, Greeks, Armenians and Syrians.[48] The precarious nature of frontier society also dictated that in the absence of male guardians, some women had the opportunity to act as feudal lords and could contribute directly to the military defence of the Holy Land, endorsing military expeditions, defending sieges, and paying and provisioning troops. Some lent their aid to crusaders: Joinville recalled that a small ship amongst the fleet sailing from Cyprus to Egypt had been given to him by his first cousin Eschiva of Montbéliard, widow of Balian of Ibelin, lord of Beirut.[49]

Women who remained behind in the West also helped to provide for the Holy Land by acting as reliable regents or financing crusaders. Some crusaders sold land to family members, including women, in order to raise funds for the expedition or returned home to burden their families with severe debts.[50]

---

[45] *Eracles*, 68–9.

[46] Yvonne Friedman, 'Women in Captivity and their Ransom during the Crusader Period', in Michael Goodrich, Sophia Menache and Sylvia Schein eds *Cross-cultural Convergences in the Crusader Period: Essays Presented to Aryeh Grabois on his 65th Birthday* (New York, 1995), 77.

[47] Hamilton, 'Women', 143.

[48] Phillips, *Defenders*, 19–20.

[49] Joinville, 84.

[50] Riley-Smith, *First Crusaders*, 149–50.

Epstein asserts that women gave more charitable donations to the crusades than men in medieval Genoa, although this was the pattern for most charitable donations, possibly because a woman's property was often moveable wealth.[51] Women also supported crusading by giving money and endowments to the newly established military orders.[52] By 1200, Innocent III in his papal bull *Quod super his* asked women to pray collectively for the success of crusade expeditions, and offered spiritual benefits if they donated cash or financed a knight instead of going on crusade.[53] Even the spiritual support of specific holy women could be influential. Philip of Flanders is known to have written to Hildegard of Bingen for her advice on the eve of his departure for the Holy Land in 1177.[54]

Marie of Champagne, daughter of Louis VII and Eleanor of Aquitaine, provides an excellent example of how the course of a noblewoman's life could be affected by crusading without ever taking the cross. She had been betrothed to her husband Count Henry I in 1153, after he had accompanied her parents on the Second Crusade. When Henry decided to return to the Holy Land in 1179 she acted as regent for him. He died shortly after his return in 1181, and thereafter Marie acted as regent until the accession of her son Henry II in 1187. After the young count reached his majority, his mother was again required to function as regent because of the crusades.[55] In 1190, Henry II of Champagne took part in the Third Crusade, and his unforeseen marriage to Isabella of Jerusalem meant that he stayed in the East until his death in 1197.[56]

Medieval Perceptions of Women and Crusading

ECCLESIASTICAL PERCEPTIONS

Authors of crusade narratives had two main reasons for avoiding the subject of women. First, a crusade expedition was by nature a military undertaking. Women were eclipsed by the martial feats of men that writers celebrated in their histories, and were customarily marginalised to the roles of onlooker or victim. Second, women were actively discouraged from crusading by the Church. According to Robert of Rheims, Pope Urban II considered female

---

[51] Steven A. Epstein, *Genoa and the Genoese 958–1528* (Chapel Hill, 1996), 118.

[52] See Alan J. Forey, 'Women and the Military Orders in the Twelfth and Thirteenth Centuries', *Studia Monastica* 29 (1987), 63–92.

[53] See Brundage, 'Crusader's Wife', 434.

[54] Miriam Rita Tessera, 'Philip Count of Flanders and Hildegard of Bingen: Crusading against the Saracens or Crusading against Deadly Sin', in Edgington and Lambert, *Gendering the Crusades*, 77–93.

[55] See also 162 below.

[56] Theodore Evergates, 'Aristocratic Women in the County of Champagne', in Theodore Evergates ed. *Aristocratic Women in Medieval France* (Philadelphia, 1999), 81–5.

participants without proper guardianship to be 'more hindrance than help, a burden rather than a benefit', but he included the sick and aged amongst this group, so gender was not the only grounds for refusing permission.[57] Woman could take part, but only if they accompanied husbands, brothers or legal cus-todians, and the message was reiterated in later crusade encyclicals. The earliest example of the commutation of a woman's crusade vow came when Emerias of Altejas took the cross for the First Crusade, but was absolved by Isarn, bishop of Toulouse, in return for founding a hospice for the poor, St Orens, in 1098. She was told that she could serve God better at home by giving charity to the poor.[58] Henry II's 1188 ordinances in preparation for the Third Crusade prohib-ited the participation of women unless they served a practical purpose, as in the case of laundresses.[59] In the thirteenth century, Innocent III's decision to allow women spiritual benefits for financing knights was undoubtedly designed to reduce non-combatant numbers on expeditions as well as raise cash, but it did at least recognise women's desire to contribute to the crusade effort.[60]

From an ecclesiastical perspective, women created a dilemma because they were entitled to prevent husbands from taking the cross through the marriage vow (in the twelfth century at least), but if they went on crusade they might slow the army and, worse, tempt crusaders into sexual sins which would lead to the loss of God's favour.[61] Maier asserts that the authors of model crusade sermons, such as Jacques of Vitry and Eudes of Châteauroux, also portrayed women as an impediment to crusading, accusing them of either 'actively trying to stop their husbands from taking the cross or being, together with children, the reason why men did not want to go on crusade'.[62] Concerns about non-combatants causing logistical problems on crusade expeditions were not neces-sarily gender-specific, as they often included the young, the aged, and the sick and the poor. On the other hand, the threats of prostitution or miscegena-tion with indigenous 'pagan' women were undoubtedly governed by ideas about gender and race. Siberry has demonstrated that sins were seen to be ultimately

---

[57] RR, 729.

[58] *Histoire générale de Languedoc*, ed. Joseph Vaissète, Claude Devic and Auguste Molinier, 16 vols (Toulouse, 1872–1904; reprinted Osnabrück, 1973), vol. 5. cols 756–8, no. 401 – CCCXXII. See Riley-Smith, *First Crusaders*, 108, and Geldsetzer, *Frauen*, 182.

[59] Gervase of Canterbury, 'Gesta Regum', in William Stubbs ed. *Gervasii Cantuariensis Opera Historica*, RS 73 (1879), 2.32; idem., 'Chronica', in William Stubbs ed. *Gervasii Cantuariensis Opera Historica*, RS 73 (1879), 1.409. Roger of Howden, *Chronica* ed. William Stubbs, 4 vols, RS 51 (London, 1868–71), 2.337, and idem., 'Gesta Henrici Secundis', in William Stubbs ed. *The Chronicle of the Reigns of Henry II and Richard I*, 2 vols, RS 49 (1867), 2.32; WN, 1.274.

[60] For papal attitudes towards women and crusading, see Rousseau, 'Home Front and Battlefield', 31–44.

[61] See Chapter 5, *passim*.

[62] Christoph T. Maier, *Crusade Propaganda and Ideology* (Cambridge, 2000), 65.

responsible for military defeats on crusade, and relations with women were often at the root of that sinfulness.[63] These ideas will be explored more fully in later chapters, but it should be noted that sometimes women were simply believed to be a disruptive influence. The *Itinerarium* blamed the riot in Sicily in October 1190 on the actions of one hot-headed woman. On being offered an unsatisfactory price for bread, she 'attacked the man with a stream of abuse, barely restraining herself from hitting him with her fist or pulling out his hair', and this inflamed other citizens into violence.[64]

PERCEPTIONS OF WOMEN AND WARFARE

Boys are accustomed to engage in battles such as this. Girls are accustomed to root for the clash of arms.[65]

The links between love and prowess in chivalric culture meant that women were often portrayed as admiring the martial expertise of knights.[66] This convention was reflected even in the earliest crusade histories. Several First Crusade sources mentioned the support received from Christian women who watched the progress of crusaders from the walls of Antioch, and how they applauded secretly.[67] The *Chanson de Jérusalem* asserts that women encouraged the crusaders in battle by reminding them of their 'heavenly reward'.[68] Robert of Clari described how ladies and maidens watched the battle between the emperor and Fourth Crusaders commence from the walls and windows in Constantinople, admiring the Franks: 'And they were saying to one another that our men seemed like angels, they were so beautiful, because they were so finely armed and their horses so finely accoutred.'[69] Evidently he was unlikely to have been privy to the conversations of the ladies on the walls, and faced with the prospect of attack by a hostile force, the good looks of their enemies can hardly have been foremost in their minds. This image, however, fits in with the courtly conventions of the tournament and women's approval of male prowess.

---

[63] Siberry, *Criticism*, 69–108.

[64] *Itinerarium*, 158; trans. Nicholson, 159; Ambroise, 1.10–11, lns 627–40. The riot is also mentioned by Ralph of Diceto, 'Ymagines Historiarum', in William Stubbs ed. *The Historical Works of Master Ralph de Diceto*, RS 68 (London, 1876), 2.85, and Roger of Howden, *Chronica*, ed. W. Stubbs, RS 51 (London, 1868–71), 3.56, but no mention is made of the woman selling bread.

[65] GT, 698; trans. Bachrach and Bachrach, 147.

[66] Richard Kaeuper, *Chivalry and Violence in Medieval Europe* (Oxford, 1999), 219–25. See also David Crouch, *The Birth of Nobility: Constructing the Aristocracy in England and France, 900–1300* (Harlow, 2005), chapter 12, 'Noble Women: The View from the Stands'.

[67] GF, 284; PT, 76; GN, 192.

[68] *La Chanson de Jérusalem*, ed. Nigel Thorp [The Old French Crusade Cycle] (Tuscaloosa, 1992), 6.112.

[69] RC, 49; trans. McNeal, 75.

It is also extremely reminiscent of a passage in the *Canso d'Antioca*, where the supernatural forces which appeared at the siege of Antioch were described as all accoutred in white and seeming like angels.[70] This particular description is unique to the Occitan tradition in First Crusade histories, and Robert was from north-eastern France, the manuscript fragment is dated to the late twelfth century. Robert was a lay knight steeped in chivalric tradition, and may not have been unaware of the parallel. He also employed the disapproval of women as a shaming device; the same ladies criticised the emperor for cowardice when he withdrew back into the city.[71] The charge of effeminacy was commonly used by Latin authors to imply cowardice, most famously against the Greeks,[72] but also against errant crusaders. Henry of Huntingdon accused Count Stephen of Blois of fleeing 'like a woman' from the siege of Antioch in 1098.[73] Everard III of Le Puiset reputedly turned the tide of the battle for Jerusalem, scorning those about to flee for their lack of masculinity: 'Are you men of Francia? I do not think it dignified to give the name of French women to you ... Shake off your fear. Demonstrate the manliness of your homeland.'[74]

Authors of crusade narratives sometimes employed female characters in masculine roles within their texts to highlight male chivalric ideals, but it is unlikely that women acted as warriors on crusades. *Fragilitas sexus* was the conventional description applied to medieval women to explain their exclusion from warfare, and they were also sometimes described as unfit to bear arms.[75] Crusade narratives supported this view: the *Itinerarium* records that women encouraged their male relatives to go on the Third Crusade, but regretted that they could not take part 'because of the weakness of their sex'.[76] There are occasional mentions of women fighting during crusade battles and especially during sieges, but these cannot always be verified. William of Tyre, in writing his account of the assault on Jerusalem, tells how 'women, forgetful of their sex and unmindful of their inherent fragility, were presuming to take up arms and fought manfully beyond their strength'.[77]

---

[70] *Canso d'Antioca*, 201.

[71] RC, 51.

[72] See Matthew Bennett, 'Virile Latins, Effeminate Greeks and Strong Women: Gender Definitions on Crusade?', in Edgington and Lambert, *Gendering the Crusades*, 18.

[73] Henry of Huntingdon, *Historia Anglorum*, ed. and trans. Diana Greenaway (Oxford, 1996), 436–7. For more detail see James A. Brundage, 'An Errant Crusader: Stephen of Blois', *Traditio* 16 (1960), 380–94.

[74] GT, 698; trans. Bachrach and Bachrach, 147.

[75] See Michael R. Evans, '"Unfit to Bear Arms": The Gendering of Arms and Armour in Accounts of Women on Crusade', in Edgington and Lambert, *Gendering the Crusades*, 44–58; and McLaughlin, 'The Woman Warrior', 193–209.

[76] *Itinerarium*, 33; Nicholson 48 translates this as the 'fragility of their sex', but, significantly, *ignavus* could be interpreted as cowardice, or an un-warlike nature.

[77] WT, 403.

This does not appear in the historical narratives of contemporary eyewitnesses, but a contingent of women is to be found in the *Chanson de Jérusalem*.[78] The *Chanson d'Antioche* also describes a battalion of women at the eponymous siege in 1098, but both passages have been interpreted as humorous episodes.[79] Accounts of individual female warriors do appear in conjunction with crusade texts, but often borrowed heavily from the realms of classical fiction. One Greek source for the Second Crusade tells of female warriors 'more mannish than Amazons' in the German contingent, bearing lances and weapons astride their horses, and dressed in masculine clothes.[80] Eyewitness Muslim sources for the Third Crusade also recorded Frankish women dressed for battle, and Guibert of Nogent likened female archers in Kerborgha's army to the huntress Diana outside Antioch; but the presence of female warriors was treated as indicative of either weakness or barbarity in a foe, and was sometimes a deliberate literary device.[81] A defeated enemy could also be described in feminine terms in order to emphasise the masculinity of victory on the battlefield. When Tancred defeated a Turkish army near Nicaea, he 'raised up the morale of the soldiers of Christ and turned the enemy into women.'[82]

Bearing in mind caveats about using female warriors to criticise or shame an enemy, some incidents where Christian women take up arms in Latin sources seem a little more authentic, if comical on occasion. Thomas of Froidmont described his sister Margaret of Beverley garbed in a breastplate and an impromptu helmet made out of a pot, carrying water to soldiers on the walls during the 1187 siege of Jerusalem, where she was wounded by a stone missile.[83] One rather gruesome Third Crusade account tells how women used knives to slit the throats of prisoners taken from a captured galley at Acre, their feminine weakness prolonging the pain of their dying enemies.[84] During the Fifth Crusade women stood armed guard over the camp and killed the Muslims who fled from a failed attack on Damietta.[85] Within the constraints of this study it has not been possible to make more detailed reference to the sources for the Albigensian Crusade, but it is notable that there is an account of women

[78]   *La Chanson de Jérusalem*, 108–9, 112. William may have found support for this story in Albert of Aachen. He mentions that women were present in the crowd who stormed the city walls after they had been breached. AA, 408–9, 430–1.

[79]   Edgington, ' Sont çou ore les fems', 157.

[80]   Niketas Choniates, *O City of Byzantium: The Annals of Niketas Choniates*, trans. Harry M. Magoulias (Detroit, 1984), 35.

[81]   Nicholson, 'Women on the Third Crusade', 338–40.

[82]   GT, 78; trans. Bachrach and Bachrach, 39.

[83]   TF, 478–9.

[84]   *Itinerarium*, 33.

[85]   Powell, 'Women on the Fifth Crusade', 300.

operating a siege engine against crusaders, and even a female castellan at the siege of Lavaur in 1211, Giraude de Laurac.[86]

Authors may have emphasised women's involvement as a means of discrediting heretical movements, but women were known to play important roles in such sects – especially the Cathar heresy.[87] In Spain, Ermengarde, viscountess of Narbonne, led her troops to aid the siege of Tortosa in 1148, although Bennett questions how far her generalship extended.[88] Mazeika has also highlighted instances of settler women fighting to protect Christian settlements in the Baltic.[89] If women did fight, it was only in the absence of suitable male warriors or when the odds seemed overwhelming; and they usually were praised for it in masculine terms. Women who became involved in fighting were encroaching on a male role that was fundamental to the construct of medieval masculinity. Fighting women could demonstrate chivalrous qualities, bravery in particular, but in order to keep masculinity intact, women had to be seen as transcending their gender. Conversely the men who failed to take the cross or demonstrated cowardice were reduced to womanly status. The *Itinerarium* mentions how wool and distaff were sent to those men who were too cowardly to take up the cross, 'hinting that if anyone failed to join this military undertaking they were only fit for women's work'.[90]

As crusade propagandists used chivalric ideas to appeal to the values of knights, so they used the *fragilitas sexus* that purportedly prevented women from taking up arms themselves to encourage knights to provide them with protection. The Church had long attempted to forbid knightly violence against not only ecclesiastics, but other members of society who could not defend themselves: the poor, widows, orphans and women in general. The abuse of helpless Christians in the East was a common theme even in the earliest calls for crusade, and sometimes the suffering of women was used in order to appeal to the chivalric sensibilities of the nobility in the West. Raymond of Aguilers recounted the abuses perpetrated against the Christian women of Tyre.[91] Robert of Rheims' version of Urban's speech emphasised how women were defiled at the hands of the Turks: 'What can I say about the evil rape of women, of which it is worse to speak than to be silent?'[92] The nature of religious warfare, however, meant that attitudes towards Muslim women differed. Those who died at the hands of crusade armies were sometimes perceived as victims, but

---

[86] James Bradbury, *The Medieval Siege* (Woodbridge, 1992), 135–7.

[87] Malcolm Barber, 'Women and Catharism', *Reading Medieval Studies* 3 (1977), 45–62.

[88] Bennett, 'Virile Latins', 26–7.

[89] Mazeika, 'Women Warriors', 229–48.

[90] *Itinerarium*, 33; trans. Nicholson, 48. Cf. Sarah Lambert, 'Crusading or Spinning', in Edgington and Lambert, *Gendering the Crusades*, 1–15.

[91] RA, 129–30.

[92] RR, 728.

most authors considered their deaths to be justified and even used them to exaggerate the extent of the slaughter.

PERCEPTIONS OF NOBILITY

Noblewomen, like noblemen, were judged by their actions as well as their ancestry. Their political roles as patrons and intercessors made them worthy of comment in narrative histories, but they were unable to achieve honour on the battlefield like their male counterparts. The difficulty in defining the noblewoman therefore largely stems from the association of nobility with warfare. How far the nobility were associated with the 'knightly class', and by what point the two become indistinguishable (if at all) has stimulated much historical debate. For some, the twelfth century seems to have been a benchmark for nobles adopting knightly ideals. Keen asserted that chivalry was inextricably associated with both martial and aristocratic values, and that from the mid-twelfth century it 'frequently carries ethical or religious overtones'.[93] This development must have owed something to the cultural impact of knightly participation in the crusade movement. The 'orders' model of society which associated the nobility with their military role (*pugnantes*), and the limited legal rights that women enjoyed, have led some to question the perceived place of women in medieval society; Shahar described them as comprising a 'Fourth Estate'.[94] However, contemporary historians such as Orderic Vitalis saw women functioning perfectly well within those three socio-economic groups.[95] The term 'nobility' itself encompassed a variety of implications beyond its military association. It was applied to an economic or land-owning 'class', to bloodline and noble descent, and it was used as a descriptive term to embody the range of values associated with 'noble' conduct.[96]

Despite claims that patrilineal inheritance was marginalising women from power during this period, there is evidence to suggest that a noblewoman's lineage remained fundamental to family dynasties and helped to establish her 'nobility' – especially when she did not have access to the battlefield as a means for social advancement.[97] The noblewoman also had clearly defined duties which revolved around roles in the family. As a daughter she was expected to

---

93 Keen, *Chivalry*, 2. For further definitions, see Jeremy duQuesnay Adams, 'Modern Views of Medieval Chivalry, 1884–1984', in Chickering and Seiler, *Study of Chivalry*, 41–89.

94 Shulamith Shahar, *The Fourth Estate: A History of Women in the Middle Ages*, 2nd edition (London, 1991).

95 Marjorie Chibnall, 'Women in Orderic Vitalis', *Haskins Society Journal* 2 (1990), 105.

96 See Crouch, *Birth of Nobility*; idem., *The Image of the Aristocracy in Britain 1000–1300* (London, 1992), 3; Chickering, 'Introduction', in Chickering and Seiler, *Study of Chivalry*, 1–38; Matthew Strickland, *War and Chivalry* (Cambridge, 1996), 21.

97 See Chapter 4, *passim*.

be obedient, and as a wife she managed the household; she had an obligation of maternity to provide an heir, and to care for her children's interests in the absence of her husband. Certain qualities were desirable at all stages: chaste behaviour and moral fibre, usually represented by piety. In terms of active participation in the ruling 'class', noblewomen were restricted in their control of property, but could exert power in a number of ways. Some women did experience a degree of autonomy in land-ownership, usually heiresses and widows, but this was dependent on their age and political situation. More often, women fulfilled important roles as intercessors with male kin, and extended patronage through their own circles of influence. The crucial function of marriage in medieval power politics meant that noblewomen often had the opportunity to play an important role in historical events. In fact, their significance in this area often meant that they were involved in arranging matches between families. Parsons asserts that 'noblewomen's unique participation in matrimonial politics did afford them opportunities to claim power and to achieve some degree of self-realisation.'[98]

The nobility as a social group shared certain legal privileges but medieval society was not the static hierarchical system that the 'orders' model would suggest. While birthright and inheritance of land were increasingly vital components to nobility, rulers were still able to confer and take away titles for personal or political reasons, and relationships of patronage could dramatically affect social status. In this period of increased prosperity, the wealthy were able to buy land and titles, which sometimes fell vacant as a result of warfare. Naturally, crusades acted as a catalyst for this kind of social mobility, compounding high death rates through disease, famine and war with access to booty and new landed wealth. A lucky crusader could improve his social position either by conquest or marriage, but this social fluidity worked both ways: the fortunes of war could reduce knights to foot soldiers and dispossess established nobility.[99] William of Tyre recounts how famine in Antioch during the First Crusade reduced some of the nobility to beggary, while others chose to starve rather than behave in a manner beneath their status.[100] Both Ambroise and the *Itinerarium* tell of nobles reduced to eating grass during the famine at the siege of Acre.[101] There were also accounts of nobles stealing bread rather than ask for charity, ashamed to beg in public because they came from noble stock.[102] Conversely, even an impoverished noblewoman from the Latin East could be a desirable marriage partner if she had a claim to land; but as the situation of

98 John Carmi Parsons, 'Mothers, Daughters, Marriage, Power: Some Plantagenet evidence 1150–1500', in *Medieval Queenship*, 65.

99 See GF, 6 and 458, for the author being one of these. See also GN, 168–9.

100 WT, 315.

101 Ambroise, 1.68–9, lns 4251–6; *Itinerarium*, 127.

102 *Itinerarium*, 130–1; Ambroise, 1.69, lns 4273–304.

the settler society deteriorated in the thirteenth century, titles alone were not always enough to secure a woman's fortune.

Ultimately, perceptions of women in medieval literature were governed by a variety of traditional ideas and contemporary concerns about gender, social status, family role, and individual character, but there was no set hierarchy for these categories. Authors combined elements of all of them in describing both women and men in order to find models which best suited their purposes. They also had to produce 'credible' history using eyewitness accounts, incorporate their version of historical 'events', and provide sufficient interesting detail. To do otherwise ran the risk of losing their audience, or, worse, patronage.

These three chapters have established the context in which crusade histories wrote about women; the following four will go on to consider how life-cycle stages and the key perceptions associated with them affected the portrayal of women in narratives of crusading and the Latin East.

◆ *Part II* ◆

♦ 4 ♦

Daughters

Daughters and Medieval Society

THE aristocratic focus of crusade narratives made it inevitable that evidence about daughters was heavily weighted towards the lineage, inheritance and betrothal of young noblewomen. To a lesser extent, their character and training were also discussed. This chapter will centre predominantly on unmarried aristocratic daughters, but heiresses will be discussed both before and after wedlock in matters pertaining to their birthright. Dowry was critical to a woman's social position and will be considered here in reference to the negotiations preceding marriage, although it will also feature in later chapters on wives and widows. Sexual status was also a measure of daughterhood – the term *virgines* was sometimes used to describe young unmarried women instead of *filiae* or *puellae*. This term could also apply to celibate women of any age, however. Many entered convents after married life and were not technically virgins, but as Wogan-Browne remarks, 'the relations between "technical" and "spiritual" virginity are constantly and revealingly negotiable.'[1] Women religious will be discussed here in relation to the issue of virginity because of its association with daughterhood, but those who were known to have entered monasteries after marriage will be considered in the relevant chapters. The following section will briefly explore the traditional views about daughters which medieval authors drew from classical and biblical writings, as well as the social conventions that influenced them during the time of the crusades. To begin, some of the general historiographical problems raised by the study of childhood and the life-cycle stage of daughterhood must be considered.

DAUGHTERHOOD AND CHILDHOOD

Schulz asserts that there are two main paradigms present in the historiography of childhood: those who believe that the concept of childhood was essentially a modern historical phenomenon and did not exist in medieval terms;[2]

---

[1] Jocelyn Wogan-Browne, *Saints' Lives and Women's Literary Culture: Virginity and its Authorisations* (Oxford, 2001), 41.

[2] James A. Schulz, *The Knowledge of Childhood in the German Middle Ages 1100–1350* (Philadelphia, 1995), 2, 3, 8–9. For an example of this view, see Philip Ariès, *Centuries of Childhood*, trans. Robert Baldick (London, 1962), 33. Other recent publications on childhood include Shulamith Shahar, *Childhood in the Middle Ages*, trans. Chaya Galai (London, 1990); Danièle Alexandre Bidon and Didier Lett, *Children in the Middle Ages: Fifth–Fifteenth Centuries*, trans. Jody Gladding (Notre Dame, 1999); and Nicholas Orme, *Medieval Children* (New Haven, 2001).

and those who saw childhood as a natural occurrence, 'governed by immutable laws'.[3] It is a problem that also affects the study of gender. Basic biological differences govern both men and women, but one cannot apply universal or timeless qualities to either sex. Gender identities are combined with criteria that are subject to change; thus imposing modern values in lieu of evidence will not suffice. The very few descriptions of parental nurture do not prove that perceptions of daughterhood remain unchanged, nor can the dearth of existing evidence be taken to mean that daughters were completely disregarded within medieval society. Women seldom appeared in official documents before they were married unless they were entitled to an inheritance, and accordingly many historical studies have been weighted towards heiresses, wives and widows, although recent attempts have been made to address this imbalance.[4] Male domination of medieval literary culture meant that most young women were only deemed worthy of attention when they were of marriageable age, and in this context they attracted both appreciation and criticism.[5]

There were three specific stages of childhood according to most authors: *infantia* covered the period up to age seven, then came *pueritia*, which lasted until fourteen for boys, and twelve for girls. Daughters were considered to mature earlier because of classical ideas about their physical imperfection; thus twelve was the canonical age of marriage for girls, although many married later. After *pueritia* came *adolescentia*, which lasted until adulthood, but there was no specific age denoting the transition.[6] Marriage was usually a sign of maturity for both men and women, but the age of partners varied widely over economic and social boundaries. Aristocratic daughters might be married as early as seven or eight, but women of lesser status often had to work for their dowry, raising the age of marriage. Although this diversity is problematic for the historian of the adolescent woman, particularly when male 'youth' was more obviously structured, Phillips asserts that there was a definable period of adolescence for women – maidenhood. This was 'understood by many as the "perfect age" of woman's life and was therefore an important ideal of femininity'.[7] During adolescence children of both sexes took on roles more strongly defined by gender, but a degree of information and opinions about their earlier lives can be ascertained.

---

3 Schulz considers Shahar's work to be an example of this approach. *Ibid.*, 2, 5–6.

4 See Katherine J. Lewis, Noel James Menuge and Kim Phillips, eds *Young Medieval Women* (Stroud, 1999); and Kim M. Phillips, *Medieval Maidens: Young Women and Gender in England c. 1270–c. 1540* (Manchester, 2003).

5 Schulz, *Knowledge of Childhood*, 258.

6 Shahar, *Childhood*, 22. See 264–5 n. 3 for a comprehensive assessment of medieval texts referring to these stages of childhood.

7 Phillips, *Medieval Maidens*, 17, 7.

TRADITIONAL VIEWS ON DAUGHTERHOOD:
EDUCATION AND PARENTAL NURTURE

The participation of noblewomen in literary culture suggests that some, at least, received scholarly training, but this was not a priority in the education of daughters. Aristocratic women were largely trained in practical arts that they would need on marriage: skills for managing the household and providing hospitality. Girls were normally instructed orally; according to Phillips, reading literacy only existed where it 'supplemented oral culture'.[8] Convent schooling was the choice of the elite, because it provided for spiritual welfare as well as safeguarding the chastity and reputation of its pupils, but medieval parents tended to spend less on educating daughters and sent them away from the family home less frequently than boys.[9] The emphasis on practical skills meant that literature about the education of daughters developed slowly, and even then writers such as Vincent of Beauvais championed the moral aspects of educational pursuits for women over the intellectual.[10] Obedience was the key characteristic required of daughters; thus discipline and training were to form an important role in providing this.

Patriarchal society and religious doctrine at the time of the crusades demanded that children of both sexes honour and obey both father and mother. Most mothers were involved in childcare, at least in the early years, but practices such as wet-nursing and fostering, as well as educational training outside the household, sometimes limited that role. Noble fathers were rarely involved with their daughters until arranging their marriage, and even then women usually assisted in this process.[11] Contemporary beliefs about the nature of women and lust exacerbated parents' fears about protecting their daughters. Based on classical ideas about physiology, early Christian teaching considered women to be more inclined towards physical passion than men, as they were driven by their lack of innate heat to reproduce,[12] which made guarding adolescent girls all the more vital. The book of Ecclesiasticus suggests: 'You have sons? Train them and care for them from boyhood. You have daughters? Guard their bodies and do not show a joyful face to them.'[13] Such traditional sources present a bleak view of the relationship between parent and child, but must be treated with caution as it is impossible to say whether they were representative of

---

[8] *Ibid.*, 62.

[9] Shahar, *Childhood*, 221.

[10] Nicholas Orme, *From Childhood to Chivalry: The Education of the English Kings and Aristocracy 1066–1530* (London, 1984), 106.

[11] For example, see 88 below.

[12] Aristotle, 'Historia Animalium', trans. D'Arcy Wentworth Thompson, in *The Works of Aristotle* (Oxford, 1910), 4.608b.

[13] Eccles 7:25–6.

medieval experience. It is certain, however, that medieval society was strongly affected by the bonds of kinship, through both male and female lines.

LINEAGE AND INHERITANCE

On marriage, a woman became subject to her husband in patriarchal society, and her role as a wife was perceived to supersede her previous status as a daughter. The predominance of husband–wife relations over the parental link, while sanctioned by church doctrine, did not always work in practice. Wives often remained in contact with their parents and siblings after marriage, playing a diplomatic role between families.[14] When a match foundered, parents or kin would often intervene, especially if the union had not produced children. Wives were sometimes criticised for influencing husbands to extend patronage to their own relatives, thus elevating their position as daughter in one family over their role as a wife in another. Some women continued to be described as daughters even after marriage, as medieval historians continued to emphasise both maternal and paternal ancestry, despite arguments that there was a growing trend for patrilineal inheritance.[15] This followed the biblical and Roman practice of listing ancestors, and was also evidenced by the growing popularity of genealogical histories, reflecting contemporary ideas about the importance of noble birthright.[16] As a result of eleventh-century church reforms, there was a drive to proscribe relationships within the prohibited seven degrees,[17] placing further emphasis on the interconnections between maternal and paternal family lines. Often a woman was described as a daughter of a particular family without referring to her personal name, demonstrating that lineage provided an aristocratic woman with her status and identity, and was perceived to be far more important than individuality.

Daughters of the nobility were valued, but medieval authors usually assumed that parents preferred sons.[18] Louis VII famously remarked that before the birth of his first son, Philip, in 1165, 'we have been terrorised by a multitude of daughters'.[19] Louis IX's wife reputedly employed William of Auvergne to tell her husband of the birth of their first child, Blanche, because she was afraid he would be angered by having a daughter instead of a son.[20] A son and heir was most desirable to fulfil military commitments, but rivalry amongst too many

---

[14] See Hugh M. Thomas, *Vassals, Heiresses, Crusaders and Thugs: The Gentry of Angevin Yorkshire 1154–1216* (Philadelphia, 1993), 108.

[15] See 159–60 below.

[16] Dunbabin, 'Discovering a Past', 3.

[17] See 104 below.

[18] Shahar, *Childhood*, 43–5.

[19] *Monuments historiques*, ed. Jules Tardif (Paris, 1866), 300, Letter 588.

[20] Stephen of Bourbon, *Anecdotes Historiques, Legendes et Apologues*, ed. Albert Lecoy de La Marche (Paris, 1877), 388 n. 1.

male kin could endanger the smooth transition of power. Daughters, on the other hand, were necessary for the creation of alliances with other families. Disputes and negotiations were often sealed with a marriage arrangement as an insurance policy. The arrival of a daughter was only a real disappointment when a male heir was desperately needed.

It has been argued that great changes were occurring in the systems of inheritance in the period prior to the First Crusade, whose impact was still being felt while crusading was at its height. According to Herlihy, from the beginning of the eleventh century bilateral inheritance was in decline, and the exclusion of women meant that the daughter was 'treated as a marginal member of her father's lineage'.[21] In Duby's study, *The Knight the Lady and the Priest*, the lay aristocracy and the priesthood were seen to preserve their ruling power by deliberately excluding women from inheritance.[22] Leyser, however, called Duby's approach to daughters 'somewhat phallocentric', arguing that not all women were 'at the mercy of their violent men folk, and could only seek refuge or endure captivity in nunneries'.[23] The idea that a trend towards patrilineal primogeniture in land holding marginalised aristocratic women from power has been challenged on two counts – first, that a defined period of transition from indiscriminate agnatic and cognatic inheritance to primogeniture cannot be clearly identified, and second, that such a view fails to take into account the difference in constructions of female power based on life-cycle roles.[24] In any case, lords were usually reluctant to leave their lands and possessions to more distant relatives, and where there was no suitable male heir, daughters did inherit. Contemporary administrative developments such as commuting feudal services for cash aided an heiress to fulfil her land-holding obligations, but legal rights for women in such situations were still limited. Parents, guardians or feudal lords usually made arrangements for an heiress to marry as soon as possible. As a result, heiresses were often married underage, and while this provided a certain amount of political stability, problems could ensue if the match later proved unsuitable. Once married, her husband assumed control of her inheritance excluding such lands as she held for her dower; but marriage also signalled a woman's 'entrée' into public life and her exercise of public

---

[21]   David Herlihy, *Medieval Households* (Cambridge, MA, 1985), 82.

[22]   See Georges Duby, *The Knight the Lady and the Priest*, trans. Barbara Bray (New York, 1983).

[23]   Conrad Leyser, 'Custom, Truth and Gender in Eleventh Century Reform', in Robert N. Swanson ed. *Gender and the Christian Religion* (Woodbridge, 1998), 79.

[24]   For criticisms of the notion that primogeniture became *de rigueur* in France from the early eleventh century, see Theodore Evergates, 'Nobles and Knights in Twelfth Century France', in Thomas N. Bisson ed. *Cultures of Power: Lordship, Status and Process in Twelfth Century Europe* (Philadelphia, 1995), 17–28; and Constance Bouchard, 'Family Structure and Family Consciousness among the French Aristocracy in the Ninth to Eleventh Centuries', *Francia* 14 (1986), 639–58. See also Johns, *Noblewomen*, 2–3, 195.

power in a variety of forms.[25] In general, heiresses had little freedom of choice in partner and had an obligation of marriage and maternity to produce an heir for their lands. However, an heiress might also be permitted to remain a widow after the death of her husband if she already had a minor heir whose interests might be compromised by her remarriage.

BETROTHAL

Marriage and the protocols by which it was arranged underwent profound changes during this period. There was a new emphasis on the mutual consent of both partners, although most marriages were still arranged by parents or elders to benefit the wider family. The issue of consent may have afforded some autonomy to the marriage partners, but it made the crime of abduction much more difficult to establish. Any question over a daughter's sexual continence, whether voluntary or through rape, could seriously affect her value as a bride, and penalties were accordingly severe for both men and women.[26] The betrothal, effectively a statement of intent to marry, was not unique to this period, but its customs developed rapidly alongside other measures to protect the interests of the two families involved in a marriage.[27]

Once a suitable marriage partner was selected, negotiations established the exact terms of the match. When the betrothal had taken place, a young noblewoman might be brought up in the court of her intended to familiarize her with the way of life she would enter into upon marriage. A dowry, the gift of the bride's family, was also negotiated, and could take different forms, ranging from hard cash to property. Cash was usually preferred, but it would often be invested, to provide a regular income and as surety for the bride's family should the marriage dissolve or fail to produce offspring.[28] The marriage arrangements usually entailed some form of dower for the bride in case her husband died. In some parts of Europe the groom's family also gave a *morgengaben*, or 'morning gift', but during the high Middle Ages there was a general decrease in this practice; thus it fell progressively to the bride's family to provide a competitive dowry to attract a suitable husband.[29] Depending on a daughter's age, a certain amount of time could elapse between the betrothal negotiations and the wedding itself. During that period, contracts were often broken if a more suitable alliance arose, which could lead to legal complications.[30] Although

---

[25] Johns, *Noblewomen*, 2.

[26] See James Brundage, *Law, Sex and Christian Society in Medieval Europe* (Chicago, 1987), 47, 107, 119.

[27] See 103–6 below.

[28] Evergates, 'Aristocratic Women in the County of Champagne', 91–2.

[29] See Diane Owen Hughs, 'From Brideprice to Dowry in Mediterranean Europe', *Journal of Family History* 3 (1978), 262–96.

[30] Evergates, 'Aristocratic Women in the County of Champagne', 91.

dowry had no official place in canon law, if it was not forthcoming after a marriage some of the nobility argued that they had a legitimate case to dissolve the union.

VIRGINITY AND THE CLOISTER

The Church championed celibacy as a means to salvation, but this was at odds with the requirements that a society based on kinship had for daughters, namely, their use in marriage alliances. The enforcement of clerical celibacy during the tenth and eleventh centuries excluded women from having an active role in church affairs through a priestly husband. Lay women attracted to a devout life could patronise the Church for spiritual benefits if they had sufficient means, but otherwise they were relegated to a cloistered role. Convents usually housed daughters of the nobility, many of whom entered nunneries at an early age,[31] although others entered convents as discarded wives or widows, having discharged their duties to the family. Some daughters rebelled against an impending marriage, but medieval authors only approved this when it involved a commitment to chastity, as in the case of Christina of Markyate.[32] Despite their disobedience, medieval chroniclers usually applauded the courage of such women; they were seen to rise above the weakness of their gender and triumph over the demands of the flesh, becoming idealised examples of virginity. Accordingly, most ecclesiastics encouraged leniency for those women with a genuine monastic vocation. During the fifth century St Jerome had written at length on the benefits of virginity and detriments of marriage. Virginity was the holiest state to which a woman could aspire. It was through the miraculous conception of Jesus in the womb of the Virgin that the curse laid upon Eve in the Garden of Eden was lifted. The idea of temptation through Eve and redemption through Mary was a common motif in ideas about the nature of women in medieval society. [33]

The Virgin Mary was perhaps the most important symbol of medieval womanhood, and while she is often associated with the imagery of motherhood and authority, her virginity also had crucial significance. Phillips has argued that, despite motherhood and living into old age, and even in images of her death, assumption and coronation as queen of heaven, Mary was continually portrayed at that period of life in which she was seen to have achieved perfection: maidenhood.[34]

---

[31] Margaret Wade Labarge, *Women in Medieval Life: A Small Sound of the Trumpet* (London, 1986), 29.

[32] Georges Duby, *Love in Twelfth Century France*, trans. Jane Dunnett (Oxford, 1994), 25. See also *The Life of Christina of Markyate, a Twelfth Century Recluse*, ed. and trans. Charles. H. Talbot, 2nd edition (Oxford, 1987).

[33] For example, St Jerome, 'Letter to Eustochium', in Jacques-Paul Migne ed. *Patrologia Latina* 22 (Paris, 1877), cols 394–425.

[34] Phillips, *Medieval Maidens*, 49–50.

The rise of her cult during the central Middle Ages undoubtedly had repercussions for the shaping of imagery for adolescent women. Other religious role models provided for daughters included the virgin martyrs: chaste women who died for the Christian faith, sometimes as a result of refusing marriage or sexual intercourse. Saint Foy, whose cult flourished at the monastery of Conques during the tenth and eleventh centuries, was a particularly striking example of a female child martyr, and in her *passio* much emphasis was placed on her youth and beauty.[35]

Saints' lives were very popular and considered to be suitable didactic texts for young women.[36] Such hagiographies were heavily concerned with the issue of chastity, and highlighted the contradictory societal requirements that daughters faced. They were considered to be available for marriage from age twelve, but had to remain chaste until their marriage took place, and this 'peculiar mixture of sexual availability and virginity' characterised the 'maiden'.[37] In accordance with these social and literary conventions, most of the individual daughters mentioned in crusade narratives were young women on the eve of marriage.

Daughters in the Narratives of Crusading and the Latin East

THE second part of this chapter will assess how such conventions influenced the narratives of crusading, incorporating some minor adaptations to accommodate the nature of the source material. For example, when considering the issue of parental nurture, the primary focus will be the relationship between father and daughter – 'paternal nurture'. This is for two reasons: first, to avoid extensive repetition of the subject matter when motherhood is considered; and second, because accounts of the relationship between fathers and daughters often highlight more effectively the gender characteristics of men and women. The categories from the previous section will be further subdivided where appropriate. For example, the source material is weighted heavily towards the inheritance and lineage of daughters in the Latin East; therefore they will be discussed in a separate category and subdivided by social status. A further section will cover the role of those daughters who did not stand to inherit lordship but whose betrothal negotiations were crucial to international diplomacy, especially in marriages arranged between the nobilities of Byzantium, western Europe and the Latin East. These differences aside, the structure will complement that of the preceding section, following a brief introduction to general views about daughters and crusading.

---

35 *Liber miraculorum sancte Fidis*, ed. Auguste Bouillet (Paris, 1997). For more detail on the Virgin in the context of crusading, see 163–7 below.

36 For a recent study, see Wogan-Browne, *Saints' Lives*.

37 Phillips, *Medieval Maidens*, 7.

DAUGHTERS AND CRUSADING

The daughter is possibly the most elusive female character in narratives of the crusades. Many chroniclers attested to the fact that women of all ages were present on crusades, but when children were mentioned their gender was not often specified. For most daughters the journey was considered too dangerous, thus some featured in 'departure scenes',[38] although wives and sons were usually the focus.[39] If a daughter was of suitable age, a betrothal or marriage might be arranged before leaving. Count Hugh of Vermandois gave his daughter Isabel (Elisabeth) in marriage to Robert, count of Meulan, before setting out in 1096.[40] Other daughters were entered into convents.[41] Some daughters and young women evidently did take the cross – many crusade narratives describe 'young women' and 'girls' accompanying armies travelling to the East, but these should be treated with a certain amount of caution. Different groups of women, described by age, social status or family role, often appeared in formulaic lists of 'types' of crusaders. This was at least in part a literary convention for demonstrating the popularity of an expedition: the variety of crusaders reflected the sheer magnitude of the response. Crusading was seen to reach across social boundaries, rich and poor, young and old, male and female, and authors used its universal appeal to emphasise its miraculous nature and divine origin.

The presence of young women on crusade was also used to indicate that an expedition lacked moral purity. Guibert of Nogent criticised William IX of Aquitaine for bringing a 'crowd … of young girls' with him on the ill-fated 1101 crusade.[42] The duke already had a reputation for debauchery, enhanced by his disputes with the papacy and the erotic courtly verse attributed to him.[43] William's troops were decimated near Heraclea; thus in Guibert's view the duke was duly punished for his licentious ways. Peter the Hermit's followers attracted similar criticism:

> … as they did not in any way turn from fornication and unlawful relationships there was excessive revelling, continual delight with women and girls who had set out for the very purpose of frivolity,

---

[38] For examples, see AA, 2–3, 478–81; WT, 140.

[39] See 113–17 below.

[40] OV, 5.30–1. Orderic may have been mistaken in his date for this marriage, however. According to Grocock and Siberry, Robert was married to Humberga of Le Puiset, but this is unlikely. See Gilo of Paris, *Historia Vie Hierosolimitane*, 127 n. 6; and 231 n. 210 below.

[41] For arrangements pertaining to families in charters left behind by the First Crusaders, see Riley-Smith, *First Crusaders*, 135–9.

[42] GN, 313.

[43] See Lindsay, *The Troubadours*, 3–24.

and boasting most rashly about the opportunity offered by this journey.[44]

Peter's contingent, famously known as the 'Peasants' Crusade', came to a disastrous end at Nicaea in late 1096, and the failure of this divinely ordained expedition could only be explained in terms of the moral turpitude of most of its participants. Other popular movements that attracted criticism, such as the so-called Children's Crusade of 1212, demonstrate that young women as well as men were motivated to take the cross for spiritual reasons.[45] Recent scholarship suggests that these crusaders were not in fact children, but rural poor lacking in the social status afforded by wealth or marriage, and influenced by preachings of apostolic poverty.[46] Contemporary chroniclers stressed that the crusade included women and girls, as well as boys and young men. The Ebersheim chronicle told how 'everyone that heard [the message], both boy and girl, having left their parents received the sign of the cross', and asserts that the host was made up of 'an infinite number of servants, maids and virgins'.[47] Other commentators described 'boys and girls, not the younger ones but also adults, married and virgin'.[48] Bearing in mind what Dickson calls the 'mythistorical fame' of the Children's Crusade, it is unsurprising that over the course of time the story was gradually reinterpreted by chroniclers, and the presence of young women was used to question the authenticity of participants' spiritual motivation.[49] The annalist of Marbach was critical of the movement from the outset, and described with a certain satisfaction the miserable homecoming of the few who returned:

> Thus consequently deceived and confused, they began to return ... turning back barefoot and famished, having been made objects of derision to

---

[44] AA, 48–9.

[45] For recent assessments of source material for the Children's Crusade, see Peter Raedts, 'The Children's Crusade of 1212', *JMH* 3 (1977), 282–9; Gary Dickson, 'The Genesis of the Children's Crusade (1212)', in his *Religious Enthusiasm in the Medieval West: Revivals, Crusades, Saints* (Aldershot, 2000), 1 n. 1; and *idem.*, 'Stephen of Cloyes, Philip Augustus and the Children's Crusade', in Barbara N. Sargent-Baur ed. *Journeys Toward God: Pilgrimage and Crusade* (Kalamazoo, MI, 1992), 83–105.

[46] Raedts, 'The Children's Crusade', 295–300.

[47] *Chronicon Ebersheimense*, ed. Ludwig Weiland, MGH SS 23 (Hanover, 1874), 450.

[48] *Annales Marbacenses*, ed. Hermann Bloch, MGH *Scr. Rer. Ger.* 9 (1907), 82. For references to boys, girls, men and women taking part, see *Continuatio Annales Admuntenses 1140–1250*, ed. Wilhelm Wattenbach, MGH SS 9 (1851), 592; Ogerius Panis, *Cafari et continuatio Annales Ianuensis, 1198–1219*, ed. Karolus Pertz, MGH SS 18 (1863), 131; and Johannes Codagnelli, *Annales Placentini Guelfi*, ed. Oswald Holder-Egger, MGH *Scr. Rer. Ger.* 23 (1901), 42.

[49] Dickson, 'Genesis', 7.

everyone,[50] for very many of the girls had been raped and had lost the flower of their virginity.[51]

Another chronicler remarked, 'many girls who had marched out virgins, were returning pregnant'.[52] Criticism of the movement may have stemmed from its lack of official status as a crusade, because 'no one encouraged or proclaimed it'.[53] Its failure served to reinforce that it was not divinely ordained, and the Children's Crusade became 'a cautionary tale, a homily against future recurrences'.[54] Women, older and younger, were undoubtedly involved in this large-scale popular movement, but their role was ultimately reduced to a dishonourable sexual fate, illustrating the dangers that awaited flighty young women who took the cross against the advice of the Church.

EDUCATION

Details about the education of daughters were not a priority for the authors of crusade narratives. Any brief references to schooling were usually limited to the tutor or institution to whose care a young daughter was entrusted. In *Gesta Dei per Francos*, we are told that Arnulf of Chocques, the first Patriarch of Jerusalem, began his career as a tutor to the nun Cecilia, a sister of Robert Curthose.[55] Robert had apparently promised Arnulf a bishopric in reward for his duties, so the education of a noblewoman could elicit lucrative patronage.[56] This information, however, comes at the beginning of Guibert of Nogent's scathing attack on Arnulf's iniquitous rise to power, and it is possible that Guibert intended to insult the patriarch by suggesting that his mediocre education made him suitable for the teaching of women only.[57] Ranulf Higden asserted that Berengaria of Navarre, wife of Richard the Lionheart, was 'beautiful and learned', and this was borne out by Ambroise's recollection that the daughter of Isaac Comnenus was sent to her for tutelage, although he did not specify that this was of a literary nature.[58]

Runciman asserted that the frontier nature of society in Outremer, with its language barriers and constant warfare, made it impossible to found Latin

---

50 Cf. Lamentations 3:14.

51 *Annales Marbacenses*, 82–3.

52 *Chronicon Ebersheimense*, 450.

53 *Chronicae regiae Coloniensis continuatio prima*, ed. Georg Waitz, MGH SS 24, 17.

54 Dickson, 'Genesis', 3.

55 GN, 290.

56 *Ibid.*, 290–1.

57 Guibert described him as 'Not dull in dialectical learning, although he had made the least use of grammatical texts'. *Ibid.*, 290.

58 Ranulf Higden, *Polychronicon*, ed. Joseph R. Lumby, 9 vols, RS 41 (1882), 8.106; Ambroise, 1.34, lns 2086–9.

schools of any established reputation.[59] It is well known that William of Tyre, one of the most celebrated historians of the twelfth century, received much of his training in Bologna and Paris, and this enabled him to become tutor to the future King Baldwin IV of Jerusalem.[60] There was a literate culture in the Latin East, however, as evidenced by the production of ornate manuscipts in Acre during the thirteenth century.[61] In common with western practices, noble daughters in the East were sometimes educated in convents. William tells us that Queen Sibylla of Jerusalem spent her early years in the convent of St Lazarus at Bethany, and was brought up by her aunt, the Abbess Yveta, youngest sister of Melisende.[62] Melisende's gift of books to the community at Bethany suggest that there was a degree of literacy at the convent, and prayers written for a woman in the Psalter attributed to her patronage imply that she may have been literate in Latin.[63] Anna Comnena's history, while undoubtedly unique for its time, shows that it was acceptable for a Byzantine noblewoman to be educated to a high degree.[64] Perhaps intermarriage between Latin and Byzantine high nobility influenced cultural attitudes towards the education of daughters.[65] In terms of upbringing, William of Tyre stressed that Theodora, wife of Baldwin III, had been 'nurtured in the innermost sanctum of the Impe-rial palace'; thus in both aristocratic societies seclusion was important, if not always in a convent.[66] A literate education, however, had no place in the crite-ria that made a daughter attractive for marriage, and was superseded by other qualities such as virginity, lineage, wealth and beauty.

After the fall of Acre, Pierre Dubois, writing in 1306–7, thought educated young women could be instrumental to the recovery of the Holy Land. He pro-posed that they could be trained in theology and logic, and then given as wives to Oriental Christians and Muslims, converting them to Christianity. In sup-port of the effectiveness of his plan, he cited the biblical example of Solomon, who despite his reputation for wisdom was persuaded by his wives to turn

---

[59] Runciman, *A History of the Crusades*, 3.489–92.

[60] Hans E. Mayer, 'Guillaume de Tyr à l'École', *Mémoires de l'Académie des sciences arts et belles lettres de Dijon* 127 (1988), 257–65.

[61] See Derbes and Sandona, 'Amazons and Crusaders', *passim.*; and David Jacoby, 'Society, Culture, and the Arts in Crusader Acre', in Weiss and Mahoney, *France and the Holy Land*, 97–137.

[62] WT, 962.

[63] *Ibid*, 710. For an assessment of the Psalter see Jaroslav Folda, *The Art of the Crusaders in the Holy Land 1098–1197* (Cambridge, 1995), 137–63.

[64] Laiou suggests that literacy amongst the women of the Byzantine aristocracy was increasing during the eleventh and twelfth centuries. Angeliki E. Laiou, 'Women in Byzantine Society', in Mitchell, *Women in Medieval Western European Culture*, 91.

[65] William of Tyre refers to the influence of eastern wives, presumably including Armenian and Byzantine women. See 124 below.

[66] WT, 843.

to idolatry. Education was to be a key factor in his plans: girls should attend schools to learn languages and basic doctrine to communicate Latin Christian ideas; not only were they to focus on men, but they could learn medical skills in women's ailments to gain the confidence of prospective female converts.[67] Such a vision may not have been a realistic one, but it acknowledged that non-combatant women could contribute to the cause of Christianity in the East, especially as the possibility of a military solution receded.

Paternal Nurture

Medieval views on the parental care of a father for a daughter are reflected by an anecdote concerning Count Joscelin 1's journey back to Edessa after his escape from imprisonment at the hands of the Turk, Belek, in 1123. Fulcher of Chartres recorded how an Armenian peasant and his family led Joscelin to safety, accompanied by a small daughter.[68] He asserted, rather unconvincingly, that Joscelin carried the child as they rode in order to pretend to others that she was his own, as proof that he had hope of descendants. Fulcher described Joscelin's inability to care for the crying child:

> … nor was there a wet-nurse present, who could suckle her or calm her with lullabies. On account of this he thought about deserting in fear the companion so harmful to him and advancing more safely alone.[69]

Joscelin was probably concerned that the noise would draw attention to him during his flight, but the anecdote supports the notion that noble fathers were unaccustomed to handling their children, who were commonly given to nurses. Joscelin persevered with this most difficult task, however, as he did not wish to offend the peasant, and later rewarded him with money and an ox for his protection.[70] In Orderic Vitalis' *Historia*, the peasant was a Saracen, and they travelled to Antioch, not Tell Bashir. Joscelin wanted to travel in disguise, and so exchanged clothes with the peasant, who pretended to be the count for the rest of the journey. The young girl was described as six years old and the Christians took turns to carry her amongst themselves: she was a part of Joscelin's subterfuge. According to Orderic, the peasant was later rewarded not only with baptism and riches, but also by the betrothal of his daughter to a Christian knight.[71] Orderic thus developed the story to indicate that Christian rulers in the East attracted Muslims to their faith through exemplary lordship, and could raise the social status of those who had served them well, as long as baptism took

---

[67] Pierre Dubois, *De Recuperatione Terre Sancte: Dalla 'Respublica Christiana' ai primi nazionalismi e alla politica antimediterrania*, ed. Angelo Diotti (Firenze, 1977), 153–5.

[68] FC, 684. For the full account see 683–6. Belek was a nephew of Il-Ghazi, ruler of Mardin.

[69] *Ibid.*, 685.

[70] *Ibid.*, 685–6.

[71] OV, 6.114–17.

place. The peasant helped Joscelin because he had lived more happily amongst the Christians than the Turks, and it was this attraction to the Frankish way of life and Christian religion that earned him a great reward.[72]

A further example of paternal care for a daughter comes from a rather unexpected source. Despite being portrayed as a deceitful and corrupt ruler, Isaac Comnenus of Cyprus was credited by the *Itinerarium* for genuinely loving his daughter.[73] Apparently, when Isaac heard that she had been captured, 'he was so overwhelmed with violent grief that he almost went out of his mind'.[74] She is described as 'his only daughter … on whom his spirit depended',[75] and on being allowed to see her after she had been taken hostage, he was overjoyed, 'and he hugged her affectionately and kissed her insatiably again and again, while his tears flowed copiously'.[76] The description was possibly intended to ridicule Isaac in accordance with perceptions of the Greeks as effeminate, but public expressions of emotion were considered appropriate for men in certain circumstances, usually in mourning or penitence.[77] The emperor's daughter was his only heir, and in King Richard's hands was a symbol of his lost power, but Isaac was also portrayed as genuinely concerned for her personal safety. Such accounts make it hard to accept that daughters were always unwelcome or unimportant children. Unfortunately for the emperor, Richard sent Isaac's beloved daughter back to France with his own wife and sister, where she married Raymond VI of Toulouse in 1199.[78] Her story did not end there, however. She had evidently separated from Raymond by 1202, as she took part in the Fourth Crusade with her new husband, whom Geldsetzer asserts was probably Thierry, an illegitimate son of Count Philip of Flanders.[79] Ernoul tells how Thierry had married her in Marseilles with the intention of pressing her claim to Cyprus, and they travelled direct to Syria with the Flemish fleet to present themselves to King Aimery of Jerusalem and demand her inheritance, whereupon they were summarily dismissed.[80]

Despite ideas about the obedience of daughters, some did flout the authority of their parents, especially after they married. One who received severe criticism as a result was Alice of Antioch. The consequences of her actions for her

---

[72] Cf. the story of Melaz, 68–70 below.

[73] 'Her father loved her more than any other creature'. *Itinerarium*, 202; trans. Nicholson, 193.

[74] *Itinerarium*, 202; trans. Nicholson, 193. Ambroise, 1.33, lns 2018–23.

[75] *Itinerarium*, 202–3; 2.14.

[76] *Itinerarium*, 203; trans. Nicholson, 194. Ambroise, 1.33, lns 2053–6.

[77] See 232–3.

[78] Ernoul, 269; and Roger of Howden, *Chronica*, 3.228. She was Raymond's fourth wife, following his short-lived marriage to Joanna of Sicily. Ambroise, 2.61 n. 161.

[79] Geldsetzer, *Frauen*, 191.

[80] Ernoul, 352–3.

role as a mother and widow will be dealt with in the following chapters, but Alice was also portrayed as a disobedient daughter. On the death of her husband, Bohemond II, in 1130, she openly challenged the authority of her father, King Baldwin II of Jerusalem, by claiming the principality of Antioch.[81] This was the first of three attempts to gain the city. As a feudal lord it was the king's duty to protect the interests of the legitimate heir, Bohemond's daughter Constance, but in William of Tyre's account he was portrayed as a father chastising his daughter. When Baldwin appeared at the gates of Antioch with an army, Alice was unable to maintain her support, and fearful of his judgement she took refuge in the citadel while negotiations took place. [82] According to William, it was the familial bond that prevailed; the king was angry, but on account of paternal affection he was persuaded to be lenient. At the instigation of advisers, Alice presented herself before her father 'prepared to accept his judgement', and showing due obedience.[83] Her father even allowed her to keep the important dower lands of Latakia and Jabala, although this was apparently an attempt to induce her not to make a further challenge. Baldwin still felt unable to trust Alice or the Antiochene aristocracy, so he made the nobles of Antioch swear an oath of fealty to Constance: 'For he feared the malice of his very own daughter, lest she attempt to cause the aforementioned minor to be disinherited, just as she had done previously.'[84] Accordingly, William asserted that it was only after her father's death that Alice was confident enough to try to seize Antioch again.[85]

Another example of rebellion against parental power is the legend of Melaz, to which Orderic Vitalis devoted a considerable amount of attention.[86] It is generally accepted that Bohemond of Taranto was captured by the Danishmend, Malik-Ghazi, in 1100 and spent several years as a hostage in Niksar before his release in 1103, which, according to Albert of Aachen, was secured through Bohemond's own negotiations and by payment of a ransom of 100,000 bezants.[87] The *Miracula Sancti Leonardi*, written before 1111, which recorded Bohemond's pilgrimage to the shrine of St Leonard near Limoges in 1106, attributed his escape to the intervention of the saint and a Christian wife of Malik-Ghazi.[88] Orderic, writing *circa* 1135, asserted that it was Malik-Ghazi's daughter Melaz who helped the prince to escape. Chibnall proposes

---

[81] For full details of this early bid for power see WT, 623–5.

[82] *Ibid.*, 624.

[83] *Ibid.*, 624.

[84] *Ibid.*, 625.

[85] See *ibid.*, 636.

[86] OV, 5.358–79.

[87] AA, 680–7.

[88] *Miracula Sancti Leonardi*, in AA SS, Nov. 3, 160–8. See also Marcus Bull, *Knightly Piety and the Lay Response to the First Crusade: The Limousin and Gascony c. 970–c. 1130* (Oxford, 1993), 242–8.

that Orderic may have heard the story from one of Bohemond's retinue, perhaps at the wedding of Bohemond and Constance of France.[89] Unfortunately
there is no corroborative evidence to support Orderic's assertion that Roger
of Salerno married a Turkish princess – if he had it would surely have been
counted amongst the recriminations against him for the disaster at the Field of
Blood in 1119.[90] The story of Melaz does not appear in any other contemporary
sources, but the theme of a Muslim princess falling in love with a Christian
captive later developed into a literary *topos* of Old French poetry, suggesting a
link with oral tradition. Orderic's version may be the earliest written example
of its kind, but it is rather different in tone from the rest of his history, containing extensive dialogue and literary devices, suggesting that he may have been
using an alternative source.[91]

The name Melaz, translated literally from the Greek, $\mu\acute{\epsilon}\lambda\alpha\varsigma$, means 'black' or
'swarthy',[92] but otherwise Malik-Ghazi's daughter was described in fairly con-
ventional terms for a noblewoman. De Weever has demonstrated that these
conventions also existed where the heroine of a *chanson de geste* is a Saracen
woman: 'the poets invariably fall back on the literary tradition of the ideal heroine in its appropriate rhetorical and linguistic rigidities', thus 'whitening' her.[93]
She was beautiful, wise, and wealthy, and the only factor that distinguished
her significantly from a Christian daughter was the authority she held in her
father's household.[94] This was justified in Orderic's eyes, however, as her disobedience to her father was not a crime but an example of divine intervention.
God had aided Bohemond 'through the wit and help of the daughter of the
enemy', and Orderic compared her with biblical heroines such as Judith and
Bithiah.[95] Like Kerbogha's mother in the *Gesta Francorum*, Melaz championed
the superiority of the Christian faith over the Muslims.[96] In this case, however,

[89] Abbot Suger of Saint Denis, *Vita Ludovici Grossi Regis*, ed. and trans. Henri Waquet
(Paris, 1964), 46–8. OV, 5.359, n. 3.

[90] See 130 below.

[91] See Frederick M. Warren, 'The Enamoured Moslem Princess in Orderic Vitalis and
the French Epic', *Publications of the Modern Language Association of America* 29 (1914),
341–58. De Weever briefly refers to Warren's article but does not consider the role of
Melaz in Orderic's history, a decision presumably governed by disciplinary restraints.
Jacqueline de Weever, *Sheba's Daughters: Whitening and Demonising the Saracen
Woman in Medieval French Epic* (London, 1998), 36.

[92] The Greek derivation of the name has led Warren to suggest that the story was of
Syrian or Byzantine origin, although it may have been influenced in part by Spanish
epic poems such as *Mainet*, and the early Old French version of the *Prise d'Orange*.
Warren, 'Enamoured Moslem Princess', 345–6, 349–51.

[93] Weever, *Sheba's Daughters*, xii.

[94] OV, 5.358. See also Warren, 'Enamoured Moslem Princess', 356–7.

[95] OV, 5.358–9, 5.376–7.

[96] See 190–1 below.

the extent of her belief led her to convert, repudiating her father and his beliefs: 'the religion of the Christians is holy and honourable, and your religion is full of vanities and polluted with all filth'.[97] She was initially attracted to the religion through her admiration of Frankish military prowess, in accordance with western courtly conventions.[98] Orderic was keen to emphasise that she retained her virtue, and her relationship with Bohemond was not portrayed as a sexual one. He did assert, however, that she 'loved the Franks', and the way he described her introduction to the Christian faith was reminiscent of physical fulfilment: in 'subtle discourse', she learnt by 'constant discussion interspersed with sighs'.[99]

Her womanly wisdom and cunning were displayed when she tricked her own father and devised the plan for Bohemond's release. The prince's role was reduced to that of a warrior following directions. Her father, on discovering her treachery, called her a 'shameless harlot' and referred to the Franks as her lovers, but Bohemond, seeing her distress, duly came to her rescue. The reward that Melaz received for her efforts was marriage, and, unusually, she was given a choice of spouse. This was because her father initially offered her to Bohemond, but Orderic wanted to portray Bohemond as a reluctant bridegroom, more concerned with the fight against the infidel and duty to God than marriage; thus she was persuaded to take Roger of Salerno instead. Orderic conveniently ignored the fact that, shortly after his release from captivity, Bohemond married the daughter of Philip I of France.[100]

Continuing Orderic's theme of proper noble behaviour, the Franks are continually praised as true to their word throughout this episode, and this is particularly evident when they had surrounded their captor but did not attack because they had sworn an oath to Melaz. Orderic described how 'all looked towards her, waiting for what she might command', and she held command over the Franks 'like she was their lady'.[101] She was greatly afraid of the wrath of her father, but armed with her new honourable friends, and, perhaps most crucially, her new faith, she was able to defy his authority with just cause. Her conversion was treated rather more seriously than Orderic's portrayal of the daughter of Yaghi-Siyan, who was bitterly upset on her release from captivity because she would no longer be allowed to eat pork.[102]

---

[97] OV, 5.368–9.

[98] There are marked similarities with the ideas he expresses through another female Muslim character, Fatima, sister of Belek. See 193 below.

[99] OV, 5.358–61.

[100] Abbot Suger of Saint-Denis, *Vita Ludovici Grossi Regis*, ed. and trans. Henri Waquet (Paris, 1964), 47–9.

[101] OV, 5.366–7.

[102] *Ibid.*, 5.372–3. Ibn al-Athir states that Bohemond was released for the sum of 100,000 dinars and the promise to release Yaghi-Siyan's daughter, whom he was holding hostage. Ibn al-Athir, *Extrait du Kamel-Altevarykh*, RHC Or. (Paris, 1872), 1.212.

Lineage and Inheritance

Lineage and rights of inheritance were crucially important to historians of the crusades and the Latin East when describing individual women. A crusader's marriage to a daughter of high lineage could help to raise the profile of crusading and the settler society in the Levant and galvanise support from the nobility of western Christendom. After his visit to the shrine of St Leonard in 1106, Bohemond of Taranto married Constance, the daughter of King Philip I.[103] Many chroniclers recorded this event and consistently referred to her pedigree – Bohemond was considered to have made an excellent marriage for himself. Guibert of Nogent aimed to capitalise on the link between the royal house and Bohemond's heroic status to enhance French prestige:

> Since his family hailed from Normandy, which constitutes a part of France, he will most assuredly be considered to be Frankish on account of this, because he had now obtained by marriage the daughter of the King of the Franks.[104]

The marriage was yet another achievement of a great hero, and formed part of his publicity drive to encourage crusaders to join the expedition he had planned for 1107. Countess Adela of Blois provided the wedding feast for her fallen husband's comrade in Chartres, and Bohemond's appeal for crusaders was timed to follow directly after this event – presumably the nobles attending the wedding were his target audience.[105]

Chroniclers often mentioned the ties of kinship between crusaders and the Levantine nobility in order to preserve and cultivate those dynastic links, and to promote crusading. In discussing the line of Fulk v of Anjou, king of Jerusalem, William of Tyre emphasised his important connections in the West.[106] Fulk's daughter Sibyl married Thierry of Flanders, and they and their son Philip were well known crusaders to the Holy Land in William's time – Amalric I even named his first daughter after her aunt, Sibylla.[107] When the Latin kingdom was in crisis in 1184–5, it was to Fulk's grandson, Henry II of England, that Patriarch Eraclius' mission appealed for aid.[108] Dynastic links to First Crusaders were particularly significant, both to the royal house and the baronage

---

[103]   FC, 482–3. Her marriage to Hugh of Troyes had been annulled.

[104]   GN, 106. He later refers to this marriage as 'obscuring the base origins of his ancient ancestors'. GN, 138.

[105]   OV, 6.73. Suger, *Vita Ludovici Grossi*, 46–50.

[106]   WT, 633. See 121–2 below. Thierry travelled to the Holy Land four times, once with his wife, and Philip was specifically targeted by an appeal (WT, 926) and travelled to the Holy Land on crusade in 1177. WT, 980–7, 994–6.

[107]   *Ibid.*, 869.

[108]   Roger of Howden, 'Gesta', 335–7.

who wished to assert the legitimacy of their positions. When a crusader married into a well-established Levantine family it brought him great prestige and was duly noted by historians. William of Tyre listed amongst the significant achievements of crusader Reynald of Marash his marriage to the daughter of the count of Edessa, Agnes of Courtenay.[109]

Inter-relations between the nobilities of the Latin East and the West were not without problems, however. For practical reasons, heirs from the West were occasionally unable to take on an inheritance in the East. This was sometimes because of economics, commitments at home, or even the delay entailed by the journey to the Levant, as demonstrated by Eustace of Boulogne's failure to prevent his cousin, Baldwin of le Bourcq, from taking the throne of Jerusalem in 1118.[110] These connections ran both ways, however: families who had settled in the eastern Mediterranean also had claims to fiefs in Europe, and became embroiled in political disputes there. Joinville recounted how discord arose between the French baronage and Count Thibaut IV of Champagne. Queen Alice of Cyprus, daughter of Isabella of Jerusalem, became a focal point for Thibaut's enemies in their disputes with the count and his allies between 1230 and 1234.[111] She had a claim to his inheritance as the elder daughter of Henry II of Champagne, the elder brother of Thibaut's father, and she was induced to visit France in 1233. In return for peace, Joinville asserted, Louis IX had to provide her with estates worth 2,000 *livres* a year, together with a lump sum of 40,000 *livres*.[112] However, he failed to mention that Louis also profited from the 1234 settlement in a manner which enabled him to increase his power over Thibaut's lands.[113]

In terms of the inheritance of daughters, most histories of crusading and the Latin East gave precedence to the royal house of Jerusalem, as even western chroniclers were always interested in the dynamics of succession to the ruling house of the Holy City. There are a few examples of daughters from western aristocracies whose inheritance featured in relation to histories of crusading: Mathilda, countess of Tuscany, was one such, but like many heiresses, Mathilda's political life did not really take shape until after her marriage and widowhood.[114] Eleanor of Aquitaine was possibly the most influential western heiress of the twelfth century, and her roles in the Second and Third Crusades drew considerable attention. As an heiress, Eleanor's birthright bought her some freedoms, but 'marriage re-emphasized her sex which ... relegated her to the

[109] WT, 772.

[110] *Ibid.*, 550. See Alan V. Murray, 'Baldwin II and his Nobles: Baronial Factionalism and Dissent in the Kingdom of Jerusalem', *Nottingham Medieval Studies* 38 (1994), 61–2.

[111] See Richard, *Saint Louis*, 42–7.

[112] Joinville, 50. See Joinville, 46–50, for a full account of the affair.

[113] Richard, *Saint Louis*, 46.

[114] See 205 below.

position of Lady in relation to her Lordly husbands'.[115] Her activities as a wife
and mother were perceived to supersede her role as a daughter, but it was the
importance afforded to her as an heiress, and her dynastic links to Prince Raymond of Antioch, which affected the course of the Second Crusade, and had
serious ramifications for her first marriage.[116]

Another reason for the high profile of Levantine heiresses in crusade texts
was the fact that inheritance by daughters occurred with regularity in frontier
society where lords and knights were often taken captive or killed on the battlefield. Accordingly, succession laws in the Latin kingdom of Jerusalem were
inclined to treat women more favourably than those in the West. According
to Philip of Novara, there was an early *assize* that enabled women to inherit
– a decision that Prawer argues provided an added incentive and assurances to
prospective settlers:

> The knight who had devoted his life to the service of king and country
> was assured that if chance did not grant him a male heir, he could leave to
> his daughter the fief he had acquired through hardship and danger. He
> was thus more strongly attached to his new country.[117]

As the Latin occupying force was relatively small, female succession to property
and land was crucial to the transmission of power throughout the Levant. In
order to provide the greatest manpower per area of land, knights were prevented for a time from holding more than one fief. According to Philip of
Novara, this meant that even if there were a male heir, a woman could inherit if
he was unable to perform the necessary service for that fief.[118] Daughters even
challenged male siblings for the right to inherit, but inevitably the daughters
who held authority were obliged to marry and remarry, in order to provide
stability to the succession of power. From around the time of Baldwin II, noble
heiresses in the Latin kingdom of Jerusalem were required to marry by law so
that their husbands could provide military service.[119] Women could, therefore,
be forced to marry, but jurists in the East attempted to curtail the rights of the

[115] John Carmi Parsons and Bonnie Wheeler, 'Lady and Lord: Eleanor of Aquitaine', in
Bonnie Wheeler and John Carmi Parsons eds *Eleanor of Aquitaine, Lord and Lady*
(Basingstoke, 2002), xiv.

[116] See 131–4 below.

[117] Prawer, *Crusader Institutions*, 25.

[118] Philip of Novara, *Livre*, RHC Lois I.559–60. See also Peter W. Edbury, 'Women and
the High Court of Jerusalem according to John of Ibelin', in Damien Coulon, Catherine
Otten-Froux, Paul Pagès and Dominique Valérian eds *Chemins d'outremer: Études sur
la Méditerranée médiévale offertes à Michel Balard*, 2 vols (Paris, 2004), I.285–6.

[119] As widows, heiresses were encouraged to remarry until the age of sixty, following
the advice of St Paul. Brundage, 'Marriage Law', 270–1. See also Prawer, *Crusader
Institutions*, 27, and Edbury, 'Women', 288–9.

lord in arranging marriages, while accepting that they were a necessity.[120] They stipulated that only those women who inherited a fief with personal military service attached to it were required to marry, but that the lord must provide three candidates suitable to her rank from whom she (or her family) could choose, thus preserving the appearance of a consensual match. She did have the right to refuse, but ultimately this could result in the loss of her fief.[121] During Amalric's reign in the second half of the twelfth century, partible inheritance was enforced if there was more than one female heir, again with the intention of maximising the feudal levy available to the crown. This rule did not apply to the major baronies, or the royal house of Jerusalem, and to an extent created a two-tier system of government, preserving the power of the established noble families.[122] Still, marriage to an heiress with a claim, even one not in possession of her lands, could attract a suitor who had the means to take back his prospective wife's inheritance. This gave legitimacy to a knight's territorial ambitions, and thus dispossessed women were often married to crusaders in order to give men from the West an incentive to fight and reclaim lost land. Most importantly, it encouraged them to settle and contribute to the permanent feudal levy that was necessary to the continued survival of a Latin presence in the East.

The importance of lineage was underlined by the case of Agnes of Courtenay. Like Isabella I of Jerusalem, she had four husbands,[123] even though her inheritance was decimated by the fall of Edessa in 1144. She benefited little from the death of her first husband, Reynald of Marash, at Inab in 1149, or when the remains of her inheritance were sold off to the Byzantine Empire in 1150.[124] She did receive a cash pension for this, which provided ready finance for military activity and patronage, but she lacked the landed wealth which would increase a patrimony. Nonetheless, she was still considered to be a desirable marriage partner at that time by both Hugh of Ibelin and Amalric, brother of King Baldwin III and then count of Jaffa.[125] Ultimately it seemed that lineage was her key attraction, but by the time she married Reynald of Sidon other factors had increased her appeal – she was the mother of a king, and had gained extensive dower lands from her third husband Hugh of Ibelin.

---

[120]   St Ambrose condemned those who attempted to force remarriage by law. St Ambrose, *De Viduis*, cols 273–4.

[121]   Brundage, 'Marriage Law', 269–70. See also Edbury, 'Women', 287–8.

[122]   For the assize referring to the partition of inheritance between brothers and sisters, see Philip of Novara, *Livre*, 1.542.

[123]   Reynald of Marash, Amalric count of Jaffa, Hugh of Ibelin and Reynald of Sidon.

[124]   WT, 781–2.

[125]   See Hamilton, 'Titular Nobility', 198. See 144–5 below.

Heiresses and the Royal House of Jerusalem

The marriage of crusaders to heiresses from the indigenous Christian population was fundamental to the establishment of a Latin aristocracy in the East from the outset. In 1098 Baldwin of Boulogne, later King Baldwin I of Jerusalem, married the daughter of an Armenian noble called Taphnuz, who was a son of Prince Roupen of Armenia.[126] The power given to Baldwin by this marriage was emphasised by Albert of Aachen: 'he made the whole land and region tributary to him'.[127] Taphnuz was said to occupy many fortresses and defences in the mountains, to which he appointed Baldwin his heir.[128] While such marriages were the customary way to secure titles to land, there were alternatives: Baldwin had already gone through an adoption ceremony to inherit the city of Edessa. Fulcher of Chartres asserted that Thoros, the duke of Edessa, chose Baldwin as his heir 'for he had neither son nor daughter'.[129] Had there been a female heir, she would probably have been married to Baldwin.[130] There were other aristocratic Armenian daughters who married crusaders – not all were heiresses but instead brought large cash dowries which helped the settlers to fulfil their military commitments.[131] At this early stage of settlement in the East, marriages with existing Christian communities were central to cementing alliances in a largely hostile environment.

No account of inheritance by women in the Latin East could be complete without considering the problems posed by daughters and their succession to power in the royal house of Jerusalem. Evidently these were high-profile women who have attracted the attention of historians, medieval and modern. This chapter, however, will attempt to focus specifically on perceptions about their role as royal daughters and heiresses in the relevant narratives. The question of inheritance in the royal house of Jerusalem was inherently shaped by the fact that the kingship began as elective. This was a practice imported from the West, and reflected the cooperative nature of the leadership of the First Crusade. Friction between the baronage and the crown of Jerusalem was rife throughout the twelfth century, but for the most part the need for strong kingship was recognised – in fact, recent scholarship suggests that the monarchy

---

[126] Sometimes called Tafroc. Murray asserts that he is thought to have been Thathoul, lord of Marash. Alan V. Murray, *The Crusader Kingdom of Jerusalem: A Dynastic History 1099–1125* (Oxford, 2000), 182.

[127] AA, 258–9.

[128] *Ibid.*, 188–9. See also WT, 453.

[129] FC, 210. See also WT, 235.

[130] Hans E. Mayer, 'Études sur l'histoire de Baudouin Ier Roi de Jérusalem', in *Melanges sur L'Histoire du Royaume Latin de Jérusalem* (Paris, 1984), 51.

[131] See 142 below.

was far more stable than had been thought.[132] By the late 1120s, under the rule of Baldwin II, the position of the monarchy had strengthened to the point where an inherited crown was a real possibility, even though he had no male heir. Baldwin had four daughters, and he used all of them relentlessly to fulfil his political aims, arranging marriages not only to provide security for the kingdom of Jerusalem, but also to cement dynastic links with the other principalities. Alice was married to Bohemond II of Antioch, and Hodierna to Raymond II of Tripoli. The youngest, Yveta, became abbess of what was to become one of the richest nunneries in the kingdom. It was the eldest, Melisende, however, who was to be Baldwin's heir, making a pivotal diplomatic marriage for the crown.[133]

Melisende was destined for a western husband. A marriage within the Levantine nobility would have caused friction, and more importantly the kingdom desperately needed the military retinue that a western bridegroom could bring. However, Baldwin was not free to dispose of his daughter as he saw fit. Melisende's husband would be a king, and the baronage had to be consulted over their future ruler. Count Fulk V of Anjou was chosen 'by the universal counsel of all the princes, ecclesiastical as well as lay'.[134] This collective decision was undoubtedly influenced by the tradition of elective kingship, but reflected precedents in noble diplomacy with the West such as the offer of the throne to Charles the Good in 1123 during Baldwin's captivity.[135]

After Fulk was chosen, Baldwin sent a special embassy to the West to arrange the marriage.[136] Melisende's special position as designated heir to the throne of Jerusalem was evidenced in the charters of the Latin kingdom, and has been discussed in detail by Mayer.[137] He suggests that when the marriage was transacted in 1129 it was intended that Fulk should be the sole heir to the kingdom, but on his deathbed Baldwin probably reneged on this agreement, and Melisende, Fulk and their son (the future Baldwin III) inherited jointly. William asserted that the king 'handed over to them care of the realm and full power'.[138] This meant that Baldwin II considered the kingship to be hereditary rather than elective, and wished 'to ensure that the throne of Jerusalem would

---

[132]   See Steven Tibble, *Monarchy and Lordships in the Latin Kingdom of Jerusalem 1099–1291* (Oxford, 1989), 186–8.

[133]   Edbury and Rowe, *William of Tyre*, 82–3.

[134]   WT, 618.

[135]   See Alan V. Murray, 'Baldwin II and His Nobles: Baronial Factionalism and Dissent in the Kingdom of Jerusalem, 1118–1134', *Nottingham Medieval Studies* 38 (1994), 69–75.

[136]   For a detailed assessment of the political background of the arrangement of this marriage, see Phillips, *Defenders*, 19–43.

[137]   Mayer, 'Studies in the History of Queen Melisende of Jerusalem', *Dumbarton Oaks Papers* 26 (1972), 93–182; and 'The Succession to Baldwin II of Jerusalem', *Dumbarton Oaks Papers* 39 (1985), 139–47.

[138]   WT, 625.

remain in his family and not go to the house of Anjou'.[139] Baldwin might have been able to pass the throne directly to his grandson Baldwin III, but in an age of high infant mortality it was important to stipulate that, should anything happen to the younger Baldwin, Melisende would be the mother of future heirs to the throne. The success of Baldwin II's policy drew a striking contrast to Henry I's failed attempt to secure the throne of England for his daughter Mathilda, and it is a testament to the strength of the royal house of Jerusalem at this time. The transition of power was not entirely smooth, however, and Melisende's political activities as a wife, mother and widow remained fundamentally characterised by her rights as an heiress.[140]

Later in the twelfth century, lack of a healthy male heir made daughters crucially important to the succession once again. Four women – Sibylla, Isabella I, Maria and Isabella II – inherited the throne of Jerusalem consecutively from 1186 to 1228. Problems began as early as 1163, when Baldwin III died without heirs, and his brother Amalric took the throne. His position was relatively secure, but the dissolution of his marriage to Agnes of Courtenay cast doubt over the claims of both their children, Sibylla and Baldwin.[141] One of the conditions that Amalric requested of the patriarch for this separation was a petition for their legitimisation, and Pope Alexander III ruled in their favour.[142] The *Eracles* group of continuations, however, asserted that the children were not legitimate, presumably influenced by the Ernoul text and his predisposition towards the Ibelin contingent.[143] By the time of his death in 1174, Amalric did have a legitimate daughter, Isabella, by his second wife Maria Comnena, who became Balian's stepdaughter on his marriage to the dowager queen.

Possible illegitimacy was not the only problem facing the royal house. Baldwin IV was the son and nephew of Amalric and Baldwin III respectively, but was stricken with leprosy. Not only was he periodically incapacitated through bouts of sickness, but he was unlikely to find a marriage partner, let alone produce an heir. As a result of his illness, he could have been passed over in favour of Sibylla, but she was only fifteen on the death of her father, and unmarried. Political instability would result whether she was married off quickly to a Levantine noble, or waited for a suitable husband from the

---

[139] Mayer, 'Queen Melisende', 100–1.

[140] See 134–5, 185–8, 213 below.

[141] See Hans E. Mayer, 'Die Legitimität Balduins IV von Jerusalem und das testament der Agnes von Courtenay', *Historisches Jahrbuch* 108 (1988), 63–89. See also 144–5 below.

[142] WT, 869. Hamilton, *The Leper King and his Heirs: Baldwin IV and the Crusader Kingdom of Jerusalem* (Cambridge, 2000), 26.

[143] '... for when her mother separated from her father the children were not declared legitimate', *Eracles*, 20; *The Conquest of Jerusalem and the Third Crusade*, trans. Peter W. Edbury (Aldershot, 1996), 14.

West.[144] Thus Baldwin was chosen and Sibylla was nominally accepted as heir-apparent, but the knowledge that Baldwin would not produce an heir meant that his two sisters became focal points for ambitious lords to vie for power. Baldwin's youth and illness also fomented political divisions. The early months of his reign resulted in the murder of seneschal Miles of Plancy who was acting as regent. Even before this event Raymond III of Tripoli had made a bid for the regency because Miles was failing to provide coherent government.[145] According to the *Eracles* chronicle, Raymond wanted regency for ten years even if Baldwin IV died, to allow time for the Pope, the German emperor and the kings of England and France to adjudicate between the sisters.[146] Thus, following the pattern established by Baldwin II, the kingdom intended to look once more to the West to solve its succession problems created by the inheritance of daughters. In the meantime, an appropriate marriage was organised for Sibylla by the High Court to a western husband of a suitable pedigree: William of Montferrat.[147] The marriage was short-lived, but produced a male heir, Baldwin V.

On the death of Baldwin IV in 1185 both Sybilla and Isabella were bypassed in favour of the young Baldwin V. Ernoul claimed that Baldwin IV had made this decision in 1183 because he was concerned that the claims of the rival sisters would cause open dissension. Sybilla and her husband were not granted the regency; it went to Raymond III of Tripoli by the agreement of the barons.[148] After Baldwin V's death in 1186, however, Sibylla took the throne with the support of a considerable sector of the nobility. The mission of Patriarch Eraclius to the West in 1184–5 had proved unsuccessful in securing the support of a western king, and conflict between the seneschal, Joscelin of Courtenay, and the regent, Raymond III, meant that the Latin kingdom was without secure leadership. There were fears that Raymond himself had designs on the throne, as he was the grandchild of Baldwin II through his mother, Hodierna.[149] However, Sibylla was the elder of the two sisters directly in line to the throne, and had already proven her ability to produce a male heir, which earned her the support of several magnates. She was also prepared to take swift action on the death of her son, which the hostile *Eracles* chronicler attributed to the machinations of her uncle, Joscelin.[150] The coronation required a city closed to outside influence, however. Reynald of Châtillon had to ask for the assent of the

---

[144] Consanguinity was also a risk if she married one of the barons. See Hamilton, *Leper King*, 39–41.

[145] WT, 963–4. For more detail, see Hamilton, *Leper King*, 84–93.

[146] *Eracles*, 20.

[147] WT, 977. See 227.

[148] Ernoul, 115; *Lateinische Forsetzung*, 51.

[149] See Hamilton, *Leper King*, 217–18.

[150] *Eracles*, 30–1.

assembled crowd: 'We wish with your approval to crown Sibylla, the daughter of king Amalric and the sister of King Baldwin. For she is the closest heir to the kingdom.'[151]

Reynald thus emphasised that her claim was based not only on her position as daughter to Amalric, but also on her relationship as a full sister to Baldwin IV. By doing this her supporters could deny that Sibylla's claim required external adjudication, and were able to justify breaking the oath they had taken to support Raymond's regency. An heiress, however, needed a husband for military duties, as Patriarch Eraclius reportedly asserted: 'Lady, you are a woman; it is fitting that you should have a man by you who can help you govern your kingdom.'[152]

The main obstacle to Sibylla's inheritance was not her possible illegitimacy, but hostility towards her second husband, Guy of Lusignan. William of Tyre portrayed Guy in a particularly unflattering light, and his reputation suffered further in continuations of William's work because of his role in the defeat at Hattin.[153] William of Newburgh asserted that the Levantine nobles were disgruntled because Guy was a foreigner, although this cannot have been the sole issue.[154] Previous suitors for both Melisende and Sibylla (Fulk and William of Monferrat) had been chosen specifically because they were from the West. Guy's marriage to Sibylla had been controversial from the start,[155] and his period of regency in 1183 compounded resentment towards him, to the extent that the king removed him from power and even attempted to annul the marriage.[156] Hamilton asserts that by doing so, Baldwin effectively stated that Guy was not suitable for the kingship.[157] Several chroniclers give the impression that Sibylla was only accepted as the heir because she had already agreed to divorce Guy, explaining the need for subterfuge at his coronation.[158] It is a testament to the strength of Sibylla's claim and the authority gained by consecration that she managed to retain Guy as her husband despite opposition, but it is notable that she was only able to do so after she had been accepted as queen.

The coronation itself was not an end to the matter; *Eracles* tells how

---

[151] *Eracles*, 32; trans. Edbury, 25.

[152] *Eracles*, 33; trans. Edbury, 26.

[153] WT, 1048–50. Smail blames the influence of the chronicle of Ernoul over the Old French continuations for this view, although Hamilton points out that the Latin continuator was quite sympathetic to Guy. See Raymond C. Smail, 'The Predicaments of Guy of Lusignan 1183–87', in Kedar *et al.*, *Outremer*, 163; and Hamilton, *Leper King*, 217.

[154] WN, 1.256.

[155] For further detail, see 224–7 below.

[156] For Guy's relationship with Baldwin IV, see Smail, 'Predicaments', 159–76.

[157] Hamilton, *Leper King*, 194.

[158] In particular, Roger of Howden, *Chronica*, 315–16. For further examples see Benjamin Z. Kedar, 'The Patriarch Eraclius', in Kedar *et al.*, *Outremer*, 195–8.

Raymond III of Tripoli then planned to overthrow Guy of Lusignan by crowning King Amalric's other daughter, Isabella.[159] Unfortunately Isabella's husband and erstwhile pretender Humphrey IV of Toron threw himself on Sibylla's mercy, foiling the plans of the disgruntled and rebellious barons. This action led him to be considered a coward and effeminate by some chroniclers, and perhaps sealed his fate with regard to his later divorce. With Raymond's claim superseded by a crowned queen and no alternative king-consort to rally opposition to Guy, the majority of the barons went to pay homage to Sibylla and her husband. The consequences were clear: an heiress needed a suitable husband to come into her inheritance, especially in the Latin East where active military leadership and inducing cooperation amongst the nobility were paramount to providing stability.

Guy of Lusignan maintained his position as king during Sibylla's lifetime, even after the battle of Hattin when little enough of the kingdom remained, but in 1190 the queen and her two heiresses, Alice and Maria, died of sickness at the siege of Acre. Ambroise lamented the youth and valour of Sibylla, and the turmoil caused by the early death of mother and daughters.[160] The *Itinerarium* suggested that some accused Guy of foul play in the death of Sibylla and her daughters, but this seems very unlikely as the kingdom passed 'by right of inheritance' to Isabella, undermining his claim.[161] He remained king of Jerusalem for nearly two years before Isabella was crowned, steadfastly holding on to his title. He was only successful for that long because the Latin kingdom was still experiencing the turmoil engendered by Saladin's victories, and because he had support from Third Crusade leader Richard the Lionheart. Conrad of Monferrat was the natural opponent for Guy in the leadership of the kingdom. He had already shown himself to be a capable military commander at the siege of Tyre, and had opposed the claims of Guy and Sibylla over the city.[162] However, a serious challenge to the leadership was not possible without the claim to the throne that an heiress could bring. According to *Eracles*, Conrad of Monferrat pursued a match with Isabella immediately on the death of Sibylla, approaching her mother Maria Comnena for help. She was described as persuading her daughter to separate from Humphrey, or else 'she could have neither honour nor her father's kingdom' – she would not gain her rightful inheritance.[163] Isabella's marriage to Humphrey was challenged on the official grounds that Isabella had been underage, exposing the problems in arranging preemptive marriages for prospective heiresses.[164] William of Tyre records that the

---

[159] *Eracles*, 33–4.

[160] Ambroise, 1.63, lns 3891–8.

[161] See *Itinerarium*, 97; and Ernoul, 267. *Eracles*, 105; trans. Edbury, 95.

[162] This had occurred in the summer of 1189.

[163] *Eracles*, 105; trans. Edbury, 95–6.

[164] *Eracles*, 106.

marriage took place in 1180 when Isabella was 'barely eight years old', but it had been reaffirmed when Isabella came of age in 1183, as many were aware: Saladin had famously besieged the wedding ceremony.[165] Ensuring that an heiress married early was paramount to providing political security, but in the Latin East it was hard to predict which alliances would be the most beneficial, especially when military disasters radically altered the power balance. Humphrey, like Guy, was deemed an unsuitable king-consort. In contrast, Conrad, the 'hero of Tyre', was seen to have the dynamic qualities and military leadership required to hold the crown.[166]

Isabella's marriage did not automatically confer kingship on her new husband, however. There was still the position of Guy of Lusignan to consider, notwithstanding the fact that the kingdom itself, her inheritance, was largely in the grip of the enemy. The final settlement appears to have been made collectively in July 1191, through the mediation of the barons and western crusaders, Richard I in particular. The marquis was recognised as consort to the heir, and as a reward for his role at Tyre he received the hereditary right to that county, including the city of Tyre, Sidon and Beirut. Conrad would receive the crown if Guy died, but only, the *Itinerarium* declared bitterly, 'because he had married the heir to the kingdom; although he had done so wickedly and forcibly in hope of becoming king'.[167] If all three – Guy, Isabella, and Conrad – died, the decision over the succession would fall to King Richard, underlining once more the import of western influence in this matter. By 1192, however, it was becoming increasingly clear that Guy's kingship was untenable. He had lost his position as king-consort and his attempts to build support by patronising Poitevins could not redeem the loss of Jerusalem. King Richard offered him Cyprus instead – for a fee. Guy accordingly renounced the throne, a decision which Hamilton asserts had the repercussion that henceforth 'any ruler who held the crown matrimonial was only a king consort'.[168]

After Conrad's assassination in April 1192, Isabella was given almost immediately to her third husband, Henry II of Troyes, count of Champagne and nephew of Richard I. Some thought the marriage was celebrated too swiftly for decency, especially as she carried a child, but again the urgent need for military leadership overrode customary sensibilities.[169] According to the *Itinerarium* the

---

165 WT, 1012; See 128 below.

166 For further details on the divorce, see 145–7 below.

167 *Itinerarium*, 235–6; trans. Nicholson, 222.

168 Bernard Hamilton, 'King Consorts of Jerusalem and their Entourages from the West from 1186 to 1250', in *Die Kreuzfahrerstaaten als multikulturel Gesellschaft*, ed. Hans E. Mayer (Munich, 1997), 13–24.

169 Eracles asserted she was married within four days of Conrad's death. *Eracles*, 143–4; trans. Edbury, 116. It was eight days according to Ralph of Diceto, 'Ymagines Historiarum', 2.104. From a Muslim perspective, 'Imād al-Din recorded shock because Isabella was pregnant with Conrad's child when she remarried.' 'Imād al-Din al Isfahāni,

count himself did not pursue the match, but consented under pressure from the French and Latin magnates, and only when 'the marchioness [Isabella] came to the count of her own accord and offered him the keys of the city'.[170] The author implied that Isabella had some autonomy in the matter, but he was probably trying to defend Richard against claims that he had forced the match – *Eracles* accused the king of making false promises to his nephew in order to get him to agree to the marriage.[171]

When Henry of Champagne went to assert his authority over the cities and castles now under his dominion, he took Isabella with him.[172] The *Itinerarium* asserted, rather romantically, that this was 'as he could not yet bear to be parted from her', but the fact that Henry needed Isabella's physical presence shows that his grip over the kingdom was still not secure – she was the visual symbol that legitimised his authority.[173] Undoubtedly, Guy of Lusignan still had ambitions for the kingship. His brother, Aimery of Lusignan, remained constable of the kingdom, and Guy supported the Pisans in an unsuccessful revolt against Henry during 1193, but died in 1194, leaving Cyprus to Aimery.[174] After Henry's death in 1197, Guy's dynastic ambitions were realised when Aimery became Isabella's fourth husband. Aimery himself may have commissioned the *Livre au Roi* in 1205, a text whose purpose, amongst other things, was to clarify important issues such as the exact position of the queen's consort, inheritance and regency.[175] Isabella's consecutive marriages were axiomatic examples of the duties of an heiress in such a weakened political climate. Her sister Sibylla had been able to exercise a degree of autonomy in her second choice of marriage partner, but the loss of Jerusalem and much of their inheritance meant that the kingdom stood in dire need of whatever a marriage with Isabella could buy, whether funds from the West, military expertise or a baronage united behind its choice of leader.[176]

Isabella died in 1205 and was succeeded by the eldest of her five daughters, Maria of Monferrat (daughter of Conrad), who was roughly fourteen. John of Ibelin was regent, and once more the High Court looked to the West for

Conquête de la Syrie et de la Palestine par Saladin, trans. Henri Massé (Paris, 1972), 377. In any case this went against established custom; see 224 below.

[170]   *Itinerarium*, 348; trans. Nicholson, 312–13.

[171]   *Eracles*, 143.

[172]   *Itinerarium*, 349.

[173]   *Itinerarium*, 349; trans. Nicholson, 314.

[174]   Jonathan Riley-Smith, *The Feudal Nobility and the Kingdom of Jerusalem, 1174–1277* (London, 1973), 153–4.

[175]   Riley-Smith, *Feudal Nobility*, 155. Greilsammer questions whether it was indeed written for the monarchy; see *Le Livre au Roi*, ed. and trans. Myriam Greilsammer (Paris, 1995), 87–106. For the date, see 83–6.

[176]   After the Third Crusade, the kingdom consisted of Acre and Tyre, and the lordships of Caesarea, Jaffa, Cayphas and Arsuf.

support and advice: in 1208 Philip II of France was asked to choose her a husband. She married John of Brienne in 1210, but died two years later. John then acted as regent for their infant daughter, Isabella II, until 1225 when she married Emperor Frederick II. Despite his conflicts with the Ibelin family, and the fact that he was designated a regent rather than a king after Maria's death, John campaigned tirelessly for aid to the Latin kingdom, both in western Europe and the Latin Empire of Constantinople, and took a major role in the Fifth Crusade. The marriage of his daughter to Frederick II, however, heralded a period of absentee Germanic rulers of the kingdom until 1268. The policy of marrying heiresses to important rulers from the West (who had other commitments and priorities), and the ensuing rivalry amongst Christian settlers who were effectively stranded in a power vacuum, contributed to the eventual undoing of the kingdom.[177] Isabella II did not even see her husband's dubious coronation: she had been crowned a bare three months before her marriage and died in 1228, having given birth to a male heir, Conrad. Ultimately, Maria and Isabella II did not live long enough to mature into the political life of the Latin East. They survived only scant years after their nominal transition to adulthood through marriage, and although they performed their dynastic duty by continuing the royal line, they scarcely drew the attention of historical narratives. These were more concerned with the men who acted on their behalf.

The only other female heiress who challenged the succession in the late thirteenth century was Maria of Antioch.[178] By this point in time, a precedent had been established whereby consanguinity, and not primogeniture, qualified inheritance of the throne, and although she had a legitimate claim, she was turned down by the High Court in favour of Hugh of Antioch-Lusignan in 1269. His comparatively shaky case included an argument that neither Maria nor her mother had been designated heir, although this was irrelevant in the eyes of the law. His success was interpreted by his own grandson as evidence that the crown of Jerusalem would be passed to any male heir in favour of a female one, but may also have been to do with the fact that Maria was over forty and unmarried.[179] Maria later added to political intrigue in the kingdom by selling the crown to Charles of Anjou in 1277. Very little information about the character of these latter thirteenth-century heiresses filtered through into the historical narratives of the Latin East for this period. Their only real impact was the power vacuum left in their wake. Chroniclers of the later period were more concerned with the growing aggression of the Mamluks, the failures of

---

[177] See Christopher Marshall, *Warfare in the Latin East, 1192–1291* (Cambridge, 1992), 37–46.

[178] There were cases of female regency during the thirteenth century; see 189–90 below.

[179] *Documents Relatifs à la successibilité au trône et à la régence*, in RHC Lois 2.421. See also Riley-Smith, *The Feudal Nobility*, 221.

crusaders, and the internal political struggles of barons and imperial legates, Italian trading communities and the military orders.

DAUGHTERS OF THE LEVANTINE NOBILITY

It was not only the crown of Jerusalem, however, that relied on the inheritance of daughters to secure political alliances. The minority of Antiochene heiress Princess Constance was characterised by continual clashes between her mother Alice and the kings of Jerusalem over the regency. While much attention was devoted to the activities of her mother, Constance was viewed as little more than a dynastic pawn in her youth, as her prospective marriage was crucial to the future of the principality. According to John Kinnamos, there had been diplomatic overtures from Antioch for a marriage alliance between Constance and Manuel, the son of Byzantine Emperor John II Comnenus.[180] Bearing in mind the support that Alice was able to muster against Baldwin II and later Fulk, it is plausible that she or her allies were seeking an alternative protector to the king of Jerusalem.[181] An alliance with Byzantium would have brought considerably more wealth to the principality and better access to protection from Muslim and Armenian encroachment than could be offered by a western lord. It has been suggested that this marriage proposal could have been part of a conscious attempt by the Byzantines to encourage the image of Manuel as a 'friend of the Latins'.[182] Instead, under the influence of King Fulk and Alice's opponents, Constance was married as quickly as possible to crusader Raymond of Poitiers at the 'unmarriageable' age of eight in the spring of 1136. Her inheritance passed to her husband, effectively quashing the aspirations of her mother and Emperor John II in one fell swoop.[183] The marriage of Raymond and Constance, in conjunction with the conflict with Leo of Armenia, handed John a *casus belli* to pursue plans that he had nurtured for some time: to establish lordship over Syria and Palestine.[184] John besieged the city successfully in 1137 and received Raymond as a vassal in the subsequent treaty.[185] The emperor then returned to the city in 1142, planning to campaign in the region of Antioch, and demanded that the city with its citadel and fortifications be surrendered to him as agreed under the terms of the treaty. This caused severe consternation amongst the Antiochene nobility, who were determined to limit Byzantine authority in the area. They claimed that Raymond had not had the

---

[180] John Kinnamos, *The Deeds of John and Manuel Comnenus*, trans. Charles M. Brand (New York, 1976), 22. See Phillips, *Defenders*, 61.

[181] See 68 above, and 183–5 below.

[182] Ralph Johannes Lilie, *Byzantium and the Crusader States, 1096–1204* (Oxford, 1993), 104, 139.

[183] WT, 662.

[184] Lilie, *Byzantium*, 109–12.

[185] *Ibid.*, 120–2.

legal authority to make such arrangements on behalf of his wife, because it was her patrimony, and, even then, she was not allowed to transfer government or land to other persons without the permission of the citizens and magnates.[186] Thus Raymond could hide behind Constance's rights as an heiress, and even give nominal acceptance to limitations placed upon him as a consort, when it was politically expedient.

Despite the social mobility afforded by frontier society, marriage part-ners were still expected to have an appropriate pedigree, and some lords were criticised for marrying heiresses in their wardship to those of lower status for financial gain. Such a story was used to explain the antipathy between Ray-mond III of Tripoli and Gerard of Ridefort: it sprang from an earlier marriage agreement that had turned sour. Raymond had apparently promised Gerard the daughter of William Dorel, heiress to Botron, but a rich Pisan named Plivain apparently offered a substantial cash sum for her, which Raymond accepted.[187] It was not unheard of for rich merchants to 'purchase' noble status by a marriage agreement, but it was usually frowned upon. *Eracles* wrote:

> it was said that he put the maiden on a balance with gold on the other side, and that the gold she weighed, and more, was given to the count; in exchange for this great sum the count granted her to Plivain.[188]

Gerard, we are told, was very angry because 'the count had given her to a peas-ant', and went on to join the Templars in a fit of pique. Marriage to an heiress was a crucial move in the career of a knight who had ambitions in the Latin East. Perhaps it was the fact that another suitable match could not be found which spurred Gerard to enter monastic life, although *Eracles* implied that it may also have been a vocational decision following an illness.[189]

Members of established noble families in the Latin East also benefited from marriage to heiresses. The Ibelins have been described by Mayer as 'a family which, at all times, placed great importance on concluding marriages which would accelerate their family's rise to the top'.[190] In particular, the marriage of Barisan (Balian the elder) to Helvis, lady of Ramla, was a significant factor in raising his family's profile. Mayer suggests that Helvis held a position as an heiress similar to that of Melisende, with Barisan as her consort, and although her brother Renier challenged successfully for the patrimony when he came of age in 1143–4, King Fulk was obliged to soften the blow by giving the newly

---

[186]   WT, 701–2.

[187]   *Eracles*, 45; Ernoul, 114.

[188]   *Eracles*, 46; trans. Edbury, 38–9.

[189]   Hamilton argues that this story may well have factual origins, despite what Morgan calls its 'caractère folklorique'. Hamilton, *Leper King*, 146–7; *Eracles*, 46 n. 1.

[190]   Hans E. Mayer, 'Carving up Crusaders: The Early Ibelins and Ramlas', in Kedar *et al.*, *Outremer*, 108–9.

built fortress of Ibelin to Barisan. Renier then died in 1146–8, and the lordship of Ramla fell to Barisan again, and later their son Hugh.[191] William of Tyre, however, did not consider Helvis significant beyond her later remarriage to Manasses of Hierges.[192] Throughout the twelfth century the Ibelins' dynastic policy grew ever more ambitious. Ernoul went as far as to suggest that Baldwin of Ibelin, lord of Ramla, entertained hopes of marrying the heiress to the throne of Jerusalem (Sybilla), and was deeply upset by her marriage to William of Monferrat.

Patronage involving marriage to an heiress was also used to heal political rifts in settler society. The *Eracles* chronicler told how Reynald of Sidon made a fortuitous marriage to another Helvis, the daughter of his old enemies Balian of Ibelin and Maria Comnena.[193] *Eracles* dated this marriage to after Balian's release from captivity and the capture of Beaufort, but it probably took place before 1189.[194] Reynald had been a key figure in the politics of the Latin East leading up to the battle of Hattin. Powerful in his own right as lord of Sidon, and the final husband of Agnes of Courtenay, he had held some influence over her son, Baldwin IV. Although he and his wife were apparently opposed to the Ibelin faction and Raymond III of Tripoli after the marriage of Sibylla and Guy of Lusignan in 1180, Agnes of Courtenay died between September 1184 and 21 October 1186, possibly before February 1185.[195] Only a marriage soon after that date would give sufficient time for Reynald to have produced the children for whom he supposedly sought safe conduct in his negotiations with Saladin in 1189.[196] It was uncertain whether Reynald had been involved in the conflict over Sibylla's succession, and Hamilton cites this marriage to Helvis as an indication that some kind of agreement had been reached between the two camps before July 1187, and possibly even before Baldwin v's death.[197]

In the latter days of the Latin settlement, heiresses with a claim could be a disruptive influence on an already unstable political system. In 1288, the so-called 'Templar of Tyre' recorded how Lucienne of Apulia, the sister and heir of Bohemond VII of Antioch-Tripoli, was sent by her husband, Narjot III of Toucy, to claim her inheritance on her brother's death. She was supported by the Hospitallers of Acre, but faced opposition from the Genoese and the

---

[191]   *Ibid.*, 115–18.

[192]   See 220 below.

[193]   *Eracles*, 81–2.

[194]   John L. LaMonte, 'The Lords of Sidon in the Twelfth and Thirteenth Centuries', *Byzantion* 17 (1944–5), 199–200.

[195]   Hamilton, *Leper King*, 158, 214 n. 17.

[196]   See Bahā' ad-Din, *The Rare and Excellent History of Saladin*, trans. Donald S. Richards (Aldershot, 2002), 91; Imad ad-Din, *Conquête de la Syrie*, 160; and Ibn Al-Athīr, *Extrait du Kamel-Altevarykh*, RHC Or. (Paris, 1872), 1.738–9, who specifically mentioned a wife and children.

[197]   Hamilton, *Leper King*, 218 and n. 31.

Tripolitans, who had organised themselves into a commune. The dispute was eventually resolved through face-to-face negotiations between Lucienne herself and Genoese admiral Benedetto Zaccaria, presided over by Hospitaller commander Boniface of Calamadrana. The 'Templar' emphasised her personal role in diplomacy, but she was constantly surrounded by advisers from the military order. She later endured the siege of Tripoli in 1289 with two other 'grans dames', Sibylla of Armenia and Margaret of Antioch-Lusignan, before escaping when the city fell to Sultan al-Malik al-Mansur.[198]

A consequence of warfare in the Latin East was that large numbers of nobles could be dispossessed of their inheritances *en masse*. When the remains of the county of Edessa were sold to the Byzantines, William of Tyre portrayed nobles of high birth weeping and distressed at being forced to leave the homes of their ancestors.[199] When daughters were disinherited in this way, attempts were made to find suitable husbands for them, but some may have been compelled to marry beneath their status. *Eracles* related that when Guy of Lusignan, himself dispossessed of a kingdom, parcelled out his new lands in Cyprus to other refugees from the Holy Land, he tried to match them to suitable partners. As well as the knights, sergeants and burgesses who came, there were also *dames juenes* [*sic*], *orphenins* and *orfenines* whose husbands and fathers were lost in Syria. He gave generously to these men, even though some of them were Greeks and even Arabic scribes, and '… had them marry the women on their arrival as befitted their station, and provided for them out of his wealth so that those that married them would be well satisfied'.[200] Heiresses, even dispossessed, were often wards of the crown and could therefore expect some protection from kings. On the Third Crusade, King Richard gave generous gifts to noble Palestinian virgins and widows at Messina in 1191.[201] Further examples of largesse often included widows, because like daughters with an inheritance, the future of most aristocratic women rested on their access to landed wealth, and if left without the protection of male relatives or inheritance through the fortunes of war, they often had to rely on charity.[202]

BETROTHALS AND INTERNATIONAL DIPLOMACY

Marriage negotiations did not revolve exclusively around the inheritance of property. Betrothals of aristocratic daughters also featured in the narratives of crusading and the Latin East when their outcome had some political ramification for crusaders or settlers. A daughter's lineage and dowry could be just

---

[198] *Les Gestes des Chiprois*, in RHC *Arm.* (1906), 2.801–3. See also Paul Crawford, *The 'Templar of Tyre': Part III of the Deeds of the Cypriots* (Aldershot, 2003), 95–100.

[199] WT, 783.

[200] *Eracles*, 139; trans. Edbury, 114.

[201] *Itinerarium*, 172.

[202] See 228–9 below.

as critical as land to forging dynastic links between families. A more cordial relationship between the Byzantine Empire and the Levantine nobility after the Second Crusade meant that there were several marriage alliances between the imperial and royal houses which featured prominently in texts related to crusading and the Latin East. Such betrothals could have an effect on international politics even when they went awry, as demonstrated by the proposed match between heiress Constance of Antioch and Manuel Comnenus.[203] Negotiations were often lengthy because of political intrigue and the distance over which envoys had to travel: the negotiations of Amalric's envoys for the hand of Maria Comnena took two years.[204] Bertha/Irene of Salzburg had to wait almost four years in Constantinople before her wedding to Manuel Comnenus while diplomats wrangled over the marriage negotiations, ostensibly because of her lineage: she was the sister-in-law of King Conrad III OF Germany rather than a blood-relative.[205]

After Bertha's death in 1159, Manuel sought a new alliance with the nobles of the Latin East. An imperial letter arrived from Manuel inviting Baldwin III's decision on one of two candidates: Melisende of Tripoli or Maria of Antioch.[206] Baldwin chose Melisende, perhaps because he wanted to avoid strengthening the emperor's hold over Antioch. In the previous year, the emperor had secured Baldwin III's support through his marriage to Theodora Comnena, enabling Manuel to force the abject submission of Prince Reynald in 1159 and enter the city of Antioch in triumph.[207] The emperor had accepted overlordship of the city on moderate terms, in comparison to his predecessors, but intentions displayed by a dynastic match with Maria of Antioch may have added insult to injury for the discomfited Antiochene nobility. Manuel initially seemed to accept Baldwin's judgement, sending envoys to Tripoli to negotiate, and marriage preparations were initiated.[208] William of Tyre described a great number of expensive ornaments, from gold jewellery to silver kitchen utensils and harnesses for horses, that were prepared by her mother, Hodierna, and aunt, Queen Melisende.[209] Count Raymond even built twelve galleys and equipped

---

[203] See 84 above.

[204] WT, 913. Lilie suggests that the negotiations dragged on until the Byzantines were faced with a new threat to their ambitions in Italy from the Holy Roman Empire. Lilie, *Byzantium*, 197.

[205] See Michael Angold, *The Byzantine Empire, 1025–1204*, 2nd edition (London, 1997), 193.

[206] Although this agreement does not appear in the Byzantine sources, Magdalino asserts that 'it was fully in the spirit of the settlement of 1159 that Manuel should use Baldwin as his broker in his dealings with the other crusader princes'. Paul Magdalino, *The Empire of Manuel I Komnenos 1143–1180* (Cambridge, 1993), 72 and n. 166.

[207] WT, 845.

[208] John Kinnamos asserts that envoys were sent to Tripoli in 1160. Kinnamos, *Deeds*, 158.

[209] WT, 856.

them to convey the nobles who had gathered in Tripoli to the wedding. William's detailed description of these preparations provides a stark contrast to the conduct of the Greek officials towards the lady and her family. He asserted that:

> Meanwhile, during all this time the Greeks investigated each thing to a hair's breadth, and pried further into the morals of the girl by examining the state of the hidden secret parts of her body …[210]

Evidently for such a potentially important bride it was crucial to establish her virginity, and her ability to bear children evidenced by menstruation, but William seems to imply that her treatment went beyond normal scrutiny. After a year had passed, it seemed clear that they were playing for time. The envoys were summoned to court and told either to reject the marriage and refund the money already spent, or to stop delaying.[211] The matter was only settled when Baldwin sent an envoy of his own to Manuel, who returned with unfavourable news: Manuel had lost interest. This was a matter of some embarrassment for the king because of his role in the negotiations:

> On understanding this the king stopped the negotiation, accounting it a great dishonour that the marriage, which he believed to have been contracted by his mediation and brought to a conclusion by his offices, should come to nothing …[212]

Baldwin withdrew from the discussions at once, and the envoys, fearing Raymond's wrath, left by boat as quickly as possible. They claimed to be returning to Constantinople, but according to William the king later found them at Antioch, deep in negotiations with Princess Constance about her daughter Maria: 'they were having daily and friendly consultation'; they also held letters sealed in gold from the emperor guaranteeing that any marriage agreement would be ratified.[213] William presented it as a testament to Baldwin's character that, despite this great insult offered him by the emperor, he intervened on behalf of his kinswoman, because 'she was a ward and robbed of the care of a father'.[214] It seems more than likely, however, that his job was already done. Constance was an experienced regent capable of conducting negotiations, and Manuel's desire to secure the match was obvious. Baldwin's involvement, if indeed it did occur, was probably little more than an exercise in saving face, and reflected his own desperate need to maintain the Byzantine alliance.

The reasons behind Manuel's change of heart are not entirely clear. Byzantine

---

[210] Ibid., 856.

[211] Ibid., 856.

[212] Ibid., 857.

[213] Ibid., 857.

[214] Ibid., 857.

historian Niketas Choniates simply glossed over the incident: as far as he was concerned, Maria was one candidate of many offered to the emperor, and was accepted for conventional reasons of beauty and lineage.[215] Kinnamos, on the other hand, admitted that Melisende had been the first choice, but recounted a story about mysterious illnesses which ruined her beauty and made her unable to travel. This, combined with a probably unfounded rumour about her possible illegitimacy, made her an unworthy candidate for the position of empress, and forced the envoys to break off the engagement.[216] Kinnamos also specified that two sets of envoys were sent, suggesting that Manuel's decision to accept Melisende had not been definitive. John Kontostephanos headed the embassy to Tripoli, and Basil Kamateros to Antioch, and the *Hodoiporikon* of Constantine Manasses suggests that the two embassies were united in Antioch to conclude the negotiations for Maria.[217]

The majority of modern historians accept the view that Manuel was driven to break an existing agreement with Melisende by a specific event – the capture of Reynald of Châtillon by Muslims, which left the principality of Antioch extremely vulnerable.[218] It seems very plausible that it was the effect of this news, in combination with a possible appeal from Constance of Antioch (including an offer of marriage to Maria), which led to Manuel's change of heart. Unfortunately the chronology of events does not bear witness to this for two reasons. In the first place, Runciman's idea that Constance appealed to the Byzantine emperor for help immediately after Reynald's capture with a simultaneous offer of marriage to Maria is unfounded. Lilie argues convincingly that this was a separate event which took place after the marriage.[219] Secondly, John Kontostephanos appears to have set off for Jerusalem in the spring of 1160 to approach Baldwin III before going on to Tripoli.[220] William of Tyre asserted that the negotiations for Melisende went on for a year before she was finally rebuffed, and she was still described as *futura imperatrix Constantinopolitana* in a charter of 31 July 1161.[221] William was also very clear about the date of Reynald of Châtillon's capture – 23 November 1161 – as Hamilton has shown.[222] The marriage between Maria of Antioch and the Emperor Manuel reportedly took place in December

---

[215] Choniates, *O City of Byzantium*, 65–6.

[216] Kinnamos, *Deeds*, 158–9.

[217] *Ibid.* See Lilie, *Byzantium*, 186 n. 183.

[218] For Reynald's homage, see WT, 845, and capture, WT, 851–6.

[219] Runciman, *A History of the Crusades*, 2.358; Lilie, *Byzantium*, 187 n. 189.

[220] Lilie, *Byzantium*, 184 n. 176.

[221] RRH 1.96, no. 366; see Lilie, *Byzantium*, 185 n. 177.

[222] Bernard Hamilton, 'The Elephant of Christ: Reynald of Chatillon', in Derek Baker ed. *Religious Motivation: Biographical and Sociological Problems for the Church Historian* (Oxford, 1978), 98–9 n. 13.

1161.[223] Bearing in mind the lengthy preparations usual for an imperial bride (judging by the expense that Raymond of Tripoli had been put to), as well as the time it would take Maria to travel to Constantinople,[224] it seems impossible that the marriage negotiations could be brought to a conclusion so quickly, had they not already been long underway. It is possible that William was in error and Prince Reynald's capture took place in November 1160, as many historians accept.[225] If so, it does not prove that this event provoked Manuel to change his mind, as the Byzantine envoys took several more months to extricate themselves from negotiations for Melisende. Count Raymond was certainly furious with the emperor when he rejected his sister without reason, 'as if the daughter of some common person'.[226] He handed over the wedding ships to pirates with orders to devastate Byzantine territory and pillage without mercy. Either Manuel had alternative reasons of his own for rejecting the match, based on information from the envoys, or was keeping his options open from the start, allowing Count Raymond to misinterpret the situation. Perhaps Baldwin III had encouraged Raymond in his certainty that the marriage would go ahead, as the king took a very personal role in negotiations and was present in Tripoli when news of the rejection arrived. Baldwin had evidently counted rather too heavily on his own influence with his new ally, based on their recent cordial relations. He was certainly quick to distance himself from Raymond when Manuel revealed his intentions, and rather than defending his humiliated count, he invited himself in on the negotiations for Maria of Antioch as soon as he found out about them.

Melisende of Tripoli's tale highlights the fact that marriage negotiations were at the very heart of alliances and enmities between the Latin East and Byzantium during this period. Following Baldwin III's marriage to Theodora, his brother King Amalric married Manuel's great-niece, Maria Comnena, in 1167. Both brothers were aware that dynastic links to the imperial family meant large cash dowries and access to potential military support, which had dwindled from the West in the wake of the failed Second Crusade.[227] William of Tyre asserts that Baldwin's marriage to Theodora was first and foremost to provide heirs, but especially to relieve some of his poverty, as she

---

[223] Kinnamos, *Deeds*, 160.

[224] Even if she travelled by sea it may have taken several weeks. The south to north route was more complex to navigate, notwithstanding winter conditions, and necessitated many coastal stops on the way. See John Pryor, *Geography, Technology and War: Studies in the Maritime History of the Mediterranean 649–1571* (Cambridge, 1992), 89–90, 95–8.

[225] For example, Magdalino, *Empire*, 72; Phillips, *Defenders*, 142. Lilie, *Byzantium*, 184 n. 174, asserts that the dates are not clear.

[226] WT, 858.

[227] For the diplomatic and financial aspects to these marriages, see Phillips, *Defenders*, 132–4, 154–9.

brought 100,000 *nomismata* as a cash dowry.[228] After Manuel's defeat at Myriocephalum in 1176, however, the fortunes of the Byzantine Empire began to wane. The emperor decided to secure an alliance with the West through the betrothal of Agnes/Anna, daughter of Louis VII, to his young son by Maria of Antioch, Alexius II.[229] Although the marriage was not associated with a particular crusade, it drew the attention of several authors on the subject.[230] William of Tyre was actually present for the event in Constantinople in 1180, and told how Manuel conferred the imperial insignia upon the two betrothed, although Alexius was scarcely thirteen and Agnes barely eight.[231] Manuel died shortly afterwards and Maria of Antioch's regency for Alexius II was very unpopular, predominantly because of dissatisfaction with the *Protosebastos* Alexius Comnenus, Manuel's nephew. Manuel's cousin Andronicus Comnenus then came to political power amid a wave of violent purges against the Italians in Constantinople in 1182, and although this was not indicative of sentiments towards Latin Christendom as a whole, western chroniclers certainly interpreted it as such.[232] William of Tyre expressed shock that these events could occur when Greeks and Latins had long lived side by side as friends and even intermarried.[233] By 1183 Andronicus had murdered Maria of Antioch and Alexius II, claiming Agnes of France for himself. Chroniclers in the West were outraged by these acts, and in order to blacken his reputation further they wrote about his nefarious relationships with other women.[234] He had already had two scandalous affairs with members of his own family,[235] and his treatment of Agnes was yet another example of the perfidy and inconstancy of the Greeks. Andronicus' reign was short-lived, but his impact on western consciousness was such that even Fourth Crusade chroniclers such as Robert of Clari mentioned the story of Agnes. Andronicus' treatment of the princess was a great insult to the French: it exposed corruption at the heart of the Byzantine Empire, and helped to justify their later conquest of Constantinople. English chronicler William of Newburgh described Agnes' plight with some sympathy:

---

[228] WT, 833–4.

[229] Lilie asserts that Manuel specifically attempted a *rapprochement* with both France and England in the second half of the 1170s. Lilie, *Byzantium*, 213.

[230] Agnes' fate featured in the Old French continuations of William of Tyre, which then influenced other authors such as William of Newburgh and Robert of Clari. Robert's account of the betrothal was very similar to that of Ernoul. See RC, 19, and Ernoul, 47. It even appeared in a very short fragment on Louis VII: see *Fragmentum historicum vitam Ludovici VII*, in RHGF 12 (Paris, 1877), 286.

[231] WT, 1010.

[232] Jonathan Harris, *Byzantium and the Crusades* (London, 2003), 111–19.

[233] WT, 1024.

[234] For example, see WN, 1.224.

[235] Eudokia and Theodora; for the latter see 218–19 below.

In this way the daughter of the king of the French was cheated of her desired and promised marriage in the realm of the Greeks, and tainted by concubinage to a most evil man, she was even deprived of her honour.[236]

Others were more critical: despite its origins at Châlons sur Marne in the Champagne region, the chronicle of Alberic of Trois Fontaines blamed Agnes for bringing the French royal family into disrepute. Alberic suggested that she had not married Alexius II at all, but had squandered her first bride's gift, and was living in sin with the Byzantine noble, Livernas Branas, until their marriage was legitimised in 1205.[237] Robert of Clari told how the French barons at Constantinople enquired after Agnes and were informed that she had married Livernas.[238] Robert expressed surprise that Agnes met them with very bad grace and asserted that she felt no kinship with her native land; she spoke to them through an interpreter and claimed to know no French at all.[239] It seems, however, to be a fairly obvious result of the policy of sending young noblewomen to be brought up in the court of their betrothed. On the one hand it enabled them to acclimatise, but on the other it could weaken ties of loyalty to their native families and undermine their role as potential diplomats. They were also extremely vulnerable to political change.

Evidently, daughters of the nobility were valuable commodities that required careful protection both before and after marriage if they wished to maintain their status. A virtuous reputation was all the more important if the daughter were to be a queen. The *Itinerarium* described rather scathingly how Isabella of Jerusalem was sequestered after her abduction from Humphrey of Toron and before her marriage to Conrad of Monferrat, 'so that the actual doing of the injury should avoid ill-repute'.[240] Essentially this was a damage limitation exercise; Isabella was bound to be the subject of scandal, and if she was confined she could at least be portrayed as innocent of wilful wrongdoing. Conveniently it kept her husband from trying to win her back, of course.

Traditionally, daughters as prospective brides demanded an escort, not only to guard the large dowries they travelled with, but also to provide security for their person so that there could be no question over their sexual integrity. Margaret of Reynel, the niece of John of Brienne, was escorted to Egypt by none other than Cardinal Pelagius in order to marry Balian Grenier, lord of Sidon, at Damietta in 1218.[241] Berengaria of Navarre was accompanied to her

---

[236] WN, 1.225.

[237] ATF, 870.

[238] RC, 54. See also *Ernoul*, 390.

[239] RC, 54.

[240] *Itinerarium*, 120.

[241] *L'Estoire de Eracles Empereur*, in RHC Occ. 2 (1859), 332.

marriage ceremony by Richard I's most prestigious female relatives, Eleanor of Aquitaine and Joanna of Sicily. *Eracles* asserted that this was so that Richard's betrothed would go with greater honour, but also so that the marriage would take place all the sooner and Eleanor's ambitions would be fulfilled.[242] Both Eleanor and Joanna were probably expected to groom the girl in the skills she might need, familiarising her with Richard's court. Similarly, envoys and bridal attendants related to the highest nobles of the Empire accompanied Manuel's niece Theodora on her journey to Syria for her marriage to Baldwin III; and 'illustrious and magnificent nobles' of the imperial family attended Maria Comnena as an escort.[243]

The betrothal of King Richard to Berengaria of Navarre during the Third Crusade was seemingly a surprise, at least to his fellow crusader Philip II of France, as Richard had a prior agreement to marry his sister, Alice.[244] Their betrothal had taken place in 1169, and had been re-established by the French kings at every possible opportunity, but Richard capitalised on the crusade expedition to postpone the actual marriage once again. When Richard finally reneged on this agreement it caused great discord between the two kings on crusade, and was probably a major factor in Philip's decision to return home.[245] *Eracles* blamed Eleanor of Aquitaine for the new match, though the *Itinerarium* was careful to call Berengaria 'the king's future wife'[246] and said that '... he had desired her very much for a long time', 'since he was first count of Poitou'.[247] No mention was made of Alice. Richard of Devizes asserted that it was because Richard had growing suspicions about Alice's virtue that he considered Berengaria as an alternative, but still argued that this was a match 'for which he ardently longed'.[248] There is a record of the gift of a *tenencia* to Berengaria by her father in 1185, which suggests her betrothal negotiations began well before the crusade, but there is no specific mention of Richard.[249] His eventual refusal to marry Alice on the highly insulting grounds that his own father Henry II had compromised her soured Philip's attitude towards him further. Richard's mother escorted Berengaria to Sicily by ship to meet Richard, and when King Philip became aware of this

---

[242] *Eracles*, 111–12. See 180–1 below.

[243] WT, 843, 913.

[244] See John Gillingham, 'Richard I and Berengaria', in his *Richard Cœur de Lion* (London, 1994), 119–31, for a detailed account.

[245] *Eracles*, 121.

[246] *Itinerarium*, 175; Nicholson, 173, translates *futuram* as 'intended'.

[247] *Itinerarium*, 175; trans. Nicholson, 173. Ambroise also emphasised this point. Ambroise, l.19, lns 1148–9. See *Eracles*, 111.

[248] Richard of Devizes, *Chronicon*, 26.

[249] Ann Trindade, *Berengaria: In Search of Richard the Lionheart's Queen* (Dublin, 1999), 54.

he reputedly encouraged Tancred of Lecce to hamper Berengaria's progress from Naples to Messina, but without success.[250] Richard's attraction to the new marriage revolved around the large cash dowry that he could use on crusade, and securing an ally close to his lands in the south of France to protect his interests there against Raymond v of Toulouse. Richard had taken a large risk by angering his fellow crusader Philip of France in this way, but the Vexin had been offered as part of Alice's dowry, and by impugning her sexual integrity Richard could maintain his own claim to the region if she remained unmarried. Gillingham asserts that marrying Berengaria while under the protection of the crusade meant that Philip could not immediately mount an attack upon him, and was ultimately 'an ingenious diplomatic device deliberately adopted by Richard in order to cut his way through a thicket of political problems'.[251]

VIRGINITY, CAPTIVITY AND THE CLOISTER

Despite the exhortations of ecclesiastical propagandists in favour of young women with a vocation for the cloister, aristocratic daughters were often too important as marriageable commodities to enter the convent, especially in the Latin East. One highly placed noble daughter who entered a nunnery in her youth was Yveta, daughter of Baldwin ii. To an extent, the fact that she was the youngest of four sisters meant that she was least likely to inherit, and as such was more 'disposable'. A comparison can be drawn with Henry, the fourth son of Adela of Blois, who, 'lest she was seen to have brought forth children for secular purposes only', gave him to the monastery at Cluny.[252] Yveta's three sisters had made the highest marriages possible, and Baldwin may have struggled to find her a partner of similar standing. Crucially, however, she had been held hostage by Muslims as a child. In 1125, the king paid a cash ransom for his five-year-old daughter.[253] Despite her youth, Friedman argues that captivity may have ruined her marriage prospects by casting a slur on her sexual integrity.[254] According to *Estoires D'Outremer* and Ernoul she could never marry because she had been a captive.[255] Yveta was subsequently entered into the convent of St Anne's in Jerusalem.[256] However, Melisende, who was renowned for her own piety, patronised the church of St Lazarus at Bethany and built a new convent suitable to her sibling's rank. Fittingly, this

---

[250] Roger of Howden, *Chronica*, 3.95–9; and 'Gesta', 2.157–60.

[251] Gillingham, 'Richard i and Berengaria', 120. For the marriage itself, see 127 above.

[252] WN, 1.31.

[253] FC, 770.

[254] Friedman, *Encounter Between Enemies*, 183.

[255] *Estoires d'Outremer*, 45; Ernoul, 5.

[256] See 142 below.

site was also associated with the two sisters of Lazarus – Mary and Martha.[257] In practical terms Melisende made sure that the property was defensible, demonstrating the precarious nature of life for female religious in the Latin East. [258] William of Tyre explained that Melisende had spiritual motives in founding the convent: she was concerned for her own soul and those of her relatives. There were also important issues of status to consider '... for it seemed undignified to her that a king's daughter should be under the authority of any mother superior in the cloister, as if a person from the common populace.'[259] Although an experienced abbess, Mathilda, was initially installed, Yveta duly took on the position created for her at some time between 1144 and 1157.[260] Evidently, social hierarchy was still a key issue even within the religious community. Melisende wanted Bethany to be richer than any other monastery or church – it was intended to be a statement of royal wealth and power as well as piety.[261] In supporting her sister's vocation she enhanced the prestige of the monarchy, negated the earlier slur on Yveta's sexual status, and gained a firm ally in the Church, which was useful in her later political conflicts.

The defences at Bethany emphasised the fact that women from all social backgrounds involved in crusade expeditions or settlement frequently risked capture, slavery and death in hostile territory. If women were of a suitable age for manual labour, of pleasing enough appearance, or rich enough to be worth a ransom, it was irrelevant whether they were a daughter, wife, mother, or widow. Distinctions between the types of women taken captive were largely imposed by crusade chroniclers themselves, usually to indicate the barbarity of an enemy. Women were undoubtedly subjected to sexual violence, torture and death in what was essentially a time of brutal warfare, but authors of crusade narratives made use of such events, emphasising the youth and beauty of women in their descriptions of sexual violence to incite pity in their audience, and to fan the flames of religious hatred. In the society of western Europe the rape of virgins was usually punished with greater severity than that of other women, and the authors of crusade narratives specifically emphasised the virginity of captives as a reminder to the audience of their imminent sexual degradation.

Albert of Aachen recounted the capture of a nun from Trier who had joined Peter the Hermit's army. After the crusaders took Nicaea she was ransomed, but she had been raped repeatedly and, in considerable distress, sought purification at the hands of Bishop Adhémar of le Puy. Afterwards,

---

[257] See Denys Pringle, *The Churches of the Crusader Kingdom of Jerusalem*, 3 vols (Cambridge, 1993–2007), 1.123–37.

[258] WT, 709.

[259] *Ibid.*, 709.

[260] *Regesta Regni Hierosolimitani*, 1.84, no. 327; Geneviéve Bresc-Bautier, *Cartulaire du Chapitre du St. Sépulchre du Jérusalem* (Paris, 1984), 108 no. 38.

[261] WT, 709.

her Turkish captor, 'inflamed with passion for the nun's outstanding beauty', persuaded her through messengers and with promises to abscond with him.[262] He even promised to become a Christian, and, 'deceived by his blandishments and vain hope', she rushed back to the illicit union.[263] It is possible that the story had some basis in fact, although Albert admitted it was heard at second hand.[264] He gave details about her convent, St Mary at the Granaries, and asserted that Duke Henry of Esch recognised her personally. Through his account of these events, Albert demonstrated understanding that she had been forced to do wrong before, but stated that no one could fathom her reasons for returning to this man 'unless it was because her own lust was too much to bear'.[265] He blamed the natural weakness of women for her decision. Whether authentic or not, this story was clearly included to serve as a didactic and cautionary tale, one of several in Albert's history focusing on the ruin of a monastic who took the cross in defiance of the Pope's orders.[266]

Sexual violence against Christian women was often used to motivate crusaders and illustrate the suffering of the eastern Christians. At Artah, during the First Crusade, Armenian Christians reputedly overthrew their Turkish overlords because their wives and daughters had been raped.[267] Guibert of Nogent, while freely admitting that he changed the wording of his original source, [268] described women suffering multiple rape to show Muslim irreverence for laws Christians held dear. He accused them of turning churches into brothels, and making virgins into public prostitutes.[269] The juxtaposition of mothers and daughters in these vivid scenes of rape where parent and child were forced to dance and sing while watching each other suffer was specifically calculated to arouse horror at the cruelty of the enemy. It also emphasised their lack of reverence for laws about secondary incest, that is, to fornicate with both a mother and her daughter.

Albert of Aachen told how Kilij Arslan's forces killed the infirm, clergy, old women and infant boys of Peter the Hermit's army, 'and put them all to the sword, regardless of age', but 'they took away only young girls and nuns, whose faces and figures seemed to be pleasing to their eyes, and beardless and

---

[262] AA, 328.

[263] Ibid.

[264] '... it is known from those who tell the story'. AA, 328.

[265] Ibid., 328.

[266] See 182–5 below.

[267] AA, 358–9.

[268] 'Moreover, although I am reluctant to insert that letter into this little work in its entirety, it pleases me to set forth certain elements of its meaning in the guise of my own words' (the text of the letter follows). GN, 101. For the original letter, see 'Epistula Alexii Komneni imperatoris ad Robertum I comitem Flandrensem (ca. 1088)', in Hagenmeyer, Die Kreuzzugsbriefe, 129–36.

[269] GN, 102.

attractive young men'.[270] Similarly, Kerbogha's terms for Christian surrender at Antioch demanded 'all their unbearded youth', as slaves, including 'girls who are still virgins' – any who were married, bearded or grey-haired would be killed.[271] The purpose for which these slaves were taken is left to the imagination but the focus on physical beauty suggests it was a sexual one. There was also a strong fear of racial pollution through miscegenation. First Crusader Raymond of Aguilers warned that the caliph of Egypt killed any Franks over twenty years of age from his base in Ascalon, but intended to keep the rest for a breeding programme with men and women of his own country so that he could have 'a warlike race ... from Frankish origin'.[272]

Recent work by Hay explores the use of gender bias in accounts of the massacres of the First Crusade. Hay acknowledges that there was undoubtedly torture and killing, but suggests that chroniclers had a vested interest in exaggerating these. He subscribes to Cole's view of an ideology of religious pollution and purification in crusade narratives,[273] and considers the language of massacre to be a literary motif which not only justified crusaders' violence but distorted it as well.[274] Attitudes to the enslavement and murder of Muslim women and children were not uniform. It has been suggested that although Bohemond was the undoubted hero of the early stages of the *Gesta Francorum*, the author's opinion of him became less favourable after his dispute with Raymond of Toulouse at Antioch.[275] In particular, the author seemed critical of Bohemond's actions at Marra, where he slaughtered the general populace but offered the Saracen leaders and their families safe conduct, then betrayed them and sold them into slavery.[276] Perhaps his shock at Bohemond's lack of attention to status prompted him to record this. As noble hostages were often worth a significant ransom,

---

[270] AA, 42–3. See also WT, 153.

[271] AA, 318–19. See also WT, 327.

[272] RA, 155. In fact it was not the caliph, but his general who was operating from Ascalon at the time.

[273] Penny J. Cole, "'O God, the Heathen have come into Thy Inheritance" (ps. 78.1). The Theme of Religious Pollution in Crusade Documents, 1095–1188', in Maya Shatzmiller ed. *Crusaders and Muslims in Twelfth Century Syria* (Leiden, 1993), 84–111.

[274] See David Hay, 'Gender Bias and Religious Intolerance in Accounts of the "Massacres" of the First Crusade', in Michael Gervers and James M. Powell eds *Tolerance and Intolerance: Social Conflict in the Age of the Crusades* (New York, 2001), 6. Cole, *Preaching of the Crusades*, 23, 29. For the most detailed longitudinal study of these massacre accounts and attitudes towards them to date, see Benjamin Z. Kedar, 'The Jerusalem Massacre of July 1099 in the Western Historiography of the Crusades', *Crusades* 3 (2004), 15–75. Kedar concludes that about 3000 Muslim men and women died in the initial massacre of 15 July, but that further purges may have occurred when the garrison surrendered and left for Ascalon on 17 July, perhaps taking other inhabitants with it.

[275] Emily Albu has challenged the view that the *Gesta* idealises Bohemond. See Emily Albu, *Norman Histories: Propaganda Myth and Subversion* (Woodbridge, 2001), 145–79.

[276] GF, 407–8.

they could expect special treatment; as Hay asserts, 'the idea that crusaders would wantonly destroy the only sources of wealth keeping most of them alive should be relegated to the realm of historical fiction'.[277] Presumably the profits from the slave-trade were not so lucrative as a noble ransom: slaves were inconvenient in terms of logistics and required a market for sale. Robert of Rheims asserted that Bohemond only had the old and infirm killed: 'he ordered to be saved the adolescents and adults of more mature age, both healthy in body and strong, and [ordered them] to be led to Antioch so that he could sell them'.[278] The captives had to be sufficiently youthful and physically fit (presumably to survive hard labour, rather than for sexual purposes) and would be sold to raise money. Perhaps Robert emphasised these factors to alleviate concerns that the crusaders were indulging in sexual relations with the Muslim slaves. This sentiment was echoed by Fulcher of Chartres' description of Caesarea's capture in 1101:

> Indeed, there were a few of the male sex whose lives were spared. But a great many more women were granted mercy, so that they could serve as handmaidens and could always turn hand mills. When [the Franks] had captured them, they bought and sold them amongst themselves in turn, whether beautiful or unsightly, and the men also.[279]

Fulcher was keen to preserve the sexual reputation of crusaders.[280] His assertion that crusaders were unconcerned about the looks of their female slaves underlined the idea that their slaves were for practical rather than sexual purposes. Conversely, Guibert of Nogent, who had read Fulcher's account, simply wrote that the crusaders spared no one, 'except the girlish youth to be kept for servitude'.[281]

In an unusual twist to these motifs of conquest and sexual activity, when Albert of Aachen described the attack of Kilij Arslan on Bohemond's camp at Dorylaeum it was the Christian women who favoured slavery or prostitution in preference to embracing their chance of martyrdom. Again, indiscriminate killing set the tone: 'women both married and unmarried were beheaded along with men and little children'.[282] As a result,

> Stunned and terrified by the cruelty of this most hideous killing, girls who were delicate and very nobly born were hastening to get themselves dressed up, they were offering themselves to the Turks so that at least,

---

[277] Hay, 'Gender Bias', 10.

[278] RR, 849.

[279] FC, 403.

[280] See 138–9 below.

[281] GN, 347.

[282] AA, 130–1.

roused and appeased by love of their beautiful appearance, the Turks might learn to pity their prisoners.[283]

These women evidently hoped that having the appearance of wealth or beauty might increase their chances of survival. This episode has strong parallels with Albert's harrowing account of a massacre in Jerusalem which does not appear in other sources. On the third day after the initial conquest took place, he asserts that those whom the crusaders had previously spared for the sake of money or pity were beheaded or stoned, regardless of age or sex, including noble ladies, pregnant women and very young children. They embraced the Christians, begging for their lives even as their throats were slit.[284] The range and vulnerability of the victims described were designed to indicate the totality of the holocaust. Robert of Rheims, however, asserted that there were female, as well as male, survivors after the capture of Jerusalem:

> When they had carried out this indescribable slaughter, they yielded somewhat to nature and saved the lives of many of the young, as much men as women, and committed them to their slavery.[285]

Albert may have been inspired by ideas about religious pollution and purification; his account of the speech of Daimbert after the capture of Jerusalem includes a reference to cleansing the holy places.[286] He clearly disapproved of the massacre of Jews at Mainz and used the same imagery of age and gender to demonstrate his abhorrence of the crusaders' actions.[287] His vivid description and strong language suggest either a horror of violence, or a passion for gory details, reflecting the contemporary trends in the *chansons de geste*. At first glance, women offering themselves to crusaders in the midst of a bloodbath at Jerusalem might be interpreted as an attempt to denigrate Muslim morality, but the similarity to his earlier description of the actions of Christian women at Dorylaeum and sympathy for the Jewish women at Mainz suggests that it was the gender of these victims rather than their religious affiliation that concerned the author. Kedar asserts that Albert's account 'plainly reveals his compassion for the victims'.[288] However, when one considers these stories in conjunction with those of the nun of Trier, Florina of Burgundy and Adalbero's courtesan,[289] a further message emerges: any woman who became involved with the crusading army, noble or common, nun or harlot, Christian, Muslim or Jew, was likely to come to grief.

[283] *Ibid.*

[284] AA, 440–3.

[285] RR, 868.

[286] AA, 480–1.

[287] *Ibid.*, 50–3 and 56–9.

[288] Kedar, 'Jerusalem Massacre', 23.

[289] For Adelbero's courtesan, see 152 below; for Florina, see 215.

When considering massacre accounts, age, as well as social status and gender, was a powerful emotive tool in the hands of crusade authors. Perhaps pity was shown more easily to the young: Robert of Rheims lamented young boys and girls whose lives had been cut short in the reputedly brutal sack of Albara.[290] It should be remembered, however, that the tragedy in the minds of medieval authors was not the deaths of Muslims, but their stubborn resistance to accept Christianity. This is amply demonstrated by Rothelin's account of Robert of Artois' attack on the Muslim camp near Mansurah in 1250, where girls and old people were slaughtered indiscriminately: '... it was sad indeed to see so many dead bodies and so much blood spilt, except that they were enemies of the Christian faith'.[291]

The perceived vulnerability of youth meant that young women were entitled to the protection of their parents. One of the worst crimes any parent could commit was to sell a daughter into prostitution; in the *Liber Augustalis*, mothers who did so were to have their noses slit.[292] Guibert of Nogent was outraged by a Byzantine law that supposedly promoted and capitalised upon the prostitution of young girls by forcing a parent who had several daughters to put one in a brothel, which was then taxed.[293] He also asserted that the emperor tried to entice the Franks to aid him by promising them the most beautiful women. Guibert scornfully dismissed this as a futile lure: first, because the Franks had impeccable self-control; and second, because Greek women were not preferable to the beauty of France itself. Ultimately it was the prostitution law of this dreadful tyrant 'that was the very reason the strongest adversity had fallen upon him and his followers'.[294] Alexius was not the only emperor to be criticised for mistreatment of daughters; Andronicus who seized power in Constantinople from Alexius II Comnenus apparently raped beautiful nuns and the daughters of his own knights or burgesses.[295] This, to a western audience, epitomised his perversion of the traditional responsibilities of a lord: to uphold Christian values and protect the interests of his vassals.

In fact, crusaders came under criticism from Christian authors for committing sexual crimes against young women, especially virgins, while *en route* to the Holy Land. These were the kind of crimes with which military defeats were associated. Guibert lists virgins amongst the Hungarian women raped by

[290] RR, 840

[291] Rothelin, 604; *Crusader Syria in the Thirteenth Century: The Rothelin Continuation of William of Tyre with Part of the Eracles or Acre Text*, trans. Janet Shirley (Aldershot, 1999), 95.

[292] *Die Konstitutionen Friedrichs II von Hohenstaufen für sein Köhngreich Sizilien*, ed. and trans. Hermann Conrad, Thea von der Lieck-Bukyen and Wolfgang Wagner (Cologne, 1973), 342–3.

[293] GN, 93.

[294] *Ibid.*, 104.

[295] *Eracles*, 27.

crusaders from the unruly contingent of Peter the Hermit.[296] Raol, author of *De Expugnatione Lyxbonensi*, criticised the men of Cologne and the Flemings because they 'insulted maidens' and looted independently, blaming this for some of the crusaders' early losses.[297] At the time of the Third Crusade, English crusaders who stopped in Lisbon were accused of defiling women and daughters by force, and flouting the king's ordinances.[298] The rape of virgins often signified impending divine retribution for sexual sins. Joscelin II of Edessa had a reputation for lust, and William of Newburgh asserted that he had abducted and raped the beautiful daughter of an unnamed citizen. In retaliation this citizen betrayed him, allowing Zengi's forces into Edessa to sack the city in 1144.[299]

Finally, although the majority of the examples mentioned here have focused on the ways in which virginity and maidenhood were abused, it should be noted that, on certain occasions, virgins could act as examples to crusaders. St Agatha and another unnamed virgin feature in Raymond of Aguilers' account of Stephen of Valence's vision of Adhémar of le Puy and the Virgin Mary during the First Crusade.[300] The importance of the Virgin to crusaders will be discussed in due course,[301] but the appearance of Agatha here is also significant. She was famously tortured and sent to the stake for resisting the advances of the prefect of Sicily during the reign of Emperor Decius in the third century, but an earthquake frightened her erstwhile captors into giving her a reprieve, and she later died in prison. A paramount example of sexual virtue, she is customarily portrayed with pincers and instruments of torture. Raymond was well aware of her significance, and perhaps he mentioned her by name when others did not because her story echoed the hardships that crusaders had suffered, as well as their need to reject sexual temptation.

---

[296] GN, 122.

[297] DEL, 177.

[298] Roger of Howden, *Chronica*, 3.45.

[299] WN, 1.59.

[300] RA, 127. For Agatha's story see AA SS, *Februarii* I (1936), 595–623.

[301] See 163–7 below.

◆ 5 ◆

Wives

Wives and Medieval Society

MARRIAGE has always played a prominent role in the formation of social bonds in western Europe, from Antiquity to the present day. In medieval society it usually involved a financial and legal transaction which enabled a new economic unit to provide for the propagation of the family line, but it also had links with the 'mysterious and terrifying world of sexuality and procreation – in other words, the realm of the sacred'.[1] During the medieval period the Church took increasing control over marriage as a sacred institution and attempted to regulate it through ecclesiastical courts, but old secular customs, Roman, Germanic, or tribal, were still prevalent in practice. From the eleventh century onwards, there was increasingly rigid legislation not only over marriage, but also over the sexual act itself. In order to understand the potential effects of crusade and settlement on perceptions of wives in medieval narratives, traditional and contemporary ideas about marriage, sex, property and influence must be considered.

MARRIAGE: TRADITION AND THE REFORM PAPACY

Celibacy and continence were traits admired by the early Christian theologians, but marriage was a sacrament, and arguments in its favour did not just follow the Pauline view that it was the lesser of two evils.[2] In the Bible, woman was created to be man's helpmeet, and this sacrosanct relationship had existed from the beginning of Creation.[3] This idea formed the cornerstone of the argument in favour of adhering to a wife's advice – as long as she counselled temperance and mercy. Wives were expected to be obedient to their husbands, following Eve's subordination to Adam as punishment for her transgression in Eden.[4] A woman's counsel could be heard, but should not rule a husband's actions. Eve had advised her husband wrongly, and as a result wives who were seen to stimulate corruption or aggression were often compared to her.

In Brooke's view, the eleventh century provided the turning point, when 'the cult of celibacy among the clergy staged a remarkable revival, and the gap between the sexual morals expected of the laity and clergy

---

[1] Georges Duby, *Love and Marriage in the Middle Ages*, trans. Jane Dunnett (Oxford, 1994), 4.

[2] 1 Cor 7:1–17, 25–40.

[3] Gen 2:18.

[4] Gen 3:16.

widened'.[5] The Reform Papacy of the eleventh century made a concerted effort to stamp out Nicolaism and had a strong impact on the way contemporary clerics portrayed marriage within their texts. Many contemporary historians were particularly critical of any lapses.[6] The sexual purity offered by clerical celibacy was not the only relevant issue, however. The ban on clerical marriage helped to protect transactions of land and benefices within the Church, and accordingly the sons of priests and concubines were not allowed to become priests themselves unless they had already made a monastic profession.[7]

Reformers wished not only to eradicate clerical marriage, but also to ensure that all marriages came under the control of church courts and were monogamous, indissoluble, consensual, and exogamous (in order to prevent intermarriage). Other types of legally permissible unions, such as concubinage, were outlawed. All sexual activity was to come under the jurisdiction of the Church, and any extra-marital sex would be punishable accordingly.[8] There was increased legislation surrounding the ceremony of marriage, incorporating the reading of banns and witnesses. The congregation largely favoured reinforcing the legality of the marriage bond, for a union often represented the most important social and economic transaction that a family undertook. However, as Duby asserts, the very need for legislation demonstrates that there were often exceptions to the rule.[9]

During this period the prohibitions about relative degrees of kinship in marriage were reinforced, making it difficult for inter-related families to maintain a hold on land in particular areas. Excommunication was decreed appropriate for anyone who married within the prohibited seventh degree. Such legislation could not be enforced entirely successfully, however. As medieval society adapted to the new vision of marriage it also began to utilise its strictures to their advantage. For example, consanguinity did not often prevent marriages between inter-related partners, but became a useful tool if one sought to divorce the other. Periodically, it was necessary for marriages to be dissolved if a political alliance had turned sour, or a couple could not produce children, or through simple incompatibility. As Bouchard asserts, "the" church did not exist as a monolithic entity', and despite the best efforts of the Reform Papacy during the Investiture Contest, royal and noble families still retained influence over the appointment of important bishoprics and abbacies at a local level; thus dispensations for separation could almost always be arranged.[10]

---

[5] Brooke, *Medieval Idea*, 41.

[6] See William of Tyre on Gervase archbishop of Rheims. WT, 547.

[7] OV, 5.15.

[8] Brundage, *Law, Sex*, 183.

[9] Duby, *Love and Marriage*, 4–5.

[10] Constance Bouchard, 'Eleanor's Divorce from Louis VII: The Uses of Consangunity', in Bonnie Wheeler and John Carmi Parsons eds *Eleanor of Aquitaine, Lord and Lady* (Basingstoke, 2002), 224.

Perhaps the most contentious issue raised by the theological renovation of marriage was the relative value of consent and consummation in validating a union. Gratian proposed in his *Decretum* (*c.* 1140) that a couple who expressed mutual consent entered into a *matrimonium initiatum*, an initiated marriage, and it only became a *matrimonium ratum*, a validated marriage, on consummation in sexual union.[11] This, however, implied that the marriage of Joseph and Mary, who were considered not to have indulged in sexual activity, was in some way incomplete. It was Peter Lombard who finally provided the view that was accepted as official church doctrine. He defined a betrothal as consent given in the future tense, but decreed a marriage to be valid when consent was expressed in the present tense.[12] However, marriage in the medieval period did not end with the spiritual licensing of sexual interaction between two partners, nor with the successful union of two family groups governed by political and economic interests. The physical relationship between man and wife after marriage also gave canonists, and chroniclers, cause for concern.

Marriage was no boundary to the sin of lust, and although marital sex was a conjugal right for the purposes of procreation, there were increasingly harsh restrictions on 'extraordinary voluptuousness'.[13] *Amicitia* between a husband and wife was approved of and supported by the command of St Paul: 'Husbands, love your wives, even as Christ also loved the Church, and gave himself for it.'[14] This was because Eve had been formed from Adam's flesh – 'He that loveth his wife loveth himself'.[15] Still, authors who were in favour of marriage were not necessarily 'pro-feminine'; they could equally be misogynistic and some considered the marital bond necessary to restrain the natural lust of women, demonstrated by the oft-quoted words of St Paul: 'it is better to marry than to burn.'[16]

Despite the Church's ruling on consent, consummation remained an important aspect of medieval marriage. The delicate balance between the spiritual and physical aspects of marital life was illustrated by the popular story of Tobias and the archangel, a tale that Brooke asserts was 'known to all the faithful'.[17] Tobias, having wooed and won his wife with the help of the archangel, apparently spent three nights in prayer before the consummation.[18] William of St Pathus' *Vita* of Saint Louis claimed that the king and his wife, Margaret of Provence, also undertook a three-night vigil before consummating their

---

[11] See Brundage, *Law, Sex*, 235–9.

[12] *Ibid.*, 264.

[13] Brundage, *Law, Sex*, 239–242, 278–88.

[14] Eph 5:25.

[15] Eph 5:28.

[16] 1 Cor 7:9.

[17] Brooke, *Medieval Idea*, 43.

[18] *Ibid.*, 194.

marriage.[19] William may have 'borrowed' the story to add strength to the case for Louis' canonisation. The couple went on to have thirteen children; thus perhaps it was important to present the saint showing physical restraint and respect both for his wife and for God. However, William had been Margaret's confessor for eighteen years and wrote at her behest, so there may have been an element of truth to the tale. Such an example shows that consummation, a necessary part of marriage, could be conducted so as not to detract from the pious and spiritual aspects of a person's behaviour. Some chroniclers and fictional writers did portray happily married couples who loved and respected each other, if not, perhaps, in terms of modern-day expectations. However, as the majority of marriages in the medieval period were based upon dynastic criteria rather than physical attraction, adultery remained a genuine problem despite social and religious restraints. Accordingly romance literature, the language of fantasy and escapism for a rigidly organised group – the aristocracy – appears to have focused largely on notions of illicit love unsanctioned by the bonds of marriage.

EXTRA-MARITAL RELATIONS: ADULTERY AND PROSTITUTION

Adultery was a common theme in the Bible, and found its way into most early Christian writings and penitentials, but the term was not always consistently defined. It could be used to describe prostitution, sex between married and unmarried persons, clerical concubinage – in fact, any form of illicit sex outside marriage. This creates problems for the historian when trying to define prostitution in its medieval context. Prostitutes were generally categorised by terms such as *meretrix* or *mulier fornicatrix*. They were occasionally referred to as *mulieres prostitutae*, but it was sex outside the bonds of matrimony, or the number of partners a woman had, rather than accepting payment, that defined a prostitute. Prostitution in the modern sense, selling sex for money or food, undoubtedly took place in medieval society, but the label could be applied to all illicit, non-marital sexual acts which endangered the soul through the sin of lust.

The risks of adultery were reiterated consistently in sermons and penitentials, testifying to the regularity of its occurrence, but on the whole, the repentant adulterer could expect forgiveness. The paramount role model for the Church in this matter was Mary Magdalene, and it is not surprising that in the 'guilt-ridden' society created by ecclesiastical reform, the cult of a penitent sinner should enjoy renewed popularity.[20] Adulterous partners in a marriage were encouraged to repent and solve their differences – infidelity alone

---

19 William of St Pathus, 'Vie de Saint Louis par le Confesseur de la Reine Marguerite', in RHGF 20 (Paris, 1840), 110.

20 Members of the Reform Papacy, including Leo IX, were known to have patronised her cult. See Jean Leclercq, *Monks on Marriage: A Twelfth Century View* (New York, 1982), 89, 95.

was not sufficient grounds for divorce. For unmarried women, the solution of the twelfth-century reformers was to encourage the rehabilitation of prostitutes, either making them suitable for marriage or creating religious houses for them. In 1199 Fourth Crusade preacher Fulk of Neuilly founded the house of Saint Antoine for 'public women'.[21] The law did make provision for the fact that some women were forced to dishonour their marriage bonds through rape, whether in isolated incidents sometimes linked to abduction, or on a large scale during times of war. More often than not, however, victims incurred punishment along with the rapist. Classical role models used to illustrate the rape of wives included Lucretia and Helen – Lucretia's tragic demise and the Trojan War fought on Helen's behalf served as ringing indictments of the dangers and unhappiness caused by physical beauty and the temptation of illicit lust.

WIVES, POWER AND AUTHORITY

The biblical subjugation of wives to their husbands was used to justify a woman's lack of legal status in medieval society. The husband was head of the household, and the legal owner of any property held by his wife. In practice, however, the relationships between families and land ownership in medieval society were far more complex. Some women retained rights over the property that they had brought into the marriage and performed administrative functions on its behalf. Livingstone challenges the idea that the women's experience of power was limited exclusively to their role as widows in the twelfth century. Based on evidence from the Chartrain region of France, she asserts that many widows had, as wives, 'been partners with their husbands and commanded significant authority in their own right'.[22] The extent of a dowry was often a determining feature of the wife's power in respect to her husband, reflecting the wealth and position of her own family. In Champagne, wives retained a 'strong attachment' to lands that were given as dowry, and often tried pass them on to daughters when they married in turn. Similarly allodial lands held by wives could be passed on to the Church or monasteries, although the consent of husband and heirs was usually necessary.[23] Dowry was not a binding feature of the marriage contract in canon law, but the Church considered it a useful way to publicise a marriage, and protect the rights of both parties involved.[24]

As well as the property and dowry she brought into a marriage, a noble wife

---

21 ATF, 877; Ralph of Coggeshall also asserted that Fulk criticised 'adulterous women' – 'fornicarias mulieres'– and called them back to the path of salvation. Ralph of Coggeshall, *Chronicon Anglorum*, 81.

22 Amy Livingstone, 'Aristocratic Women in the Chartrain', in Evergates, *Aristocratic Women*, 71.

23 Evergates, 'Aristocratic Women in the County of Champagne', 92.

24 Michael M. Sheehan, 'The Influence of Canon Law on the Property Rights of Married Women in England', in James K. Farge ed. *Marriage, Family and Law in Medieval Europe: Collected Studies* (Cardiff, 1996), 21.

had access to other routes of influence which were less easily documented, but effective nonetheless. Depending on her personal relationship with her husband, she could act as a diplomat between important families, or become a conduit for those seeking favour or patronage at the court of her spouse. Her traditional role as a mediator and 'helpmeet' meant that she could advise her husband on political matters, as long as she was not perceived to be the decisive partner. However, the sexual origins of a wife's persuasive power were often mistrusted.[25] In her husband's absence, a noble wife might even be expected to take on more of the practical duties of lordship. Crusades notwithstanding, husbands could leave their domain for considerable periods of time because of war, feudal services or pilgrimages in the normal course of noble life in medieval Europe. A wife could act in her husband's stead in court, make donations, support his vassals, and even direct warfare on his behalf, although she was increasingly unlikely to take to the field herself.[26] In the comital family of Flanders during this period there was a particularly strong tradition of wives acting as regents for their husbands. Clemence, wife of Robert II, was a diligent and capable regent during the First Crusade, and Sibyl acted as regent for her husband Thierry during his crusading expeditions between 1138–9 and 1147–9. Despite her advanced stage of pregnancy, Sibyl responded to the aggressive encroachment of Baldwin IV of Hainault by raising an army to defeat him and negotiating a truce.[27]

Wives in the Narratives of Crusading and the Latin East

THE role of the crusader's wife deserves special consideration, as the perceptions associated with it have already attracted scholarly interest.[28] Crusading and settlement created specific problems for the marriage bond, supplemented in crusade narratives by stylised departure scenes. When individual wives came to the attention of contemporary historians of crusading, they were usually described in terms conventional for women: by lineage, character, piety and prudence. Kinship ties between the Latin East and the rest of Christendom also meant that authors emphasised the marital relationships connecting crusaders and settlers. Their histories reflected contemporary ideas about what made a marriage partnership succeed or fail and the authority that wives

[25] See Sharon Farmer, 'Persuasive Voices: Clerical Images of Medieval Wives', *Speculum* 61 (1986), 517–43.

[26] Livingstone, 'Aristocratic Women', 62–8. See also McLaughlin, 'The Woman Warrior', 193–209.

[27] Karen S. Nicholas, 'Countesses as Rulers in Flanders', in Evergates, *Aristocratic Women*, 123. See also Thérèse de Hemptinne, 'Les épouses de croisés et pèlerins flamands au XIe et XIIe siècles: l'exemple des comtesses de Flandre Clémence et Sybille', in Balard, *Autour de la Première Croisade*, 83–95.

[28] See especially Brundage, 'Crusader's Wife'; and *idem.*, 'Crusader's Wife Revisited'.

exerted in the household. They also addressed the threat of captivity peculiar to crusading and its repercussions for the marriage bond. The sin of adultery and the distinctions between licit and illicit sex formed a large part of the discourse about marriage which strongly influenced perceptions of wives in contemporary narratives. In crusade histories, noble wives and the unlawful sexual activities of the general host tended to eclipse the role played by wives of lower social status, but they will be discussed where evidence permits.

WIVES AND CRUSADING: THE 'CANONICAL QUANDARY'

From the outset, wives posed a specific obstacle to canonists with regard to crusading. The crusade vow made a married crusader temporarily unable to fulfil the conjugal debt, leaving both partners vulnerable to the temptation of adultery. The possibility of a wife's infidelity during an expedition was undoubtedly a real concern for crusaders as well as canonists and preachers. In 1148 the Moorish population of Lisbon reportedly taunted crusaders that their wives would be conceiving bastards during their absence.[29] However, crusaders' wives were not kept in chastity belts as popular myth supposes, and canonists were concerned that the rights of both married partners should be upheld. From the very first expedition a crusader needed the consent of his wife before taking the cross, in much the same way that mutual consent was required for a vow of continence. Urban II's letter to the people of Bologna dated September 1096 states explicitly that 'care should be taken lest young married men heedlessly set out on this journey without the consent of their wives'.[30] In direct contradiction to this, men were largely encouraged by preachers and the authors of crusade chronicles to leave against the wishes of their wives. James of Vitry recounted an exemplary story about a man who was locked indoors by his wife to prevent him from attending a crusade sermon, but he listened through a window and then jumped through it in order to take the cross.[31] Gerald of Wales recounted how Rhys ap Gruffudd, prince of South Wales, was keen to take part in the Third Crusade, even going as far as making all the preparations, 'until his wife … turned him away from his noble purpose, having ascertained his weaknesses, insisting effectively in her feminine manner'.[32] A woman from Cardigan physically restrained her husband from taking the cross by hanging on to his cloak and belt, and was awakened by a terrible voice three nights later. The speaker claimed she had deprived him of a servant and warned that she would lose that which was most dear to her. On returning to sleep, a divine retribution was exacted – she lay on her own child in her sleep and killed the child. Her

[29] DEL, 131.

[30] Heinrich Hagenmeyer, *Die Kreuzzugsbriefe aus den Jahren 1088–1100* (Innsbruck, 1901), 138. See Brundage, 'Crusader's Wife', 429.

[31] James of Vitry, Sermon 2:37, ed. and trans. in Maier, *Crusade Propaganda*, 120–1.

[32] GW 'Itinerarium', 6.15.

husband went to the local bishop with the story and took the crusade vow there and then. His wife raised no further objections, sewing the cross into his clothing with her own hands.[33]

In truth, many who took the cross did not redeem their crusade vows, and one cannot rule out commitments to wives or families as a contributory factor. This is supported by the fact that Innocent III removed the necessity of a wife's consent for crusading in the decretal *Ex multa* of 1201.[34] On balance, crusaders sometimes had good reason to fear for the safety of wives and property: Tyerman notes two English cases where the wives of absent crusaders were murdered.[35] To this end the special protection of the Church was granted to the wives and families of crusaders – protection which enabled Sibyl of Flanders to appeal to the archbishop of Rheims and the Pope for aid against Baldwin IV of Hainault.[36] Wives and children were consistently at the heart of protective arrangements in crusade encyclicals and narratives. Marriage represented one of the major transactions of a medieval person's life, including a considerable exchange of land and material goods as well as the hope of continuing the family line, all of which were invested in wives and the children they bore. The safeguarding of families was probably Urban II's idea. There is no extant encyclical for the First Crusade, but *circa* 1108 Guibert of Nogent asserted that Urban had cursed all those who might dare to harm the wives, sons, and possessions of crusaders within the next three years with anathema.[37] The earliest known example of a bishop protecting the property of a crusader occurred in 1107, when Bishop Ivo of Chartres attempted to uphold a claim of Hugh II of Le Puiset against Count Rotrou of Perche. This acted as a test case which explored some of the loopholes in the protection offered to crusaders, and was referred back and forth between ecclesiastical and secular courts.[38] The First Lateran council of 1123 and Eugenius III, in *Quantum Praedecessores* (March 1146), reiterated that the wives, sons, and possessions of crusaders would remain under the protection of the Church.[39] In *Divina Dispensatione* I (October 1146) Eugenius enjoined Italian crusade preachers to emphasise the protection offered to the families of crusaders. He also wished to impose strict penalties for opportunists: anyone who took advantage of a crusader's absence to harass his family

---

[33] *Ibid.*, 6.113.

[34] Brundage, 'Crusader's Wife', 434.

[35] See Christopher Tyerman, *England and the Crusades, 1095–1588* (London, 1988), 210–11.

[36] Nicholas, 'Countesses as Rulers', 123. See 108 above.

[37] GN, 117.

[38] See Riley-Smith, *First Crusaders*, 136; and Ian S. Robinson, *The Papacy 1073–1198: Continuity and Innovation* (Cambridge, 1990), 337–8.

[39] Eugenius III, *Quantum Praedecessores*, 91, in Rolf Grosse, 'Überlegungen zum Kreuzzugsaufruf Eugens III von 1145/6: Mit einer Neuedition von JL8876', in *Francia* 18 (1991), 85–92.

should be placed in chains in public and excommunicated.[40] The charters left by crusaders often made specific provisions for wives while they were away or in the event of their death. Some involved money or endowments to religious houses for the protection of wives and children. In 1180, Ralph, a crusader from Duri near Amiens, left a charter donating some of his lands to the Church. They would remain in his hands for his lifetime, and in his wife's should he predecease her. Agnes, his wife, was present and consented to the proceedings although she did not appear as a witness.[41] In some cases the illness of a partner could prompt care arrangements and even provide the impetus to crusade. At some point between 1129 and 1132, a knight called Guy Cornelly of Til-Châtel went to Jerusalem and became a Templar because his wife had contracted leprosy 'by the mysterious judgement of God'. She and their three daughters were to be cared for at the abbey of St Bénigne de Dijon.[42]

For those crusaders who intended to settle, wives were crucial to the establishment of a Latin population on all fronts where religious war was waged: in the Baltic, in Spain and in Outremer. At the time of the Third Crusade, Ralph Niger accepted the necessity of women for repopulating conquered territories, but thought that they should not accompany armies to the East: they should rather be sent for once the land had been pacified.[43] Of those husbands who took part in the First Crusade together with their wives, both Raymond IV of Toulouse and Baldwin of Boulogne can be said to have harboured territorial ambitions in the East.[44] According to William of Malmesbury, Raymond had no inclination to marry, and was satisfied to call his 'natural' son Bertram heir, but on the eve of the First Crusade he married Elvira of Leon-Castille, demanding 'a treaty of perpetual peace' as a dowry.[45] This act was presumably undertaken to help fill his wallet and provide some security for his heir before

[40] Eugenius III, *Divina Dispensatione 1*, ed. Paul Kehr, in *Papsturkunden in Italien: Reiserberichte zur Italia Pontificum*, 6 vols [Acta Romanorum Pontificum] (Rome, 1977), 2.108–10.

[41] This was often the case: female family members were sometimes asked to provide consent to charters pertaining to them, but seldom acted as witnesses. See Slack, *Crusade Charters*, 84–5, no. 13.

[42] 'occulto Dei judicio'; see *Cartulaire générale de l'ordre du Temple 1119?–1150*, ed. G. A. M. J. A. d'Albon (Paris, 1913–22), 19, no. 27, and Riley-Smith, *First Crusaders*, 159.

[43] Niger, *De Re Militari*, 227.

[44] Raymond's wife was Elvira of Leon-Castille. See OV, 5.276 and n. 2; WM, 1.697, 701; FC, 320; GN, 134. See 169 below. Baldwin of Boulogne took Godvere of Tosny and she died during the journey. AA, 182–3; WT, 164, 221, 453. See also Geldsetzer, *Frauen*, 185–6.

[45] WM, 1.697. In fact, the marriage to his unnamed first wife, Bertram's mother, was dissolved, and he married another woman in 1080 before his union to Elvira. WM, 2.346–7. It was traditionally thought that Baldwin's marriage to Godvere also took place on the eve of the crusade in 1096, but Mayer suggests a more likely date of 1090. Mayer, 'Baudouin 1er', 41.

leaving. The fact that certain crusaders were prepared to take wives with them might indicate an intention to settle, but Elvira returned home on Raymond's death in 1105.[46] Other couples travelled back to the West together after their pilgrimage vows had been fulfilled. Hadvide of Chiny, who accompanied her husband Dodo of Cons-la-Grandville on the First Crusade, gave a bejewelled chalice and expensive vestments to St Hubert en Ardenne on her return.[47]

It was often more advantageous for a crusader with territorial ambitions to travel to the Holy Land as a bachelor or widower. Some married *en route* to or from the Holy Land, though whether to fellow participants or women from the communities they passed through is not always clear. Odo of Deuil relates how some Second Crusaders had to be re-baptised in the orthodox style in order to marry while travelling in the Byzantine Empire.[48] William of Newburgh told how Robert Curthose returned from the Holy Land with a wife to whom he was betrothed on the journey.[49] After the First Crusade, those nobles who intended to settle often married into the existing population in order to secure property and alliances, although Murray asserts that Christian women of a suitable class must have been rare.[50] Both Baldwin of le Bourcq and Joscelin 1 followed the precedent set by Baldwin 1 and took noble Armenian brides.[51] Marrying Muslim women was always frowned upon. Fulcher of Chartres asserts that some crusaders did, initially, but only with the prerequisite of baptism.[52] It is difficult to ascertain rulings on marriage during the early phase of settlement because the laws of the kingdom were destroyed when Saladin took Jerusalem in 1187.[53] There were attempts to regulate sexual behaviour between Christians and Muslims at the council of Nablus in 1120,[54] but laws on this and other marital concerns only survive from the thirteenth century, largely in works of the 1260s by Philip of Novara and John of Ibelin. Both Prawer and Brundage have used the marriage laws of the *Livre des Assises de la cour des Bourgeois* (c. 1240) to compare Levantine marriage law with customary and Roman law

[46] WM, 1.701. She bore him a child during this time. See 169 below.

[47] *Chartes de l'abbaye de Saint Hubert-en-Ardenne*, ed. Godefroid Kirth, 2 vols (Brussels, 1903), 1.82, no. 63. See Riley-Smith, *First Crusaders*, 149; and Geldsetzer, *Frauen*, 188. Murray asserts that Dodo received a low profile in accounts of crusading because of his marriage to Hadvide and an enmity between the counts of Chiny and the Ardennes-Bouillon family. Murray, *Crusader Kingdom*, 192.

[48] OD, 57.

[49] WN, 26. This was Sibyl, whose father was Geoffrey of Conversano, a cousin of Bohemond of Taranto.

[50] Alan V. Murray, 'Daimbert of Pisa, the *Domus Godefridi* and the Accession of Baldwin 1 of Jerusalem', in Murray, *From Clermont to Jerusalem*, 87.

[51] WT, 482, 635.

[52] FC, 748.

[53] Riley-Smith, *Feudal Nobility*, 133.

[54] Brundage, 'Prostitution', 60.

in Europe.[55] According to Philip of Novara, after the conquest of Jerusalem in 1099 women were allowed to choose their husbands freely, or at least in accordance with the wishes of their families. This freedom was curtailed by the aforementioned restriction to a choice of three candidates for heiresses and widows, probably around the time of the reign of Baldwin II.[56] At a lower social level, burgesses retained the right to marry as they chose, but marriage between serfs from different lordships was forbidden.[57]

DEPARTURE SCENES

When they described the departure of crusaders, wives held a special significance to the authors of crusade narratives: they represented the sexual and worldly lives abandoned by the participants. Fulcher of Chartres illustrated this view amply:

> Then husband told wife the time he was expecting to return, and that if he was to keep his life, by God's grace, he would return home to her. He commended her to the Lord, kissed her lingeringly, vowing as she wept that he would return. She, however, fearing that she would never see him again, could not support herself, tumbled lifeless to the ground, mourning for her love whom she was losing in this life just as if he were dead already. He, as if having no compassion, although in truth he had, and as if he had no sympathy whatever for the tears of his wife or the grief of his friends, although suffering secretly, he departed thus, steadfastly and unyielding in spirit.[58]

This dramatic and enduring image of a wife abandoned was further compounded by the romantic and idealistic portrayal of crusaders during the Victorian era, both in poetry and art.[59] Departure scenes were also represented in popular songs[60] and contemporary art: Maier has recently identified three crusaders leaving their family in a *bible moralisée* of the thirteenth century, which reflects almost exactly the kind of image portrayed in narratives.[61] In truth,

55 Prawer, *Crusader Institutions*, 358–411. See also Brundage, 'Marriage Law', 258–71.

56 Philip of Novara, *Livre*, RHC Lois I, 588. See 73–4 above.

57 Prawer, *Crusader Institutions*, 204–5.

58 FC, 163.

59 Elizabeth Siberry, 'The Crusader's Departure and Return: A Much Later Perspective', in Edgington and Lambert, *Gendering the Crusades*, 177.

60 See William C. Jordan, 'The Representation of the Crusades in the Songs Attributed to Thibaud, Count Palatine of Champagne', *JMH* 25 (1999), 27–34; and William E. Jackson, 'Poet, Woman and Crusade in Songs of Marcabru, Guiot de Dijon, and Albrecht von Johansdorf', *Medievalia* 22 (1999), 268–76.

61 The women are portrayed tearing at their hair. Christoph T. Maier, 'The *Bible Moralisée* and the Crusades', in Edbury and Phillips, *The Experience of Crusading: Western Approaches*, I.211–15.

there probably were scenes of distress when crusaders embarked on these potentially fatal journeys. Odo of Deuil, an eyewitness to the Second Crusade, wrote of their departure:

> The crowds and the king's wife and his mother, who nearly perished because of their tears and the heat, could not endure the delay; but to wish to depict the grief and wailing which occurred then is as foolish as it is impossible.[62]

However, descriptions of leave-taking in many of these sources often relied on formulaic components, and it has been suggested that they were a deliberate statement emphasising the exclusion of women, and making crusading a gendered event – a military and male preserve.[63] Chroniclers invariably admonished crusaders not to let thoughts of loved ones sway them from their religious duty. Crusaders were encouraged to leave the 'alluring charms' of their wives in Baudri of Bourgueil's account of Urban's speech. Robert of Rheims used the scriptural authority of Matthew to persuade those who were held back by affection for their wives and families to take up the cross.[64] The bishop of Oporto's speech in *De Expugnatione Lyxbonensi* praised crusaders for leaving behind the 'alluring affection of wives', alongside infants and adult children.[65] The maternal role of wives was also emphasised by William of Tyre who described them 'carrying young children and those suckling at the breast in their arms' as they bade farewell to husbands taking part in the First Crusade.[66] The love of children, as well as the idea of home, wider kin and property, were also factors exerting an inhibiting influence on the crusader, but the relationship between man and wife held further significance.

The physical sacrifices incurred by taking the cross went beyond the rigours of the journey alone: renouncing the world of the flesh enhanced the penitential qualities of crusading. Riley-Smith, in his seminal article on 'Crusading as an Act of Love', has demonstrated how crusade sermons and encyclicals promulgated a specialised vision of fraternal love that was couched in terms of kinship to appeal to their lay audience.[67] Crusaders were encouraged to sever their earthly family ties on behalf of a wider Christian community whose obligations of kinship superseded their own. The sacrifice of separation was endured by

---

[62] OD, 19.

[63] See Lambert, 'Crusading or Spinning', 3–6.

[64] BB, 15. RR, 728. Matt 10:37 and 19:39. For similar examples see RA, 117, and AA, 2–3, 478–81.

[65] DEL, 71. Phillips asserts that Raol may have been influenced by Guibert of Nogent in his description. Jonathan Phillips, 'Ideas of Crusade and Holy War in the Conquest of Lisbon', in Robert N. Swanson ed. *The Holy Land, Holy Lands, and Christian History* (Woodbridge, 2000), 129.

[66] WT, 140.

[67] Jonathan Riley-Smith, 'Crusading as an Act of Love', *History* 65 (1980), 190–2.

both crusaders and their wives for the greater cause of Christ. These scenes were not a simple literary *topos* denigrating women as an inhibiting influence on crusaders: they affirmed the quasi-monastic status of crusaders, derived from their role as pilgrims. Ralph of Caen asserted that Godfrey of Bouillon exhibited more of the virtues of a monk than a soldier, although he took care to emphasise the duke's military prowess.[68] Guibert of Nogent described crusading as a new way of gaining salvation that could be equated with monasticism:

> … so that without having chosen from the very beginning, as has become customary, life in the monastery or some kind of religious profession, they were compelled to leave the world although still subject to their traditional freedom of practice and habits [and] to a certain extent they sought the grace of God by their own deeds.[69]

He also told how crusaders spurned castles and properties, and he highlighted the physical attributes of the women that crusaders left behind: '… the most beautiful wives were reviled like something corrupt, and formerly more valued than any jewel, the faces of dependents of either sex were scorned …'.[70] According to Guibert, abandoning worldly pleasures represented the pilgrims' contrition, which in turn enabled them to be successful crusaders. Weeping and confessing their sins, crusaders took up their arms and renounced their wives and children.[71] Thus wives became part of a broader metaphor for the corrupt and carnal world that the crusaders rejected in favour of a spiritual enterprise.

Preachers of the crusades made good use of guilt to encourage potential crusaders. They focused on sins that were perceived to be widespread in medieval society, such as adultery, to inspire penitence and a desire to take the cross.[72] On balance, the failure of crusades was seen to result from poor adherence to the spiritual requirements for the expedition. Crusaders could fail if they aroused God's wrath through their sins. Avarice was usually held to blame, but sexual sins were perceived as particularly offensive. William of Newburgh blamed the failure of the Second Crusade on a large presence of women, ostensibly encouraged by Louis VII's decision to take Eleanor of Aquitaine. He was bewitched by her beauty and could not bear to leave her behind. This set a poor example, encouraging other nobles to bring their wives (who in turn required maidservants), with the result that a multitude of women accompanied the crusaders, bringing into disrepute an army that should have been chaste.[73] However, a

---

[68] GT, 615. This contrasts with the derision implied by Eleanor of Aquitaine's complaint that she had married a monk rather than a king. See 140 below.

[69] GN, 87.

[70] Ibid., 87–8.

[71] Ibid., 266.

[72] See 129–30 below.

[73] WN, 85.

penitent lord could take his wife with him on crusade, and still be perceived as a suitable role model. Ralph of Gael and his wife Emma of Hereford had been exiled to Brittany for their part in the 1075 rebellion against William the Conqueror. Orderic Vitalis recounts how many years later 'he took the cross and set out for Jerusalem with Robert Curthose, duke of Normandy, to fight against the Turks; as a pilgrim and penitent following the way of God he died, together with his wife'.[74]

The sexual influence of wives could even have a positive effect: in an oft-cited example, Orderic Vitalis recorded the shame of Adela of Blois when her husband deserted the First Crusade at Antioch in 1098, and how she was instrumental in persuading him to take the cross again 'between conjugal caresses'.[75] While intercession was an accepted part of the wife's role, it was very rare for a woman to be portrayed using overtly sexual influence for a divine purpose, as this kind of power was largely feared and condemned. It is possible that the author employed this scenario in order to display his contempt for Adela's husband, intending it as yet another 'humorous episode'. Certainly, Count Stephen incurred the criticism of some authors for his cowardice, but in Orderic's account he died a hero and martyr through adhering to the advice of his wife. Stephen, like Ralph of Gael, was a penitent redeemed by making the ultimate sacrifice: giving his life for the cause of the crusade. Adela was cast in the traditional role of a woman approving or criticising male prowess – she emphasised to her husband that military glory and honour were important to maintaining noble status. Whether Adela truly encouraged her husband in this is open to question. She was evidently a capable regent,[76] and Stephen's reputation had suffered a great blow with the success of the expedition he had left behind. The countess was renowned for her piety, and Guibert of Nogent spoke extravagantly of her prudence, generosity, abundance, and power, hinting that she may have even out-shadowed the reputation of her martyred husband.[77] Both Orderic and Guibert referred to her as wise, but despite Adela's literary pursuits, such an accolade did not necessarily encompass academic learning when applied to women. It usually referred to a more traditional wifely trait, good counsel, which Orderic evidently perceived her to provide.

Aside from Adela, wives cited as supporting the crusade movement usually wanted to take part themselves. Orderic Vitalis asserted that 'beloved' wives lamented not because of the absence of their husbands but because they 'longed passionately to leave their children and all their riches behind and

74   OV, 2.319. See also William of Jumiéges, Ordric Vitalis, and Robert of Torigni, *Gesta Normannorum Ducum*, ed. and trans. Elisabeth van Houts, 2 vols (Oxford, 1995), 2.147. Geldsetzer, *Frauen*, 185–6.

75   OV, 5.325.

76   See Kimberley A. LoPrete, 'Adela of Blois: Familial Alliances and Female Lordship', in Evergates, *Aristocratic Women*, 7–43.

77   GN, 132.

follow their husbands on the pilgrimage'.[78] The *Itinerarium* spoke of brides encouraging husbands to crusade, although they were not destined to take part themselves.[79] Chroniclers made it clear, however, that they stayed at home, as was considered proper. In fact, Riley-Smith has suggested that wives such as the Montlhéry sisters probably did influence participation in expeditions by importing family traditions of crusading into a new household on their marriage.[80] Similarly, Lower has demonstrated the strong influence of family ties through dynastic marriage which influenced the participation in the Baron's Crusade of 1239–40.[81]

WIVES AS CRUSADERS

In accordance with common practice in medieval literature, most of the women recorded in these sources are referred to as wives.[82] This may also have reflected a real trend – of fifteen women who travelled with the crusaders between 1096 and 1101, nine travelled with their husbands, and one with her fiancé.[83] Lloyd asserts that the majority of English noblewomen who went on crusade in the thirteenth century were accompanying their husbands. He admits that women of lower social status may have been able to take the cross independently with greater ease,[84] but noble wives, whose duties included producing legitimate heirs, were subject to less social freedom. In reference to the crusading vows of Eleanor of Montfort (1240) and Eleanor of Castille (1267), Lloyd writes:

> Whether they pestered their husbands to allow them to go on crusade or whether they went under pressure is unknown, but it appears that no crucesignata of so high a social stratum fulfilled her vow independently of her consort.[85]

If, by the term 'pester', Lloyd means that wives were motivated to take part in crusades on their own account, then that may indeed have been the case. Although she may not have been of such high status, Erneburg, wife of William of Hokesour, took the cross with her husband, but when he received a dispensation to commute his vow, she journeyed to the Holy Land on pilgrimage

---

[78]   OV, 5.17.

[79]   *Itinerarium*, 33. The author also included mothers encouraging sons.

[80]   Riley-Smith, *First Crusaders*, 97–8, 169–88.

[81]   Michael Lower, *The Baron's Crusade: A Call to Arms and its Consequences* (Philadelphia, 2005), 46–52.

[82]   See 14 above.

[83]   See Geldsetzer, *Frauen*, 184–7. The remainder included a widow, a nun, and a courtesan who accompanied her lover. Nothing is known about the marital status of the goose-woman or the woman killed outside Bohemond's tent at Antioch.

[84]   An idea supported by Kedar, 'Passenger List', 272.

[85]   Simon Lloyd, *English Society and the Crusade 1216–1307* (Oxford, 1988), 77–8.

by herself in 1225–6.[86] There are also examples of wives like Alice, countess of Blois, who made the journey to the East as a widow after her *crucesignatus* husband John of Châtillon had died in 1279 without fulfilling his vows. She had taken a vow in 1266 or 1267 which she fulfilled in 1286 or 1287.[87] Derbes and Sandona tentatively suggest that she, or other crusading women during the latter part of the thirteenth century, influenced the preponderance of images of Amazons in Acre manuscripts produced at that time.[88] Such women may have been unusual, however; others lacked the confidence to complete the journey without their spouses. Edith, wife of Gerard of Gournay, took the cross with her husband, but when he died early in the course of the First Crusade, she returned home.[89]

Others may have wanted to take the cross under the influence of their own family ties rather than those of their husband. Count Baldwin IX of Flanders was the son of Margaret of Alsace, the daughter of crusaders Sibyl and Thierry, but crusading tradition also ran strong in the family of his wife, Marie of Champagne, who took the cross with him in 1201.[90] She was the granddaughter of Louis VII and Eleanor of Aquitaine and sister to Henry II of Champagne, who had taken part in the Third Crusade and become king of Jerusalem. She was also sister to Count Thibaut III, who had taken the cross but died at the outset of the Fourth Crusade. Another crusader wife, Eleanor of Castille, had strong family traditions of crusading; she was the niece of John of Brienne, king of Jerusalem, and the daughter of Ferdinand III of Castille, famed for his conquest of Andalusia.[91] She may have been influenced by her mother-in-law, Eleanor of Provence, who had been absolved of her own crusade vow[92] and whose sister Margaret was the crusader-queen of Louis IX. As the Lord Edward's wife, Eleanor, could have commuted her vows if her husband had not wished her to participate. The provision of heirs was always a possible factor in explaining the presence of a wife on a crusade, especially at a time of high infant mortality, but Eleanor had three living children when she left for the East.[93] Hamilton suggests that Edward may have wished to take his Eleanor on crusade in order to avoid the charge of adultery.[94] The prospects of a continued Latin

---

[86] *Curia Regis Rolls* 12, 9–10, no. 69.

[87] See Geldsetzer, *Frauen*, 181–2; and Purcell, 'Women Crusaders', 60. There is scope for including Joanna of Sicily in this category. See 207–9 and 215–16 below.

[88] Derber and Sandona, 'Amazons and Crusaders', 214–15

[89] 'Interpolations de Robert de Torigny', 277. Geldsetzer, *Frauen*, 185.

[90] Ralph of Coggeshall, *Chronicon Anglorum*, 130. See also Villehardouin, 2.124.

[91] Bernard Hamilton, 'Eleanor of Castile and the Crusading Movement', in Benjamin Arbel ed. *Intercultural Contacts in the Medieval Mediterranean* (London, 1996), 92.

[92] 'Annals of Waverley', in *Annales Monastici (A.D. 1–1432)*, ed. Henry Richards Luard, 5 vols, RS 36 (London, 1864–89), 2.342. See also Geldsetzer, *Frauen*, 183.

[93] Hamilton, 'Eleanor', 95–6. The eldest of these, John, died in 1271.

[94] Ibid., 96–7.

presence in the Near East were dwindling towards the end of the thirteenth century, and as a result crusaders and settlers alike were heavily criticised for their sins. Edward may have wanted to adhere to spiritual guidelines so that he would be successful in his crusade, but it could also have been a deliberate attempt to forestall external criticism in the event of military failure. The leaders of the crusade needed to be above suspicion of misconduct, and Eleanor's presence may have been a calculated act of propaganda.

Although historical narratives evinced concerns about the presence of wives on crusade and fears for their safety, their contribution to the crusade effort was sometimes acknowledged. Noble wives were singled out for praise when carrying rubble in their skirts at the siege of Archas during the First Crusade, but this was probably commented on because of their noble rather than marital status.[95] One admirable woman, mortally wounded while filling a ditch at the siege of Acre during the Third Crusade, reputedly begged her husband to leave her body there to aid the work.[96] It has been argued that Ambroise did not intend this story to be taken seriously, recorded as it was between a tale about a knight attacked while relieving himself[97] and a further humorous anecdote concerning a Turkish emir who immolated his own genitals with Greek fire intended for Christian siege engines.[98] In the *Itinerarium*, however, the latter story is preceded by two different, less amusing stories, and these anecdotes as a whole are described as 'miraculous' and 'not unworthy of being brought to the attention of posterity'.[99] The author drew from Ambroise but reorganised the section with tales from alternative sources and endeavoured to imbue them with moral rather than humorous purpose. He was keen to stress the marital status of the woman: she begged her husband to fulfil her wish by the sacrament of marriage and their vows.[100] This suggests that the author was keen to legitimise the story as a genuine act of piety rather than an amusing anecdote: as such it was more in keeping with the religious tone he added to Ambroise's account.[101]

WIVES, POWER AND AUTHORITY

The political activities of noble wives were largely perceived to rely on their marital relationship, and crusade histories were often polarised about the benefits and detriments of such influence. When their persuasive power was considered beneficial, wives counselled temperance and mercy, and could even further the

---

95 GN, 264.

96 *Itinerarium*, 101–2; Ambroise, I.58–9, lns 3632–60.

97 Ambroise, I.58, lns 3578–619.

98 *Ibid.*, I.59, lns 3656–94. Edgington, 'Sont çou ore les fems', 161. Ailes and Barber concur that these stories are for the purpose of entertainment. Ambroise, 2.22.

99 *Itinerarium*, 103, 104, 98–9.

100 Nicholson, *Chronicle*, 106 n. 229.

101 *Ibid.*, 14–15.

cause of Christianity. Albert of Aachen described how Omar, the emir of Azaz, was persuaded by his Christian wife to give allegiance to Godfrey of Bouillon. Omar did have a political incentive for opposing Ridwan of Aleppo, but Albert preferred to emphasise divine intervention through the wife of his knight.[102] In cases where a wife's influence over her husband was criticised, its sexual nature was usually emphasised. For example, Emperor Alexius III Angelus was said to have blinded his brother Isaac 'at the prompting of his wife [Euphrosyne] who had told him that if she were not to be empress she would never sleep with him'.[103]

In general, the military actions of their husbands assumed precedence over the actions of individual wives on crusade. For example, Berengaria of Navarre and Joanna of Sicily seem to fade away from the western narratives of the Third Crusade after Richard's marriage.[104] They were recorded moving into the royal palace at Acre after its capture, and after slaughtering the garrison there on 16 August 1191 the king left them to pursue his interests in Arsuf. The two queens spent a few months in Jaffa, before returning to Acre for the sea voyage home, and were excluded from the main decision-making processes.[105] The exclusion of women from military activity in crusade narratives can be frustrating to the historian, but in such a volatile environment their confinement was also a practical necessity.

There are some exceptions, however. Margaret of Provence, queen of France, features heavily in Joinville's history of Louis IX's crusade. As the king's marshal, Joinville had quite a close personal relationship with the queen and recorded several conversations with her during the course of the journey. Joinville characterised Margaret as both wife and mother, but first and foremost she was a queen, and during Louis' capture after the battle of Mansurah she had to take on an authoritative role. When Louis was negotiating his release from the Saracens he apparently stated that he could not guarantee that the queen would raise the money: 'he did not know whether or not the queen would consent, since, as his consort, she was mistress of her actions', although this may have been a bargaining ploy.[106] The queen also helped to keep the crusade force together in Damietta.[107] The Rothelin manuscript, however, made no mention of the queen's role in these negotiations. It stated simply that she was placed inside Damietta with some of Louis' war equipment, and resided there with the countess of Artois (Mathilda of Brabant) and

---

[102] AA, 344–7.

[103] *Eracles*, 29; trans. Edbury, 23. Byzantine sources also criticised Euphrosyne and considered Alexius a weak ruler. Barbara Hill, *Imperial Woman in Byzantium 1025–1204: Patronage, Power and Ideology* (Edinburgh, 1999), 36.

[104] See Geldsetzer, *Frauen*, 191–2.

[105] *Itinerarium*, 286, 350.

[106] Joinville, 186; trans. Shaw, 249.

[107] Joinville, 218. See 169–70 below.

the countess of Poitiers (Joanna of Poitiers-Toulouse) in houses within the city until Louis made arrangements to have them brought out after the surrender.[108]

After her early periods of regency, Sibyl of Flanders finally accompanied her husband Thierry on his third visit to the Holy Land in 1157. Her duties as a regent had been discharged by this point, as their son Philip was installed as count in the same year.[109] This was not part of a major expedition: Thierry was there to fight, and after the couple completed their vows in Jerusalem, Thierry and his forces went to stay with the king. Sibyl went to her aunt by marriage, Yveta, at the convent of Bethany for the duration of her husband's 'tour of duty'.[110] That she reputedly decided to remain in the Holy Land to enter the convent at Bethany suggests that Sibyl had genuine spiritual motivation for the journey. Although William of Tyre did not record this event, he considered her to be 'a religious and God-fearing woman'.[111] Sibyl's case demonstrates how a wife could harbour a strong desire to crusade for personal reasons, and furthermore appeal to the Church to support her vocation over the wishes of her husband. The most detailed account in these sources of her decision to stay can be found in the *Chronique d'Ernoul*:

> When the count had been in the land as long as he wished, he went to Bethany and said to his wife the countess: 'My lady, make ready, for we are returning to Flanders.' But the lady replied that God willing, she would never return to Flanders, nor cross the sea again. Despite all his entreaties she would not agree to leave that land, nor change her mind.[112]

Having failed to assert himself, the count then decided to enlist the help of the king and patriarch to persuade her.

> And when she heard they were coming, she went to the abbess and asked her for a nun's clothing; and the abbess gave it to her. When they arrived to speak to her, and found that she had been dressed in these clothes, they were filled with sorrow. The patriarch came to her and told her that she could not do this, for it was against the will of her husband. She begged the patriarch and the king to plead with the count to leave her, for God's sake; they did so, and she flung herself at his feet crying mercy, that he should for the love of God leave her there to do her penitence, for she would not stay there were it not out of penitence.

---

108 Rothelin, 593, 595, 619. In comparison to Joinville, the Rothelin manuscript seldom mentions Queen Margaret's presence on crusade.

109 Nicholas, 'Countesses as Rulers', 123.

110 Ernoul, 21.

111 'religiosa et deum timente femina'. WT, 876.

112 Ernoul, 21.

The count, when he saw this, was filled with sorrow, and was touched by her goodness, and because of the entreaties of the king and the patriarch he gave her permission to remain. She stayed behind, and the count took his leave of her, and of the patriarch and the king, and returned to Flanders.[113]

Sybil had mustered enough authority to defy the will of her husband, and won over the king and the patriarch once she had convinced them of her genuine devotion. In the final part of the story, Ernoul described Sybil's saintly life in the convent, and how Yveta and the other nuns begged her to become abbess. 'But the lady replied that, if it pleased God, she would never be abbess, for she had certainly not come there to be abbess, but to be a disciple.'[114] The author thus emphasised her humility and the strength of her vocation – the only circumstances under which the defiance of a husband's wishes could be tolerated.

As in the West, aristocratic wives of the settler society in the Latin East could exert authority as feudal lords in the absence of their husbands by defending cities and castles under siege, and negotiating peace, but again they seldom took to the battlefield themselves. Count Raymond III of Tripoli's wife defended Tiberias in his absence when Saladin's troops threatened in 1187. This event ultimately resulted in the battle of Hattin, but she herself was not blamed for incompetence in managing the siege – the decision to march was based on the perceived seriousness of the enemy threat.[115] When false news reached Jaffa of Baldwin I's death in 1101, it was his wife, aided by councillors, who sent to Tancred in Antioch for help.[116] Later Morphia, wife of Baldwin II, was said to have been involved in the negotiations surrounding his release from captivity in 1124. She was also credited with arranging an Armenian rescue mission.[117] With the help of these forces, her husband escaped imprisonment and held the tower of Kharput, where Orderic Vitalis asserted that he held the three wives of his captor Belek hostage. These Turkish women do not appear in William of Tyre's history,[118] and Orderic's portrayal of them held much in common with his account of Melaz. When Belek arrived they entreated Baldwin not to return them to their husband, offering advice and encouragement, expressing admiration for Frankish prowess and customs, and a desire to join the Christian faith. As in the case of Melaz, it was acceptable for Muslim wives to act independently

113 *Ibid.*, 21–2.

114 *Ibid.*, 22.

115 *Eracles* described her as frightened, but focused instead on the size of Saladin's army rather than any failings on her behalf; her husband evidently expected her to hold the castle unless they were severely outnumbered in which case they should take to the sea. See *Eracles*, 43–5.

116 FC, 421

117 OV, 6.114–15.

118 WT, 568.

from their husbands as long as it was for the Christian cause.[119] Wives were also able to accept homage on behalf of an absent partner. Although Marie, the wife of Baldwin IX of Flanders, never reached Constantinople to be crowned, Alberic of Trois Fontaines asserted that she accepted homage from Bohemond V of Antioch in her husband's stead before she died at Acre.[120]

The intercession associated with wives was not reliant on her the relationship between a wife and her husband alone. On occasion she was uniquely placed to approach others on behalf of her spouse. Cecilia of France, wife of Count Pons of Tripoli, went out to meet King Fulk of Jerusalem when Zengi had besieged her husband in Montferrand (Bārīn). Although the king was on his way to relieve Antioch, William recounts that she pleaded with 'most urgent perseverance, in the feminine manner' for the king to go to her husband's aid, and that he, 'moved by her very great persistence', set out accordingly to relieve the fortress.[121] Unfortunately he was intercepted by Zengi and met with a terrible defeat.[122] William also mentions that Cecilia was Fulk's sister, but whether this would have influenced his decision in favour of her husband was open to question. Cecilia was born of the adulterous union of Bertrada of Montfort and Philip I of France, a match which had brought shame to Fulk's family.[123]

Dynastic links through marriage provided an essential conduit for negotiations and appeals for aid. Imperial brides were also perceived to hold considerable influence and held a diplomatic role in the Byzantine court.[124] William of Tyre suggested that the hospitality shown to King Conrad III of Germany in Constantinople after the failure of the Second Crusade was at least in part at the request of Emperor Manuel's wife, Bertha of Salzburg.[125] When Prince Alexius IV Angelus was disinherited by the usurpation of his father's throne (Isaac II Angelus), it was Philip of Swabia, king of Germany (who had been married to Irene, Isaac's sister), whom he approached for support.[126] Another wife who acted as an ambassador for her husband was Marie of Brienne, the wife of Latin emperor Baldwin II of Constantinople. She approached Louis IX for aid in Cyprus during his first crusade expedition, as the French king had

[119] OV, 6.116–21.

[120] ATF, 884. As Alberic is the only source to mention this event, there have been some questions over its veracity. Wolff has shown that there is corroborative evidence in a letter of Pope Innocent III to the patriarch of Jerusalem in 1213. See Röhricht, Regesta Regni Hierosolymitani, 1.232, no. 863. Robert Lee Wolff, 'Baldwin of Flanders and Hainault, First Latin Emperor of Constantinople: His Life, Death and Resurrection, 1172–1225', Speculum 27 (1952), 289. See also Andrea, Contemporary Sources, 306 n. 118.

[121] WT, 638.

[122] OV, 6.494–7.

[123] See 129–30 below.

[124] For an assessment of their patronage, see Hill, Imperial Women, 153–80.

[125] WT, 749.

[126] Gunther of Pairis, Hystoria Constantinopolitana, ed. Peter Orth (Hildesheim, 1994), 127.

already shown himself willing to lend financial support to their cause. Joinville described how he came to meet her at Paphos, and escorted her to Limassol to be welcomed by Louis and Margaret of Provence. As her ship containing her wardrobe had been driven away by a storm, the author showed his generosity by giving her the materials to attire herself in proper style. Joinville was very impressed by her, describing how he and many others pledged to support her, although ultimately the king was unable to finance an expedition.[127] At other times, however, heeding the advice of an oriental wife could have fatal results. William of Tyre asserted that 'Our ... Eastern princes, greatly affected by the influence of women, spurn the medicines and healing practice of our Latins, having faith only in the Jews, Samaritans, Syrians and Saracens.'[128] In his opinion such trust was misplaced and resulted in the death of Baldwin III, who was poisoned by pills given to him by the count of Tripoli's physician.

Noble wives may have been excluded from giving advice on military matters, but some showed awareness of the martial world. Eleanor of Castille commissioned an Old French translation of Vegetius' *De re militari* for her husband Lord Edward during their stay at Acre.[129] Margaret of Provence only acted as a political leader on crusade while her husband was in captivity, but as an intercessor she exercised her persuasion on Louis IX several times during the course of their crusade, with varying degrees of success. She had a role in the decision-making process, apparently: 'the queen and all the council agreed' that they should disembark near Hyères but Louis wished to carry on to Aigues-Mortes. However, Joinville made it clear that the queen's influence was not without limits. True to the somewhat egocentric style of his narrative, he recounted that it was only after he himself advised Louis that the king agreed to disembark, a decision which 'greatly delighted the queen'.[130] Margaret also interceded with Louis for six men who returned late from the island of Pantelleria: 'the queen and all of us did what we could to make the king change his mind', but to no avail.[131] Perhaps she felt responsible for the situation, as she had asked Louis to send the men to gather fruit for their children. On another occasion during the sea voyage, Margaret wished to make a vow of pilgrimage, but told Joinville that she could not without the king's permission, presumably because of the marriage vow. Joinville advised her to commission a silver ship for Saint Nicholas instead, thus exercising her own patronage and forgoing the need for permission to travel.[132]

127 Joinville, 76–8.

128 WT, 859.

129 Hamilton, 'Eleanor', 101.

130 Joinville, 358; trans. Shaw, 326–7.

131 Joinville, 352; trans. Shaw, 324–5.

132 Joinville, 344–6.

LOVE AND MARRIAGE

In a successful marriage, wives acted within the confines of a licit sexual union and were usually perceived as demonstrating the traditional qualities attributed to noblewomen: lineage, piety and beauty. Like daughters they were sometimes described as chaste despite their duty to provide an heir, meaning that they were faithful to their marriage vows and avoided adultery. Women were often perceived as having more choice in a second marriage, therefore love or physical attraction was often discussed in the context of remarriage, but the limited descriptions of marital relationships in crusade narratives demonstrate that love was perceived to be a consistent feature of the marital bond. Conrad of Monferrat's wife, Theodora Angela, warned him of treachery and allowed him to escape the aftermath of the Branas revolt against Emperor Isaac II in 1187, 'because she loved him so much'.[133] Later, Isabella of Jerusalem did not want to marry Conrad because 'she loved Humphrey, her husband'.[134] Excessive love could be dangerous: John of Salisbury asserts that Louis VII loved Queen Eleanor 'almost beyond reason', and 'passionately, in an almost childish way', which had negative ramifications for the Second Crusade.[135]

When authors discussed love they were often imposing their own interpretations on the activities and relationships of their subjects, but this does not preclude the possibility that love did exist within some marriages. As Gillingham asserts, the reality of medieval marriage was 'complicated by love and the expectation of love'.[136] Joinville's description of the secret trysts between Louis IX and Margaret of Provence in the early days of their marriage suggests they had a genuine fondness for each other, but he also chastised Louis for being too detached from his family.[137] McCannon has interpreted the relationship between Louis, Margaret and Joinville in his history as a form of classic love triangle.[138] Of particular import is an embarrassing incident that occurred on the return journey from the Holy Land. A fire, started by an errant chambermaid, swept through the queen's cabin at night, and Joinville witnessed her running out of her room naked to throw her burning bedclothes overboard. Joinville, wishing to portray himself as the consummate gentleman, pretended

---

[133] *Eracles*, 59; trans. Edbury, 51, and see 23 n. 33. See also Thomas R. Boase, *Kingdoms and Strongholds of the Crusaders* (London, 1971), 141–2.

[134] *Eracles*, 105.

[135] John of Salisbury, *Memoirs of the Papal Court*, ed. and trans. Marjorie Chibnall (London, 1956), 53, 61.

[136] John Gillingham, 'Love, Marriage and Politics in the Twelfth Century', in *Richard Cœur de Lion*, 244.

[137] Joinville, 326; trans. Shaw, 313.

[138] Afrodesia E. McCannon, 'Two Capetian Queens as the Foreground for an Aristocrat's Anxiety in the Vie de Saint Louis', in Kathleen Nolan ed. *Capetian Women* (London, 2003), 171–5.

not to have seen anything, but his reticence did not fool the king, who seemed to display some jealous anger.[139] Joinville himself did not seem to have strong feelings towards his own spouse – he expressed regret at leaving his castle and children for the crusade, but not his wife.[140] At that time he was married to his first partner, Alice of Grandpré, following a betrothal in 1230, which occurred before he became seneschal of Champagne. There is some evidence that he tried unsuccessfully to avoid the marriage because she was no longer of suitable social standing, and this may have affected their relationship.[141]

It was important to a successful match that a wife was of good character: chaste, modest, wise – and beautiful. The 'Templar of Tyre' asserted that Margaret of Antioch-Lusignan was particularly fair of face on the eve of her marriage to John of Montfort, emphasising his role as an eyewitness, for he acted as one of her pages in that year (1269). Perhaps he was concerned that he would not be believed, as he recorded that she went on to become enormously fat, and to look like her father. This statement was not intended with any rancour, as he maintains a favourable disposition towards 'my lady of Tyre' throughout his history – in comparison, her husband, John, was stricken with gout of the hands and feet.[142]

According to the *Itinerarium*, Berengaria of Navarre was 'very wise and of good character', and Richard was attracted by her 'graceful manner and high birth'.[143] Ambroise described her in conventional poetic terms as 'a wise maiden, a fine lady, both noble and beautiful, with no falseness or treachery in her'. He asserted that the king loved her greatly and referred to her as his beloved, whom he held dear.[144] The question of the marital relationship between Richard and Berengaria has become a topic of much historical interest because they did not produce an heir: some have speculated over whether Richard had homosexual tendencies. The evidence in favour of this rests upon the fact that he and his wife became estranged, and the homoerotic overtones derived from descriptions of Richard's penitence for his sins and friendship with Philip II of France by Roger of Howden.[145] Gillingham maintains that Richard was unlikely to have indulged exclusively in homosexual activity at the risk of not providing a future heir, if he did at all.[146] These speculations are largely based on information about the couple's lives after the expedition, and do not feature prominently

[139] Joinville, 354.

[140] *Ibid.*, 68.

[141] Jackie Lusse, 'D'Étienne à Jean de Joinville: L'ascension d'une famille seigneuriale champenoise', in Dominique Guénot ed. *Jean de Joinville: De la Champagne aux Royaumes d'Outremer* (Paris, 1998), 26–7.

[142] *Les Gestes des Chiprois*, 773–4.

[143] *Itinerarium*, 196; trans. Nicholson, 189, 173.

[144] Ambroise, I.19, lns 1147, 1137, 1154.

[145] Roger of Howden, 'Gesta', 2.7.

[146] See John Gillingham, *Richard I* (London, 1994), 84.

in the narratives of crusading, which described the nuptials in some detail. The narratives also focused on the political ramifications of the royal marriage, and then largely ignored Berengaria after her wedding day.

The ceremony itself was celebrated 'in royal style' at Limassol in Cyprus on 12 May 1191. Berengaria was crowned queen amongst important churchmen and nobles, and the king was described as 'merry and full of delight, pleasant and agreeable to everyone'.[147] Roger of Howden concentrated on listing the officiating clergy and the legality of her dower, but Ambroise described the bride in more conventional poetic terms, calling her 'beautiful, with a bright countenance, the wisest woman, indeed, that one could hope to find anywhere'.[148] This contrasts with Richard of Devizes' statement that Berengaria was 'a girl more prudent than pretty',[149] but as the queen never reached England he is unlikely to have seen her himself. The same author made a curious remark about Berengaria's voyage to the island of Cyprus, stating that she embarked 'perhaps still a virgin'.[150] This may have been a rather ribald comment on the king's virility, suggesting that pre-marital sex was the norm, although given that Richard was the only chronicler to criticise Berengaria's looks it is possible that he thought the match unsuitable.[151] On the other hand, he may simply have meant that it was only by chance that she had not yet married. The choice of Cyprus for the marriage was largely governed by expediency, as the capture of the island meant that the marriage could take place away from the sphere of French influence. The couple could not marry in Sicily as Berengaria had arrived at Messina on 30 March, during the penitential season of Lent. Richard, as a leader of a crusade, could not very well break with church tradition at the beginning of such a large expedition, for fear that military setbacks would be blamed on his own lack of piety.

Eracles described the wedding with a bald statement: 'he married the maiden whom his mother had sent, in a chapel dedicated to Saint George'.[152] Considering Richard's treatment of his sister Alice, it is unsurprising that Philip was portrayed as angry at the match, but *Eracles* asserts that he acted with dignity nonetheless, embracing Berengaria on her arrival in the Holy Land: 'he was careful not to betray his feelings or show any sign of outrage at what King Richard had done to him ... [except] when he got back to France'.[153]

In some cases the celebration of a marriage could have direct military consequences. Although her betrothal took place in 1180, the actual marriage

---

147 *Itinerarium*, 196; trans. Nicholson, 189. See also Ambroise, 1.28, lns 1738–41.

148 Roger of Howden, *Chronica*, 3.110: Ambroise, 1.28, lns 1735–7.

149 Richard of Devizes, *Chronicon*, ed. and trans. John T. Appleby (London, 1963), 25.

150 *Ibid.*, 35.

151 *Ibid.*, 25.

152 *Eracles*, 121; trans. Edbury, 104.

153 *Eracles*, 121; trans. Edbury, 104.

ceremony for Isabella of Jerusalem and Humphrey IV of Toron took place in 1183 at Kerak, when Isabella reached the official canonical age for marriage. Unfortunately Saladin took the opportunity afforded by the nuptial celebrations to place the fortress under siege. William of Tyre wrote of the difficulties caused by wedding guests and extra non-combatants:

> Evidently actors, pipers and psaltery players had convened from all over the region for the day of the wedding; but their hope was dashed, for while they sought stage-plays and wedding frolics, they found the conflict of Mars and more warlike activities far removed from their different talents.[154]

Saladin deliberately targeted the wedding because he was aware that the inhabitants would be more vulnerable.[155] Certain courtesies were observed, however. Ernoul told how Stephanie of Milly, the hostess, sent Saladin some of the food from the wedding feast, and he reciprocated by preventing mangonel attacks on the tower which contained the nuptial chamber.[156] To an extent this was a form of negotiation uniquely suited to the female role, although Ernoul suggested that Stephanie and Saladin had a cordial relationship from an earlier occasion when Saladin had reputedly spent time in the castle of Kerak as a prisoner. Aside from the problem of non-combatants in the castle, the political ramifications of this situation were very serious. Important nobles attending the wedding were trapped, including Reynald of Châtillon (Stephanie's husband) and Joscelin of Courtenay; thus Baldwin IV took the decision to remove Guy of Lusignan from the regency, fearing that the remaining barons would not cooperate with him. This effectively undermined Guy's later position and led to later attempts to separate him from his wife, Sibylla.[157] Ernoul's account, however, emphasised that it was possible for the cycle of love and marriage to continue even in the very midst of war, and the marital bond achieved a degree of respect that could reach across enemy lines, for the aristocracy at least.

EXTRA-MARITAL RELATIONS

This section will begin by addressing cases of adultery amongst the nobility, and then go on to discuss the issues that chroniclers raised with regard to prostitution in the crusade host, and in the Holy Land. The crimes of fornication and adultery were often seen as indicative of the sinful nature of society, but could be rectified in the spiritual rewards of crusading. Peter the Hermit inspired

---

154 WT, 1057.

155 Ernoul, 103. See also Hamilton, *Leper King*, 192–3.

156 Ernoul, 103. After the defeat at Hattin, Stephanie appears negotiating with Saladin once more. See 230 below.

157 See 225–7 below.

adulterers, amongst other sinners, to take the cross *poenitentia ducti*, but Albert of Aachen associated this crime with the activities of repentant 'common people' rather than perceiving it as a motivating factor for clerics and nobility.[158] At the time of the Council of Clermont, William of Malmesbury claimed that 'many men, locking out their lawful wives, entered upon divorce by wrecking another man's marriage'.[159] Evidently society was still adapting to the new strictures of eleventh-century reform, but William probably had a specific and high-profile case of adultery in mind.

Aristocratic Adultery

At the Council of Clermont, Urban reiterated the excommunication of Philip I of France for abandoning his first wife Bertha of Frisia in favour of Bertrada of Montfort, the wife of Count Fulk IV of Anjou. The significance of this affair in the development of canonical rulings on marriage is emphasised by Duby, and it certainly had an impact on contemporary historians.[160] Guibert of Nogent described Bertrada's situation as an abduction in his crusade narrative, although Orderic Vitalis asserted that she was complicit in the event. Philip actually married Bertrada in 1092, but it was not considered to be a true marriage by the Church.[161] Nearly one hundred years later, William of Tyre also noted the significance of the affair, and of the relationship between Bertrada and Philip he wrote: 'he acknowledged her as if a partner of the bridal bed and companion of his concerns, afterwards treating her with the affection of a husband contrary to the laws of the Church'.[162] Philip's resulting excommunication, and its reiteration in 1095 perturbed the French aristocracy. William of Malmesbury asserts that not only were Philip's subjects relieved of their obligations to him under his excommunication, but all those who referred to 'that accursed woman, his wife,' as their 'queen' or 'lady' were also subject to the spiritual sanction, unless the two agreed to part.[163] This fear of spiritual punishment probably influenced some guilt-ridden nobles to take part in the First Crusade, but others may have been unwilling to leave their lands (and wives) vulnerable to a king who rode roughshod over the rights of an important vassal in this way. Certainly, Fulk IV of Anjou, the wronged husband,

---

[158] '... bishops, abbots, clerics, monks; then the most noble laymen, princes of different domains, and all the common people, as many sinful as pious men, adulterers, murderers, thieves, perjurers, robbers: that is to say every sort of people of Christian faith, indeed even the female sex, led by repentance, all flocked joyfully to this journey'. AA, 4–5.

[159] WM, I.595.

[160] Georges Duby, *Medieval Marriage* (Baltimore, 1978), 29–45.

[161] GN, 110. See also OV, 4.260–4, 5.10.

[162] WT, 631–2.

[163] WM, I.597.

did not take the cross although Urban II probably put pressure on him to do so.[164]

As Latin settlements flourished in the East, the ebb and flow of military success and failure meant that the sexual activities of the new inhabitants came under scrutiny from historians. Fulcher of Chartres blamed Prince Roger of Antioch for the defeat at the Field of Blood in 1119, asserting that he revelled in sin and 'he shamefully committed adultery with many others while married to his wife'.[165] Conversely, men were sometimes praised for keeping to their marriage vows, a reminder that high standards of behaviour were required of both men and women. William of Tyre criticised some of the early activities of Prince Raymond of Antioch, but noted that once married his only vice was the occasional gamble on horses – a rather odd assertion considering his later accusation of an affair with Eleanor of Aquitaine.[166] Perhaps he was referring only to Raymond's continence during the considerable period he had to wait before his child bride Constance was old enough for intercourse. In comparison, Baldwin III received criticism for dishonouring the marriage vows of others as a young man. Even though Baldwin himself was unmarried, this was inappropriate behaviour and an abuse of his power, but William considered him to have expiated these sins by later being a faithful husband to his wife Theodora. His crimes were relegated to the impulse of youth.[167]

The political bonds formed by marriage meant that some cases of adultery had very serious ramifications for political stability in the Levant. Bohemond III of Antioch incurred the wrath of both king and church by putting away his Greek wife Theodora in favour of 'a certain Sibyl … who, it is said, practised evil magics'.[168] Bohemond had political motives for dissolving the marriage as the Byzantine alliance had faltered with Emperor Manuel's death in 1180. William of Tyre, however, blamed Sibyl for leading the prince onto a path of greater evil, using the charge of witchcraft to criticise her influence and justify a match that he was otherwise unable or unwilling to explain. Bohemond was excommunicated, and later an interdict was placed upon the whole principality. Many of the Antiochene nobility were also critical of his actions, and Bohemond, unwilling to make peace, drove away some of his most valued lords through this marriage, weakening his principality at a crucial point in the run up to Hattin.[169] Muslim

---

[164] John France, 'Patronage and the Appeal of the First Crusade', in Jonathan Phillips ed. *The First Crusade: Origins and Impact* (Manchester, 1997), 10–11.

[165] FC, 622–3.

[166] WT, 659.

[167] WT, 716, 843–4.

[168] WT, 1012. Lilie asserts that Bohemond married Theodora after 1175, as he was married until then. Lilie, Byzantium, 215. The *Lignages d'Outremer* asserts that his first wife was Orgueilleuse of Harim. *Lignages d'Outremer*, ed. Marie Adélaide Nielen (Paris, 2003), 83.

[169] WT, 1013–15.

sources also were aware of Sibyl and asserted that she was a spy for Saladin, corresponding with him.[170] Later, according to *Eracles*, Bohemond received his just deserts. Sibyl 'who was an evil woman' betrayed him to Prince Leo of Armenia: she arranged to have the prince, her own husband, taken captive in order to disinherit his two sons Raymond and Bohemond (later IV of Antioch-Tripoli), in favour of her own, William.[171] She was apparently enticed to do so by the prospect of marriage to Leo of Armenia, although Cahen asserts this was unlikely as Leo was already married.[172] Evidently marriage to a rich prince was seen to be the pinnacle of a malicious woman's designs. A more sympathetic chronicler might have argued that she was acting in the interests of her child, but *Eracles*, by including this proposed marriage, emphasised that she was ambitious for herself alone. In comparison, a royal mother who indulged in adultery drew no attention at all in surviving chronicles – the relationship between Plaisance and John of Jaffa is only referred to in two undated papal letters.[173]

Perhaps the most scandalous tale of adultery connected to a crusade is that of Eleanor of Aquitaine's supposed relationship with her uncle, Raymond, prince of Antioch. The queen was conspicuously absent from the narrative of Odo of Deuil, the main eyewitness source for the French contingent of the Second Crusade. She is only mentioned twice,[174] and then not by name, despite the fact that she participated in it and maintained a high profile in other contemporary texts and letters. A study of the extant manuscript of Odo's history suggests that information about Eleanor may have been excised.[175] This was probably a result of her divorce from Louis VII and remarriage to Henry II rather than misconduct on crusade – Odo's was an 'official' history of the king's crusade, and Eleanor's marriage to Louis was ultimately ended on grounds of consanguinity, not adultery.[176] According to John of Salisbury, who was in the papal curia when the couple visited the Pope on their return from the Holy Land, the king was made suspicious by Raymond's constant conversation

[170] Imad al-Din al-Isfahāni, *Conquête de la Syrie et de la Palestine par Saladin* (Paris, 1972), 139. Claude Cahen, *La Syrie du Nord à l'époque des croisades et la principauté d'Antioche* (Paris, 1940), 430.

[171] *Eracles*, 165; trans. Edbury, 128. Her involvement is supported by an Armenian chronicle. See *La Chronique attribuée au connétable Smbat*, ed. and trans. Gérard Dédéyan (Paris, 1980), 68.

[172] Cahen, *La Syrie du Nord*, 582–3 n. 3. Leo's wife was apparently Sibyl's niece. *La Chronique attribuée au connétable Smbat*, 65.

[173] See Peter W. Edbury, *John of Ibelin and the Kingdom of Jerusalem* (Woodbridge, 1997), 96–7.

[174] She appears travelling to Saint Denis while Louis VII visited a leper colony, as well as in Odo's 'departure scene'. OD, 17, 19.

[175] OD, xxiii n. 67.

[176] For a recent discussion, see Bouchard, 'Eleanor's Divorce', 223–35.

with Eleanor. He did not overtly accuse her of adultery, but ascribed a line from Ovid's *Heroides* to one of the king's advisers: 'guilt under kinship's guise could lie concealed'. He left his own opinion open to question by saying that the adviser had argued thus 'either because he hated the queen, or because he really believed it'.[177] By the time William of Tyre wrote his account, Eleanor and Louis were long divorced, and he presented Raymond as the instigator of the affair. Eleanor assented because she was imprudent and, crucially, was unfaithful, 'contrary to royal dignity and neglecting marital law'.[178] Her adultery was beneath her royal rank as a consecrated queen, and reduced her to the base nature of all women. It appears that women of noble lineage and character were expected to transcend the general standards applied to women as a gender. Other chroniclers such as Gervase of Canterbury and Richard of Devizes, writing in the 1180s and 1190s respectively, hinted at an affair without discussing it explicitly.[179] McCracken identifies this technique as a '*topos* of secrecy', implying that it was a literary device to draw attention to a scandal well known amongst contemporaries.[180]

Stories about adultery continued to multiply around Eleanor, especially after her death. In relation to the history of crusading, there were two more rumoured affairs of note. Later historians accused her of being romantically involved with Geoffrey of Rançon, the man who was blamed for the disastrous battle of Mount Cadmos – an argument based on little more than her reputation and the fact that Geoffrey was one of her vassals.[181] Over a hundred years after her crusade, she was even accused of trying to initiate an affair with Saladin, despite the fact that he could have been no more than a child when Eleanor was in the Latin East. The minstrel of Rheims claimed that, disheartened by Louis' lack of military prowess, and hearing of the fine characteristics of Saladin, 'she conceived a great passion for him in her heart'. At Tyre she tried to arrange her own abduction, with Saladin's approval, as he knew that she was 'the most aristocratic and wealthiest lady in Christendom'. The minstrel claimed that she was even prepared to give up her faith for him, and considered her to be a very evil woman, but fortunately one of Eleanor's ladies alerted the king so that he was able to capture her just as she was boarding the ship for her escape.[182] She accused her husband of cowardice, and was attracted to

---

[177] John of Salisbury, *Memoirs*, 53.

[178] WT, 755.

[179] Gervase of Canterbury, *Chronica*, 1.149; Richard of Devizes, *Chronicon*, 25–6.

[180] Peggy McCracken, 'Scandalizing Desire: Eleanor of Aquitaine and the Chroniclers', in Wheeler and Parsons, *Eleanor of Aquitaine, Lord and Lady*, 249.

[181] Curtis H. Walker, 'Eleanor of Aquitaine and the Disaster at Cadmos Mountain on the Second Crusade', *American Historical Review* 55 (1950), 857–61.

[182] *Récits d'un ménestral de Rheims au treizième siècle*, ed. Natalis de Wailly (Paris, 1876), 4–5. McCracken records a further account of her passion for an unnamed Sultan while at Antioch, from the fifteenth century. McCracken, 'Scandalizing Desire', 253–4.

Saladin because of his success on the battlefield, in keeping with the portrayal of noblewomen as audience to masculine prowess. This story was fairly characteristic of thirteenth-century representations of Eleanor. In the minstrel's eyes, 'she was not only fickle, but gave her baptised body to the infidel, betraying not only her husband, but her God, the ultimate in debauchery'.[183] Alberic of Trois Fontaines echoed William of Tyre, saying that 'King Louis divorced her on account of the unrestrained lust of this woman, who was not comporting herself as a queen, but rather showing herself to be almost a harlot'.[184] Eleanor thus became 'an emblem of the dangers of the queen's sexual intimacy with the king', and chroniclers from different backgrounds reinterpreted ideas about Eleanor to suit anxieties about sexuality and sovereignty in their own time.[185]

Ultimately, such stories make it difficult to tell whether Eleanor did have an adulterous relationship with Raymond.[186] Her quick remarriage to Henry II also drew criticism from ecclesiastical historians, although it was not at all unusual for an heiress of her standing at this time. She was even accused of having an affair with Henry's father, Geoffrey of Anjou, before he died.[187] The situation on the Second Crusade was undoubtedly born of political need, whether or not a love affair resulted. Raymond of Antioch desperately wanted the military aid that Louis could offer.[188] Eleanor, as the king's wife, was the natural conduit through which such appeals could be made; thus it was normal for Raymond to exploit his link of kinship with her. William of Tyre agrees that this was Raymond's initial intention, but, rebuffed by Louis, he began an affair with Eleanor out of spite.[189] As a powerful heiress, with her own crusading heritage from the duchy of Aquitaine, perhaps Eleanor believed that her crusade with Louis was more of a joint venture. She had taken the cross with her husband in a public ceremony, and was following the earlier example of her grandfather, William IX of Aquitaine.[190] Evidence suggests that Louis' hold over the duchy was not entirely

---

[183] Georges Duby, *Women of the Twelfth Century: Eleanor of Aquitaine and Six Others*, trans. Jean Birrel (Chicago, 1997), 7.

[184] ATF, 841. See also GW 'De Principis', 8.299.

[185] McCracken, 'Scandalizing Desire', 258.

[186] See Flori, *Aliénor d'Aquitaine*, 295–335.

[187] Walter Map, *De Nugis Curialum*, ed. and trans. Montague R. James, revised by Christopher N. L. Brooke and Roger A. B. Mynors (Oxford, 1983), 474–6; GW, 'De Principis', 8.300.

[188] See Yves Sassier, *Louis VII* (Paris, 1991), 183–9; and Phillips, *Defenders*, 90–5.

[189] WT, 755.

[190] See Elizabeth A. R. Brown, 'Eleanor of Aquitaine Reconsidered: The Woman and Her Seasons', in Wheeler and Parsons, *Eleanor of Aquitaine, Lord and Lady*, 1–54; and *idem.*, 'Eleanor of Aquitaine: Parent, Queen and Duchess', in William W. Kibler ed. *Eleanor of Aquitaine, Patron and Politician* (Austin, 1977), 9–23.

secure,[191] and without her presence he may not have been able muster the support of even the limited number of knights and barons from that region who took the cross.[192] She may well have been bitterly disappointed when Louis refused to aid her kin, or even give some acknowledgement to her right as a wife to intercede and give counsel. The result was that she was 'torn away' from Antioch, and with 'their mutual anger growing greater', the marital relationship broke down.[193] There is the possibility that Raymond, in desperate straits as he was, was prepared to use any means possible to secure aid, and when Louis was reluctant, deliberately cultivated a relationship with Eleanor which drove a wedge between the two. Either way, it seems that Raymond believed he would still be able to benefit from Eleanor's presence without the king, perhaps because she had financial or military support of her own to offer, or would in the future if she managed to divorce her husband successfully. That chroniclers opted for the simple explanation of a love affair speaks volumes about contemporary perceptions towards the influence of important women in medieval society and obfuscates the minutiae of the politics involved. There can be no definitive proof that Eleanor had a physical relationship with Raymond, but, to some extent, that question is irrelevant.[194] She was evidently keen to uphold the position of her kinsman, to the extent that she would jeopardise her marriage. Presumably from there it only took a very short step for chroniclers to believe that even such a high-profile woman as the queen of France could succumb to her innate female weakness.

Queen Melisende of Jerusalem was treated more liberally than Eleanor in William of Tyre's narrative despite rumours about an affair with her cousin Hugh II of Jaffa. Melisende's position as heiress to the kingdom meant that she did not have to be portrayed as a submissive wife, who relied on intercession with her husband for authority. William did not countenance the charge of adultery; he asserted that the real reasons for the dispute were 'unknown' but stressed the kinship between Melisende and Hugh, and that there seemed to be many arguments supporting over-familiarity between the two.[195] Hugh was accused of plotting against the king and the

---

[191] See Lindy Grant, *Abbot Suger of Saint Denis: Church and State in Twelfth Century France* (London, 1998), 161. The unrest in Poitiers during the early part of Louis' reign and the fact that Eleanor was able to transfer her inheritance to Henry II after her divorce both suggest this.

[192] Of twenty-eight major French nobles listed as taking the cross at Vézelay, only two hailed from Aquitaine, Geoffrey of Rançon and Hugh VII of Lusignan. *Historia Gloriosi Regis Ludovici VII*, in RHGF 12, 124–33.

[193] John of Salisbury, *Memoirs*, 53.

[194] See Flori, *Aliénor*, 334. He focuses on the masculine qualities attributed to Eleanor because, bucking contemporary trends, she demanded her separation from Louis, exercising her own choice. See 140–1 below.

[195] WT, 652.

episode resulted in a rebellion during 1134 which had to be put down by force.[196] Hugh was exiled, but afterwards an attempt was made on his life which left him seriously injured, and Melisende's wrath fell on those who had opposed him. Even the king himself was not safe among the queen's partisans, to the extent that he became extremely uxorious to appease her. William cited Melisende's displeasure as having twofold causes: 'to an extent even she was seen to be tainted by the disgrace of the reproachful accusation, and very great sorrow struck her on behalf of the expulsion of the count'.[197] Melisende's vengeance on the pertinent members of the court, however, suggests that as a wife and heiress she was already able to use patronage and faction to her own advantage, a situation later exacerbated by her widowhood and regency. In these circumstances, intimating that the conflict was a result of marital jealousy obscured the political motivation of Hugh of Jaffa's rebellion, more openly stated by Orderic Vitalis: Fulk had 'changed governors and other dignitaries too quickly and thoughtlessly'.[198] He thus excluded the established nobility distinguished by their descent from the First Crusaders and replaced them with 'Angevin strangers' and 'new flatterers'.[199] It is generally accepted that Melisende was a focal point for disgruntled nobles and was gradually being excluded from power by Fulk, therefore the matter of adultery was incidental; in fact Mayer suggests such rumours may have been started by her husband in order to create a pretext for repudiating her.[200] Riley-Smith has underlined the support of the Montlhérys in Fulk's bid for the throne, and their growing disillusionment with him, as another factor.[201] William, however, chose to represent the conflict as inspired by marital jealousy in order to trivialise the serious threat posed to Fulk's authority in the early years of his reign, and mask the king's initial unpopularity. He certainly went on to present an image of domestic harmony between the two after this time, especially when he described them setting off for the hunting party at Acre which was to cost Fulk his life in 1143.[202]

Crusading Armies and Prostitution

Canonical views on adultery and prostitution were reflected in narrative histories from the time of the First Crusade. Even in the *Gesta Francorum*, crusaders were warned against fraternising with local women during expeditions, whether Muslim or Christian.[203] At Antioch during the First Crusade,

[196] See Mayer, 'Queen Melisende', 102–11.

[197] WT, 655–6.

[198] OV, 6.390–1.

[199] *Ibid*. See also Mayer, 'Angevins *versus* Normans', 1–25.

[200] Mayer, 'Queen Melisende', 110. See also Hamilton, 'Women', 149–51.

[201] Riley-Smith, 'Families, Crusades and Settlement', 1–12.

[202] WT, 710.

[203] DEL, 177.

Stephen of Valence experienced a vision whereby Christ criticised the crusaders' behaviour:

> 'Behold, with opportune help I sent you safe and unharmed into the city, and lo, you are satisfying your many filthy pleasures with Christians and depraved pagan women, so that a great stench rises to heaven.[204]

Military failure led directly to accusations that crusaders had indulged in sexual improprieties. Henry of Huntingdon gave a minimal account of the Second Crusade, whose outcome he considered to be a direct result of the crusaders' sexual behaviour. The expedition, he asserted, 'came to nothing, because God despised them. For their incontinence, which they practised in open fornication, rose up in the sight of God. They also greatly displeased God by their adulteries.'[205]

The very presence of women was seen to be divisive. As well as the irate baker-woman who started a riot in Messina, other women were seen to foment trouble between the Lombards and the crusaders on the Third Crusade.[206] The Lombards apparently thought their wives were flirting with the crusaders. 'They were led on by jealousy, because some of the pilgrims had been chatting to their wives – but they did this more to annoy their husbands than with adultery in mind.'[207] Brothels in the Holy Land were also responsible for corrupting crusaders. The *Itinerarium* asserts that the French had fallen into disrepute at Tyre, enjoying wine and dancing girls and frequenting houses of ill repute:

> For although it was thought that their devotion had led them to come to the Holy Land on a true pilgrimage, they had left the military life and indulged in the amatory life, with songs about women and bawdy feasting.[208]

Thus the failures of the French contingent were not only a result of these sins, the author questioned their very motivation for undertaking the expedition. This was a serious charge, especially in the light of the emphasis on 'right intent' for a successful crusade. The author did, however, note that some were shocked at their compatriots' behaviour.[209] He also admitted that Richard's army had suffered the same problem in Acre, where he described them polluting the city with their addiction to wine, women and other pleasures.[210]

The solution to this problem, we are told, was that no women should leave the

[204] GF, 337. See also GN, 219; RR 821; PT, 99.

[205] Henry of Huntingdon, *Historia Anglorum*, 752–3.

[206] See 45–6 above.

[207] *Itinerarium*, 158; trans. Nicholson, 158. See also Ambroise, 1.10, lns 611–14.

[208] *Itinerarium*, 330–1; trans. Nicholson, 299.

[209] Ibid., 331.

[210] Ibid., 248.

city to accompany the army apart from laundresses 'who would not be a burden nor a cause of sin.'[211] This reiterated guidelines of 1188: that crusaders should not have female company except possibly washerwomen of good repute.[212] According to Ambroise, laundresses 'were as good as monkeys for getting rid of fleas.'[213] The confinement to Acre was not applied universally, however. At least two women were outside the city after this point, as Bahā ad-Din recorded that the daughter of an English knight was captured and put to death.[214] She was travelling in a large party from Beirut, and did not have the chance to reach the comparative safety of Acre. He gave less detail about the other woman, only referring to her as a Frank, but she may also have been a noblewoman, and therefore perceived to be above the suspicion of prostitution.[215]

Labels of sexual promiscuity and acceptance of institutionalised prostitution were often used to denigrate non-Latin society. As well as Guibert of Nogent's attack on Greek attitudes to prostitution,[216] Saladin reputedly began his rise to power through the taxation of prostitutes in Damascus.[217] Prostitution within the crusade army was treated differently. Like many armies, the crusaders attracted camp followers, but it is hard to tell whether they came from the West – 'professionals', or female participants falling into financial hardship during the course of the journey – or whether they were accumulated from the locations that the crusaders passed through. In truth, there was probably a mixture of all three, with the high death rates on crusade acting as a catalyst to the formation of new relationships not governed by formal marital arrangements. Guibert of Nogent told of the severe punishments for illicit sex at the camp outside Antioch, which he considered just. He asserted that crusaders feared even to speak of prostitutes or brothels in case God's displeasure manifested itself through death on a pagan sword. Any unmarried women who fell pregnant (children were unmistakable evidence of illicit sex) were considered to be prostitutes and subject to horrible punishments with their pimps.[218]

Strictly speaking, as the crusade was a pilgrimage, crusaders were not supposed to indulge in any sexual activity, even if their wives accompanied them. However, most authors were less concerned about crusaders indulging in sexual relations than the fact that they were doing it outside the bonds of marriage. Guibert of Nogent criticised the activities of Peter the Hermit's followers in

[211] *Ibid.*, 248; see also Ambroise, 1.92, lns 5688–9.

[212] See 45 above.

[213] 'd'espucer valeient singes'. Ambroise, 1.92, ln. 5691, trans. 2.110.

[214] Bahā' ad-Din, *The Rare and Excellent History of Saladin*, 170. See also Nicholson, 'Women on the Third Crusade', 399; and Geldsetzer, *Frauen*, 189.

[215] Bahā' ad-Din, *The Rare and Excellent History of Saladin*, 177.

[216] GN, 104. See 101 above.

[217] *Itinerarium*, 10–11.

[218] GN, 196.

Hungary because 'they repeatedly dishonoured marriages',[219] even though they were Christians who had offered their hospitality to the crusaders. Peter himself, however, was praised for making prostitutes morally acceptable for husbands.[220] In Raymond of Aguilers' history, St Andrew expressed dismay at the sins and adultery of crusaders, 'although it would be pleasing to God if you would take them in marriage'.[221] Writing of the Fourth Crusade, Greek chronicler Niketas Choniates praised the continence of Baldwin IX of Flanders:

> ... for as long as he was separated from his dear wife, he never so much as glanced at another woman ... most important, twice a week in the evening he had a herald proclaim that no one who slept within the palace was to have sexual intercourse with any woman who was not his legal wife.[222]

The fact that crusaders needed constant reminders about their behaviour suggests that adultery was a genuine problem. Some historians record the expulsion of prostitutes from crusader camps during expeditions in order to appease divine wrath. This apparently occurred outside Constantinople in 1204, and at St Louis' behest during his attack on Damietta in 1249.[223] The most famous example occurred at the siege of Antioch in 1098, when Fulcher of Chartres asserted that married as well as unmarried women were a danger to crusaders' sexual purity: 'they expelled the women from the army, the married as well as the unmarried, lest by chance they were displeasing the Lord, polluted as they were by sordid activities and luxuries'.[224] This account seems to have been the unique addition of Fulcher, and it is questionable how accurate it was, given that the author was not present at Antioch himself. His view reflects those of authors such as Ralph Niger, Henry of Huntingdon and William of Newburgh – any women on crusade, even wives, could be the cause of sexual sin.

Miscegenation was another issue that concerned the authors of crusade narratives. Unsanctioned relations with Muslim women quickly became an excuse not only for the failures of crusades, but also for the setbacks of Latin settlement in Outremer. *Eracles* explained that Jerusalem had fallen in 1187 as a result of sin: 'no one should wonder that the land of Jerusalem was lost, for they committed so much sin in Jerusalem that Our Lord was extremely angry'.[225] Like Ralph Niger, he specifically cited the cautionary tale of the Midianite women from Flavius Josephus, implying that the settlers had been weakened by lying

---

219 *Ibid.*, 122.

220 *Ibid.*, 121.

221 RA, 97.

222 Choniates, *O City of Byzantium*, 328.

223 RC, 72. Joinville, 94.

224 FC, 223.

225 *Eracles*, 49; trans. Edbury, 42.

with the enemy.[226] Writing even earlier, Walter the Chancellor showed concern that adulterous wives in Antioch were influenced by eastern ways and were acting as prostitutes in the run up to the first era of Antiochene wars. He told of women who, 'having scorned their husbands' beds, served unchastity in the lewd brothel', and solicited at crossroads for customers. According to Walter, 'they were available for a price whatever the weather and would lie down with anyone who wanted', even the unwilling.[227] He emphasised their desire for profit and indiscriminate sexual behaviour as recognised aspects of prostitution. He blamed a plague of locusts on the sins of Christians, and criticised not only prostitution but also lust within the marriage bond which was influenced by exposure to eastern culture. He told how men had special jewelled coverings made for their wives' shameful parts, 'not to clothe the appearance of their shame or to restrain the flame of lust, but so that that which was forbidden might inflame more hotly those people who did not desire legitimate pleasures.'[228] Fortunately, in Walter's opinion, the earthquake of 1114 brought about universal repentance, and men and women gave up their immorality for the sackcloth and ashes of penance.[229]

After their successful defeat of Kerbogha's army, Fulcher of Chartres made the odd assertion that when they found the women of his camps 'the Franks did nothing else evil to them, except that they thrust their lances into their bellies'.[230] It is uncertain whether he meant that women were simply raped and not murdered, or that they were killed and the sexual purity of crusaders was preserved against Muslim 'pollution' through intercourse. Bearing in mind Fulcher's story about expulsion of women from the camp at Antioch, and his description of the crusaders' indifference to the looks of women captured at Caesarea, the latter argument seems more persuasive.[231] Perhaps Fulcher was attempting to reinforce the image of the crusaders' renewed spiritual purity; they had repented their earlier shameful behaviour and gained victory at Antioch, thus they could not be seen to fall from grace before marching on the Holy City itself.

SEPARATION

Despite the best efforts of the Reform Papacy to make marriages indissoluble, certain unions were simply untenable. Consanguinity was cited on a regular basis to facilitate a divorce, but in fact this excuse probably covered a multitude

---

[226] *Eracles*, 47–8. Niger, *De Re Militari*, 227.

[227] WC, 62; trans. Asbridge and Edgington, 79.

[228] *Ibid.*

[229] *Ibid.*, 83–4.

[230] FC, 257; trans. Ryan, 106.

[231] FC, 243, 403. See 138 and 99 above.

of other reasons, political and personal.[232] William of Tyre asserted that relationship problems experienced by Hodierna and Raymond II of Tripoli 'arose from marital jealousy', but did not specifically state that it was a matter of adultery, nor who was to blame.[233] Queen Melisende was unable to reconcile her sister with Raymond and was planning to take Hodierna back to Nablus. However, the separation was more permanent than either of them expected, as shortly after they left Tripoli Raymond was murdered by Assassins.[234]

Despite the purported affair between Eleanor of Aquitaine and Raymond of Poitiers, most contemporary sources cited the official reason for her divorce from Louis VII, consanguinity. Evidently this was not the real issue, for rumours of consanguinity were rife from the early years of their marriage, and after their divorce both promptly remarried partners who were at least as closely related to them – Henry II and Constance of Castille.[235] In John of Salisbury's account, Eleanor had asked for the separation at Antioch when Louis had refused to let her stay behind, on the grounds of consanguinity. Despite this, the same adviser who warned Louis about Eleanor and Raymond encouraged the king to remain married, as a divorce would be extremely damaging to his prestige.[236] William of Tyre saw Eleanor's adultery as a major factor in the divorce, but asserted that Louis decided to end the union on his own terms.[237] The fact that Louis went ahead with the divorce even though he risked losing Aquitaine was a surprise to some – William of Newburgh described how the French were unable to retain the duchy and pined with envy.[238] Perhaps Louis genuinely believed he had the resources to hold on to Eleanor's inheritance – he continued to style himself as duke until 1154.[239] It is interesting that even though William of Newburgh blamed the failure of the Second Crusade on the presence of Eleanor and her women, he did not mention the rumour of her adultery. He put the separation down to a coolness developing between her and Louis because of the failure of the crusade itself: she was no longer convinced of her husband's prowess on the battlefield or in the bedroom. Eleanor reputedly complained about her lack of conjugal rights – that 'she had married a monk, and not a king' – and her growing desire for a match with Henry II.[240]

[232] It was for this reason that the Fourth Lateran Council reduced the number of degrees from seven to four in 1215.

[233] WT, 786.

[234] Ibid., 786. See also 187 above.

[235] James Brundage, 'The Canon Law of Divorce in the Mid-Twelfth Century: Louis VII and Eleanor of Aquitaine', in Wheeler and Parsons, Eleanor of Aquitaine, Lord and Lady, 215. Bouchard, 'Eleanor's Divorce', 231.

[236] John of Salisbury, Memoirs, 53.

[237] WT, 770.

[238] WN, 1.94.

[239] Brown, 'Eleanor of Aquitaine Reconsidered', 9.

[240] WN, 1.93.

Current scholarship largely accepts that the main reason for the separation was Eleanor's failure to produce a male heir.[241] The Capetian monarchy of the twelfth and thirteenth centuries was keen to encourage the image of stability by providing a continuous sequence of male heirs clearly designated by the practice of anticipatory succession. Eleanor and Louis had been married for fifteen years, and had only produced one daughter. Marital differences, whatever their nature, could have been reconciled for the sake of retaining the duchy of Aquitaine. Eugenius III's attempt to encourage a *rapprochement* between the two demonstrates that the Church still upheld the indissolubility of marriage even in consanguineous matches.[242] Eugenius even achieved a degree of success as Eleanor fell pregnant shortly afterwards, but when the child proved to be another girl, Louis decided to go through with the divorce.

Royal marriages seemed similarly fluid in the early history of the kingdom of Jerusalem, as demonstrated by the case of Baldwin I. After only a few years, Baldwin put aside his second wife, commonly known as Arda, the Armenian princess he had married on his arrival in the East.[243] A variety of reasons for the divorce were espoused by contemporary historians, and as both Mayer and Hamilton assert, the almost complete silence of Baldwin's chaplain and chief apologist Fulcher of Chartres on the subject is telling.[244] According to Guibert of Nogent, Arda was following her husband from Edessa to Jerusalem by ship when she was captured by pirates. On her release, Guibert described her fate:

> ... the king himself having doubts, not without reason, about untrustworthy pagan insatiability, straightway abstained from his own marriage bed, and having changed her garb, left her with other nuns in the house of Anne, the blessed mother of God's Virgin mother. In truth, it pleased him to live in a celibate manner, because his struggle was not against the flesh and blood, but against the rulers of the world. [Eph. 6.12][245]

Guibert's knowledge of these events suggests that the separation must have taken place between 1102 and 1108; William of Tyre's chronology indicates some time before 1105. However, Guibert's version of events fails to explain why Baldwin did not divorce Arda immediately, as her capture supposedly took place in 1100 and she was still queen in 1102.[246] Guibert's history was composed at least

---

[241] Brundage, 'Canon Law of Divorce', 217.

[242] Bouchard, 'Eleanor's Divorce', 225, 231.

[243] Hagenmeyer notes that she is referred to as Arda, but there is no contemporary authority for her name. FC, 422 n. 7. See also Hamilton, 'Women', 144.

[244] In the context of separation he only mentions Arda's reinstatement; see 143 below. Mayer, 'Baudouin Ier', 53–4, Hamilton, 'Women', 145.

[245] GN, 349.

[246] Mayer, 'Baudouin Ier', 56–7.

five years before Baldwin's marriage to Adelaide of Sicily in 1113, which would puncture his theory about the king wishing to live a celibate life. Writing in the 1180s, William of Tyre could afford to be more critical of Baldwin's actions:

> ... without an examination of the case he put her away, contrary to the law of marriage [since] she had been neither convicted nor confessed of guilt ... and forced her to become a nun against her will ...[247]

The convent of St Anne consisted of only three or four women at this time, but in return for taking Arda they received considerable royal patronage. Later it was to become one of the most wealthy monastic houses in the Latin kingdom, with its own market in Jerusalem.[248] William recorded that others accused her of breaking her marriage vows, but still considered the divorce illegal. He also accredited Baldwin with a financial motive for the separation. Apparently some thought that

> this was done so that by marrying a more noble and more wealthy woman he might improve his condition, and on account of his poverty, which was oppressing him heavily, he was considering acquiring wealth from elsewhere by the name of dowry.[249]

The importance of the wealth that a marriage could bring was reflected in the match made by Baldwin I's cousin, Baldwin of le Bourcq. He married Morphia, daughter of the Armenian duke, Gabriel of Melitene (Malatya): 'receiving with her under the name of dowry a very large and very much needed sum of money' (50,000 gold bezants).[250] At a time when the Latins were establishing themselves in the East through almost continual warfare, the ready cash that a dowry could bring was crucial to financing expeditions.[251] Albert of Aachen asserted that Arda's marriage had been celebrated with incalculable pomp but explained that her father had only paid 7,000 bezants of the agreed dowry of 60,000, putting off the rest of the payment until a later date.[252] This later instalment never materialised; thus Albert considered Baldwin to be justified in putting Arda aside, and Taphnuz, fearing retribution, fled to his strongholds in the mountains.[253]

---

[247] WT, 495–6.

[248] See ibid., 496; Thomas S. R. Boase, *Castles and Churches of the Crusading Kingdom* (London, 1967), 13.

[249] WT, 496. For more information on Adelaide's dowry, see 209–10.

[250] WT, 482.

[251] Mayer supports the idea that Jerusalem had great need of money at the time. Mayer, 'Baudouin Ier', 59–60.

[252] AA, 188–9.

[253] Ibid., 360–1; see also WT, 350. Mayer asserts that Albert, writing before 1120 and shortly after Baldwin had repented his misdemeanour by taking Arda back, was keen to uphold the honour of the Lotharingian dynasty. Mayer, 'Baudouin Ier', 52.

If Baldwin had put aside Arda for urgent financial reasons, however, it is curious that he waited for such a long time to remarry and gain a new dowry.

William of Tyre's attitude to Arda herself was somewhat ambiguous. Despite showing a degree of sympathy for her plight, he also told a scandalous story about her which does not appear in contemporary texts such as those of Fulcher or Guibert. Although at first the queen appeared content with her new monastic life, she later approached the king and 'by false stories' persuaded him to let her visit Constantinople on the pretext of raising patronage for the convent. Apparently, when she got there,

> She began to give all her attention to sordid and impure things and having discarded the habit of religion, was prostituting herself to all who came, with care neither for her own reputation nor the queenly honour which she had held previously.[254]

As Hamilton points out, this tale is unlikely to hold any truth, for if it was widely known Baldwin could never have reinstated her as he did later.[255] The inclusion of this tale makes it hard to ascertain William's true attitude. He may simply have been repeating gossip, or it is possible that he considered Baldwin responsible for Arda's fall from grace, by denying her the conjugal rights to which she was lawfully entitled and consigning her to a vocation which she had not chosen willingly. There are also parallels with his portrayal of Eleanor of Aquitaine's adultery; Arda's actions were not suitable to her previous status and 'queenly dignity'.

As a result of this dubious separation, when Baldwin married Adelaide of Sicily in 1113, many considered the match to be bigamous. By the time he married the dowager countess he was forty-two, and still without heirs. Perhaps he was waiting for Arda to fade from public memory, or affairs of state prevented him from making a suitable new match.[256] Unfortunately the union with Adelaide also disintegrated, and in 1116 he returned his new wife to Sicily, reinstating Arda.[257] Fulcher of Chartres explained that Baldwin was unwell and feared death, therefore he put aside the woman he had wed unlawfully because Arda was still alive.[258] William of Tyre concurred, adding that Baldwin, in remorse and penance, confessed and promised to make amends, restoring his first wife to the honour of which he had deprived her.[259] He was unlikely

---

[254] WT, 496.

[255] Hamilton, 'Women', 145.

[256] Mayer suggests that there may even have been rumours that he had homosexual tendencies. Mayer, 'Baudouin 1er', 58.

[257] See 209–10 below.

[258] FC, 601.

[259] WT, 542.

to gain financially from this decision, and if he was motivated by the need for a successor he could have taken a new, younger bride with a dowry; thus his motives may have been genuinely pious. Murray, however, argues convincingly that Baldwin made this decision on the advice of his nobles, who were more concerned that Roger II of Sicily would have a legitimate claim to the throne under the terms of the marriage agreement should Baldwin die.[260] Albert of Aachen added that the separation was a condition of Pope Paschal II for the reinstatement of the patriarch of Jerusalem, Arnulf, in 1116.[261] Although Baldwin reinstated his Armenian wife, it appears that she never returned to take up her position, and the king died childless in 1118.

It is undoubtedly significant that both of Baldwin's dissolved marriages failed to produce an heir, but marriages could end in divorce even if the couple procreated successfully. King Amalric of Jerusalem was forced to put aside his wife Agnes of Courtenay before he could succeed to the throne in 1163. Most contemporary chroniclers agreed with William of Tyre's assertion that her marriage to Amalric was dissolved on the grounds of consanguinity at the order of the patriarch of Jerusalem. It has been argued that the move was in order to exclude Agnes and other dispossessed Edessan noblemen from rising to power over the established baronage.[262] Mayer, however, believes that the annulment of Agnes' marriage had little effect on Edessan prominence in the kingdom. Based on evidence from the *Lignages d'Outremer* and William of Tyre, he asserts that Agnes was already married to Hugh of Ibelin when her match with Amalric took place in 1157.[263] Crucially *Eracles* asserted that Amalric required a 'dispensation to legitimise the lady and her children'[264] – Agnes would not have needed a dispensation from the Pope if it were only a relatively minor matter of consanguinity; thus adultery or bigamy was the more likely cause. As a result, Agnes became 'a *femme fatale* of the Latin East', accused of affairs with Aimery of Lusignan and patriarch Eraclius when he was archbishop of Caesarea.[265] Hamilton has dismissed this argument, however, on the grounds that patriarch Fulcher, who was known to oppose the marriage, would undoubtedly have excommunicated the couple for bigamy.[266]

[260] Murray, 'Baldwin II and his Nobles', 63.

[261] AA, 860–3. For William of Tyre's account of Arnulf's role, see 218 below.

[262] Hamilton, 'Titular Nobility', 197–203.

[263] Hans E. Mayer, 'The Beginnings of King Amalric of Jerusalem', in Kedar, *Horns of Hattin*, 128–30. For the account of Agnes being forced to marry Amalric, see *Lignages d'Outremer*, 79. Mayer points out that William of Tyre used exactly the same terminology to describe their relationship as the bigamous marriage between Baldwin I and Adelaide of Sicily. See WT, 869–70, 552.

[264] *Eracles*, 20; trans. Edbury, 13.

[265] Mayer, 'Beginnings', 134. These accusations came from Ernoul, 59, 82.

[266] Hamilton, *Leper King*, 25.

If the marriage was indeed bigamous, it is surprising that William of Tyre did not mention it, given his antipathy towards Agnes. He is believed to have had a personal grudge against her because she successfully championed his rival Eraclius to the patriarchate of Jerusalem.[267] He could have accused Agnes of neglicting her marriage vows and blamed her feminine weakness and inconstancy without overtly criticising his own patron. In a comparable example, the author of the *Itinerarium* managed to blame Isabella of Jerusalem for agreeing to marry Conrad of Monferrat, even though he seemed to comprehend that she had little choice in the match.[268] William could even have accused Agnes of seduction; he already considered her to be 'a woman most hateful to God, and ill-natured in her avarice'.[269] After the divorce he asserted that Amalric stayed unmarried for a time, but Agnes married Hugh of Ibelin *statim*; and when Hugh died, she was criticised for entering into another consanguineous marriage with Reynald of Sidon, which was possibly bigamous because Amalric was still alive.[270] From these examples it seems that William was determined to create the impression of a woman governed by lust, yet he chose to give a detailed account of the degree of relationship between the two partners, as if to prove that consanguinity was the only reason for the dissolution of the marriage. It is also one of the only instances in his history when he openly relied on a woman, Abbess Stephanie of St Mary the Great, for testimony. Traditionally women were not used as witnesses to support an historical argument, but it seems that in areas of genealogy a woman was perceived to have some expertise.[271] This woman in particular was described as very old, 'a woman devout and noble in body and mind'.[272] As a nun, her reliability as a witness was unimpeachable, and crucially she was the daughter of Joscelin 1 of Edessa, thus a relative of Agnes. By utilising her testimony, William definitively defended Amalric and by extension Agnes herself against any other charges of impropriety in their union.

The separation of Isabella 1 of Jerusalem from Humphrey of Toron and her marriage to Conrad of Montferrat also caused considerable controversy. A witness to the papal court asserted that she had been abducted from the tent next to her husband at the camp outside Acre, although he suggested it

---

[267] See Morgan, *The Chronicle of Ernoul*, 41–2.

[268] See 146 below.

[269] WT, 1019.

[270] *Ibid.*, 870. It had been thought that the marriage between the two was annulled, but this was based on a misinterpretation of William's comments. See Rudolph Hiestand, 'Die Herren von Sidon und die Thronfolgecrise des Jahres 1163 im Köngreich Jerusalem', in Kedar *et al.*, *Montjoie*, 77–90; and Hamilton, *Leper King*, 33–4.

[271] See Elisabeth van Houts, *Memory and Gender in Medieval Europe 900–1200* (London, 1999), 65–92.

[272] WT, 869.

may have been with her tacit approval.[273] Even the *Eracles* chronicle expressed concern:

> God knows if this sentence was in accordance with the law, for the lady was not in the power of her husband but was in the power and control of the marquis who married her as soon as the sentence had been given.[274]

Given the initial similarities of the *Eracles* chronicle to the pro-Ibelin, *Ernoul* group of texts for the period 1184–97,[275] it is surprising that the author was critical of the marriage, as it secured the kingdom for Balian's stepdaughter Isabella. Criticism of Conrad at this point in the text was certainly at odds with the more positive portrayal of his earlier feats at Tyre. Gillingham has suggested that the *Eracles* narrative was supplemented by versions of a later 'anecdotal' text; and if the pro-Ibelin source ended in 1187, a theory that Edbury finds persuasive, this may well account for the discrepancy in views.[276]

Ambroise and the *Itinerarium*, on the other hand, had no qualms about expressing their disapproval of Conrad's actions. The English contingent supported Guy of Lusignan as the rightful king, and Conrad's refusal to aid the siege of Acre during a time of famine branded him an enemy and a criminal in their eyes. Ralph of Diceto implied that Conrad and Isabella's union was ill omened, as a group of crusaders were captured on the same day as their wedding.[277] Both the *Itinerarium* and Ambroise record the archbishop of Canterbury's opposition to these actions, and attempted to throw further doubt on the legitimacy of the marriage by asserting that it was bigamous and that Conrad had two living wives already.[278] Their opinion of Isabella herself was ambivalent. The *Itinerarium* stated that she was forcibly abducted like Helen of Troy, but then quoted Virgil on the inconstancy of women, asserting that she was complicit because of her womanly nature:

> The female sex is weak, and she rejoices at each new embrace, spitting out those she knows and swiftly consigning them to oblivion. The girl is easily taught to do what is morally wrong, willingly accepted the advisor's

---

273 Innocent iii, 'Litterae ejusdem de incestuoso matrimonio comitis Henrici (anno 1200)', *Patrologia Latina* 26 (3), col. 981, cited in Jonathan Riley-Smith, *The Feudal Nobility and the Kingdom of Jerusalem, 1174–1277* (London, 1973), 115.

274 *Eracles*, 107; trans. Edbury, 97.

275 Morgan, *The Chronicle of Ernoul*, 117–37.

276 As a result, Gillingham asserts, these histories 'cannot be taken as reliable accounts of the 1190s or as expressions of the view of the "native" baronage at the time'. Gillingham, 'Roger of Howden on Crusade', 147 n. 33. Edbury, *The Conquest of Jerusalem*, 5.

277 Ralph of Diceto, 'Ymagines Historiarum', 2.86.

278 *Itinerarium*, 22. See also Ambroise, 1.66–7, lns 4121–38. Conrad supposedly had one wife in the West, and his second wife Theodora Angela was still alive in 1195–8; see Charles M. Brand, *Byzantium Confronts the West 1180–1204* (Cambridge, MA, 1968), 80, 84, 119.

shameful instructions, and soon she is not ashamed to say that she was not carried off but went with the Marquis of her own accord.[279]

A potentially lucrative marriage did not always fulfil its promise, and this could be another reason for separation. In the early 1240s, Ralph of Nesle, count of Soissons, married Alice of Cyprus, and tried to press the claim of his new wife to the throne of Jerusalem. His hold over the lordship was weak, however, 'for those who had put him there, that is his wife's relations, had more authority and power than he had, so that he seemed to be nothing but a shadow.'[280] Alice had considerable political experience as in 1218 she acted as regent for her infant son Henry I of Cyprus, but she had encountered problems with her powerful lieutenant, Philip of Ibelin.[281] In 1225 she had married Bohemond V of Antioch-Tripoli, but this union was short-lived. They divorced in 1228, apparently because of personal differences, but perhaps again because Bohemond had been unable to break the Ibelin hold over Cyprus. Later, the Ibelin family continued to obstruct her ambitions for power in the kingdom of Jerusalem. In 1243 they accepted her as regent at Acre, for she was closest heir to the current king, Conrad, but it had already been decided that fortresses should remain in the hands of Balian of Ibelin, lord of Beirut, and Philip of Montfort.[282] According to the Acre continuation, after Tyre had been recovered from the imperialists, they refused to hand the city over to Ralph and Alice, now claiming uncertainty over the succession.[283] Ralph and his allies lacked the resources to enforce their will over such strong opposition. Having reached a stalemate, 'angry and disappointed, he [Ralph] threw it all up, left his wife and went home to his own country.'[284] Ralph had married Alice in expectation of exercising the power to which she had a claim. She must have been in her early to mid-forties when they married and was unlikely to produce more children, so the position that he could gain through marriage was probably his main motivation for the match. When this was not forthcoming, he evidently considered the arrangement invalid and terminated the agreement.

WIVES AND CAPTIVITY

There were also specific perceptions about wives and captivity. A wife was a symbol of a man's worldly goods, and was often associated with booty. In felicitous circumstances, a noble wife could be of great importance as a hostage, but

---

[279] *Itinerarium*, 121–2; trans. Nicholson, 124.

[280] *L'Estoire d'Eracles Empereur*, 420; trans. Shirley, 128.

[281] See Peter W. Edbury, *The Kingdom of Cyprus and the Crusades, 1191–1374* (Cambridge, 1991), 49–51.

[282] 'Les Gestes des Chiprois', in RHC *Arm*, 2.730–2. See Edbury, *Kingdom of Cyprus*, 81–2.

[283] *L'Estoire d'Eracles Empereur*, 423.

[284] *Ibid.*, 420; trans. Shirley, 128.

a combination of noble birth and the bonds of marriage was no guarantee for personal safety. Albert of Aachen lamented the loss of over one thousand 'delicate and beloved wives', who were 'very noble women and eminent matrons', at the 1101 battle of Paphlagonia in Anatolia.[285] The husbands who survived fled the battlefield leaving their wives to be raped, killed or chained by the Turks, who sent them as slaves into countries where they could not speak the language, to be treated like dumb animals.[286]

Captivity also brought with it the stigma of infidelity which had repercussions for the marriage bond, as Guibert's account of Arda's captivity demonstrated. While rape did occur, a mixture of ignorance, the desire to denigrate Muslim practices, and fears about racial pollution led authors to endow their enemies with an insatiable sexual appetite which was perceived to make sexual intercourse the inevitable consequence of captivity. Guibert of Nogent said that the Turks were rapists, who had no consideration for shame or the marriage bond.[287] He described Islam as a new licence for sexual depravity: 'the desire for pleasure was hidden under the excuse of procreating children not of their wives but of a great number of whores'.[288] In his account of Kerbogha's letter to the Persians the atabeg charged them to procreate with wives and prostitutes to oppose the Christians.[289] Evidently their profligacy was not only due to sexual depravity but was also part of a conscious effort to present a threat to the Christian religion, an idea that was reinforced by fears about inter-breeding.[290]

In the thirteenth century the Rothelin continuator emphasised the polygamy of Saif al-Dīn, Saladin's brother. Not only did he have many wives, he had even more concubines, 'according to the laws of Mohammed'.[291] He differentiated these from the Assassins, however: 'these unbelieving Muslims ate pork and lay with their own mothers, sisters, daughters and all the women they could get, contrary to the law of Muhammad'.[292] Frederick II was accused of becoming so intimate with the Saracens that he assumed similar morals and customs, employing eunuchs to guard his many women.[293] As a result of these kinds of perceptions about the Muslim enemy, some noble wives never transcended the sexual slur that a period of captivity entailed. William of Tyre told how Renier of Brus, lord of Banyas, graciously took back his wife after she had been imprisoned for two years, but:

[285] AA, 610–11.
[286] Ibid., 572.
[287] GN, 102.
[288] Ibid., 98.
[289] Ibid., 212.
[290] See 98 above.
[291] Rothelin, 522; trans. Shirley, 35.
[292] Rothelin, 523; trans. Shirley, 35.
[293] Rothelin, 526.

Realising afterwards, however, that she had not conducted herself with sufficient prudence amongst the enemy and she had not observed with enough caution, in the manner of noble matrons, the sanctity of the marriage bed, he put her away from him …[294]

The guilt was portrayed as hers, rather than extended to her captors. She was apparently content to accept the charge of infidelity and entered a convent in Jerusalem in order to expiate her sins. William evidently wanted to demonstrate that the lord of Banyas had acted honourably in this matter, as he emphasised that Renier waited until she died before marrying again.[295]

Some captured wives were never returned. The wife of Folbert of Bouillon (Emeline)[296] was taken captive in a raid near Edessa, we are told by Albert of Aachen, because of her 'forme elegantis', and her husband was beheaded. Despite her good looks, her captor ordered that she should be treated honourably until he had ascertained the worth of her ransom, which suggests that captors were inclined to treat noble hostages well.[297] In the end, however, a Turkish mercenary 'who saw Folbert's wife and was inflamed with excessive love and eager desire'. He asked for her in marriage instead of his wages.[298] Emeline's chances of ransom may have perished with her husband if she had no access to wealth of her own from the West, and she was duly given in marriage to her admirer. She may even have had a beneficial effect on her suitor: Albert noted that the knight, 'happy at his marriage', continued to fight for the emir of Azaz, who later allied with Christian princes against Ridwan of Aleppo.[299] In marked contradiction to the attitudes of these chroniclers, it is notable that the closest example we have of a biographical account of a woman's experiences on crusade, Thomas of Froidmont's Hodoeporicon, makes no reference to a sexual threat posed by Muslim captors, although his sister Margaret of Beverley was apparently unlucky enough to have been captured twice. Evidently he may have wished to protect his sister's reputation, but he focused on the hard labour she was forced to carry out during her period of slavery – gathering stones and chopping wood – and the privations and beatings she had to endure.[300]

Wives were also affected by the captivity of their husbands. William of Tyre recounted with some relish the capture and ignominious demise of the dissolute count Joscelin II of Edessa, whose conduct contrasted poorly with the

[294] WT, 656. See also Friedman, 'Women in Captivity', 83.

[295] Ibid, 656.

[296] Geldsetzer, Frauen, 185.

[297] AA, 344–5.

[298] Ibid.

[299] 'nuptiis his laetatis'. Ibid.

[300] She was ransomed once at Jerusalem and for a second time by a generous citizen of Tyre. TF, 478–80.

exemplary life of his wife Beatrice. The city of Edessa had fallen to Nureddin in 1144, but the count still controlled some fortresses based around his stronghold at Turbessel. However, Joscelin was captured in 1150 and his wife had the thankless task of rallying the shattered remnants of the county in his absence.

> His wife in truth, a modest woman, sober and God-fearing, such as God loves, had stayed behind with her minor son and two daughters; and as far as she was able, with the advice of those nobles who had remained, she was striving to rule the people and was governing the province against enemies, working hard enough to supply arms, men and food, surpassing womanly strength.[301]

Joscelin remained in captivity until his death in 1159, leaving his wife effectively widowed.[302] Ultimately, Beatrice was unable to maintain her husband's patrimony, and with the agreement of King Baldwin III, sold its remaining fortresses to the Byzantine Emperor Manuel in return for a yearly pension for herself and her children.[303] William did not blame Beatrice for taking this option, but saw it as the natural result of Muslim advances and King Baldwin's inability to protect those fortresses in addition to his own realm and Antioch.[304]

As booty, the wives and children of a defeated enemy were a source of potential wealth, but allowing them to go free was usually a sign of good faith. The *Gesta Francorum* was highly critical of the Byzantine Emperor Alexius when, 'brimming with empty words and hostile plans', he allowed the Turks to leave Civetot (Kibotos) with their wives and children, depriving the crusaders of the booty which they had earned.[305] Later, wives determined the intentions of Syrian and Armenian spies at Antioch. The fact that their wives remained within the city was indicative of treachery.[306] It was a customary and recognised sign of submission and commitment that a Turk who wished to pay homage to a Frankish leader should involve his wife, sometimes giving her as a hostage as a sign of good faith. Count Raymond of Toulouse sent a Turk named Bohemond to negotiate after the victory at Ascalon, and Raymond of Aguilers described how 'he came to us with his wife and arms'.[307] The presence of a wife was therefore used to gauge the honourable intentions of her husband.

One Muslim leader with a reasonably good reputation when it came to the treatment of female hostages was Saladin. In the aftermath of Hattin, his

301 WT, 775.

302 *Ibid.*, 774.

303 *Ibid.*, 781–2.

304 *Ibid.*, 781–2.

305 GF, 191.

306 *Ibid.*, 244; GN, 171. Raymond of Aguilers, however, asserted that despite the fact that the Turks had given wives to the Armenians and Greeks, they were prepared to join the crusaders as soon as they could escape. RA, 64.

307 RA, 159.

advance across the Latin East engendered a wave of dispossessed Christians, but he seems to have allowed them several opportunities to escape. He agreed to Count Joscelin's terms for the surrender of Acre, allowing the citizens forty days to leave with their wives and possessions, and similar terms were made for Christians at Ascalon.[308] On his way to besiege Tyre, Saladin allowed Balian of Ibelin an escort to go to Jerusalem and find his wife, children and household before going to Tripoli.[309] Balian had agreed to stay in the city for one night only, but broke the terms of the agreement in order to help negotiate the surrender of Jerusalem. Saladin provided him with a knight to escort his dependants to Tripoli nonetheless.[310] Muslim sources mention the departure from Jerusalem of a nun who had been the widow of a king, which may refer to Maria Comnena. The newly widowed Stephanie of Kerak was allowed to go free with all her possessions.[311] Saladin also allowed Queen Sibylla to leave Jerusalem before he besieged the city, for he was concerned that he could not ensure her safety if the city was taken.[312] Still, after Jerusalem was captured only those wealthy enough to pay the required ransom escaped slavery, despite Balian of Ibelin's attempts to negotiate the liberation of some of the poor.[313]

Clerical Marriage and Concubinage

At the beginning of the crusade period the Church was still struggling to enforce its views on clerical marriage, and occasionally these were represented in historical narratives of crusading. Clerical marriage was still practised openly in the Byzantine Church, and Guibert of Nogent criticised their persistent adherence to what he saw as a misinterpretation of scripture.[314] Despite the papacy's attempts to enforce celibacy, several Latin priests and prelates continued to keep mistresses. Monks in particular were discouraged from crusading because it contravened their commitment to cloistered life and risked closer association with women. This did not prevent their involvement, however: ecclesiastical authors often included cautionary tales about secular and religious clergy on crusades, focusing on their relations with women as a means for criticism. Albert of Aachen described a man and a woman who committed adultery outside Antioch and were beaten through the crusader camp.[315] Guibert insisted that the man was a monk, exacerbating the depth of his crime:

308 Eracles, 56–7, 62.
309 Ibid., 57.
310 Ibid., 63.
311 Ibn Al-Athīr, Extrait du Kamel-Altevarykh, 709. Imād al-Din, Conquête de la Syrie, 105.
312 Eracles, 62.
313 Ibid., 69.
314 GN, 93.
315 AA, 228–9.

Meanwhile a certain monk belonging to a religious community very well known to all, who had departed in flight from the confines of his monastery, undertook the journey to Jerusalem, moved not by piety but by a whim. Having been caught there with a certain woman, if I am not in error, convicted by an ordeal by fire, that miserable woman and her lover were led around through all parts of the camp by order of the bishop of Le Puy and others to the fear of observers, and naked they were beaten most cruelly with whips.[316]

The monk's motivation for crusading and his ultimate folly clearly demonstrated Guibert's contempt for monastics who took the cross in defiance of the Pope's ordinances. Albert of Aachen recounted how a certain unnamed woman of great birth and beauty was caught unawares by a Turkish raid from Antioch while 'dicing' in an orchard garden with a young archdeacon of royal blood named Adelbero. Their comrades escaped, but Adalbero had his head cut off, and the woman was taken into the city, where 'they tormented her all night with the unchaste intercourse of their excessive lust, showing no kindness towards her'.[317] After this they killed her publicly on the ramparts, and fired her decapitated head (along with Adelbero's) out at the Christian army with a mangonel.

Albert's inclusion of this story in his narrative had a twofold function: it warned against engaging in licentious activities on crusade, and acted as a deterrent to noblewomen and clerics who took the cross for frivolous reasons. The fact that he was careful to mention the name and lineage of the clerk involved suggests that contemporaries may have been able to corroborate the story. Brundage interprets it as explicitly sexual, and a warning that 'crusaders who indulged in irregular sexual exploits might meet a sudden and particularly unpleasant death', but the tale also had further dimensions as an indictment of clerical concubinage.[318]

Arnulf of Chocques, the first Latin patriarch of Jerusalem, was also criticised for his libidinous activities on the First Crusade. Raymond of Aguilers said that good clergymen objected to Arnulf's election to the Jerusalem patriarchate, first because he did not have the right qualifications, and second, because he was accused of incontinence on the journey. He had become the object of 'vulgar stories'.[319] William of Tyre also recounted these accusations with great animosity and criticised Arnulf for leading an unchaste life even after his election. He may have vilified the patriarch in order to alleviate some of the scandal attached to Baldwin I. William described the king as being led astray by the wicked patriarch, who also orchestrated his bigamous marriage to Adelaide. Arnulf's origins were also emphasised: he was the son of a priest, and acting

---

[316] GN, 196.

[317] AA, 208–11. This was Adelbero of Luxembourg, archdeacon of Metz.

[318] Brundage, 'Prostitution', 59.

[319] RA, 154.

against canon law by receiving a benefice without having made a monastic profession. He was a threat to church hierarchy and the impartial distribution of church lands. Indeed, he was even accused of dowering his niece, who married Eustace Grenier, with church lands.[320]

The Ernoul and *Eracles* continuations expanded upon William of Tyre's antipathy for another patriarch of Jerusalem, Eraclius. Whether or not the patriarch was Agnes of Courtenay's lover as Ernoul claimed,[321] both sources asserted that the patriarch kept a mistress called Pasque of Riveri, the wife of a draper from Nablus. Apparently they had an arrangement whereby she would come to stay with him in Jerusalem for a fortnight or more with her husband's consent, and the couple were well paid for the privilege. When her husband died, we are told, Eraclius took her in and bestowed such great riches upon her that a stranger may have thought her a countess, and the people of the city nicknamed her the 'patriarchess'.[322] *Eracles* recorded with some relish the discomfiture of the patriarch when he was informed, during a *parlement* with the king and his barons, that his mistress had given birth to a daughter.[323] William of Tyre became an altruistic campaigner for the patriarchate in the *Eracles* account, opposing Eraclius because he knew of his indiscretions rather than for his own gain. God, however, permitted the election of Eraclius because of the sins of the people of Jerusalem.[324]

These accounts were undoubtedly influenced by the fact that Patriarch Eraclius' loyalties lay for the most part with Sibylla and her husband Guy of Lusignan, rather than the Ibelins. Kedar has championed the reputation of Eraclius, arguing that the indiscretions of such a high-profile clergyman would surely have been denounced more widely had they been common knowledge at the time.[325] It is significant, however, that this was not a simple matter of unsanctioned clerical marriage: the hostile chroniclers stressed that Pasque of Riveri was already married, and that the arrangement was made for financial benefit, compounding Eraclius' sins further. In the *abrégé* version popularised by Bongars' influential edition of crusade texts in the seventeenth century, Eraclius preferred to stay with his mistress than join the battle at Hattin, and as a result of his affairs and the abuses of the clergy, the first kingdom of Jerusalem fell to Saladin.[326]

---

[320] WT, 421–2, 454–5, 519.

[321] See 144 above.

[322] See Ernoul, 86–7; and *Eracles*, 51.

[323] Ernoul added to the scandal by asserting that this was during a council of war, and referring to the lady explicitly as his wife.

[324] *Eracles*, 51.

[325] Kedar, 'The Patriarch Eraclius', 182–3. Evidently after Hattin, the sins of the patriarch, like the supposed incompetence of Guy of Lusignan, evolved into justifications for military failure.

[326] Kedar, 'The Patriarch Eraclius', 184.

6

Mothers

Mothers and Medieval Society

THE historian of women, while recognising that motherhood is biologically exclusive to the female sex, must be careful to avoid applying 'universal' values or innate qualities to mothers, as their experiences were affected by a variety of criteria including wealth, social class, and individual perspective. It is true that medieval women were often defined solely by their unique capacity to produce children, but not all of them became mothers, especially where relatively high rates of celibacy existed. Even then, pregnancy and birth only formed part of the parental process – the conventions surrounding child rearing and the interaction between parents and children are, like gender, subject to social change. When focusing on the medieval period, a further layer of complexity is added by the specific problem of male authorship in relation to the female experience of motherhood. Self-evidently biological and social restraints limited men's experience of motherhood, but relationships with their own mothers as well as medical knowledge and tradition helped to form opinions that varied with individual authors. A medieval male perspective on the maternal role, no matter how alien it may seem to modern women, can still provide valuable evidence about how motherhood was perceived by contemporaries.

TRADITIONAL VIEWS ON MOTHERHOOD

The reliance of medieval authors on tradition allows for a fairly consistent literary construct of motherhood for this period. The biblical command to 'Honour thy father and thy mother' is described by Blamires as fundamental to the case for women, and allowed mothers a measure of authority that was not bestowed upon any other female role.[1] 'Profeminist' authors invoked what Blamires calls the 'obligation-to-your-mother's-womb' on a regular basis, asserting that women deserved respect because they suffered to bring forth life.[2] In the Christian tradition, children, male and female, were expected to obey both parents. Joinville recorded how, on his deathbed, Louis IX instructed his son Philip to 'Honour and respect your father and mother, and obey their commands.'[3]

Eve and Mary dominated Christian perceptions of motherhood in the medieval world. Other biblical role models for mothers did exist but were often

---

[1] Blamires, *The Case for Women*, 70–95.

[2] *Ibid.*, 72.

[3] Joinville, 404; trans. Shaw, 348.

limited to Old Testament examples of matriarchs whose importance lay primarily in the explanation of the lineage of the people of Israel.[4] As a wife, Eve had succumbed to temptation in the Garden of Eden, and motherhood was her punishment, but also her means of redemption: 'I will greatly multiply thy sorrows and thy conception; in sorrow thou shalt bring forth children.'[5] She became the mother of the human race, and effectively provided the means to create the celibates and virgins who achieved God's grace. Thus it was a woman's capacity for childbirth that redeemed her from Eve's sin: 'she shall be saved in childbearing, if they continue in faith and charity and holiness, with sobriety'.[6] This idea was also fundamental to the growth of the cult of the Virgin Mary, for as the mother of Christ, she was the source of redemption for all humankind.

Mary had dual capacity as both virgin and mother. While her virginity provided her with unquestioned sanctity, it was her authority as a mother and her ability to intercede with Christ that accorded her a unique position amongst the saints. Mary's unattainable perfection through her virginity meant that she was probably a confusing role model for expectant mothers. The growth of the cult of St Anne, the Virgin's mother, may suggest that she was a more amenable alternative.[7] While imagery of the Virgin contained few elements of earthly motherhood, she embodied everything about a mother's benign influence. As a role model she represented the virtues of grace and mercy that were often applied to queens and noblewomen. She was depicted as *Maria Regina*, the Queen of Heaven, from as early as the fifth century. A woman unrivalled in power and above the criticisms of earthly womanhood, she was often used as a symbol by secular queens and the papacy. Blanche of Castille, the mother of crusader Louis IX, was portrayed in the likeness of Mary during the mid-thirteenth century, but interestingly it was in her guise as the bride of Christ.[8]

PREGNANCY AND MOTHERING

In terms of physiology, Aristotle believed that women's menses provided matter that was then transformed by the seed of the male, thus giving women little more status than a vessel in the procreative process.[9] Ecclesiastical writers in general were far more concerned about regulating the sexual relationship

---

4 John Carmi Parsons, 'The Pregnant Queen as Counsellor and the Medieval Construction of Motherhood', in John Carmi Parsons and Bonnie Wheeler eds *Medieval Mothering* (New York, 1996), 39–61.

5 Gen 3:16.

6 1 Tim 2:15.

7 Leyser, *Medieval Women*, 123, 128; Shahar, *Fourth Estate*, 99–100.

8 Mary Stroll, 'Maria Regina: Papal Symbol', in Anne J. Duggan ed. *Queens and Queenship in Medieval Europe* (Woodbridge, 1997), 173, 175, 177.

9 Elisabeth Badinter, *The Myth of Motherhood: An Historical View of the Maternal Instinct* (London, 1981), 9.

between husband and wife than its ultimate consequence: parenthood. As a result of Eve's transgression, motherhood and the procreation of children was the mitigating factor that allowed favourable views on marriage. According to St Augustine, intercourse was only acceptable when entered into for the procreation of children, even within marriage. Sex for any other reason engendered the sin of lust, especially if efforts were made to prevent conception, or to abort a pregnancy.[10] There were contemporary medical treatises relating to the act of childbirth, and most well-educated authors would have been aware of theories about conception, as it formed a fundamental part of the contemporary philosophy behind human existence. In practical terms, men were unlikely to be present for an actual birth, as women and midwives were most commonly in attendance, but they had some experience of the conventions surrounding it.[11] When Margaret of Provence nearly died in childbirth, King Louis IX of France kept a vigil at her bedside despite his mother calling him to attend affairs of state.[12] Guibert of Nogent described his own difficult birth in some detail; presumably he had heard the story from his mother. She was 'racked with continuous pain', and her family, fearing for her life, promised the young Guibert (if he survived) to a monastic life under a vow to the Virgin Mary.[13] Guibert described himself as almost an aborted foetus when he was born, and the callous remarks of the woman at his baptism provide fodder for the arguments of Ariès that high infant mortality in the medieval period led to a lack of sensitivity towards children.[14]

If Ariès espoused a bleak view of the parental role in medieval society, Shahar has agreed that in ecclesiastical literature, at least, 'children are often depicted as a burden and also indirectly as the cause of sin'.[15] Parenthood had a place at the heart of the discourse about the benefits and detriments of marriage and virginity, and authors also reflected concerns about wealth and the rising population engendered by the economic boom of the eleventh and twelfth centuries. Bernard of Cluny expressed concern in the twelfth century that 'ever growing is the horde of men who lack religious piety, whose desire to marry and whose unrestrained proliferation are the outcome of a fleshly lust which knows no bounds'.[16] These views were not exclusively masculine; they were shared by the

---

[10] See St Augustine, 'De Nuptiis et Concupiscentia', in *Patrologia Latina* 44 (Paris, 1865), vol. 10.i, cols 413–74.

[11] See Becky R. Lee, 'A Company of Women *and* Men: Men's Recollections of Childbirth in Medieval England', *Journal of Family History* 27 (2002), 92–100.

[12] Joinville, 332. See 178–9 below.

[13] 'diutinis ergo cruciatibus agitata'. Guibert, *Autobiographie*, 18.

[14] Guibert, *Autobiographie*, 18–20.

[15] Ariès, *Centuries of Childhood*, 128; Shahar, *Fourth Estate*, 103.

[16] Bernard of Cluny, *De Contemptu Mundi*, ed. Hermon C. Hoskier (London, 1929), book 2, cited in Shahar, *Childhood*, 9.

women religious who also lived a celibate life and believed that the primary role of a woman was not motherhood, but service to God.[17]

Motherhood and the qualities associated with it could also be applied to non-female subjects. Pregnancy and childbirth as purely physical roles are restricted to mothers, but men, cities, kingdoms, religious figures and institutions were all capable of displaying 'motherly' qualities. As Parsons and Wheeler assert:

> Maternity is a biological fact, rooted in the female body through birth, yoked to breast-nurture through infancy. But mothering is an activity ... [it] is culturally constructed, [and] grounded in specific historical and cultural practices.[18]

Although many examples which employ mothering qualities are based on biblical and literary *topoi*, they can provide a means to interpret contemporary cultural perceptions of motherhood, especially in historical narratives where information is otherwise relatively scarce.

MOTHERS AND EDUCATION

Women had been excluded from teaching in the Bible because Eve had advised Adam to disobey God,[19] but as women were to be saved through childbearing, motherhood allowed some flexibility from this stricture. Mothers were largely accepted as the educators of their children in medieval society, at least during their earliest years.[20] In noble society, men usually took over the formal education of boys, which began at age seven, but mothers still had a role in providing religious and moral guidance, usually by oral means. Mothers could also control the continuing education of their children by securing the appointment of a preferred tutor. Guibert of Nogent told how his mother chose his tutor and ensured that he gave up all his other students to concentrate on her son.[21] Of her own education, he wrote, 'you would have thought her a mellifluous bishop rather than the illiterate woman she was', demonstrating that a high standard of oral knowledge could still be imparted by women even if they were not literate.[22] Guibert's mother also experienced dreams and visions, sometimes in relation to Guibert himself, who believed in her powers of prophecy. He asserted that she had foreseen certain events that had already come true, and others that

---

[17] Shahar, *Fourth Estate*, 106.

[18] John Carmi Parsons and Bonnie Wheeler, 'Medieval Mothering, Medieval Motherers', in *Medieval Mothering*, x.

[19] 1 Tim 2:12–15.

[20] Janet L. Nelson, 'Gender, Memory and Social Power', in Pauline Stafford and Anneke B. Mulder-Bakker eds *Gendering the Middle Ages* (Oxford, 2001), 192.

[21] Guibert, *Autobiographie*, 26–30.

[22] *Ibid.*, 168; trans. Archambault, 73.

he expected to.[23] Guibert evidently subscribed to the tradition of mysticism: a means whereby women were enabled to speak with authority on religious matters.

Mothers also led by example, and piety was a key component of perceptions about them. In common with perceptions about the Virgin Mary, the 'good' mother was portrayed as almost asexual, despite the tangible evidence of her sexual activity: children. According to Guibert, his mother would have preferred to remain a virgin,[24] but having submitted to intercourse as a dutiful wife she had redeemed herself through agonising childbirth and by dedicating her last son to the Church. Accordingly she deserved honour and obedience, especially as she was content to live the rest of her life in chastity. She was pious and authoritarian, overseeing Guibert's education by a tutor who used physical punishment, and although this disturbed her she was pleased at her son's determination to continue his lessons.[25]

Orderic Vitalis was also a child oblate: he entered the abbey of Saint-Évroul in Normandy at age ten. In terms of parenting, he made no reference to his mother, except to say that he himself was half-English – he gave more attention to his tutor, Siward, who schooled him from age five. As there were serious health risks involved in childbirth at this time, Orderic's mother may simply have died, but his father, Odelerius, was a Norman priest and therefore it is possible that there was some shame attached to his parents' union. As a child, he recalled his sorrow at leaving for Normandy, but it was only he and his father who wept. His mother, again, was conspicuously absent.[26]

While mothers were often praised for educating their sons in a proper fashion, their educational influence over their daughters could be treated with suspicion. Later vernacular poets drew from classical sources and often used the link between mother and daughter to elicit misogynist arguments against women as a gender. Some mothers were perceived as teaching their daughters tricks to deceive and ensnare men, when they were no longer young or attractive enough to do so themselves. Walter Map used this to argue against taking a wife on account of the legacy of Eve, for disobedience 'will never cease to stimulate women to be unwearied in following out what they have derived from their mother'.[27] Chaucer's wife of Bath told of tricks she learnt from her mother to deceive her husband.[28] The vituperative Le Jaloux in Roman de la Rose accused his mother-in-law of corrupting and prostituting her own daughter (his

[23] Ibid., 128–30, 168.

[24] Ibid., 76–84.

[25] Ibid., 32–42.

[26] OV, I.2, 6.553.

[27] For examples, see Walter Map, De Nugis Curialium, 293.

[28] Geoffrey Chaucer, The Wife of Bath, ed. Peter G. Beidler (Boston, 1996), 64.

wife).[29] His role in the text was obviously intended to exaggerate the case against women, and demonstrates that, in the worst circumstances, mothers were cast as greedy, manipulative, and actively teaching their children to do wrong for their own personal gain.

REGENCY AND MATERNAL AUTHORITY

Prior to this period kinsmen gravitated towards their more successful relatives, so that maternal kin were sometimes more prominent.[30] Despite the purported shift towards primogeniture,[31] there is evidence to suggest that links to maternal kin remained strong during the time of the crusades. The inheritance of Godfrey of Bouillon, crusader-king of Jerusalem, relied on his mother, Ida. William of Malmesbury asserted that Godfrey was 'more distinguished on his mother's side, and claimed descent from Charlemagne.'[32] Similarly, Tancred's links through his mother Emma to Bohemond and the Guiscard line were far more celebrated than his paternal heritage from Marquis Odo the Good.[33] Stephen of Blois' claim to the English throne through his mother Adela provided sufficient justification for many nobles to oppose the female heiress, Empress Mathilda, in civil war. The status of a noblewoman may have originated with her lineage, but once married, her most important function was to provide an heir, or else her position as a wife could be threatened. Poulet asserts that 'fertility' was the 'cardinal virtue' of queens, and the same held true for most noblewomen.[34]

Tradition and education imbued mothers with a certain degree of authority, but the only occasion when a noble mother was specifically sanctioned to take political power on behalf of her children was in the absence of her husband, sometimes as a wife, but usually when she was a widow. As the authority attached to regency was so closely associated with the bond between mother and child, however, it will be considered in this chapter. Regency was based on the premise that maternal love encouraged a woman to act in the interests of her child. Despite the political problems that stemmed from limits on the military role of women, this was perceived to be a safer alternative than entrusting a minor's patrimony to a male relative who might have a claim. Successful female regents only survived by adopting masculine characteristics, but women were perceived as easily induced to enjoy the trappings of power for their own

---

[29] Guillaume de Lorris and Jean de Meun, *The Romance of the Rose*, trans. Frances Horgan (Oxford, 1994), 142–3.

[30] Leyser, 'Maternal Kin', 128.

[31] See 58–9 above.

[32] WM, 1.655–7.

[33] GT, 605.

[34] André Poulet, 'Capetian Women and the Regency: The Genesis of a Vocation', in Parsons ed. *Medieval Queenship*, 103.

benefit. Conflict usually ensued when a mother was seen as unwilling to relinquish her position, a problem exacerbated by the fact that there was no uniform
age for a minor's transition to legal authority. In the Latin East, John of Ibelin's
Discourse on the Regency asserted that a mother had the right to administer
lordships in the case of a minor heir, which was usually common practice in
the West. When it came to the throne, however, regency over the kingdom was
to be entrusted to the nearest relation, whether male or female, on the mother's
side if the claim was matrilineal, or the nearest male relation on the father's side
if the claim was patrilineal. John's agenda was political, however, as he sought
to justify Ibelin dominance over the royal house of the mid-thirteenth century
in legal terms.[35] Both Baldwin III and Baldwin V inherited the throne through
their mothers before this law was consigned to writing, but Hamilton asserts
that it was designed specifically to exclude the mother of a minor from the
regency if he or she inherited the throne from their father, and therefore 'almost
certainly' dated from Baldwin IV's reign, relating to the separation of Amalric
from Agnes of Courtenay.[36]

Mothers in the Narratives of Crusading and the Latin East

To begin, a brief outline of mothers' involvement in the crusade movement will be provided, before going on to consider perceptions about the
Virgin Mary. The Virgin demands separate attention from worldly mothers.
Her dual role as virgin and mother added to her unique qualities; her association with Christ and the Holy Places was also significant to the authors of
histories about crusading and the Latin East. Queens and noblewomen were
considered to share some of her maternal qualities, but they also had more
earthly and practical characteristics influenced by their wealth, status and
fertility.

The activities associated with mothers such as pregnancy, childbirth and
education will be addressed, as well as the literary conventions of 'mothering'.
More detailed portrayals of maternal relationships with children were usually
included by medieval authors when they related to regency, therefore any such
accounts will be discussed in this chapter even if they apply to widows. One
particularly intriguing example features a Muslim woman conversing with her
son: the mother of Kerbogha, atabeg of Mosul. Her appearance in several
First Crusade sources is sufficiently unusual to be treated as a separate case
study.

---

[35] John of Ibelin, *Le Livre des Assises*, ed. Peter W. Edbury (Leiden, 2003), 804–10.

[36] Hamilton, *Leper King*, 84.

MOTHERS AND CRUSADING

The mothers of crusaders were seldom mentioned as taking the cross. Evidently, chroniclers might have found it hard to extol the deeds of a hero who went on crusade with his mother, but many of the women who took the cross were mothers already, or indeed, became mothers while on crusade.[37] Lack of reference to mothers on crusade can largely be accounted for by the fact that they were more likely to be described as wives if they undertook the expedition with their husbands. Emma of Hereford took part in the First Crusade with her adult son, Alan of Gael, but Orderic Vitalis only mentions the crusade of husband and wife.[38] In practical terms, crusaders were less likely to be accompanied by parents, not necessarily because of old age or illness,[39] but because many still had duties to the family that kept them in the West, even if some of them wished to end their days in the Holy Land. In any case, age was not a barrier to travel for older women such as Ermengarde, countess of Brittany.[40] Even aged women of lower social status took part in crusades, though narratives emphasised that they might not withstand the rigours of the journey.[41] By the time of the Third Crusade, Eleanor of Aquitaine was in her late sixties, and escorted her son's fiancée all the way from Iberia to Sicily. She could not have taken the cross herself, however, as she was required to protect Richard's inheritance in his absence.[42] Blanche of Castille was renowned for her piety, but there is no evidence to suggest that she ever planned a pilgrimage to Jerusalem herself. As an experienced regent, Blanche's duty was to stay behind and care for her son's kingdom. Her reluctance at Louis' decision to take the cross was noted by several authors.[43]

Affection for parents or mothers was sometimes perceived as holding

---

[37] See 167–70 below.

[38] See OV, 2.318; and Geldsetzer, *Frauen*, 185.

[39] As chroniclers reiterated, many participants were pilgrims suffering from the effects of old age and illness, attracted by the spiritual benefits of the crusades. Riley-Smith has shown that several male First Crusaders must have been past fighting age. See Riley-Smith, *First Crusaders*, 107.

[40] See 41 above.

[41] During the First Crusade Tancred reputedly offered aid to a weakened, starving old woman who was about to cross the Vardar river. GT, 607. As well as the use of old age and youth in emphasising indiscriminate slaughter in massacre accounts, discussed above, the aged and infirm were often targeted for moving slowly – for examples, see WT, 183 and RA, 36. Guibert of Nogent compared the speed of the crusade army to that of an old woman, as it marched into battle outside Antioch in 1098. GN, 237–8.

[42] Ambroise wrote that Richard 'sent back his mother to look after his land that he had left, so that his honour would not decrease'. Ambroise, 1.19, lns 1155–7; trans. 2.47.

[43] See 177–8 above.

crusaders back.[44] However, the *Itinerarium* spoke of mothers encouraging sons to crusade (as well as brides urging husbands), and Gerald of Wales recounted the example of a pious mother from Cardigan who gave up her only son to the crusade, thanking the Lord for granting him the opportunity to serve a holy cause.[45] Riley-Smith has shown that mothers could be influential in spreading the crusade idea to their children as well as to their husbands: 'the period was one in which mothers could take a real interest in their children, but it may be that the influence of women on recruitment was more indirect', such as introducing a new chaplain to the household.[46] Generations within families built up a tradition of crusading,[47] aided by the support and encouragement of pious mothers.

In fact, by assuming responsibility at home many women became enablers, rather than inhibitors, of the crusade movement. It was Ida of Lorraine who stepped in to negotiate with the abbot of St Hubert in his dispute with her son, Godfrey of Bouillon. The abbot had threatened Godfrey with excommunication, which could have prevented him embarking on the expedition, but Ida calmed the situation by giving him the church of Sansareux. This enabled her son to go on crusade with a clean bill of spiritual health.[48] Orderic Vitalis recounts how Count Geoffrey II of Mortagne, the father of First Crusader Rotrou, fell ill and entrusted the estate to his wife Beatrice, to watch over on her son's behalf. He gave her 'prudent instructions', and enjoined both her and his nobles to keep peace and ensure that their son's inheritance remained intact.[49]

Some mothers took a more active role in helping to finance crusaders while they were in the East. Ernoul records how Henry II of Champagne left his inheritance to the care of Countess Marie:

> He handed it over to his mother to govern and protect, and for as long as he lived she delivered to him the income of the land. With this he paid the debts he incurred at Acre; she sent him payment [every year].[50]

---

44   See 113–17 above.

45   *Itinerarium*, 33. See 117 above; GW 'Itinerarium', 6.133.

46   Riley-Smith, *First Crusaders*, 98.

47   It has been argued that crusading trends within families were not universal, however. Some noble houses who had been badly affected by the Flemish civil war were reluctant to take the cross during the preaching of the Second Crusade. See Jonathan Phillips, 'The Murder of Charles the Good and the Second Crusade: Household, Nobility, and Traditions of Crusading in Medieval Flanders', *Medieval Prosopography* 19 (1998), 55–76.

48   *Cantatorum sive chronicon Sanci Huberti*, ed. Karl Hanquet (Brussels, 1906), 203–6, 338–40. See Riley-Smith, *First Crusaders*, 128.

49   OV, 6.395.

50   Ernoul, 291.

On hearing of the troubles of her son Louis IX in the East, Blanche of Castille immediately mobilised to provide reinforcements and funding for the flagging crusade, ruthlessly enforcing ecclesiastical tithes to provide the king with the resources necessary for his upkeep.[51]

The propagation of Frankish society in settler areas of the Levant was a crucial factor in maintaining aristocratic power, and the obligation of maternity was reflected in the contemporary marriage laws. Brundage described a *militia cubiculi* of women serving the kingdom in the marriage bed rather than on the battlefield.[52] At times of military hardship, however, children could become the focus of the sins of mothers in settler society. Fulcher of Chartres asserts that before the battle against al-Afdal in 1105, the inhabitants of Jerusalem all fasted, even to the extent that mothers curtailed their breastfeeding.[53] When Saladin was besieging Jerusalem in the days before the Third Crusade, *Eracles* describes how repentant mothers cut off their children's hair in basins of cold water in front of Mount Calvary, throwing away their shorn locks.[54] It is inevitable that camp followers as well as wives became mothers during the course of crusades, but pregnant unmarried women were likely to face punishment, as their condition was an infallible indication that illicit sex had taken place.[55]

THE VIRGIN MOTHER

The Virgin mother was treated with reverence in the narratives of crusading, which often recorded crusaders appealing to her for aid. As a saint and the mother of Christ she held foremost place as an intermediary, and because crusaders were pledged to protect the Holy Land, Christ's 'patrimony', she was the natural conduit through which they could appeal to her son. When the armies of the First Crusade were besieged by Kerbogha inside Antioch, the *Gesta Francorum* records how the priest Stephen of Valence had a vision of Christ, Mary and St Peter. Christ was angry at the sins of crusaders, but both the Virgin and Peter interceded, 'begging and praying to him, to help his people in this trouble'.[56] Guibert of Nogent in recording the same incident called her 'the Virgin of invincible piety and always the intercessor with God for the human race, Mary'.[57] Raymond of Aguilers, who was keen to emphasise visions and portents surrounding the expedition, asserted that the Virgin appeared to Stephen without St Peter, and spoke to her son directly

---

[51] Gérard Sivery, *Blanche de Castille* (Paris, 1990), 238–43.

[52] Brundage, 'Marriage Law', 270–1.

[53] FC, 494.

[54] *Eracles*, 67.

[55] GN, 196; see 137 above.

[56] GF, 338.

[57] GN, 219.

on behalf of the Christians: 'these are the ones for whom I so often pray to you'.[58]

Raymond also recorded how a priest called Ebrard prayed to a statue of the Virgin mother in Tripoli for several days, begging for her intercession on behalf of the crusaders at Antioch.[59] Peter Bartholomew, who underwent an ordeal of fire to uphold the veracity of the Holy Lance, claimed to have had a vision of the Virgin Mary and Bishop Adhémar, in which they told him that Raymond, the author of this history, was having doubts about the miraculous find. Peter accused Raymond of supporting him outwardly, but secretly requiring proof that the Lance was a true relic of Christ. In response, Raymond 'burst into tears' and Peter advised him to pray to Mary and St Andrew, reassuring him that he would be forgiven.[60] Raymond's agenda throughout his history was clearly to support his lord the count of Toulouse against Bohemond, whose contingent opted for scepticism on the discovery of the Lance.[61] He did not intend to foster doubts about the relic, but used the example of his own misgivings as a device to defend it against further criticisms. The account also showed Peter's strong charismatic power and manipulation of his position through visions, which he evidently used to ascertain the loyalty of people around him.

Raymond records that Stephen of Valence had another vision of Bishop Adhémar and the Virgin, en route to Jerusalem. On this occasion, Mary did not speak. Adhémar acted as an intermediary: through him, the Virgin indicated that she wanted Adhémar's relic of the True Cross to be carried with the army, and for Stephen to give a ring to Raymond IV of Toulouse. The deceased bishop claimed that it would bring God's aid should Raymond call upon it in her name.[62] On hearing of this vision, Count Raymond was apparently sufficiently moved to send for Adhémar's cross and hood from Latakia, demonstrating the influence such visions had on the leaders of the crusade, and the importance of acting upon them for the morale of troops. Here the Virgin appeared in a more authoritative rather than intercessory role. Adhémar relayed questions to her and responded to her commands; she was perceived as too important to speak to Stephen directly.[63]

It is conceivable that the Virgin, untainted by sexuality, was more readily received as a nurturing mother-figure by celibate ecclesiastics. Joinville's history included a story about a monk who witnessed the Virgin visit the holy abbot

[58] RA, 74.

[59] Ibid., 117.

[60] Ibid., 123–4.

[61] See Colin Morris, 'Policy and Visions', 33–45.

[62] RA, 128.

[63] For a further discussion of the roles played by the visions of Stephen of Valances and Peter Bartholomew, see John France, 'Two Types of Vision on the First Crusade: Stephen of Valences and Peter Bartholomew', Crusades 5 (2006), 1–20.

of Cheminon one night in his sleep. She pulled his robe back over his chest, 'so that the night air might do him no harm'.[64] The crusaders themselves were keen to earn her regard by observing festivals pertaining to her. During the First Crusade, the army remained at Caphalia to celebrate the Purification of Holy Mary, in February 1099.[65] The day after the Saracens were defeated in battle near Jaffa in 1101, the Christians gathered in the tent of the king to hear the mass of the Nativity of the Blessed Mary before returning to the city.[66] When Second Crusader Alvisus, bishop of Arras, was on his deathbed, he asked for the festival of the Blessed Virgin to be celebrated early, and 'gave his soul to the Virgin, whom he remembered with such devotion'.[67] Later, when the expedition reached Adalia, the crusaders celebrated the feast of the Purification of the Virgin, despite deluging rains.[68]

There were extensive sites dedicated to the Virgin in the Holy Land, and their appearance in descriptions of the Holy Places of Jerusalem demonstrates that devotion to her as well as to Christ was important to prospective pilgrims. Before besieging Jerusalem, a group of knights including Tancred visited the Basilica of the Blessed Mary in Bethlehem. On hearing of the capture of Jerusalem, crusaders such as Bohemond of Taranto and Baldwin of Boulogne came to celebrate Christmas there. Fulcher of Chartres told how 'we wanted to assist personally with the prayers throughout the night at the manger where the venerable mother Mary bore Jesus'.[69] It was at this church that Baldwin I was crowned in 1101.[70] As this site was believed to be the birthplace of Christ, and was associated with the kingship of David, it was a natural place for the assertion of Latin Christian dominance to begin. Mary featured heavily in descriptions of the Holy Places in the *Gesta Francorum*, and in the thirteenth-century Rothelin continuation. The latter source based its account on *The Condition of the City of Jerusalem*, a text written in Old French towards the end of the twelfth century.[71] Many of the stories in this text focused on the maternal role of the Virgin, giving domestic vignettes of her life with the young Jesus and locating them geographically, such as the stream where she used to send him to fetch water, or a spring in Egypt where she was said to have washed Jesus' clothes.[72]

---

[64] 'pour ce que li vens ne li feist mal'. Joinville, 68; trans. Shaw, 195.

[65] RR, 852.

[66] FC, 417–18.

[67] OD, 44–7.

[68] *Ibid.*, 128–9.

[69] FC, 280, 332.

[70] *Ibid.*, 384–5.

[71] Shirley, *Crusader Syria*, 2.

[72] Rothelin, 513–15.

Crusaders revered relics of the Virgin as well as the sites connected with her. Raymond of Aguilers records how Saint George appeared to Peter Desiderius, chastising him for leaving behind relics, including a vial of the blood of the Virgin Mary and the martyr Thecla.[73] The Rothelin continuation described a wooden tablet carved with an image of the Virgin that produced a healing balm, kept at a nunnery in Saidnaiya. It was apparently so powerful that even Muslims revered it.[74] Gunther of Pairis mentions two Marian relics amongst his list of holy objects brought back by Abbot Martin after the conquest of Constantinople. These included a relic from the place where Mary departed from the Sepulchre, and a relic of her milk. The abbot also brought Philip of Swabia a tablet containing relics centred on a carving of the Lord's Passion, with the Virgin Mary and John the Evangelist standing on either side.[75] During the establishment of the Latin Empire of Constantinople, when Greeks ambushed Henry of Flanders during a raid, they called upon the Virgin and were rewarded with victory. They also captured the icon of Mary, which was believed to bring success in battle, and had great symbolic importance to the authority of the Byzantine emperor. It was also a rich treasure covered in precious stones and the Venetians demanded it as the price for supporting Henry as emperor.[76] Abbot Martin, before his departure on the Fourth Crusade, delivered a sermon in the Church of the Blessed Virgin in Basel, and according to Gunther of Pairis, 'he commended himself and his companions to the Blessed Virgin, humbly begging that she intercede for this new army before her son'.[77] Many of the relics that he stole were intended as gifts for her, as thanks for keeping him and his companions safe from so many extreme dangers.[78]

The Virgin was sometimes perceived as the protector of crusaders. Joinville told of a squire who fell off a ship on the return from Louis ix's crusade. When he was recovered by one of the king's galleys the squire told how he had prayed to Our Lady of Vauvert, and she had carried him by the shoulders and kept him safe. The author had such faith in this miracle that he had it depicted on the walls of his chapel at Joinville, and in another stained-glass window at Blécourt.[79] The Virgin was also an emotive figure on the battlefield. The First Crusaders carried a banner depicting her, which had been captured at Antioch.

---

73   RA, 134. Thecla was persuaded by St Paul to give up her betrothed and was condemned to death.

74   Rothelin, 513–14. See Bernard Hamilton, 'Our Lady of Saidnaiya: An Orthodox Shrine Revered by Muslims and Knights Templar at the Time of the Crusades', in Swanson, Holy Land, Holy Lands, 207–15.

75   GP, 176–7, 179–80.

76   RC, 66, 107.

77   GP, 116; trans. Andrea, 73.

78   GP, 173.

79   Joinville, 356.

Raymond of Aguilers considered that the decapitation of Turkish prisoners followed by crusaders displaying their heads on stakes was God's vengeance for their defilement of the Virgin's banner.[80] Insults to Christ's mother were not to be tolerated, and inflamed the crusaders at the siege of Lisbon during the Second Crusade. Raol described how

> they constantly attacked the blessed Mary, Mother of the Lord, with coarse insults and abusive and shameful words, declaring it unworthy of us that we should venerate the son of a poor woman with as much reverence as if he were God himself.[81]

Mary thus became the focus of doctrinal attack for the Muslims arguing against the divinity of Christ, and in contrast was a rallying point for the defence of Christianity.

Perhaps the only other mother whose portrayal held an echo of spiritual authority and featured prominently in crusade narratives was the Empress Helena, mother of the Emperor Constantine who was canonised for discovering the True Cross in Jerusalem. This event was marked by an annual celebration on 3 May in the Latin Church, and her story was well known in medieval Europe and celebrated in Anglo-Saxon poet Cynewulf's *Elene*.[82] Helena's resting place was remarked upon in Robert of Clari's description of the marvels of Constantinople.[83] The Rothelin continuator told of a place in the Holy Sepulchre dedicated to St Helena, where she was believed to have found the relics that made her so famous.[84] In some senses the story of Helena and the True Cross was used in crusade narratives to legitimise the renewed presence of Latin Christianity in the East, capitalising on her association with her son Constantine and his role in bringing Christianity to the Roman Empire.

PREGNANCY AND MOTHERING

Pregnancy and childbirth were perceived to form an established part of the natural order; therefore when Ekkehard of Aura gave an account of the signs and portents around the First Crusade, he included unusual pregnancies.

> What should I say about those times [when] a certain woman remained pregnant for two years, and at length birthed from her womb a talking son; and likewise a little infant double in all limbs, and another with two heads ...[85]

---

80 RA, 58.

81 DEL, 131.

82 See Cynewulf, *Elene*, ed. Pamela O. E. Gradon (London, 1958).

83 RC, 86.

84 Rothelin, 495.

85 Ekkehard, *Hierosolimita*, RHC Occ. 5.19.

It is tempting to suggest that these improbable occurrences demonstrate Ekke-hard's limited understanding of the practicalities of childbirth, but to do so would take his work out of context, as the literary and biblical sources from which he drew were filled with such examples. It is interesting, however, that he accepted these reports as genuine but dismissed the story of the divinely inspired goose-woman as fictitious – probably because the latter involved a woman claiming spiritual authority.[86] Albert of Aachen described in more detail how the difficult conditions on the march south from Dorylaeum on the First Crusade affected pregnant mothers:

> For indeed, very many pregnant women, their throats dried up, their wombs withered and all the veins of the body drained by the indescrib-able heat of the sun and that parched region, gave birth and abandoned their own young in the middle of the highway in the view of everyone. Other wretched women rolled about next to their young on the common way, having forgotten all shame and modesty because of their extreme suffering in that drought. They were driven to give birth not by the due order of months or because their time had come, but were forced by the raging of the sun, the fatigue of their travels, the swelling of their thirst, their long distance from water. Their infants were discovered in the middle of the plain, some dead, some half alive.[87]

William of Tyre also recounted these details, noting that Albert was the only one to record them.[88] Albert was especially concerned about women taking the cross for frivolous reasons, so perhaps he intended to remind his audience about the physiology that made women unsuitable for the journey. He was at pains to express, however, that the story did not spring from hearsay but from participants who had also suffered during the march. His account demon-strated that he was aware of the natural time-limit for pregnancy and that vari-ous health problems linked to the consumption of inadequate food and water and physical stress could bring on premature birth. In a similar vein, Robert of Rheims told of starving women suffering famine once inside Antioch, unable to produce milk to suckle their sons.[89]

As the crusade host were often chastised for their sexual activities, it is inevitable that pregnancy and childbirth occurred in the course of expeditions, whether as a result of licit or illicit sex. For the most part, however, a specific birth was very seldom recorded unless the child was of sufficient status.[90]

---

[86]   *Ibid.*

[87]   AA, 138–41.

[88]   See also WT, 217–18.

[89]   RR, 815.

[90]   For a list of children born during crusades or on pilgrimage to the Near East, see Geldsetzer, *Frauen*, 213–15.

Elvira of Leon-Castille bore Raymond IV of Toulouse a son, Alfonso-Jordan, while he was campaigning in Tripoli, but returned with the child to the West after her husband died in 1105.[91] Margaret of Beverley was reputedly born while her parents were on a pilgrimage to the Holy Land, although this would remain unknown were it not for her brother's account of her adventures.[92] Noblewomen who were at an advanced stage of pregnancy were sometimes prevented from taking on the rigours of the expedition. Marie of Champagne delayed her departure on crusade because of pregnancy, but did eventually journey as far as Acre after her child was born.[93] The risk to very young children on such difficult journeys was also recognised. Mabel of Roucy, wife of Hugh II of Le Puiset, went with her husband on the 1107 crusade, but stopped in Apulia to give birth to a son (Hugh II of Jaffa). As the child's health was fragile he remained there to be brought up by relatives, while Mabel went on to settle in the East.[94] Mabel was the niece of Bohemond of Taranto, which probably influenced their participation in his crusade, and led to her husband receiving the county of Jaffa.[95] On his death, she was remarried to a certain Count Albert from Liège, and they died soon afterwards, so effectively she had little contact with her son.[96]

In the thirteenth century, Eleanor of Montfort remained in Brindisi to give birth to a son, Simon, as the Baron's Crusade travelled through in 1240, and Eleanor of Castille had a daughter, Joan, at Acre in 1272. On Louis IX's crusade, his brothers Charles of Anjou and Robert of Artois both became fathers. Beatrice of Provence bore Louis of Anjou during the sojourn in Cyprus of 1248–9. Mathilda of Brabant gave birth to Robert II of Artois in 1250, just a few months after her husband died at the battle of Mansurah. Margaret of Provence gave birth to John-Tristan in 1250, Peter in 1251, and Blanche in 1253.[97] Joinville went into considerable detail about her experience giving birth to John-Tristan in Damietta. It was indeed a dramatic situation: her husband was defeated and imprisoned, and she was trapped inside the city. She was terrified by the news of Louis' capture, and hallucinating that her room was full of Saracens, to the extent that she feared that the child might die. To comfort her she had an old knight lie beside her bed and hold her hand. The name of the knight went unmentioned, but the emphasis on his age was probably in order to justify his presence in such an intimate setting.[98] As the situation

91 WM, 2.701.

92 TF, 477.

93 Villehardouin, 2.124.

94 WT, 651. La Monte, 'The Lords of le Puiset on Crusade', 102–4.

95 Riley-Smith, *First Crusaders*, 172.

96 WT, 651. This was Albert of Namur, lord of Jaffa.

97 See Geldsetzer, *Frauen*, 213–15.

98 Joinville, 216–18.

worsened, the queen asked the knight to cut off her head rather than let her be captured. The child was born safely, but Margaret had to break the traditional confinement in order to persuade the Italians in the city not to flee. She begged them to take pity on her poor weak child and wait for her to recover, and in return she would arrange the feeding of the army. She was successful, but in the end she had little time to convalesce before the city was surrendered.[99] Margaret is usually characterised as a wife rather than a mother throughout Joinville's history, and in this case her duties as Louis' queen even transcended the traditions surrounding motherhood. However, Joinville evidently thought it more conceivable that she would appeal to the Italian contingent to stay through her vulnerability as a mother rather than her diplomatic power as queen of France. Despite the restrictions on sexual activity for the common host, noblewomen and queens like Margaret were seldom criticised for having children while on crusade: they were fulfilling what was seen to be an essential duty, the provision of heirs.

Muslim mothers appeared rarely in the narratives of crusading, and few of these limited references touch on the subject of childbirth. For the most part, like other women, they were associated with the spoils of war. Some authors denigrated their enemies by suggesting that Muslim women had irreverent attitudes towards pregnancy and motherhood. Both Fulcher of Chartres and Guibert of Nogent recorded that women were killed at Caesarea because they were believed to be perverting their maternal capacity by hiding bezants in their wombs. This description may, however, have been influenced by the work of Flavius Josephus.[100] Guibert recorded how women were brought to Antioch by the Turkish army specifically for breeding purposes, but fled when Kerbogha lost the battle, leaving their newborn babies to be found by the crusaders, more concerned for themselves than their children.[101] William of Tyre, however, recounted a legendary tale about Baldwin i's capture of the wife of a powerful Saracen noble. She was heavily pregnant, and he treated her courteously, leaving her to be found by her husband with food and water, a maid to assist her, two camels, and his own cloak. A universal respect for motherhood was, in this case, seen to transcend the boundaries of religion, at least for 'a woman of such high rank'.[102]

While there were few detailed references to the act of childbirth itself, the imagery associated with it was sometimes applied to the crusaders and their enemies. Chroniclers often compared the sounds of suffering or dismay to the cry of a woman in labour, drawing on imagery from biblical sources such

99   Joinville, 218.

100   FC, 404; GN, 347. See FC, 404 n. 21, for other versions.

101   GN, 225.

102   WT, 464.

as Jeremiah and Isaiah.[103] Thus Robert of Rheims described the sorrow of Turkish troops at the death of a Turkish emir: 'a trembling seized them, here there was sorrow as if from a woman in labour, and there was a cry of lamentation'.[104] Joinville described the noise made by sick soldiers during Louis ix's crusade, as barber-surgeons cut away rotting flesh from their gums. He recounts that 'it was pitiful to hear around the camp the cries of those whose dead flesh was being cut away; it was just like the cry of a woman in labour'.[105] Whether authors drew from personal experience or borrowed from biblical sources they demonstrated awareness and even sympathy for the physical suffering that childbirth entailed.[106] Guibert, conscious of his own mother's experience, used the analogy of relief after the pain of childbirth to describe the First Crusaders' approach to the Holy Sepulchre in Jerusalem.

> Omnipotent God, what intimate feelings, what happiness, what grief they felt there, when after things unheard of and never experienced by an army from any age, like the tortures of birth, they saw themselves to have reached the new joys of their desired vision, just as if new-born children![107]

Ecclesiastical imagery often focused on the maternal or 'mothering' qualities of the Church.[108] Fulcher of Chartres described the institution as: 'our mother of course, by whose milk we were reared, from whose training and example we benefited, and by whose advice we were protected'.[109] In his account of Pope Urban's speech at the Council of Clermont, Baudri of Bourgueil used maternal imagery to call for the defence of the eastern Church, which had given the West divine milk through the teachings of the evangelists.[110] William of Tyre was highly critical of the military orders, whom he considered arrogant and corrupted by wealth. He likened them to rebellious children, ungrateful to their mother, the Church.[111] In De Expugnatione Lyxbonensi, the bishop of Oporto used vivid imagery of the Church as a mother crying for help to persuade the crusaders not to press on to Jerusalem without first aiding the Iberian Church.

---

[103] See Isa 13:8 and 21:3, Ps 48:7, and especially Jer 4:31, 6:24, 22:23, 50:43. See also Jer 49:24: 'Damascus is undone, she is put to flight, trembling has seized on her: anguish and sorrows have taken her as a woman in labour.'

[104] RR, 787.

[105] Joinville, 166; trans. Shaw, 239.

[106] Leyser, Medieval Women, 124.

[107] GN, 282.

[108] See Jo Spreadbury, 'The Gender of the Church: The Female Image of Ecclesia in the Middle Ages', in Swanson, Gender and the Christian Religion, 93–103.

[109] FC, 152.

[110] BB, 14.

[111] WT, 818.

To you the mother church, as it were with her arms cut off and her face disfigured, appeals for help; she seeks vengeance at your hands for the blood of her sons. She calls to you, verily, she cries aloud. 'Execute vengeance upon the heathen and punishments upon the people' ... Therefore ... raise up the fallen and prostrate church of Spain; reclothe her soiled and disfigured form with the garments of joy and gladness ... Now, as worthy sons of the mother church, repel force and injury ...[112]

It was common practice in medieval literature to consider cities and countries as feminine, and where applicable maternal imagery was also used. Orderic Vitalis told how Urban II 'urged the children of Jerusalem to set out boldly to the rescue of their Holy Mother'.[113] After the capture of Tyre in 1124, Fulcher of Chartres exclaimed: 'Justly the mother Jerusalem is pleased with her daughter Tyre at whose right she sits crowned henceforth.'[114] Oliver of Paderborn described the captured city of Damietta on the Fifth Crusade as an adulterous wife who had returned to her husband, and would now bring forth Christian progeny to defend the faith in the city.[115] Guibert of Nogent recorded how Peter the Hermit was reprimanded by Bohemond for his desertion at Antioch:

When [France], the mother, after God, of virtue and constancy has sent forth men most pure all the way to this place, you, useless babbler and most corrupt of all people, you, she brought forth to her own disgrace and infamy, she had you and henceforth it was just as if she had birthed a monster.[116]

As well as institutions and places, the nurturing aspects of 'mothering' were used to describe the behaviour of men. Ambroise described Richard the Lionheart leading his fleet 'as the mother hen leads her chicks to food'.[117] Fulk v of Anjou was compared to Martha in his care for the kingdom of Jerusalem.[118] That most masculine of heroes, Tancred, was compared to a hunting lioness abandoning its prey on realising its young were under threat, and later to a tigress who has

---

[112]   DEL, 79. See Susanna Throop, 'Vengeance and the Crusades', *Crusades* 5 (2006), 21–38, for comparable examples on the theme of vengeance. She refers to this passage, but does not comment on its gendered aspects.

[113]   OV, 5.19.

[114]   FC, 737.

[115]   '... and you who first conceived bastards, will henceforth bear legitimate sons to the faith of the son of God, firmly possessed by the doctrines of Christ.' Oliver of Paderborn, 'Historia Damiatina', in Hermann Hoogeweg ed. *Die Schriften des Kölner Domscholasters, späteren Bishofs von Paderborn und Kardinal Bischifs von S. Sabina* (Tübingen, 1894), 229.

[116]   GN, 181.

[117]   Ambroise, 1.20, lns 1245–6; trans. 2.48. See also *Itinerarium*, 179.

[118]   WT, 637.

just given birth.[119] These examples demonstrate that there was a strong sense of maternal identity which, even when not applied to actual mothers, can shed light on perceptions of motherhood and the concept of 'mothering'. Descriptions of the nurturing and protective activities of mothers demonstrate that medieval authors expected strong personal bonds to exist within parent–child relationships, and that women had a role in providing wisdom, moral guidance and protecting their families, to an extent. Mothers deserved to be treated with respect, but as women they were also vulnerable, and could be betrayed by ungrateful children, and corrupted or debased at the hands of an enemy.

MOTHERS AND EDUCATION

> The monastic rule did not teach you this,
> Nor the woman who gave you birth ...[120]

So Guibert of Nogent upheld the value of mothers as moral instructors when he chastised Peter the Hermit for leaving the monastic life to go on crusade – and for his immoderate eating. The mothers who were praised in narratives of crusading for educating their children well were invariably involved in their religious education. Adela of Blois was praised by Orderic Vitalis because she 'carefully brought up her young sons to defend the Church'.[121] He wrote of Constance, mother of Bohemond II of Antioch, that she looked after him 'as a mother should' until he came of age, although she anxiously prevented him from taking up his inheritance until Baldwin II had been released from prison.[122] Joinville accredited Blanche of Castille with the spiritual training of her son, Louis IX:

> As for his soul. God kept it from harm through the good instruction he received from his mother, who taught him both to believe in God and to love him, and brought her son up in the company of religious minded people. Child as he was, she made him recite all the Hours, and listen to sermons on days of high festival. He always remembered how she would sometimes tell him that she would rather he were dead than guilty of committing a mortal sin.[123]

Blanche was renowned for her strict piety, and Joinville seems to have held her in great esteem, but there is evidence to suggest that he may have considered

---

[119] He was described as a lioness when his troops were threatened by Byzantines at the crossing of the river Vardar, and likened to a tigress in his speed crossing Bythnia. GT, 608–9, 630.

[120] GN, 180.

[121] OV, 6.42–3.

[122] Ibid., 6.132–5.

[123] Joinville, 40–2; trans. Shaw, 181–2.

her approach too harsh and overbearing.[124] This did not preclude a loving relationship between a royal mother and her children, however. The 'Templar of Tyre' told how the mother of Conradin, grandson of Emperor Frederick II, feared that her child would be poisoned, and brought him up with twelve children of identical age, showing them 'equal affection'.[125] Blanche kissed the son of St Elizabeth of Thuringia on the forehead assuming that his mother must have done so many times. This suggests that she too offered physical demonstrations of affection to her own children. Louis' reaction to her death implied genuine fondness for his mother, although Joinville thought his behaviour rather excessive.[126] In any case, he believed that it was through Blanche's instruction and nurture that Louis gained the moral framework which later enabled him to become a saint.

Another mother who was given credit for the pious achievements of her sons was Ida of Lorraine. Ralph of Caen praised both the secular and divine virtues of Godfrey of Bouillon, attributing the latter to his mother: 'in his eagerness for war look to the father, in his cultivation of God behold the mother'.[127] Guibert of Nogent described her as a learned Lotharingian aristocrat, most remarkable for her innate serenity and devotion to God. He attributed the success of her three crusading sons, Godfrey, Baldwin and Eustace, to her piety and nurturing skills:

> The rewards of her sons were due, so we believe, to her remarkable long-standing religious commitment … These three, not in any way departing from their mother in honesty, were distinguished by many glorious deeds of arms and at the same time not lacking in modesty. The glorious woman was wont, when she wondered about the end of that journey and her own sons' fortune, to tell how she had heard a prediction from her son the duke's mouth, something made a long time before the start of that pilgrimage.[128]

Honesty was evidently seen as another key characteristic that mothers could impart to their sons: Joinville asserted that he knew his father's name was Simon because he had his mother's testimony, and believed it unquestioningly.[129] Ida's prediction, however, became a staple feature of later fictional literature about Godfrey of Bouillon, and was included in William of Tyre's history:

> The mother of these great princes was a religious and saintly woman pleasing to God, and while they were still of tender years, filled with

[124]   For example in her interference with Louis' marriage. See 178–9 below.

[125]   *Les Gestes des Chiprois*, 739–40.

[126]   See 179 below.

[127]   GT, 615; trans. Bachrach and Bachrach, 37.

[128]   GN, 129.

[129]   Joinville, 26.

divine spirit, she foresaw the future circumstances and the station which was being prepared for them in adulthood, just like something predicted by an oracle. Now, one time, while they were playing together around their mother, in the manner of children, and provoking each other in turn they often took refuge in her lap, and having hidden under her cloak, it so happened that their father Count Eustace came in, a man of great renown. When they were challenging each other and brandishing their hands and feet, which had been covered by the cloak worn by their mother, the count asked what it was that was stirring so often under there. It is said that she made this response: 'Three princes of great power, of whom the first will become a duke, the second a king, and the third a count.' This prophecy was implemented afterwards by the kind order of divine mercy, and subsequent events declared the truth of the things the mother predicted.[130]

William here presents a rather cosy vignette of domestic life intruded upon by divine prophecy. Godfrey first became duke of Lorraine through his maternal uncle, then king of Jerusalem; he was followed on the throne by his brother Baldwin, and Eustace became count of Boulogne, thus Ida's prediction was believed to have had merit. This story was but one of many legends surrounding Godfrey and his brothers. It is interesting that William chose to accept the veracity of this one while criticising others for promoting the legend that Godfrey was descended from a swan.[131] Such predictions were not unique in crusade narratives. Guibert of Nogent referred to the mother of the Byzantine emperor Alexius as a 'sorceress' who predicted that a man of Frankish origin (whom Guibert considered to be Bohemond) would take her son's life and empire.[132] The minstrel of Rheims suggested that Blanche of Castille knew, on the departure of Louis IX on crusade that she would never see him again.[133] The maternal role imbued women with a kind of innate spiritual knowledge which differed from male learning or scholarship, especially when it coincided with events that were perceived to be divinely ordained, as the example of Kerbogha's mother will demonstrate further.

REGENCY AND MATERNAL AUTHORITY

Crusading and Maternal Power

Of those who acted as regents for *crucesignati* in the West, relatively few mothers are mentioned in the narratives of crusading, unless the historical events with which they were associated affected an expedition. One of the main exceptions

---

130 WT, 427.

131 *Ibid.*, 427.

132 GN, 105–6.

133 *Récits d'un ménéstral de Rheims*, 192. See 177 below.

was Blanche of Castille, perhaps again because of Joinville's female patron.[134] When she took on the regency during Louis IX's crusade she had many years of administrative experience: her husband Louis VIII had died in 1226, leaving her in charge of the twelve-year-old heir to the throne. Even though she was a 'foreigner', 'with neither relations nor friends in the whole kingdom of France',[135] care of the kingdom had fallen to her purely by virtue of her maternal role. Blanche was in fact in quite an unusual position during Louis IX's minority. The powers bequeathed to her as regent by her late husband Louis VIII were in theory almost absolute, considering that she did not have to abide by any coronation oaths.[136] Blanche continued to play a role in Louis IX's government even after he reached his majority. Joinville consistently emphasised Blanche's piety and love for her son, reflecting the high moral standards required to justify women holding power, and perhaps to deflect criticism of the authority she commanded over Louis.

Female regency in Capetian France was not markedly unusual, although the first queen to act as regent for a son on crusade was Adela of Champagne, Philip II's mother. Evidently, Eleanor of Aquitaine was unable to act as a regent during the Second Crusade as she accompanied her husband. Had she remained, her involvement in the conflict between Louis VII and Thibaut IV of Blois in the early 1140s might have made her a controversial choice to hold political power in the king's absence. It is notable, however, that Louis did not entrust the kingdom to his mother either. Adelaide of Maurienne was passed over in favour of his friend and adviser Abbot Suger of Saint-Denis.[137]

Poulet asserts that there was no set pattern to regency in France, but mothers were more likely to be regents for minor sons than wives were for absent husbands. Louis IX was evidently satisfied with Blanche's capabilities during his minority, or he would not have entrusted her once more with the kingdom when he embarked on crusade in 1248. He did not, however, grant Margaret of Provence the same authority when he departed on crusade for a second time in 1270, but rather designated a co-regency under Simon of Nesle and Matthew of Vendôme. Poulet suggests that Margaret's son Philip III also excluded her from legislation, as an 'intriguing and authoritarian parent'.[138] She supposedly made her son Philip swear an oath to hold France under her wardship until he was thirty. On hearing this, Louis immediately got a papal dispensation to release his son from the oath.[139] This left Margaret open to criticism for abusing her position as a mother to protect her family's interests in Provence, rather

---

[134] See 37 above.

[135] Joinville, 42; trans. Shaw, 182.

[136] Poulet, 'Capetian Women', 109.

[137] See Grant, *Abbot Suger of Saint Denis*, 142–78 for Suger's role as regent.

[138] *Ibid.*, 110.

[139] Labarge, *Women in Medieval Life*, 59.

than acting in the interests of her son. As a result, she was excluded from a position of power as both a wife and a mother.

Shadis has recently emphasised the importance of Blanche of Castille's politicised activity even before she became a widow, and the significance of motherhood in providing her with her privileged position as regent.[140] Blanche was a successful regent, as long as she maintained a devout and disinterested image by emphasising that she ruled for the benefit of her son and only took up the reins of power reluctantly. Although a pious woman, the sources for Louis IX's crusade largely agree that she disapproved of his decision to take the cross. Joinville asserted that when she heard the news, 'she mourned as much as if she had seen him lying dead'.[141] The minstrel of Rheims asserted that Blanche accompanied Louis for three days on the journey from Saint-Denis, against his will. After hearing the farewells of her son, the queen replied in tears:

'My own very sweet son, how will it be that my heart can endure the parting between you and me? Truly it will be harder than stone if it does not split in two pieces, for you have been the best son to me that any mother ever had.'[142]

Matthew Paris attributed a more political motive to Blanche's attempts to persuade Louis to stay. He included her in a faction of other magnates and councillors trying to dissuade the king from the enterprise:

But his mother had more effect on him, amplifying her emotional words, saying: 'Dearest son! Listen and hearken to the counsels of your distinguished friends, without relying on your wisdom alone. Remember what a virtue it is, and how much it pleases God, to obey your mother and to follow her implicitly. Remain behind, and thereupon the Holy Land will suffer no detriment. A military expedition of [far] greater numbers could be sent there than if you had gone to that place in person. For God does not lay blame unjustly, nor does he mock. You are excused, my son, sufficiently, by what your illness did to you …'[143]

Louis was affected by his mother's plea, and initially he laid down his cross, but promptly took it up again so that he could prove his decision was not just a result of illness.[144] Blanche had given practical reasons why he should not go, but reminded him that he had a religious duty to obey her. She used a combination of advice and her authority as a mother to compel Louis to stay,

---

[140] Miriam Shadis, 'Blanche of Castile and Facinger's "Medieval Queenship"', in Nolan, *Capetian Women*, 137–61.

[141] Joinville, 62; trans. Shaw, 191.

[142] *Récits d'un ménéstral de Rheims*, 191.

[143] MP, 5.4.

[144] *Ibid.*

but ultimately he followed his own counsel. Not every source gave Blanche such precedence, however. The Acre continuation of William of Tyre placed Louis' entire family – his mother, wife and brothers – at his sick-bed, grieving and expecting him to die, and together they tried to persuade him to put aside the cross.[145] For some authors, Blanche may simply have been cast in the traditional role of female 'inhibitor'– a woman in genuine fear for her son's life. Matthew Paris, however, suggests that she and other advisers had sound political reasons for discouraging him, and were prompted by concern for the security of the kingdom upon which Louis had only recently established firm authority.[146]

Although Blanche played an important role in raising funds for her son while he was on crusade, and dealt with popular unrest, characterised by the 'Crusade of the Shepherds' in 1251, neither of these activities found their way into Joinville's narrative.[147] He did recount that the king received a letter from her when he was freed from captivity and arrived at Acre, in which she begged him to return. She was concerned about a grave threat to the security of the realm posed by King Henry III of England.[148] The fact that Louis decided to stay in the East despite the problems besetting his mother is a testament to his faith in her abilities as a ruler, although he did send his brothers home.[149] It was only when news arrived of her death, in the summer of 1253 (she died in November 1252), that Louis recognised that he would soon have to return.

Joinville expressed surprise at the grief of Queen Margaret on hearing the news. The author himself was called in to comfort her, and asked her why she was upset, 'for it is the woman who hated you most who is dead'.[150] Joinville detailed how Blanche had restricted Louis' access to his wife in the early days of their marriage; they had to arrange secret trysts when they lived at Pontoise.[151] At another time, when Blanche tried to extract her son from the bedside of his gravely ill wife, Margaret is said to have cried out: 'Alas! Whether I live or die, you will not let me see my husband!'[152] The dynamic between the two queens has been the subject of much scholarly interest: historians have debated whether it sprang from personal jealousy and rivalry, or whether there were

---

[145] *L'Estoire de Eracles Empereur*, 431–2.

[146] See Jean Richard, *Louis IX, Crusader King of France*, trans. Jean Birrell (Cambridge, 1992), 12–19, 41–61; and Sivery, *Blanche*, 229–43.

[147] See William C. Jordan, *Louis IX and the Challenge of the Crusade* (Princeton, 1979), 105–16.

[148] Joinville, 229.

[149] Joinville asserts that he said to his barons: 'I have come to the opinion that if I stay there will be no danger of losing my realm, since the Queen Mother has people enough to defend it.' Joinville, 238; trans. Shaw, 272.

[150] Joinville, 332.

[151] *Ibid.*

[152] *Ibid.*; trans. Shaw, 316.

more fundamental political issues at stake.[153] Joinville focused strictly on the personal relationship between the two, and although he may have sympathised with Margaret's exclusion from her husband's political life, he never suggested that Blanche was not entitled to her position or abused her authority. While Joinville comforted her, Margaret described her sorrow at Blanche's death as a reaction to her husband's grief and fear for her daughter in France, which demonstrated proper wifely and motherly behaviour.

Louis himself was very upset at his mother's death – Joinville asserts that he spoke to no one for two whole days, organised many services for her in the Holy Land, and sent a chest full of letters to various ecclesiastical establishments to pray for her soul.[154] In a similar vein, King Baldwin III of Jerusalem, despite considerable conflict with his mother Melisende, was described as terribly upset at her death: 'how much he had sincerely esteemed her is borne witness by these verifiable proofs as he gave himself to lamentation and would receive no consolation for many days hence'.[155]

It was with a note of sadness that William of Tyre described the last debilitating illness of Queen Melisende. He reiterated how well she had ruled the kingdom, but 'after losing her memory for some time, her body nearly consumed', she had taken to her deathbed.[156] In a touching account, he described how her sisters Hodierna and Yveta, two of the most powerful noblewomen in the Levant, cared for her assiduously in her last days, and few others were allowed to see her.

It was only Joinville, who was close to the king, who recorded Louis' grief at his mother's death. Blanche of Castille had little impact in general on the Rothelin continuation, and the Acre text referred to her death only briefly, without recording Louis' reaction.[157] The relationship between mother and son presented by Joinville has led Jordan to suggest that Louis' crusade was part of a 'broader "commitment" to the integrity of his own selfhood' in terms of liberating himself both personally and politically from his overbearing mother, but this seems rather excessive.[158] It is true that he left her with fewer powers than she had during her first period of regency – he took his seal with him, and his own curia was very active while he was on crusade.[159] However, it was Blanche's proven trustworthiness and ability which enabled him to undertake the crusade he desired, and he obviously had no fears about ambitions on her

---

153 For recent accounts, see Sivery, *Blanche*, 203–16; and McCannon, 'Two Capetian Queens', 163–76.

154 Joinville, 330.

155 WT, 858.

156 *Ibid.*, 851.

157 *L'Estoire de Eracles Empereur*, 440.

158 Jordan, *Louis IX*, 3.

159 Sivery, *Blanche*, 230, 232.

own behalf. Perhaps it was the way he had managed to maintain a harmonious power balance with his mother that made him peculiarly well qualified to mediate in the dispute between the sixteen-year-old Bohemond vi of Antioch-Tripoli and his mother, Lucienne of Segni, who was unwilling to give up the regency to her son. Both of them visited the king during his stay at Acre, and Louis fulfilled the traditional role of a western king by adjudicating between them, although Joinville makes it clear on whose side his sympathies lay. The young Bohemond reportedly recognised that he ought to remain under her guardianship for a further four years but he accused his mother of squandering his inheritance.[160] Whether this was through poor judgement or malice is open to question. Louis responded by providing military aid to the young Bohemond, and helping to persuade his mother to relinquish some of her power.[161]

Eleanor of Aquitaine, like Blanche, was perceived as an authoritarian and politically active mother, but because of the reputation she had developed as a wife and a divorcee she could not employ the shield of piety and chaste widowhood to deflect criticism so effectively. As a mother, she has been accused of neglect and favouritism when it came to her children, especially because she left behind two daughters when she divorced Louis vii. They remained in the custody of their father, and William of Newburgh asserts that they were married 'by paternal provision' to men of Louis' choice.[162] However, this was not unusual for the time, as daughters of royal blood were highly valuable commodities. It has been shown that Eleanor did on occasion take her children with her on difficult and dangerous journeys, suggesting that she desired their company.[163] Eleanor had also been involved in a serious revolt against her husband Henry ii with her sons in 1173, for which she had been imprisoned, but Richard's succession to the throne brought her freedom, and his decision to take the cross afforded her the opportunity to return to political life. Ralph of Diceto portrayed Richard as overly obedient to his mother's wishes as a result.[164]

Eracles left his audience in no doubt as to who was responsible for King Richard breaking his marriage agreement with Alice of France. Eleanor was allegedly furious when she found out that the marriage had been arranged, especially with the daughter of her hated ex-husband, and actively went out

---

[160] '... the city of Antioch is being ruined in her hands.' Joinville, 286; trans. Shaw, 296.

[161] Joinville, 286. Jordan also considers this friendship significant. Jordan, *Louis IX*, 12, 132.

[162] WN, I.93.

[163] RáGena C. DeAragon, 'Wife, Widow, and Mother: Some Comparisons between Eleanor of Aquitaine and Noblewomen of the Anglo-Norman and Angevin World', in Wheeler and Parsons, *Eleanor of Aquitaine, Lord and Lady*, 102–3.

[164] Ralph of Diceto, 'Ymagines Historiarum', 2.67–8.

of her way to prevent the union.[165] According to *Eracles* she then took it upon herself to negotiate a match with the king of Navarre for one of his daughters. Richard showed little reaction or remorse for breaking his agreement with Alice – apparently 'the king was thrilled by this proposition'.[166] If we are to believe *Eracles*' version of events, it is surprising that Eleanor did not act sooner as Richard and Alice were engaged for around twenty-five years, and seeing that Philip's sister was at the Angevin court and rumoured by some to be Henry II's mistress it is unlikely that she was ignorant of the match until she escaped confinement. This perception of Eleanor as a domineering mother has led to some historians considering Richard to be 'an irresponsible crusader, indifferent to important matters of politics like securing the succession to the throne'.[167] Coupled with speculations about his homosexuality, he has been considered a reluctant bridegroom whom Eleanor forced to marry. In fact, Gillingham argues that there is 'not a shred of evidence' that Eleanor conducted the negotiations.[168] He suggests that Richard had arranged the marriage himself before his departure: he needed Berengaria's dowry quickly to help fund his crusade venture, and an alliance with her father King Sancho VI to protect his southern lands. The negotiations had only been held up because of Richard's previous commitment to Alice.[169] Both Ambroise and the *Itinerarium* simply interpreted Eleanor's role as that of an escort.[170]

Mothers and Regency in the Latin East

A key factor in achieving approbated maternal influence was that a mother had to act in the best interests of her child. Princess Alice of Antioch was portrayed not only as an unruly daughter but also as a bad mother. William of Tyre criticised Alice's lack of regard for her own child, and for excluding Constance from her plans 'so that having disinherited her daughter, she could seize control of the principality for herself in perpetuity, whether remaining in widowhood or moving on to a second marriage'.[171] Alice seems to have believed that she had a genuine claim to power in Antioch, as the widow of Bohemond II and mother of the legitimate heir, but William considered her an unpopular ruler because of her sex: 'For in that very city there were God-fearing men, contemptuous

---

[165] It is impossible that Eleanor was unaware of the match with Alice, which was arranged in 1169, before her imprisonment.

[166] *Eracles*, III.

[167] Gillingham, 'Richard I and Berengaria', 120.

[168] *Ibid.*, 122.

[169] John Gillingham, 'Some Legends of Richard the Lionheart: Their Development and their Influence', in Janet L. Nelson ed. *Richard Coeur de Lion in History and Myth* (Exeter, 1992), 61–6.

[170] Ambroise, 1.19, lns 1143–5. *Itinerarium*, 175.

[171] WT, 624; see also WT, 635.

of the impudence and foolishness of a woman.'[172] The kings of Jerusalem also considered Alice unsuitable for political authority, as Baldwin II and later Fulk v of Anjou both took on the post of regent over Antioch rather than delegating to her. However, other women in the Latin East acted as regents, so it seems unlikely that Alice's sex alone was the cause of her exclusion from power. It is only on William's authority that we hear that Alice was deliberately trying to disinherit her daughter.[173] Asbridge argues that there is a lack of supporting evidence to suggest that this was indeed Alice's intention, especially as there are questions about William's reliability for the period in which these events occurred.[174] She may have simply been asserting control over the regency, which she considered to be her legal right as a mother. William suggested a further reason – that Alice desired to make the best possible second marriage for herself.[175] This may have been true, but did not necessarily mean she was motivated by greed. A good marriage could also have bolstered her position as regent, and helped to provide security for her daughter's principality whose future had been uncertain since the death of Prince Roger in 1119.

Cahen has argued that the Antiochenes opposed female regencies, although there was probably no legal restraint on women ruling on behalf of minors in Antioch at that time.[176] This judgement is largely based on the political experiences of Alice and Constance, as the two most prominent widows in Antioch during the twelfth century, but it is possible that age and experience, as well as gender, were the factors which conspired to exclude them from power. Alice's parents had married shortly before her father's captivity in 1103, and she was their second child. She had married Bohemond II in 1126, at which time she was presumably at least twelve and not more than twenty-one; thus she was unlikely to have been older than her mid-twenties in 1130, with only four years in a public position in the principality. In terms of experience she contrasted strongly with her sister Melisende, who had ruled jointly with her husband and son for twelve years before becoming regent in her thirties, as well as being an heiress in her own right. The age of their children may also have been signifi-cant – Constance was two on her father's death, which meant a considerable period of regency would ensue, whereas Baldwin III was thirteen, and was to come of age (officially at least) in two years' time. When Constance herself was widowed on the death of Raymond of Poitiers at the battle of Inab in 1149, her children were young. Baldwin III decided to involve Patriarch Aimery of Antioch in the rule of the principality, possibly because of the length of

---

172   *Ibid.*, 624.

173   *Ibid.*.

174   Asbridge, 'Alice of Antioch', 29–47. He also notes that the question of female regency in Antioch was 'untested' at this time.

175   See 220–1 below.

176   Cahen, *La Syrie du Nord*, 440. See also Phillips, *Defenders*, 47.

time Antioch would be without male leadership while waiting for an heir to succeed:

> For the wife of the prince, Constance, with two sons and as many daughters still underage, had been left alone to deal with public affairs and the administration of the principality, neither was there anyone to perform the duties of a prince and raise the people from despair.[177]

Constance had the same number of male children as Melisende on widowhood, but they were much younger.[178] As a result, we are told, Patriarch Aimery came forward as a protector, and William paid particular attention to his liberal use of wealth.[179] Aimery may have assumed the position as a result of his ability to provide necessary resources and finance, but as a member of the secular clergy he could not act in that all-important military capacity required of a lay ruler. It was probably also significant that Constance was only twenty-two and possibly perceived as too young for the responsibility; the past actions of her mother may also have weighed against her. For the immediate aftermath of Inab, Baldwin III assumed the official responsibility for the military protection of Antioch, but after setting affairs in order he returned to Jerusalem. At that point, he and the people of Antioch were seemingly content to leave Constance nominally in charge, with the support of Aimery, although soon afterwards he encouraged her to remarry.[180]

The current political situation was also important when considering whether to entrust power to a female regent, although in a frontier society like the Latin East there was always a heightened degree of vulnerability. Antioch's situation in the 1150s after the fall of Edessa and battle of Inab was much worse than the circumstances of the kingdom of Jerusalem on the death of Fulk V of Anjou in 1143. The newly unified Muslim threat in the North required military support which could not be provided effectively by an already over-stretched king. Antioch's need for a dynamic military ruler was more acute, hence the pressure upon Constance to remarry.

Alice of Antioch's husband had also died unexpectedly in battle, but it was probably her choice of allies that most perturbed the kings of Jerusalem when it came to the issue of her regency. In the 1130 attempt to seize power, Asbridge notes that important men of Antioch such as the constable, Renaud Masoir, and the patriarch, Bernard, did not appear in the list of nobles supporting the king, and may have supported Alice, although it was Renaud who ended up with the official position of regent in

---

[177] WT, 773.

[178] The heir, Bohemond III, was five when his father died.

[179] WT, 773.

[180] Ibid., 774. Perhaps he was unable to discuss her remarriage at that point because she was entitled to a year's mourning.

1132.[181] Apparently Alice even intended to approach the Turkish ruler Zengi, who had recently come to power in Aleppo, for aid, in order to gain Antioch for herself in perpetuity and to make her position more secure.[182] There is no corroborative evidence in Muslim sources to suggest that this accusation is true,[183] but there were examples of female rulers negotiating with Muslims in times of hardship. Melisende of Jerusalem and her son communicated with Unur of Damascus, and in the thirteenth century Isabella of Ibelin, the lady of Beirut, concluded a treaty with Sultan Baybars.[184] In particular, after Baldwin II's death, disillusionment with the rule of Fulk of Anjou meant that Alice became a rallying point for nobles dissatisfied with the new king, and her powerful accomplices included Count Pons of Tripoli, Count Joscelin II of Edessa and William, lord of Saone and Zardana.[185] She also attracted the rebels Hugh II, count of Jaffa, and Ralph of la Fontanelle to her court at Latakia in 1134.[186]

Hugh's revolt was evidence of discontent with Fulk as a ruler, but some of his problems may have been inherited from Baldwin II.[187] The exact authority of the kings of Jerusalem over principalities such as Antioch and Tripoli was still questioned, and Baldwin's policy of dynastic marriages for his daughters may have caused some concern about royal intentions. Although William of Tyre claimed that Alice had bribed him for support, Pons of Tripoli had long been concerned about the king's growing power, as he had tried to refuse Baldwin II feudal service in 1122, an act that almost led to military conflict.[188] It is not surprising, therefore, that after Baldwin II's death both the new ruler of Edessa, Joscelin II, and Pons took the opportunity provided by Alice to resist his successor, Fulk. The new king had to assert his authority first by military means, and then he was able to use the relatively weak position of Antioch to choose a suitor for Constance, Raymond of Poitiers.[189] In 1135, before Raymond's arrival, Alice had taken control of the city for a third time, and she went unopposed for a while, perhaps because of support from the new and controversial Patriarch Ralph, or the aftermath of Fulk's political difficulties in Jerusalem. The king

---

[181] Asbridge, 'Alice of Antioch', 34.

[182] WT, 623–4.

[183] Asbridge, 'Alice of Antioch', 34–5.

[184] See Mayer, 'Queen Melisende', 122–4; and Peter M. Holt, 'Baybars' Treaty with the Lady of Beirut in 667/1269', in Edbury, Crusade and Settlement, 242.

[185] WT, 636.

[186] Murray, 'Baldwin II and his Nobles', 82–3. On the basis of these visits, Asbridge argues that the date of Hugh's rebellion may have been earlier than previously thought. Asbridge, 'Alice of Antioch', 43.

[187] This was evidenced by the concern of the nobles of Jerusalem that the king was wasting too many of their resources in northern Syria, as well as the offer of the throne to Charles the Good. See Alan V. Murray, 'Baldwin II and his Nobles', 60–85.

[188] WT, 566, 636.

[189] Phillips, Defenders, 51–2.

may have been unwilling to damage the fragile reconciliation with his wife and her entourage by taking action, as William asserted that Queen Melisende supported her sister.[190] Alice also had the support of certain unnamed nobles, and once more the constable and acting regent of the city, Renaud Masoir, appears to have offered no resistance.[191] Her success was short-lived, however, as Raymond arrived and married Constance in the following year.[192] It was this marriage that eventually overturned Alice's hold on the city, as her claim to power came through regency, rather than inheritance.

William's portrayal of Alice as a devious and disruptive force in the politics of the Latin East contrasts sharply with his depiction of her sister Melisende, who participated in a civil war against her own son, Baldwin III of Jerusalem, in 1152. One might have expected severe criticism for a mother who encroached upon her son's patrimony in such a self-interested fashion; however, Melisende's capacity for administration and her right to govern were above question in William's history. This was partly because of her rights as an heiress: he emphasised that she was crowned jointly with her son.[193] He also praised her ability and, crucially, her experience:

> There was, however, his mother, a most prudent woman, having much experience in almost all worldly affairs, clearly transcending the nature of the female sex, so that she could put her hand to strong things, and strive to emulate the glory of the most magnificent princes, and follow in their endeavours without false steps. As the designated heir was still young in age, she ruled the kingdom with so much hard work, and managed affairs with such control she was said to equal her forefathers in merit for her part; and for as long as her son desired to be ruled by her counsel, the people enjoyed a longed-for tranquillity, and the business of the realm progressed with prosperity.[194]

Evidently William considered the rule of an experienced regent preferable to that of an untried youth. It is also significant that he associated Melisende's rule with peace, although she had to cope with crises such as the fall of Edessa in 1144, and the failed attack on Damascus in 1148. Her experiences as queen during the reign of Fulk had prepared her well for the intricacies of regency politics, but she had to rely on her constable, Manasses of Hierges, for military

---

190 WT, 658.

191 Asbridge, 'Alice of Antioch', 44.

192 See 220–1 below.

193 In contrast, the French translator of William of Tyre suggested that the king was crowned with his mother because the young king was as yet unmarried. 'L'Estoire de Eracles Empereur', in RHC Occ. 1.707.

194 WT, 717; see also WT, 761, for Melisende as an equal of princes at the Council of Palmarea in 1148.

leadership. Baldwin III, despite his youth, embarked on a military career soon after his father's death, but with mixed results. He had achieved some success at Wadi Musa in 1144, but met with abject failure in the Haurān region in 1147, and it has been suggested that Melisende deliberately used these to exclude her son from power, resulting in civil war.[195] William of Tyre, on the other hand, blamed the dispute on the arrogance of Manasses of Hierges and on certain nobles (probably the Ibelins) who had inflamed Baldwin against his mother.[196] These nobles argued that having come of age 'it was shameful that he should be ruled by female judgement,' 'declaring it to be unseemly that the king, who ought to rule all others, always hung from his mother's teat like the son of a commoner'.[197]

Melisende was restricted to Nablus, and her vassals refused Baldwin's summons as a king. William of Tyre's chronology becomes rather confused during this period; he asserts that this event occurred after the civil war, but Mayer argues that it happened in 1150, and was in fact the main precipitant of the war. In his view, Melisende was squeezing Baldwin out of power, effectively creating a separate court for herself with her own administration, much as Alice of Antioch had after 1132 at Latakia.[198] Crucial acts of patronage included the queen's gift of the county of Jaffa to her younger son Amalric in 1150, which might suggest that she was grooming him as a supporter,[199] and the lordship of Ramla and Mirabel to her cousin Manasses of Hierges through marriage to Helvis in 1151.[200]

Was Melisende a woman obsessed by retaining her own authority, applying the concept of 'divide et impera' even at the expense of both her sons' power? This is an image more in tune with William's perception of Alice of Antioch, and does seem rather excessive in its condemnation. It could be argued that Melisende saw Baldwin as unready for the demands of kingship: too inexperienced and inclined to take risks, evidenced by his earlier military failures. William of Tyre could have protected the reputation of Amalric by emphasising his patron's support for his 'wronged' mother without portraying him as a rebel: none of Melisende's followers were explicitly referred to as such. Mayer asserts that Baldwin was the better ruler once he had come of age, and that Melisende should have given way 'honourably and with dignity' but 'her thirst for power was greater than her wisdom'.[201] On the other hand, the fact that the Church and a considerable portion of the nobility initially supported her suggests that

---

[195] Mayer, 'Queen Melisende', 117–18, 124.

[196] WT, 777–8.

[197] Ibid., 778, 717.

[198] Asbridge, 'Alice of Antioch', 39–41.

[199] Mayer, 'Queen Melisende', 98, 124–5.

[200] Ibid., 163, 155.

[201] Ibid., 123, 122–5.

many of them shared her reservations about Baldwin III's ability, or at least his choice of supporters, who were undoubtedly an ambitious group.[202] Melisende was ultimately unsuccessful in retaining her inherited authority in the kingdom because she was a woman. It was inevitable that she had to step aside in favour of a male heir, and when matters reached a head her supporters recognised that her position was untenable; but this was not necessarily a comment on her ability as a ruler.

The conclusion of her joint rule did not end Melisende's political role in the kingdom. William of Tyre asserts that, in concert with her son, she attempted to persuade Princess Constance of Antioch to remarry, and to bring about a reconciliation between her sister Hodierna and Raymond II of Tripoli.[203] Mayer, however, asserts that this meeting of the *Haute Cour* took place in 1152 after Melisende's defeat, and it was in fact a demonstration of Baldwin III's success that he could force his mother and her supporters to participate.[204] Still, it is notable that Baldwin delegated to her in what was traditionally a more feminine field of politics, matrimonial negotiation. In 1153, with the capture of Ascalon, Baldwin III firmly established his military credentials and secured his position, but even then, William of Tyre asserts that he distributed the possessions and lands he had taken 'with the advice of his mother'.[205] Melisende was also involved in organising later military campaigns such as the capture of a fortress across the Jordan in 1157.[206] Both Melisende and her sister Hodierna were involved in the preparations for the marriage of Melisende of Tripoli in 1160, even though Baldwin's role as marriage broker proved unsuccessful.[207]

The civil war, in the view of William of Tyre, was a minor event, a temporary and unfortunate upheaval in an otherwise congenial relationship between mother and son. Edbury and Rowe suggest that it was William's respect for the authority given by consecration which made him support Melisende consistently, as he remained uncritical of queens such as Theodora and Maria Comnena, who were accused by others of acting unwisely or unjustly.[208] Lambert argues that 'Melisende was still defined by her relations with men, as wife, widow and mother, but her role as queen required her to transcend such gendered constraints', and that William emphasised her right to rule because of his own legal training and interest in the law.[209] The fact that Melisende was a

---

202 *Ibid.*, 143.

203 WT, 784–5.

204 Mayer, 'Queen Melisende', 161.

205 WT, 804.

206 *Ibid.*, 838.

207 *Ibid.*, 856. See 88–91 above.

208 Edbury and Rowe, *William of Tyre*, 65, 80–3.

209 Lambert, 'Queen or Consort', 157, 155.

particularly keen patron of the Church,[210] and praised by St Bernard of Clairvaux, may also have influenced William's opinion.

Agnes of Courtenay was not so fortunate. She came under severe criticism for wielding undue influence over her son, Baldwin IV of Jerusalem, and fomenting discord between the king and Raymond III of Tripoli.[211] A maternal regency was not possible for Baldwin IV because the marriage of his mother had been annulled, and therefore neither she nor the dowager queen Maria Comnena, who was his stepmother, had rights of regency.[212] In any case, if Agnes was an unacceptable queen-consort, whether because of bigamy or her political activities, there is no reason to suggest that she would ever have been officially recognised as a regent. When Baldwin IV inherited as a minor, no regent was chosen, but Miles of Plancy, the seneschal of the kingdom, looked after the government of the kingdom until his murder by the Brisebarres.[213] In the absence of a seneschal, Raymond of Tripoli became regent, but Agnes still exercised considerable patronage amongst the nobility and the Church through her position as the king's mother. In doing so she seems to have alienated many members of the Jerusalem baronage, and William of Tyre.[214] His bitterness towards Agnes over the patriarchal election is understandable, but he was significantly less scandalised when Melisende and her son overtly interfered with the election of the royal chancellor, Ralph, to the archbishopric of Tyre.[215]

Maria Comnena, the widow of King Amalric of Jerusalem, appears as another domineering mother, even though she never officially acted as a regent. She was seen as particularly influential in arranging the separation of her daughter Isabella from Humphrey of Toron, and her subsequent remarriage to Conrad of Monferrat. The *Eracles* continuation records that after being approached by Conrad, it was Maria who challenged the validity of Isabella's marriage, and advised her to leave Humphrey: 'This angered her mother, and she remonstrated with her repeatedly and explained that she could not become lady of the kingdom unless she left Humphrey.'[216] She also reminded Isabella of Humphrey's cowardice in not making a bid for the throne against Guy of Lusignan, and eventually Isabella consented to her mother's wishes. *Eracles* also suggested that Maria had a personal grudge against Humphrey because he hated her and tried to stop her from seeing her daughter after they married.

---

[210] See Boase, *Kingdoms and Strongholds*, 101–4.

[211] WT, 1019.

[212] Hamilton, *Leper King*, 84.

[213] See Bernard Hamilton, 'Miles of Plancy and the Fief of Beirut', in Kedar, *Horns of Hattin*, 136–46.

[214] Hamilton, 'Titular Nobility', 197–203.

[215] He was described as 'a man of considerable learning but far too worldly'. WT, 738–9.

[216] *Eracles*, 105; trans. Edbury, 95.

This was reputedly because 'he was acting on the advice of his own mother, Stephanie, the lady of Kerak', which added to Humphrey's image as a weak ruler.[217] Stephanie of Milly, heiress to the lordship of Oultrejourdain, was a powerful woman in her own right. It is entirely possible that Baldwin IV had taken the decision to marry Isabella to Humphrey in order to remove her from the influence of Maria Comena's new family, the Ibelins. In 1180, when the marriage was arranged, the succession to the throne seemed secure, as Sibylla had an infant son, and her new husband Guy had not yet fallen from grace, thus Isabella was more 'disposable'.[218]

Although *Eracles* was troubled by the legality of Isabella's divorce, Maria can still be seen to be acting in her daughter's best interests, encouraging her to inherit the kingdom of Jerusalem and to leave a husband who was a coward and prevented a mother from having access to her child. The author of *Itinerarium* was more candid in his criticism. Violently opposed to Conrad of Monferrat and Maria's second husband, Balian of Ibelin, he described Isabella's mother as godless, pliable, fraudulent and 'steeped in Greek filth from the cradle'.[219]

As problems with the succession to the kingdom of Jerusalem continued into the thirteenth century, inheritance through the maternal line became more common. In 1256 Bohemond VI of Antioch-Tripoli brought his sister Plaisance with her young son, Hugh II of Cyprus, to inherit the throne of Jerusalem.[220] Marriage to a mother who had the guardianship of a young heir could sometimes be as lucrative as marriage to an heiress, and accordingly Plaisance was married to a very powerful noble, Balian of Ibelin, son of John of Arsuf, in 1254.[221] Her regency was controversial, however, as her son's claim faced opposition. The Templars, barons, and Teutonic Knights supported Hugh along with the Venetians and Pisans, but the Hospitallers and the Genoese claimed that Hugh was not the true heir. They supported Conrad's son, as the grandson of Isabella II.[222] The marriage was dissolved in 1258 for the sake of peace between Bohemond and the lord of Arsuf, but Edbury suggests that the couple separated as early as mid-1255.[223] Although Bohemond has been seen as the instigator of this divorce, Edbury demonstrates that in fact during the time of the separation another marriage negotiation was underway between the two families; thus he argues that personal, rather than political, factors may have ultimately been responsible for the split.[224] Rothelin stipulates that the queen

[217] *Eracles*, 106; trans. Edbury, 96.

[218] Hamilton, *Leper King*, 161.

[219] *Itinerarium*, 121; trans. Nicholson, 123.

[220] *Les Gestes des Chiprois*, 742–4.

[221] *L'Estoire de Eracles Empereur*, 441.

[222] Rothelin, 634.

[223] *L'Estoire de Eracles Empereur*, 443. Edbury, *John of Ibelin*, 88.

[224] Edbury, *John of Ibelin*, 88–90.

then returned to Tripoli with her son and brother, the prince of Antioch, but power remained in the hands of John of Arsuf, who died shortly afterward. When Plaisance died on 22 September 1261, the regency of Cyprus passed to Hugh of Antioch-Lusignan.[225]

An Unusual Case Study: Kerbogha's Mother[226]

The conversation between Kerbogha and his mother in the Gesta Francorum stands out quite dramatically from the rest of the text both in style and content,[227] a fact which has in the past caused speculation that the passage was written by a collaborator on the Gesta rather than the same person.[228] Although crusade narratives occasionally portray women attempting to dissuade men from fighting, there are no distinct literary precedents for a Turkish woman attempting to prevent her own son from fighting on the basis of Christian supremacy. Kerbogha's mother occupies a significant portion of the text in those histories in which she appears; why, therefore, as a woman and a non-Christian is she given such attention? The conversation between mother and son has been described as 'camp gossip', and more recently as 'comic exchanges' to break up the text, with little or no historical value.[229] In fact, this passage deserves re-examination to determine how it fits into the Gesta and other crusade chronicles, and what it can tell us about contemporary attitudes to women, motherhood, and non-Christians.

Bearing in mind the connections between First Crusade histories,[230] it is unsurprising that certain key elements are shared in most versions of the story. Kerbogha's mother, on hearing that her son has besieged Antioch, comes to visit him from Aleppo, and begs him not to undertake battle with the Christians. While she does not doubt the prowess of her son, nor is she a Christian herself, she fears the God who fights on behalf of the Christians. Kerbogha

---

[225]   The Rothelin continuator makes no mention of an affair between Plaisance and John of Ibelin, count of Jaffa and Ascalon, which may have begun at this time. See 131 above. L'Estoire de Eracles Empereur, 443, 446.

[226]   An earlier version of this section was published as 'The Role of Kerbogha's Mother in the Gesta Francorum and Selected Chronicles of the First Crusade', in Edgington and Lambert, Gendering the Crusades, 163–76.

[227]   The conversation appears in GF, 323–30; RR, 811–14; GN, 212–16; PT, 93–6; BB, 62–4. Kerbogha's mother appears as 'Calabre' in the Chanson d'Antioche, 1.51–2, 1.268–9, 1.523–4. The passage does not appear in the version of Fulcher of Chartres or Raymond of Aguilers, nor in the later histories of Albert of Aachen, William of Tyre, Orderic Vitalis and William of Malmesbury.

[228]   Bréhier includes the speech of Kerbogha's mother in a list of suspect passages which he suggests could have been added to the original text. Histoire Anonyme de la Première Croisade, ed. Louis Bréhier (Paris, 1924), vi.

[229]   See Hill, Gesta, xvi; and August C. Krey, 'A Neglected Passage', 78 n. 47. See also Rubenstein, 'Who Wrote the Gesta Francorum', 198.

[230]   See 26–7 above.

does not initially believe her, thinking she is mad or possessed, because his forces outnumber the Franks.[231] She uses biblical quotations from David and the prophets to prove her case. Kerbogha then asks who has told her about the Christian people and their God, wanting to know the origins of her fears. She asserts that the movement of the stars has predicted the defeat and death of her son.[232] Kerbogha refuses to heed her advice and she returns disappointed to Aleppo, and, in the *Gesta* version, takes with her 'all the booty which she could assemble'.[233] Whether this was included to add to the finality of her words or simply to demonstrate the greed of the enemy is open to interpretation.

Kerbogha's mother demonstrated many values attributed to Christian mothers in addressing her son: piety, honesty, wisdom, and the requisite nurturing qualities. She was concerned for her son's welfare but careful not to offend his pride. She tried to instruct him on religious matters like a Christian mother, and demonstrated her own knowledge and wisdom accrued from various sources. A fond relationship between Kerbogha and his mother is demonstrated through the use of endearments. In the version of Robert of Rheims, his mother called him 'the solace of my old age and the only pledge of all my love'.[234] In the end, however, she was unable to persuade her son of his imminent danger, and had to leave him to his fate.

If it was 'camp gossip', the story may have been deliberately concocted to rally the Frankish troops before the battle.[235] It is even possible that Kerbogha's mother visited her son in actuality, and her departure fuelled rumours that she believed in his imminent defeat. However, such explanations are purely hypothetical and it seems more prudent to assume that she was a predominantly fictional creation, developed from some literary precedent of a mother dissuading her son from fighting. The 'reconstructed' nature of this episode is crucial when it comes to understanding the importance of the conversation in its written context. Edgington considers the dialogue between Kerbogha and his mother as similar to other conversations held between Turks in the *Gesta*: 'they must be dismissed as historical evidence, but ... they make interesting historiographical evidence'.[236] The most curious element to the conversation is that Kerbogha's mother argues in defence of Christianity, but it is not a precursor

---

[231]   GF, 325.

[232]   *Ibid.*, 328.

[233]   *Ibid.*, 330.

[234]   RR, 812.

[235]   My thanks to Professor Peter M. Holt for this suggestion.

[236]   Susan B. Edgington, 'Romance and Reality in the Sources for the Sieges of Antioch, 1097–8', in Charalambos Dendrinos, Jonathan Harris, Eirene Harvalia-Crook and Judith Herrin eds *Porphyrogenita. Essays on the History and Literature of Byzantium and the Latin East in Honour of Julian Chrysostomides* (Aldershot, 2003), 33–45.

to possible conversion, as in the case of Melaz or Belek's wives.[237] She also contrasts strongly with the mother of Timurtash of Mardin whom William of Tyre described as a warmonger, reproaching her sons with 'incessant ... urging' to take back the city of Jerusalem from the Franks in 1152.[238] Christian rhetoric, rather than issues of gender or race, is paramount to understanding the role of Kerbogha's mother within the text. Even if the conversation was conceived in tales around the camp-fire at Antioch, some medieval historians seized the opportunity to use Kerbogha's mother as a mouthpiece to explain the preordained success of the First Crusade and justify the superiority of Christianity. As such, the passage fits within the *schema* of other set-pieces in crusade narratives, but in this case a unique perspective is provided by her femininity and her role as a mother.

Whether the author of the *Gesta Francorum* was a layman of limited education, or a cleric influenced by the style of set-pieces in *chansons*,[239] the words of Kerbogha's mother justifying the superiority of Christianity can be used as further evidence to support the role of narratives in disseminating the crusade message. Even if it was initially intended by the author of the *Gesta* as a vehicle for his opinions, it comes as no surprise that others used the dialogue to impose their own interpretations. Robert of Rheims reinvented her speech using different biblical references, elaborating it into a rhetorical exercise justifying Christian supremacy, and associating the crusading army with avenging angels.[240] Perhaps his efforts were genuinely a result of wanting to correct and improve an earlier history, as he claimed, but if so he made good use of the opportunity to underline the divine origins of crusading.

The character and opinions of Kerbogha's mother also changed under different authors. In the version of Baudri of Bourgueil, she employed arguments similar to profeminine ones about the duty due to mothers; she criticised her son for entering into combat with the Franks without consulting her, and appears far more authoritative.[241] In *Dei Gesta Per Francos*, Kerbogha's mother was more critical of the Christians, calling them weak and ignorant. Her son is less affectionate towards her; he does not refer to her as 'beloved' and when she returns to Aleppo it is 'very much suspected by her own son'.[242] In contrast, Robert of Rheims played on the emotions of mother and son, and embarked

---

[237] See 68–70 and 122 above.

[238] WT, 787.

[239] See 26–7 above.

[240] The *Gesta* focused on the prophet David in Psalms and, in what Hill calls 'a rather confused recollection' of verses from Romans or Galatians, he saw the crusaders as the heirs of Christ. Hill, *Gesta*, 54. Robert of Rheims quoted more extensively from Deuteronomy, and from Exodus. RR, 812.

[241] BB, 62.

[242] 'de filio suo nimium suspecta'. GN, 216.

upon colourful descriptions of the sources for Kerbogha's mother's knowledge.[243] He also chose to omit the story claiming that Bohemond and Tancred could eat 2,000 cows and 4,000 horses in one meal – a tale that was probably intended to ridicule Kerbogha's superstitious nature. If Robert wished to tone down the comic elements of the story, it suggests that he had a more serious purpose for the conversation as a whole.

Kerbogha's mother stands out amongst the women portrayed in crusade narratives for her knowledge of the arcane. In the *Gesta* version, she predicts her son's defeat through 'observing and calculating most ingeniously'. She goes on to assert: 'I have gazed at the stars of the sky, and I have accurately scrutinised the planets and the twelve signs and innumerable other oracles'.[244] There were other accounts of Saracen women with supernatural powers in historical narratives, but these usually involved accusations of witchcraft. The *Eracles* chronicle tells of a Saracen sorceress who, captured and tortured by soldiers, admitted to casting spells 'by the devil' on their camp. She then supposedly prophesied correctly that few of them would escape capture or death, and her power was attributed to the devil.[245] Interestingly, although Raymond of Aguilers did not include the episode concerning Kerbogha's mother, he included an incident where two Saracen women were killed by the very siege engine upon which they were casting spells.[246] Orderic Vitalis, who also omitted the account of Kerbogha's mother despite his inclusion of Melaz and Fatima, described a sister of Belek, Baldwin II's captor, and 'a very experienced sorceress', who prophesied by the stars.[247] Popular sources also attested to this belief in the oracular power of Saracen women. In the *Chanson de Jérusalem*, Thomas of Marle met just such a woman on his entrance to Jerusalem, who predicted his death not at the hands of pagans or Turks, but of his overlord, Louis VI of France.[248]

Such extraordinary powers were not limited to so-called 'pagan' women; Christian women, especially mothers, were also portrayed as prophetic.[249] In connection with warfare in the Latin East, Walter the Chancellor recorded that a 'moon struck' woman made a prophecy of doom on the eve of the Field of Blood.[250] It was also acceptable for men to have knowledge of astrology. Arnulf of Chocques and a certain man in his service were credited with

---

[243] Including soothsayers, magi and prophets, oracles, entrails and animal limbs. RR, 813–14.

[244] GF, 328.

[245] *Eracles*, 47.

[246] RA, 149. See also WT, 406–7.

[247] OV, 6.125.

[248] *Chanson de Jérusalem*, 141, lns 4776–84.

[249] See 174–5 above.

[250] WC, 83; trans. Asbridge and Edgington, 120.

correctly interpreting the portents for a victorious battle at Antioch.[251] Kerbogha's mother differs from other women in that her prophecy does not come from a diabolic, crazed intuition or maternal instinct but, like the men, through her own learning and that of her soothsayers. Her knowledge and ability were portrayed as beyond that usual for a woman. Guibert of Nogent reports that, 'At these words Kerbogha was rendered dumb by the miraculous eloquence of his mother.'[252] Robert of Rheims remarked:

> No-one should be surprised that the woman spoke thus,
> For she knew the books of Moses and the prophets well.[253]

He implied therefore that some would be surprised at her ability. He also recounted that Kerbogha grew angry after his mother's prediction of his death and tried to discredit her by criticising her 'empty words' and 'unskilled rhetoric'.[254]

Kerbogha's mother does not appear in the chronicles of Fulcher of Chartres or Raymond of Aguilers.[255] Fulcher probably used Raymond's work to fill in the details about events during the crusade at Antioch, which may explain her absence from the chronicle.[256] It seems odd that Raymond, with his obvious enthusiasm for recording visions and portents, saw fit to exclude the episode, even though he probably had access to the *Gesta*. John France suggests this is because of the different 'preoccupations' and background of Raymond.[257] It is possible that Raymond may have considered the story to be 'camp gossip' not worth repeating; certainly in chronicling the events at Antioch he was more concerned with justifying the story of the Holy Lance. However, he may also have balked at ascribing Christian values to a woman and a Saracen, preferring only to give evidence of supernatural power on the side of the Christians.

Albert of Aachen also neglected to mention Kerbogha's mother. This may have been a result of his independence from the *Gesta* tradition, but Kerbogha's mother did feature in the source with which Albert was closely associated: the *Chanson d'Antioche*. Instead, Albert included another fictitious episode with parallels in the *Chanson*, a conversation between Kerbogha and Suleyman, the

---

[251] GT, 665–6. We cannot be certain, however, that Arnulf's man was a western crusader. He may have been a resident of the city of Antioch, as he mentions that his parents, wife and child were with him.

[252] GN, 215.

[253] RR, 811.

[254] *Ibid.*, 813.

[255] See n. 2.

[256] France, 'The Anonymous Gesta Francorum', 42.

[257] 'The Anonymous enjoyed retailing fabulous stories and what was probably camp gossip about, for example, Kerbogha's mother or Emperor Alexius, while the story of Mirdalin and Kerbogha playing chess as the crusaders sallied out from Antioch is the only example in the *Historia*.' *Ibid.*, 56–7. See RA, 80.

ousted Turkish ruler of Nicaea. Sent as an envoy by Yaghi Siyan, Suleyman admonished Kerbogha about the strength and superiority of the Christian army.[258] Elements of his warnings echo those of Kerbogha's mother. It is uncertain whether Albert had access to both stories, but it is possible that he combined elements of the two and omitted Kerbogha's mother in order to streamline his narrative.

The passage also raises the thorny issue of chronology in the First Crusade sources. In the Gesta, Kerbogha's mother not only predicts her son's defeat, but also that her son will die within a year.[259] Hill argues that 'the confidence of the prophecy suggests that the Author wrote it in the summer of 1098, after the Great Battle of Antioch'.[260] However, the date cited for Kerbogha's death is usually 1102.[261] If the speech of Kerbogha's mother was filled with the confidence of hindsight, why not simply be content with a prediction of Kerbogha's defeat? Why would the author put such a stricture on Kerbogha's forthcoming death? If the Gesta was completed in 1101 as is commonly believed, or possibly earlier as Colin Morris suggests, when Kerbogha was still alive, why include a prophecy that might turn out to be wrong?[262] It is likely that the author of this passage, at least, was writing with the benefit of hindsight, confident that Kerbogha was already dead. Obviously, this is not conclusive proof that the Gesta was written later than thought. Even if the author was writing in 1102, Kerbogha's mother's prediction of her son's death within a year of the battle in 1098 would still be wrong, yet the prediction is reiterated in all versions of the speech. Hill asserts that Kerbogha may have died as early as 26 October 1101, but would the Gesta, or at least this part of it, have been complete in time to be used as the original source for Raymond of Aguilers and Fulcher of Chartres in that same year?[263] A common or compiled source may indeed account for the lack of Kerbogha's mother in the accounts of Raymond and Fulcher. At present

---

[258] AA, 248–59. See also Chanson d'Antioche, 1.259–62 lns. 5048–144.

[259] 'Although you will not die as a result of this battle, you will yet in this year.' GF, 326–7.

[260] Hill, Gesta, 54 n. 7.

[261] In Ibn Al-Athir's Histoire des Atabecs de Mosul Kerbogha's death is cited as 494 (1100–1). RHC Or. (Paris, 1887), 2.31. But in Extrait du Kamel-Altevarykh it is stated that Kerbogha died near Khoy in the month of Dhū'l Qa'da 495 (between 17 August and 15 September 1102, after an illness of thirteen days. 1.208. The Annals D'Aboulfeda also has Kerbogha dying in 495. RHC Or. 1.6.

For historians who date Kerbogha's death to 1102, see BB, 63 n. a; PT, 95 n. 74; William B. Stevenson, The Crusaders in the East (Cambridge, 1907), 121 n. 3; Runciman, A History of the Crusades, 2.41; and Cahen, La Syrie du Nord, 237. Rosalind Hill asserts that Kerbogha died some time between 26 October 1101 and 14 October 1102, but gives no source. Hill, Gesta, 54.

[262] Morris, 'Gesta', 66.

[263] France, 'The Anonymous Gesta', 58. Fink asserts that Fulcher of Chartres was writing before the death of Stephen of Blois in 1102, using the Gesta and Raymond which were finished 'between late 1100 and late 1101'. Fink, A History of the Expedition

there are no obvious solutions to such questions. However, it is clear that the speech of Kerbogha's mother deserves more than the cursory attention it has attracted so far in the debate surrounding the primacy of the *Gesta* as the original source for many chronicles of the First Crusade.

In sum, Kerbogha's mother is unique in crusade literature, a knowledgeable non-Christian woman arguing in defence of Christianity without converting herself, or betraying her son.[264] Only the *Chanson d'Antioche* took the trouble to supply her with a name, Calabre, and describe her physically. At seventy years old, we are told, 'she was an old and wrinkled woman' with hair straggling down past her ears, shaggy eyebrows and completely grey hair.[265] Most authors of historical narratives did not consider a description necessary: it was the validity of her message that they wished to impress upon their audience. While her character is largely fictional, it seems that historians have been unjustified in dismissing the conversation as insignificant. Kerbogha's mother is valuable in two ways: first, for the views she supplies as a mouthpiece for propaganda on crusading; and second, for the information she provides about perceptions of non-Christian women and motherhood. Perhaps it is by virtue of Kerbogha's mother's very 'otherness', as a woman and a Saracen, that the audience would have found it acceptable for her to be well educated, conversant with the Christian faith as well as her own, and deciphering prophecies from the stars.[266] On the other hand, she may provide a mirror for the experience of Christian mothers, providing wise and devout advice to her son, acting in his best interests, but ultimately unable to protect him from his fate.

to *Jerusalem*, 20. Also see Susan B. Edgington, 'The First Crusade: Reviewing the Evidence', in Phillips, *The First Crusade: Origins and Impact*, 55–77.

In the chronicle of Albert of Aachen, Kerbogha responds to the warnings of Yaghi Siyan again with reference to his own death. 'If I am lucky enough to live, before six months shall pass I shall put these Christians to the test and find out whether they are as strong as you claim, and I swear by my god that I shall destroy them in such a way that all their posterity shall grieve.' AA, 258–9.

[264] Possible parallels could be drawn with Saracen heroines of the *chansons de geste*, although these, like Melaz (see 68–70 above), are normally required to betray their own kin to the Christians. See De Weever, *Sheba's Daughters*, xii.

[265] 'Vielle estoit et mousue', 'Li poil par les orelles li sont aval gisant / Les sorcius avoit lons et le poil tot ferrant'. *Chanson d'Antioche*, 1.268–9, lns 5253, 5263–4.

[266] Harari concurs, although he does not appear to have come across my own article published on the subject in 2001. He asserts that the anonymous chose Kerbogha's mother in order to suggest to the reader that 'if even such an unlikely person holds this view, it must be the right view'. Harari, 'Eyewitnessing in Accounts of the First Crusade', 90. He uses this 'entertaining' episode to support the view that the author of the *Gesta* was not an eyewitness.

7

Widows

Widows and Medieval Society

DURING the medieval period, life expectancy was relatively low because of disease, epidemics, warfare and poor medical care; thus the death of a marriage partner was common. Amongst the aristocracy, male life expectancy was curtailed by their traditional military role – 'because noblemen were warriors and thus subject to violent death, women could expect to be married more than once.'[1] It has been estimated that 46 per cent of aristocratic men in England who survived past the age of fifteen during the late medieval period died violently.[2] Even where death was not linked specifically to the battlefield, sustained military campaigns led to high mortality through starvation and diseases such as dysentery. Traditional noble activities such as hunting and jousting could also prove fatal. Lower down the social scale, Bennet estimates that single women (often widows) in rural English society held 10 to 15 per cent of all village holdings. She describes a rudimentary model of marriage which lasted approximately twenty years, ending in the death of a partner, with widows seemingly living on for an average of up to a decade or more.[3]

In medieval thought, the widow was perceived as quintessentially female, but she often had to act in a masculine way. Her control of property meant that she was more 'visible' in official documents than other women, whether in charters selling or donating property, in endowments to the Church, or in wills. Widows were also more likely to have access to political authority, especially if they were guardians for minor heirs. The maternal aspects of regency have already been considered, but widows also held their own rights to dower lands and property, which sometimes led to conflict with other relatives. Remarriage was the main issue which informed contemporary debates about widows: a subject on which both clergy and laity often had opposing views. Widowhood as a

---

[1] Amy Livingstone, 'Powerful Allies and Dangerous Adversaries; Noblewomen in Medieval Society', in Linda E. Mitchell ed. *Women in Medieval Western European Culture* (New York, 1999), 7–30, 17.

[2] See Thomas H. Hollingsworth, 'A Demographic Study of the British Ducal Families', *Population Studies* 11 (1957), 4–26; and Joel T. Rosenthal, 'Medieval Longevity and the Secular Peerage, 1350–1500', *Population Studies* 11 (1973), 287–93. For an earlier study based on north-west France, see Georges Duby, 'Dans la France du Nord-Ouest au XIIᵉ siècle: les "jeunes" de la société aristocratique', *Annales ESC* 19 (1964), 839–43; trans. Cynthia Postan in *The Chivalrous Society* (Berkeley, 1977), 112–22.

[3] Judith M. Bennet, *Women in the Medieval Countryside: Gender and Household in Brigstock before the Plague* (Oxford, 1987), 143–5.

'life-cycle stage' is dependent upon marital status, rather than maturity, but age was still a key factor in determining how widows were perceived. Ecclesiastical writers favoured the cloister for all widows, but recognised that remarriage was often the best or only course of action for younger women. A widow's womanly nature was considered to leave her vulnerable to vice and sexual licentiousness, not to mention predatory men. Wealth and social status also influenced the portrayal of widows – only widows who took on the trappings of true poverty were worthy of respect. Accordingly, this chapter will explore contemporary opinions about what made 'a widow indeed'.

TRADITIONAL VIEWS ON WIDOWHOOD

According to church doctrine, widows were entitled to be treated with due honour, as long as they behaved in a manner suitable to their condition. St Paul commanded that one should 'Honour widows that are widows indeed'; therefore the death of a partner was not the only qualification required. He characterised the true widow as desolate and trusting in God. She should undertake continual prayer, and care for the family that remained to her, children, nephews, and parents, to ward off the sin of *luxuria* – 'she that liveth in pleasure is dead while she liveth'.[4] Charity and humility were also necessary criteria, as long as her children were grown and her duties as a mother fulfilled.[5] Paul recommended that women under sixty should remarry, have children, and 'give none occasion to an adversary to speak reproachfully', for otherwise they would become idle gossips, susceptible to sin.[6]

Church fathers were inspired to write about widows through the discourse about marriage and celibacy as a whole. The attitude prevailed that if a woman had married once, and thus fulfilled the worldly duty required of her, she could legitimately and, indeed, ought to remain celibate. In *De Viduis* (c. 378), St Ambrose praised the sacrifice of young women who chose to remain widows, as their chastity was more arduous to maintain: 'For she certainly is the more noble who represses the heat of youth, and the impetuous ardour of youthful age'.[7] Appropriate dress was also required to make a widow, not only to demonstrate grief but also to reinforce a woman's widowed state. Other suitable signs of mourning included weeping, which had many benefits and could even be a defence mechanism for chastity.[8] Deborah was the archetypal example of a woman who, despite *fragilitas sexus*, 'showed that widows have no need of the help of a man'.[9] She governed men and led armies, but Ambrose made it clear

4   1 Tim 5:3–6.

5   1 Tim 5:10.

6   1 Tim 5:9, 11–15.

7   St Ambrose, col. 251; trans. de Romestin, 392.

8   *Ibid.*, col. 258.

9   St Ambrose, col. 261; trans. de Romestin, 398.

that he did not advocate political power for women as a rule. He interpreted Deborah's story as a parable to reassure widows that they are capable of valorous decisions, and should not rely on feminine weakness as an excuse for remarriage.

In the eyes of the medieval Church, widows were classed with other *miserabiles personae* such as orphans.[10] As a part of this group they featured consistently in clerical appeals for the knighthood to stop their violence.[11] If a widow was being forced into a new marriage, she had the nominal right to the protection of bishops and the king.[12] If she was left destitute by the death of a husband she could receive charity. If a widow was wealthy, however, she could be a lucrative source of income, whether as a patron or a prospective entrant to the cloister. Bernard of Clairvaux, one of the foremost theologians of his day, corresponded with several widows. He praised the pilgrim Ermengarde, countess of Brittany, for her humility in giving up her great estate for the cloister.[13] Conversely, he chastised Ida, countess of Nevers, for her conflict with the abbot of Vézelay.[14] Of particular interest to this study are the letters he sent to Melisende of Jerusalem, offering comfort and counsel on the death of her husband, Fulk v of Anjou. He spoke of her great power and noble lineage, but reminded her that these things are transient and changeable.[15] He warned her that, 'although a woman, you must act as a man ... so that all may judge you from your actions to be a king, rather than a queen'.[16] He saw the key to achieving this as prudence, strength, and discretion. He reassured her that although she may think 'I am only a woman, weak in body and changeable of heart', God would lend her aid to perform tasks beyond her natural strength and wisdom.[17]

In a further letter he praised her rulership and her courageous decision to remain unmarried, as a widow's humility was also becoming in a queen. The good fortune of her birth and widowhood was a 'double honour', and a gift from God.[18] Bernard also addressed the importance of acting appropriately in front of men, especially in her prominent position, equating her conduct in widowhood with the defence of her political authority:

---

[10] James A. Brundage, 'Widows as Disadvantaged Persons in Medieval Canon Law', in Louise Mirrer ed. *Upon My Husband's Death: Widows in the Literature and Histories of Medieval Europe* (Ann Arbor, 1992), 194.

[11] See Bull, *Knightly Piety*, 21–79. See also Carlson, 'Religious Writers and Church Councils', 141–71.

[12] Sheehan, 'The Influence of Canon Law', 18.

[13] Letters 116 and 117, SBO 7.296–7. See also 41 above.

[14] Letter 375, SBO 8.338.

[15] Letter 354, SBO 8.297.

[16] Letter 354, SBO 8.298; trans. James, 346.

[17] *Ibid.*

[18] Letter 289, SBO 8.205.

Before God as a widow, before men as a queen. Remember that you are a queen whose worthy and unworthy actions cannot be hidden under a bushel, but are set up on high for all men to see.[19]

Significantly, perhaps because of her role as queen, he advised her to use Jesus himself as a role model for her widowhood:

Give yourself unto him to be ruled, and to be taught how you ought to rule. Learn of him as a widow, for he is meek and humble of heart; learn of him as a queen, because he gives the poor redress and rights the wrongs of the defenceless. When you think of your dignity, bear in mind that you are a widow because, to speak plainly, you cannot be a good queen unless you are also a good widow.[20]

At the other end of the spectrum, courtly literature often portrayed widows as avaricious and foolish, sexually demanding or power-hungry. In the later medieval period, scathing literary stereotypes of the widow were epitomised by Chaucer's Wife of Bath, and Giovanni Boccaccio's *Il Corbaccio* (c. 1355) which embodied the perception of the ageing widow as *luxuria*: wealthy, lustful, malicious, even murderous.[21] In general, older women were portrayed in less than flattering terms; those past childbearing age might be ridiculed as shrivelled and worthless. Aged widows in particular were often criticised for clinging on to youthful vanities. Conversely, the main stereotype of a young widow in Old French literature was provided by the 'Widow of Ephesus' fable, a story that linked the characteristics of excessive grief and sexual availability.[22]

WIDOWS, WEALTH AND POLITICAL AUTHORITY

There was a pronounced difference between the economic positions of men and women on widowhood. As the man held the legal rights to a married couple's property, he could still provide for himself in the event of the death of a partner, and often kept the dowry from his wife's family, especially if they had children. A wife, however, had to be provided for in case the worst happened. When a husband died, the property that he owned was divided amongst his dependants, and consequently bereaved women relied on the protection of relatives and the law to support themselves. It was to address this problem that the dower, the gift of a husband to his wife on marriage, developed. The husband was expected to provide his wife with the means to support herself after his death.

---

[19] Letter 289, SBO 8.206; trans. James, 347.

[20] *Ibid.*; trans. James, 348.

[21] Giovanni Boccaccio, *The Corbaccio*, trans. Anthony K. Cassell (Urbana, 1975), 54–5.

[22] See Heather M. Arden, 'Grief, Widowhood and Women's Sexuality in Medieval French Literature', in Mirrer, *Upon My Husband's Death*, 306–7, 309. See also Marie de France, *Fables*, 92–5; and 235 below.

Like other marital customs such as dowry, canon law could not enforce the provision of a dower because of its views on consent, but supported the practice in general.[23] The dower often took the form of a specific estate or dwelling, or approximately one-third of the husband's land. A widow was usually entitled to hold this until her death even if she remarried, but local custom and tradition varied. Bennet asserts that a widow in England was entitled to one-third of her husband's property under common law, but in customary law she might be entitled to half or even the entire estate.[24] In Genoa, however, the customary right to the widow's third was taken away in 1143.[25] On a widow's death, dower land usually reverted back to her husband's heir, but a widow was sometimes entitled to distribute up to one-third of her husband's moveable goods, referred to as *legitim*, as she wished, by leaving a will.[26] In certain cases widows were even able to dispose of their dower land, especially if it had formed a part of their own dowry. It might be used as dowry for a daughter's marriage, creating a link between particular family lands and the female line.

A widow's dower was often contested and her rights to it sometimes depended upon the new heir, whether her own child or a more distant relative. In cases where the heir was a minor, a widow might become a regent and manage her child's property until he or she came of age, although both she and the child were usually in wardship. As property owners or regents, widows were able to take on more masculine roles, distributing patronage, directing their own financial affairs and even providing military service. In Champagne, the dowers of aristocratic women were increasingly focused around fiefs. Administrative developments such as secular dower letters confirmed by the feudal lord, and the recording of women who held fiefs 'in dower', appear with more regularity in the feudal registers throughout the twelfth century.[27] Such widows were self-evidently perceived as having a legitimate place within the aristocratic ruling hierarchy.

Livingstone warns against the assumption that widowhood was a universally liberating experience for women, however. While some women were able to continue traditions of administrating estates from marriage into widowhood, others had little authority as either wives or widows. In some cases widowhood may have been an aristocratic woman's first experience of autonomy, but the degree to which she exercised power still relied upon political and familial circumstances.[28] Even aristocratic widows could fall into poverty if their position was usurped by encroaching family, or their means for support was eroded

---

23 Sheehan, 'The Influence of Canon Law', 21.

24 Bennet, *Women in the Medieval Countryside*, 143–4.

25 Epstein, *Genoa and the Genoese*, 45.

26 Leyser, *Medieval Women*, 169.

27 Evergates, 'Aristocratic Women in the County of Champagne', 94–5.

28 Livingstone, 'Aristocratic Women', 68–71.

through war or other economic factors. During the thirteenth century, much of the early strength of the comital household in Flanders was encroached upon by increasingly powerful towns and the French kings exploiting a series of female regencies, despite the fact that some of these women were evidently capable rulers.[29]

REMARRIAGE AND THE CLOISTER

Following on from the ideas of the Church Fathers, some medieval canonists attempted to put strictures on the remarriage of widows,[30] but the economic, political and social bonds of their society revolved around the marital bond. Within the general population, it is likely that many remarried after the death of a partner if they had the opportunity to make a suitable match. Some may have chosen to remain unmarried, but vocational celibacy within the monastery was the lot of only a select few. Amongst the aristocracy, it might be suitable for a widow to remain unmarried and politically active as a regent, but once her children were of heritable age, a dowager could be a drain on the resources of an estate. Under these circumstances some families encouraged widows to remarry or enter a convent.

When it came to remarriage, the king or feudal overlord could intervene in cases of wardship, and their choice was not always in accordance with a family's wishes. The concerns of the nobility in England on this subject were reflected in Henry I's pledge to respect the rights of widows on his coronation, and their mention in *Magna Carta* following the 1185 *List of Rich Widows and Orphaned Heirs and Heiresses* of Henry II's reign.[31] It was common practice to levy fines on those widows who wished to remain unmarried or choose their own marriage partner. The widow of Ralph of Cornhill paid the king 200 marks, three palfreys and two goshawks to avoid marrying Godfrey of Louvain, and to retain her right to her lands with the marriage partner of her choice.[32]

Men who wished to marry widows under guardianship were also expected to pay for the privilege. When the remarriage of aristocratic widows could provide such a lucrative income, it took perseverance and wealth to purchase freedom of choice. Guibert of Nogent related in his *Memoirs* the struggle of his own mother to remain a widow against the wishes of her family, and how she sought protection in the name of Christ.[33] Her discussion with her persecutor

---

[29] See David Nicholas, *Medieval Flanders* (Harlow, 1992), 150–61. Karen Nicholas challenges the traditionally negative view of female regency in Flanders. See Nicholas, 'Countesses as Rulers in Flanders', 111–37; and de Hemptinne, 'Les épouses de croisés et pèlerins flamands'.

[30] See Shahar, 93–4.

[31] Leyser, *Medieval Women*, 171–2.

[32] From *Rotuli de Oblatis et Finibus in Turri Londinensi asservati tempore regis Johannis*, ed. Thomas Duffus Hardy (London, 1835), 37.

[33] Guibert, *Autobiographie*, 92–5.

demonstrated that young widows were perceived to desire remarriage for worldly reasons, and that the Church could preserve the rights of those who wished to remain celibate.

To an extent, the widow in medieval society represented the two extremes of female power. The wealthy noble widow with access to a considerable dower could act independently as the head of a family, command a feudal host, control her image by patronising art and literature, and politick with both Church and the nobility. On the other hand, widows were also the weakest and most vulnerable members of society, who, denied the protection of a husband, required charity and shelter.

Widows in the History of Crusading and the Latin East

WIDOWS AND CRUSADING

The role of the widow in crusade narratives has seldom been given close scrutiny beyond accounts of women left behind, grieving on the departure of crusaders. To an extent, even the wives of crusaders left in the West had attained a status akin to widowhood. In the 'departure scene' recorded by Fulcher of Chartres, the crusader's wife 'mourned him in this life as if he were dead already'.[34] Bernard of Clairvaux famously wrote to Pope Eugenius III in May 1146 that he had been so successful in preaching the Second Crusade, 'Towns and castles are emptied, one may scarcely find one man among seven women, so many women are widowed while their husbands are still alive.'[35] The Church protected the wives and families of crusaders to reassure those facing the real possibility of dying on crusade. Many crusaders' wives were destined to become widows – this was reinforced by the positive emphasis on the prospect of martyrdom as the ultimate benefit of crusading, with salvation as the grand prize. A young Welsh crusader named Gruffud reportedly remarked:

> 'What ... person of manly spirit shrinks from this journey of pilgrimage, when amongst all the troublesome things which he imagined could happen to him, nothing could be more unfortunate, nothing worse could befall him than that he might return?'[36]

Crusade charters reflect this heightened perception of impending mortality.[37] Recent studies suggest that at least one in three crusaders died on the journey, although these calculations are usually based upon the aristocracy and clergy – the death rate amongst poorer pilgrims was probably much

---

34   FC, 163. See also 113 above.

35   Letter 247, SBO 8.141; trans. James, 399.

36   GW 'Itinerarium', 15.

37   See Riley-Smith, *First Crusaders*, 135–9; Constable, 'Medieval Charters', 79–80.

higher.[38] Crusading must therefore have had a considerable impact on widow-hood in Europe, but accurately gauging its effect is difficult. A historical frag-ment pertaining to Louis VII records that many women were widowed and children were orphaned as a result of the Second Crusade.[39] The oppression of widows within medieval society was evidently a concern to Urban II, who included preying on widows, orphans and clergy in his criticism of the knight-hood in his speech at Clermont, and exhorted knights to atone for such sins by going on crusade.[40]

There is evidence to suggest that some women entered convents or remar-ried on hearing of the death of their husbands. In *circa* 1100, Ebrolda, widow of Berengar who had died in Jerusalem, joined the convent at Marcigny and left a charter donating some of her worldly goods to the monastery at Cluny.[41] In 1227, when her husband Ludwig IV of Thuringia died of a fever *en route* to joining the Fifth Crusade, Elizabeth of Thuringia (who later became a patron saint of the Teutonic Order) founded a hospital dedicated to St Fran-cis in Marburg.[42] In certain cases, it was impossible to certify whether cru-saders had died. Ida of Louvain went on pilgrimage to Jerusalem in 1106 in order to search for her husband, Baldwin of Mons, who had gone missing in Asia Minor.[43] Such women lingered in the shadow of widowhood. Remar-riage was the usual way for a widow to secure her future, but without con-firmation of her husband's death she risked committing the sin of bigamy. This was an issue of serious concern to canonists, who debated how many

---

[38] Powell asserted that 34.1 per cent of known crusaders died on the Fifth Crusade. James M. Powell, *Anatomy of a Crusade, 1213–1221* (Philadelphia, 1986), 170. Riley-Smith estimates that between 35.2 and 37.3 per cent of his sample group, which included 112 knights, 22 churchmen and 3 women, died on the First Crusade, although he uses the same system as Powell. Jonathan Riley-Smith, 'Casualties and the Number of Knights on the First Crusade', *Crusades* 1 (2002), 13–28, 18. Phillips estimates that of the German contingent on the Second Crusade, approximately one in three died. Jonathan Phillips, *The Second Crusade: Extending the Frontiers of Christendom* (New Haven, 2007).

[39] *Fragmentum historicum vitam Ludovici VII*, 286; See also Cole, *Preaching of the Crusades*, 52.

[40] BB, 14.

[41] *Recueil de chartes de l'abbaye de Cluny*, ed. A. Bernard and A. Bruel, 6 vols (Paris, 1876–1903), 5.152, no. 3804. See also Riley-Smith, *First Crusaders*, 147, 227, who has not yet managed to locate any more information on this crusader.

[42] See *Cronica Reinhardsbrunnensis*, ed. Oswald Holder-Egger, MGH SS 30, 2 vols (Hanover, 1896), 1.609–10; and Klaus Guth, 'Patronage of Elizabeth in the High Middle Ages in Hospitals of the Teutonic Order in the Bailiwick of Franconia', in Malcolm Barber ed. *The Military Orders: Fighting for the Faith and Caring for the Sick* (Aldershot, 1994), 245–52.

[43] Giselbert of Mons, *Chronique*, ed. Leon Vanderkindere (Brussels, 1904), 45. For Baldwin's death and Ida in Jerusalem, see AA, 340–59, 717. See also Riley-Smith, *First Crusaders*, 147; and Geldsetzer, *Frauen*, 209.

years a crusader's wife should wait before remarriage, if she had the right to remarry at all.[44]

Crusading did not necessarily lead to a greater number of women running fiefs, for as we have already seen, they periodically acted in a public capacity for other reasons, but the death of a husband on crusade did allow certain women to consolidate their political role. When Stephen of Blois died on crusade, it could be argued that the position of Adela of Blois did not change significantly, as she had directed the affairs of her family during both of her husband's expeditions, and she decided on Stephen's successor without censure by contemporary historians.[45] Alice of Montlhéry's husband had died before the First Crusade in 1094, but as a widow she took control of the family inheritance while her son Everard III of Le Puiset and daughter Humberga took part in the expedition. She employed her other sons to support her in various political disputes and was severely criticised for persecuting the church of Chartres. Bishop Ivo eventually excommunicated her in 1098–9.[46] At the other end of the scale, the implementation of a crusader's will could cause legal complications that might leave a widow impoverished. Crusading was expensive, and lands that had been associated with a marriage agreement might be alienated or mortgaged. After the First Crusade the widow of Geoffrey Jordan of Vendôme was excommunicated for trying to repossess a church that her husband had left to a local abbey.[47]

The close association of wealthy widows with ecclesiastical institutions meant that some helped to provide finance to prospective crusaders. Mathilda of Tuscany did not embark on crusade herself, but she was praised in crusade narratives for her protection of both Gregory VII and Urban II during the late eleventh century.[48] Mathilda and the dowager empress Agnes of Germany had considerable resources at their command and as a result featured in the plans for Gregory's proposed 'crusade' to the Holy Land in 1074.[49] As widows were usually entitled to a share in their husband's moveable goods they could be a lucrative source of ready cash, something that crusaders always needed. By the time of the Fifth Crusade, ten out of the fifteen wills in Genoa that donated money to the expedition were drawn up by women.[50] On the other hand,

[44] Brundage, 'Crusader's Wife Revisited', 243–5.

[45] WN, 1.31. See also LoPrete, 'Adela of Blois', 35.

[46] Livingstone, 'Aristocratic Women in the Chartrain', 69

[47] Riley-Smith, *First Crusaders*, 131.

[48] FC, 149. Peter Partner, *The Lands of St. Peter* (London, 1972), 129. For further details see Patricia Skinner, *Women in Medieval Italian Society 500–1200* (Harlow, 2001), 136–41.

[49] See Herbert E. J. Cowdrey, 'Pope Gregory VII's "Crusading" Plans of 1074', in Kedar, *Horns of Hattin*, 36.

[50] Powell, 'Women on the Fifth Crusade', 296. See also 43–4.

dowagers could hinder fundraising for a crusade by draining the resources of a patrimony. Joinville complained about his problems in raising sufficient cash for the crusade in 1248 because his widowed mother was still alive, and the income from his estates was no more than 1000 *livres*.[51]

It was the unique position of the widow, as a woman with access to her own money and military service, which later allowed the Church to re-think its traditional views on women taking the cross. Some widows travelled to the Holy Land with retinues of their own knights, whether to provide military aid for a specific crusade, or simply because they needed personal military protection to complete the pilgrimage. Hostiensis' *Summa Aurea* of *c.* 1253 asserted that a woman could go on crusade if she was of sufficient age, wealth, and character, even if her husband did not accompany her.[52] Evidently this was unlikely to occur unless she was a widow, and such women were still excluded from military decisions. Purcell asserts that even those who were 'acknowledged leaders of feudal hosts, were simply unarmed pilgrims, subordinate in planning, at least to the military needs of the expedition, and considered only obliquely useful'.[53]

The possibility of remarriage to widows in the Latin East was a significant factor in encouraging crusaders to the Holy Land. Based on evidence from the *Livre de Jean d'Ibelin* and the treatise of his son, James of Ibelin, a widow was entitled to half of her husband's estate, although this probably reflects the equality of marital property rights prevalent in the laws of the kingdom.[54] As women could hold fiefs in their own right, so widows could hold dower land, but like heiresses they were expected to marry to provide military service.[55] Brundage asserts, 'it is striking that the jurists of thirteenth-century Outremer expected widows to remarry as a matter of course and … [they] could be forced to remarry'. However, legal sources stipulated a 'mandatory waiting period' for widows before remarriage which had not been in use since the ninth century.[56] According to William of Tyre this was approximately one year,[57] and presumably it was reintroduced to give feudal lords time to find suitable candidates who might have to travel from the West.

WIDOWS, WEALTH AND POLITICAL AUTHORITY

A dower was one way of ensuring that the women left behind by crusaders would be provided for. Richard of Devizes emphasised that King Richard had issued an act recognising the dower of his mother Eleanor before his departure

---

[51] Joinville, 64; trans. Shaw, 192.

[52] Cited in Brundage, 'Crusader's Wife', 438.

[53] Purcell, 'Women Crusaders', 58.

[54] Brundage, 'Marriage Law', 265. See RHC Lois, 1.279–80 and 467.

[55] *Ibid.*, 267. See 73–4 above, and Edbury, 'Women', 288–9.

[56] Brundage, 'Marriage Law', 269–70.

[57] WT, 981.

on crusade, freeing her from dependence on the Exchequer by giving her an income of her own.[58] Presumably this was so that she had sufficient power in her own right to withstand challenges to her authority in his absence. Richard of Devizes went on to praise her care of the people on her dower lands, and how she resolved the dispute over the excommunication of the bishop of Ely, so that her vassals could bury their dead. He asserted that the queen demonstrated great compassion for her subjects and travelled to London to argue on their behalf with great success, for 'who could be so barbarous or hard-hearted that the lady could not bend him to her wishes?'[59] Thus Eleanor mediated with the ecclesiastical hierarchy, the Exchequer barons and the bishop of Ely in order to fulfil her own duties of lordship, as well as undertaking a role in government on behalf of her son.

Dower could also have a financial impact on crusade expeditions. During the Third Crusade, the dower received by Joanna, queen of Sicily, drew considerable attention from contemporary historians. The crusaders reached Sicily at a time when she had recently lost her husband, King William II, in 1189. It is thought that he had intended to take part in the Third Crusade with the kings of France and England. Richard I was probably expecting some kind of contribution to the expedition in terms of an equipped naval force, but in the event of William's death Joanna's dower had to suffice. It was William's naval power that had saved Tripoli from Saladin's forces after the battle of Hattin, and Gerald of Wales asserted that negotiations for a fleet had taken place as early as 1188.[60] William had left a will designating a large amount of money and one hundred war galleys to Henry II, which Richard claimed on behalf of his late father. However, Tancred of Lecce, the illegitimate son of William II's uncle, had usurped the throne and was holding Joanna captive. Richard had to extend his stay in the Mediterranean and launch an attack on Messina in order to retrieve Joanna's dower. The *Itinerarium* emphasised Richard's feelings of responsibility towards his widowed sister and asserted that Richard compelled Tancred to give up the dower on her account.[61] Even the hostile *Eracles* chronicler wrote that Joanna was pleased to see her brother on his arrival, but he did not consider the king to be entirely motivated by fraternal duty.[62] *Eracles* described Richard pleading with his sister to sell her dower and promising to repay her, but implied that the king had already made arrangements behind her back. Richard was described as 'devious and greedy' because he had already come to an agreement with Tancred over its sale.[63]

---

58   Richard of Devizes, *Chronicon*, 14.

59   *Ibid.*, 60.

60   GW 'De Principis', 245.

61   *Itinerarium*, 154.

62   *Eracles*, 104.

63   *Ibid.*, 109.

After the capture of Messina on 4 October 1190, Richard was in a better position to demand the dower from Tancred. According to the *Itinerarium*, Joanna was entitled not only to an adequate dowry but 'her share of her husband the king's treasury which belonged to her by right' – presumably at least the traditional third –'and also a gold table to be equally divided with the wife of its late owner'.[64] Richard of Devizes described Joanna's dower more fully – as well as a twelve-foot-long golden table and seat, she was to receive a silk tent, 60,000 quarters each of wheat, barley and wine, and twenty-four golden plates and cups. Most importantly for the imminent crusade, King Richard wanted the hundred galleys stipulated in William II's legacy, together with the necessary funding to supply them for two years.[65] Richard of Devizes considered this dower to have had a direct influence on the military strategy of the English king. In a speech to his followers Richard stated explicitly that it was his intention to hold Messina to ransom for it, even before the riot that supposedly initiated the taking of the city.[66] What the majority of crusade chroniclers do not mention, however, was Tancred of Lecce's agenda in capturing Joanna. Precarious as his claim to inherited power was, he was also facing a severe challenge from the Emperor Henry VI, who was claiming Sicily in the right of his wife, Constance. He was in desperate need of allies, and appears to have used these negotiations about the dower to extract support from Richard against Henry.[67] Joanna's dower became crucial, not only to the financing of the Third Crusade, but to the wider field of contemporary European politics.

Although it brought much-needed finance, Joanna's dower became another bone of contention between the French and English contingents on the Third Crusade. Unsurprisingly, the *Itinerarium* asserted that Richard kindly offered to share the money with the French contingent to support the expedition:

> Although he was not bound by the terms of the alliance to divide the money received for his sister's dowry he wished to do so out of pure liberality. This bought him glory and approval and wiped out his enemies' envy to some degree.[68]

Conversely, the French chronicler Rigord recorded that Philip only received a third of Richard's profits, and that this was his due after mediating peace between the English and Italians; in fact he thought that Philip should have

---

64   *Itinerarium*, 166; trans. Nicholson, 164–5. For Richard's demands, see Ambroise, 1.14, lns 868–73, and Ambroise, 1.16–17, lns 975–1033, for the resolution of the agreement. For a description of the dower see also Roger of Howden, *Chronica*, 3.61.

65   Richard of Devizes, *Chronicon*, 17.

66   Ibid., 21.

67   Matthews, *The Norman Kingdom*, 289.

68   *Itinerarium*, 169–70; trans. Nicholson, 168. See also Richard of Devizes, *Chronicon*, 25.

been given half of the profit.[69] According to the *Itinerarium*, only half of the 40,000 ounces of gold promised by Tancred was in fact Joanna's dower; the other half was a dowry for the usurper's daughter to marry Arthur of Brittany, Richard's nephew, and seal their alliance.[70] Of course, Joanna's dower was only one of a number of factors which led to conflict between the English and French contingents, but as disunity was a hindrance to the successful outcome of the Third Crusade, its significance should not be under-estimated.[71]

Although not strictly a crusader,[72] Adelaide of Sicily travelled to the Latin East as a widow and received considerable attention from crusade chroniclers on account of her large dower, which included men, and cash. Previously married to Roger I of Sicily, brother of Robert Guiscard, she became a widow in 1101. William of Tyre called her 'a noble, powerful and rich matron'.[73] After receiving King Baldwin I's offer of marriage, she consulted with her son Roger II, and they made a joint decision to accept, on the condition that if the union did not produce a child, Roger would become king of Jerusalem. Adelaide was probably on the cusp of her forties and, while producing a child was a physical possibility (Eleanor of Aquitaine had a child in her mid-forties), the combination of her age and high infant mortality meant that it was increasingly unlikely as the marriage progressed, so Roger's succession was a real possibility.[74] William of Tyre stated unequivocally that Baldwin desired her primarily for her wealth, although he was childless.[75] His envoys had been told to agree to any conditions, as the king barely had enough to run his household and pay his knights. Adelaide 'held everything in abundance since she was in good favour with her son', and could expect a large dowry: 'hence, he longed to relieve his own lack of wealth with her excess'.[76]

Accordingly, she arrived at Acre with grain, wine, oil, salt meat, armed men, splendidly mounted knights, and a huge amount of money.[77] Albert of Aachen, although not an eyewitness, added to this list a detailed description of the ships,

---

69 Rigord, 'Chronique', in Henri-Francois Delaborde ed. *Oeuvres de Rigord et Guillaume le Breton*, 2 vols (Paris, 1882), 106.

70 See also Ambroise, 1.19, lns 991–3.

71 See Gillingham, *Richard I*, 157, 163–6.

72 She does not appear in Geldesetzer's history, even among those of uncertain status. Geldsetzer, *Frauen*.

73 WT, 525.

74 *Ibid.*, 526–7. Murray asserts that Adelaide was probably born in 1075, making her around thirty-eight at the time of her remarriage. Murray, *The Crusader Kingdom of Jerusalem*, 179. See 143–4 above.

75 Orderic Vitalis echoed this view. OV, 6.433. Hamilton has said that Baldwin was motivated by the need for an heir, but his choice of bride does not suggest it was his primary concern. Hamilton, 'Women', 145.

76 WT, 526.

77 *Ibid.*.

armour and bejewelled vestments she brought with her, and asserted that the ship upon which she travelled was very richly decorated.[78] William of Malmesbury and Orderic Vitalis also emphasised her enormous wealth, but Orderic was extremely hostile to Adelaide and asserted that she had accumulated it by murdering her husband as well as other crimes.[79] William of Tyre makes it clear that, as a widow, Adelaide was still dependent on her son, and although she was party to the negotiations for the match, it was her son who stood to benefit if Baldwin died. Unfortunately for Roger, the marriage was dissolved,[80] and his investment, the dowry, was not returned as was common custom. Orderic Vitalis thought this a fitting end for Adelaide's crimes, but William asserted that the insult to Roger II and his mother (and the loss of their wealth) created bad relations with Sicily for some time. There is, however, evidence to suggest that William may have exaggerated on this point.[81] As Phillips points out, William was clearly not taking into account several attempts by the Sicilians to become involved in the Latin East. Roger II had interests outside the kingdom of Jerusalem: notably Adelaide distributed gifts of patronage to Prince Roger of Antioch at her wedding. Her son maintained a role in the succession through his relationship to Constance, and his opposition to Raymond of Poitiers. Later he sent envoys to Louis VII suggesting a sea route for the Second Crusade, but was turned down, probably for fear of angering the Byzantine emperor. Roger was also a target for calls for a crusade in 1150.[82] In 1174, William II of Sicily sent a fleet to Egypt which William of Tyre recorded himself.[83]

Margaret of Austria was widowed on the death of her husband, King Bela II of Hungary, in 1196, and used her dower to finance an expedition to the East. In many senses she epitomised the type of widow whom the Church considered suitable to take the cross. A 'matron' in her thirties, she had no immediate family commitments to children or her husband's family, so she sold her dower and used her wealth to gather a retinue for an expedition to the Holy Land. Crusading tradition was strong in her family, for she was the daughter of Louis VII (by Constance of Castille), and the aunt of Henry of Champagne, king of Jerusalem, through her half-sister Marie. According to the *Eracles* continuator, 'she had conceived a longing to go to Jerusalem and visit the Holy Sepulchre',[84]

78 AA, 842–7.

79 WM, 1.689; OV, 6.433. Chibnall suggests that Orderic was influenced in this by an oral source, Robert, son of William of Grandmesnil, who was an enemy of Roger II of Sicily; see OV, 6.432 n. 1.

80 See 143–4 above. For the divorce see AA 860–3.

81 OV, 6.433; WT, 542–3.

82 See WT, 641; AA 846–7. See also Phillips, *Defenders*, 113–15; OD, 10–15.

83 WT, 963. Prutz asserts that the section about Adelaide was written before that date. Hans Prutz, 'Studien über Wilhelm von Tyrus', *Neues Archiv der Gesellachft für ältere deutsche Geschictskunde* 8 (1883), 115–17.

84 *Eracles*, 193.

showing genuine pious motivation. Apparently she brought with her 'a fine company of knights',[85] and accompanied other Germans to Tyre. There was, however, a suggestion that she was rather naïve. The *Eracles* chronicler asserted, 'because the emperor had sent such a great army, she expected that he would recover the whole kingdom of Jerusalem', and 'she imagined that with the arrival of the Germans, the city of Jerusalem would be won back from the Saracens'.[86] The author could have been praising her for her devout belief in divine support for the crusade, or implying that she was unworldly and, because of her femininity, not conversant with military realities. Ultimately her hopes were unfulfilled, as she died in Tyre within eight days of her arrival, but *Eracles* mentions that she gave all her wealth to Count Henry because he was her nephew.[87] Margaret thus demonstrated all the admirable qualities in an aristocratic widow and, with the end of her married life, she gave herself over to spiritual service. Even her death benefited the cause of the Latin Christians in the Holy Land.

Other crusading widows met with a more unpleasant end. Albert of Aachen recounted the story of Countess Ida, the widow of Margrave Leopold II of Austria, who took part in the 1101 crusade.[88] Ida was counted amongst the leaders of the expedition, and presumably at least some of the 'enormous army of cavalry and infantry and of the female sex' came from her own personal retinue.[89] Other leaders included William IX of Aquitaine and Welf IV, duke of Bavaria, and Ida's comparative status was demonstrated by the fact that, like these noblemen, her oath of fealty was required by the Emperor Alexius.[90] The crusaders were eventually ambushed and defeated by Kilij Arslan at Heraclea,[91] but Albert was unsure of Ida's fate.

> Countess Ida was either captured and taken away, or was torn limb from limb by the hooves of so many thousand horses: to this very day her fate is not known, except that they say she was carried off among the many thousands of women into the land of Khorasan in eternal exile.[92]

Ida's case demonstrates how very difficult it was to discern what happened in the aftermath of battle on crusade, even to important noblewomen, especially when some were taken captive. Ekkehard of Aura also described the battle and, although he was not an eyewitness to the event, Hagenmeyer suggests that the unnamed margravine whose death he records was in fact

---

85 *Ibid.*

86 *Ibid.*; trans. Edbury, 143.

87 *Eracles*, 193.

88 AA, 626–7.

89 *Ibid.*, 624–5.

90 *Ibid.*, 626–7.

91 *Ibid.*, 628–9.

92 *Ibid.*, 630–1.

Ida.[93] Later, the *Historia Welforum Weingartensis* recounted that Ida was carried off by a Saracen prince and became the mother of Zengi, probably to explain his successful capture of Edessa through his military prowess.[94] Purcell notes that it was Ida's companion, the bishop of Salzburg (who died in a later encounter) 'who became the legendary martyr and the margravine who took a more literally mundane part in her legend'.[95] Albert of Aachen is possibly the best narrative source for the 1101 crusade,[96] but he was not an eyewitness, and his emphasis on the suffering of women throughout his history indicates that he was inclined to mistrust the participation of any women in crusade expeditions, regardless of status.[97]

Levantine widows could also command substantial dowers, which were usually discussed in the context of remarriage to the crusaders or settlers who were to benefit from their wealth. However, some women managed to maintain a degree of autonomous political power through their dowers without bowing to the pressure of a new match. After the first of Alice of Antioch's failed attempts to seize power, her father allowed her to keep the cities of Latakia and Jabala, 'which nevertheless her husband, in his final will, had intended for her, for the sake of dower at the time of marriage'.[98] In fact, Asbridge questions whether the king would even have had the right to take them away under Antiochene law at the time.[99] It was believed that Alice had gained enough wealth from her dower and the guardianship of Constance to provide expensive gifts with which to bribe both her Christian and Muslim allies.[100] William emphasised the problems and fears of the Antiochene nobility about encroaching Muslim power, and the barons appealed to the new king, Fulk v of Anjou, for aid. Fulk duly arrived and won the hearts of the people of Antioch by saving them from a Muslim attack, even those who had been swayed by Alice's patronage.[101] Therefore, in William's interpretation, Fulk weathered the conflict by acting in his capacity as military protector, in opposition to the corrupt form of monetary politics offered by Alice, a woman unable to engage in the most important aspect of medieval rulership, warfare. In fact, many of her supporters had their

---

93 Ekkehard of Aura, *Hierosolymita*, ed. Heinrich Hagenmeyer (Tubingen, 1877), 170. 'marchisiam Idam trucidatam', in Ekkehard, *Hierosolimita*, RHC Occ. 5.32.

94 'Historia Welforum Weingartensis', in MGH *Scriptorum* 21 (1869), 462.

95 Purcell, 'Women Crusaders', 58.

96 Alec Mulinder, 'Albert of Aachen and the Crusade of 1101', in Murray, *From Clermont to Jerusalem*, 69–77.

97 His accounts of Florina and Emeline of Bouillon suggest this. See 215 below, 149 above.

98 WT, 624; see 68 above.

99 WT, 636, Asbridge, 'Alice of Antioch', 36.

100 WT, 636.

101 *Ibid.*, 639.

own reasons for opposing the king, as previously discussed, so, whether money actually changed hands or not, William deliberately made use of perceptions about femininity to accuse her of nefarious activities.

Widows were evidently perceived to act in a capacity that drove them to overcome the natural deficiencies of their sex, but in some cases the situation was too desperate for anyone to rule effectively. William of Tyre saw female rule as less than ideal, and interpreted the regencies of widows Beatrice of Edessa and Constance of Antioch as a sign of divine displeasure: 'Therefore in recompense for our sins, both regions, bereft of better councillors, barely surviving by themselves, were ruled by the judgement of women.'[102] Such a statement stands in stark contrast with his approval of Melisende:

> ... left with two children still under legal age, and just as much by hereditary right, care and administration of the kingdom fell to her responsibility, acting as the legitimate guardian of her sons. With the advice of the barons of the region, strenuously and with good fortune, transcending the strength and spirit of women, she managed this up to that time.[103]

William, along with most contemporary writers, believed that rulership was an unnatural activity for women, and saw most widows in positions of power as the unhappy victims of fortune, struggling to manage tasks to which they were evidently unequal. In comparison, Melisende was bolstered by her constitutional position, but she must have exhibited a certain amount of skill as a ruler in order to transcend her sex and become a worthy exemplar in William's eyes. She also had the assets of an entire kingdom at her disposal, and retained a lucrative income from dower lands at Nablus even after the conflict with her son.[104] Beatrice, on the other hand, had nowhere near enough resources to restore the shattered infrastructure of the county of Edessa – in the end the cost was too much even for the kingdom of Jerusalem to bear. Only the fabulously wealthy Byzantine Empire had the necessary resources to preserve what remained, and William recognised that renouncing their claim to Manuel Comnenus and settling for the limited wealth afforded by a pension was probably the only viable option for the countess and her children.[105]

Sibylla of Armenia was not so fortunate: widowed and bereft of her son, Bohemond VII of Antioch-Tripoli, in 1287, she was informed by the people of Tripoli that grief made her unable to manage the city, and asked to find an alternative protector. They were unhappy with her choice, Bartholomew, bishop of Tortosa, and rebelled, founding an independent commune.[106]

[102] *Ibid.*, 775.

[103] *Ibid.*, 777.

[104] Mayer, 'Queen Melisende', 172–3.

[105] WT, 781–2; see 149–50 above.

[106] *Les Gestes des Chiprois*, 780.

REMARRIAGE

Remarriage in the Context of Crusading

In common with other medieval literature, remarriage features strongly in any mention of widowhood in narratives of crusading and the Latin East. However, while canonists were at pains to dissuade crusaders' widows from remarriage, historians did not often criticise a new union unless it was unsuitable in terms of status, organised by force or with undue haste. On the burial of Hugh of Landricourt during St Louis' crusade, John of Joinville heard six of his own knights talking loudly in the chapel. When he rebuked them for their impropriety, they laughed and said that they were arranging the remarriage of the dead man's wife. Joinville considered this most scandalous and recounted the divine justice meted out to them:

> And God took such vengeance on them that the very next day, in the great battle of Shrove Tuesday, they were all of them either killed outright or mortally wounded, so that the wives of all six were in a position to marry again.[107]

Criticisms of remarriage could also be used to denigrate the morality of the crusaders' enemies. Guibert of Nogent attempted to discredit the origins of the Muslim faith by focusing on the rich widow (presumably Khadija) who married the prophet Mohammed.[108] She foolishly allowed herself to be persuaded into the match by a corrupt hermit, and enabled the prophet's rise to power through her wealth. She had remained unmarried previously because there was no one of suitable rank available, but the widow was seduced not by Mohammed's appearance or wealth but by his prophetic power, and her desire for knowledge about past and future events. Guibert described the union as lustful and corrupt, saying that the marriage bed brought on bouts of a disease akin to epilepsy in the prophet, and, when the widow complained, the hermit claimed they were divine visitations. The widow foolishly believed these words, and accepted a marriage with a man whom Guibert considered little better than an imbecile, because of her 'womanly levity'.[109] His design was evidently to ridicule the prophet, but his scorn for the widow in this case was perhaps all the more palpable because it drew a stark contrast with the example of his own mother.[110]

In general, marriage to a wealthy widow was viewed as an easy path to power in comparison to honourable advancement through achievement on the

---

[107] Joinville, 164; trans. Shaw, 238.

[108] See Jonathan Berkey, 'Women in Medieval Islamic Society', in Mitchell, *Women in Medieval Western European Culture*, 100.

[109] GN, 96–7.

[110] See 202–3 above.

battlefield, and could be used as an insult. After Nureddin's death in 1174, Saladin took the opportunity to make himself overlord of Damascus by marrying his widow. She was the daughter of Unur of Damascus, and therefore aided Saladin's claim to overlordship of the city, but it seems that she was also capable of acting on her own behalf. When King Amalric besieged Banyas on Nureddin's death she reportedly demanded that he desist and accept a truce, 'surpassing womanly courage'.[111] The *Itinerarium*, however, bitterly lamented Saladin's good fortune in marrying the widow and gaining the status and wealth that she provided.[112]

Some widows actually took the opportunity provided by crusading to arrange a new marriage. Albert of Aachen is the only source to mention the fate of the widow Florina, daughter of the duke of Burgundy. She was making her way through Rum with the man she hoped to marry (Prince Sven of Denmark), when Turkish raiders attacked them. Albert described in tragic terms how despite six arrow wounds she clung to her fleeing mule in an attempt to escape death, but she was caught and killed along with her intended.[113] With this story Albert added to his catalogue of misfortunes which befell women on crusade, although he did not explicitly blame Florina's desire to remarry for her unhappy end.

There was definite interest in the possibilities of Joanna of Sicily's remarriage during the Third Crusade, as she was only twenty-four on her husband's death.[114] As a dowager queen she was significant enough to be visited socially by the king of France on her release from captivity under Tancred of Lecce, and Roger of Howden suggested that the recently widowed king may have wanted to marry her.[115] According to the Lyon *Eracles* it was Richard's promise to secure her a suitably rich and powerful husband which enticed her to sell her dower and give the proceeds to him.[116] This implies that Richard was playing upon his sister's perceived feminine weakness and lust. Perhaps the author saw Joanna as rewarded for her gullibility by Richard's later attempt to arrange a scandalous match with Saladin's brother, Saif al-Din. This surprising move was not simply a creation of the *Eracles* author: Bahā' ad-Din also records that such an offer took place, but that the alliance fell through because Joanna refused marriage to an 'infidel'.[117] Fear of this proposed alliance was reputedly enough to coerce Saladin into offering a truce, although Muslim sources demonstrate

[111] WT, 956.

[112] *Itinerarium*, 10.

[113] AA, 377. See also Geldsetzer, *Frauen*, 186.

[114] He died on 16 November 1189. Roger of Howden, *Chronica*, 3.29.

[115] Roger of Howden, *Chronica*, 3.56; and 'Gesta', 2.126.

[116] *Eracles*, 109. See 207–9 above.

[117] Bahā' ad-Din, *The Rare and Excellent History of Saladin*, 187, 196. Imād ad-Din also refers to these negotiations. See Gillingham, *Richard I*, 184.

that he was actually involved in the negotiations, if not in person.[118] Despite his antipathy for Richard, the *Eracles* chronicler noted that Saif al-Dīn's conversion to Christianity was a stipulation of the proposed match: even he did not have the temerity to suggest that the king of England would barter with his own sister's immortal soul. It was considered shameful even to treat with the Muslims, so bestowing a daughter of royal lineage in this way must have been controversial. Gillingham suggests that the negotiations were kept completely secret, but the *Eracles* author evidently knew about it, and as the proposal came to nothing, perhaps the *Itinerarium* and Ambroise felt justified in not mentioning it at all in order to preserve Richard's image as the model crusader.[119]

Because she was a widow, the emphasis chroniclers placed on the role of Joanna's dower and speculation about her remarriage has ultimately eclipsed the crusade of the woman herself, when her presence should not be underestimated. Whether Richard was portrayed as coming to her rescue, or abusing her trust, contemporary historians highlighted her vulnerability, although she was evidently capable of taking decisive action. When Isaac Comnenus of Cyprus tried to capture Joanna and Berengaria, it was the queen of Sicily who reputedly forestalled the emperor until her brother arrived, and she had the power to refuse a marriage partner she deemed unsuitable.[120] She was not an acknowledged leader of the host, and little is known about her activities in the Latin East beyond measures taken for the protection of the two queens, but it is likely that she did not just accompany Richard for her own safety.[121] Released from captivity, and her family duties in Sicily complete, she could easily have returned to England with her mother, Eleanor. Evidently, her role as an escort for Berengaria was crucial as far as Cyprus, and perhaps by that point she was committed to the full expedition, but it seems likely that Joanna herself had already taken the cross. She may have intended to accompany her husband to the East before his death, and thus fulfilled the vow in his honour. She had also invested heavily in the expedition, and perhaps she wished to remain close to her brother in order to ensure he protected her interests to the best of his ability.

Remarriage in the Latin East

In accordance with marital law and political circumstances, it seems that a high number of aristocratic widows in the East entered into more than one

---

[118] *Eracles*, 151. See also Gillingham, *Richard I*, 186–8, Lyons and Jackson, *Saladin*, 342–5.

[119] Gillingham, *Richard I*, 188.

[120] *Eracles*, 115; trans. Edbury, 101. The *Itinerarium*, and Ambroise, however, played down her role in order to portray Richard as the hero. *Itinerarium*, 187–8. Ambroise, l.23–4, lns 1436–46.

[121] See 120 above.

marriage. Some husbands preferred to arrange for the remarriage of their own wives, particularly if they had no heirs. On his deathbed, Bohemond of Taranto's nephew Tancred supposedly arranged just such a marriage for his wife Cecilia of France. He dowered her with two Antiochene fortresses, Arghzan and Rugia. Her husband was to be Pons of Tripoli, the son of Tancred's old enemy, Bertram of Toulouse.[122] There is some doubt about the veracity of William of Tyre's account of these events, as a considerable amount of time elapsed between Tancred's death in 1112 and the marriage in 1115. However, this may have been to wait for Pons to come of age.[123] Considering the political friction that had characterised the relationship between Antioch and Tripoli until this point, there may have been a degree of uncertainty over whether the union would come to fruition at all. Asbridge asserts that this story was probably a 'fanciful invention',[124] but it was not one of William's creation – the tale was sufficiently well known in the West to appear in William of Malmesbury's *Gesta Regum Anglorum* by 1138.[125] It is possible that contemporaries propagated the idea that the marriage was the final wish of Tancred in order to ensure that the nuptials went ahead as planned.

Following biblical guidelines, widows were no longer required to marry in the Latin East after they reached sixty, way beyond potential childbearing years, but an age at which a woman might still have a duty of care to nurture children. The provision of heirs, therefore, was not necessarily the deciding factor in the remarriage of a widow, especially if she had already had children with her former husband. The political stability provided by a husband who could perform military duties was considered to be more important. When Raymond III of Tripoli married widow Eschiva of Bures they had no children: she had several already by her first husband, and Raymond apparently loved them as if they were his own.[126] William thus emphasised the magnanimity of Raymond, portraying him as a good husband and stepfather whose regency he considered to be the best hope for the kingdom. The marriage may have been for reasons of love, but, even so, Raymond's interests were served by the marriage alone, as it provided him with the requisite wealth to pursue his political and military ends.

The fragile power balance in the Latin East demanded that to some extent the normal ecclesiastical views on remarriage were suspended, but certain individuals did attract censure. Men were sometimes criticised for taking

---

[122]   WT, 522, 636. Albert of Aachen attributed this remarriage to Baldwin I's initiative. AA 854–5.

[123]   *Ibid.*, 123. Albert of Aachen dates the marriage to 1115. AA, 701.

[124]   Thomas S. Asbridge, *The Creation of the Principality of Antioch, 1098–1130* (Woodbridge, 2000), 122.

[125]   WM, 1.705.

[126]   WT, 967.

advantage of widows, as indicated by the sources for Baldwin I and Adelaide. William of Tyre had excused Baldwin's role in the affair on the grounds of poverty, but blamed Patriarch Arnulf for deceiving the 'noble and honest woman', who 'in her own sincere manner' thought that the king was in a suitable position to make a legal marriage.[127] Adelaide was portrayed as the innocent victim of political machinations; but in direct contrast Orderic Vitalis ridiculed her in conventional terms as a widow eager for remarriage. He called her 'insatiably greedy for pomp and honour', and considered Baldwin justified in repudiating a woman 'wrinkled with age' and 'stained with many crimes'.[128] William of Tyre thought the marriage failed to produce heirs because of God's displeasure at Baldwin's behaviour. He ignored the fact that the king had no children from his two previous marriages, and that the queen's age was an issue.[129] William of Malmesbury, however, followed Orderic's line by giving dark hints about the origin of Adelaide's wealth. Ignoring her age, he said that Baldwin put her aside because 'she was afflicted with some disorder, which caused an incurable cancer to attack her privy parts'. He expressed no surprise that the marriage did not produce children, because Baldwin was a warrior 'for whom leisure was a form of illness', and he found the embraces of a wife 'repellent'.[130]

After the death of Baldwin III in 1163, his young widow, Theodora Comnena, was later seduced and abducted by her relative Andronicus. William of Tyre said that Andronicus had acted 'like a snake in the bosom or a mouse in a wallet' and absconded with Theodora to Damascus with the aid of Nureddin.[131] Despite the scandal, King Amalric probably benefited from the situation as Theodora had held the important port of Acre as her dower, and Andronicus had been enfeoffed with Beirut. Taking into account the dower of Nablus that the king had promised to his own wife Maria Comnena, Lilie estimates that 'nearly a quarter of the kingdom had come under Byzantine influence'.[132] The couple were pardoned by the Byzantine emperor in 1180, and they lived together with their children in Pontos until 1182, by which time Hamilton suggests Theodora may have died.[133] At that point, Andronicus was called to Constantinople by the opponents of Maria of Antioch, and married Agnes of France in

---

[127] WT, 526.

[128] OV, 6.433.

[129] See 209 above.

[130] WM, 1.689. The similarities between the works of Orderic and William have been pointed out by several historians, although their accounts appear to have been independent. Thompson and Winterbottom suggest that the two may have met to discuss 'work in progress'. WM, 2.255. See also 210 n. 79 above.

[131] WT, 914. For Byzantine accounts, see Kinnamos, *Deeds*, 188–9; and Choniates, *O City of Byzantium*, 80–1, 128.

[132] Lilie, *Byzantium*, 195. See also Ernoul, 15.

[133] Lilie, *Byzantium*, 195; Hamilton, 'Women', 162.

1183.[134] Even if Theodora was still alive, Andronicus was obviously unconcerned about committing bigamy, as he had two wives already when he abducted her.[135] Robert of Clari added to this story, although his grasp of the chronology was limited. He asserted that the abduction happened when Andronicus had come to escort Theodora to the wedding of Alexius II and Agnes of France in 1180, rather than *circa* 1168.[136] In his version of events, Andronicus fell in love with Theodora during the sea voyage to Constantinople, taking her by force, and then abducting her.[137] Robert was evidently unaware of the sequence of events and preferred to skip to the more salubrious features of the story, so that Andronicus could be criticised for his treacherous nature, and vilify the Greek race as a whole.[138]

Marriage to a wealthy widow may have invited criticism, but for the most part it was an accepted way of consolidating and building upon family power. It was perhaps not quite as lucrative in the long term as a marriage which brought heritable property, but even temporary access to rights over fiefs and moveable goods could help to finance military ambitions, and occasionally included other political benefits. The Ibelin family seem to have profited considerably from Balian of Ibelin's marriage to the widow of Amalric, Maria Comnena. Balian gained her dower of Nablus, weakening the royal domain, and also took control of future heir to the kingdom, Isabella.[139] After Sibylla's death he was in a position to control the crown of Jerusalem through arranging the remarriage of her daughter, Isabella, to Conrad of Monferrat.[140] In 1194, the new king, Henry II of Champagne, 'gave the office of constable to John of Ibelin, the brother of queen Isabella', undoubtedly because of their family relationship.[141] Later, when John fought followers of Emperor Frederick II at Nicosia in 1229, Gerard of Montagu was killed, leaving his wife, an important heiress named Eschiva of Montbéliard, widowed. Perhaps only within a year, she was married again – to Balian of Ibelin, lord of Beirut, even though the match was within the prohibited degrees, and earned them both excommunication.[142]

[134] See 92–3 above. Harris, *Byzantium and the Crusades*, 117.

[135] He had recently married Philippa of Antioch (sister-in-law to the emperor) and already had a wife in Constantinople. WT, 978–9. Choniates, *O City of Byzantium*, 79–80. Kinnamos, *Deeds*, 188.

[136] He may have become confused with King Amalric's marriage to Maria Comnena, which occurred while Andronicus was in the Latin kingdom of Jerusalem.

[137] RC, 20.

[138] Hamilton, 'Women', 162. For an assessment of Byzantine explanations for Andronicus' behaviour in this matter, see Lilie, *Byzantium*, 194–5 n. 218.

[139] Prawer, *Crusader Institutions*, 28.

[140] *Itinerarium*, 121.

[141] *Eracles*, 125.

[142] *L'Estoire de Eracles Empereur*, 376; and *Les Gestes des Chiprois*, 715, 721–2. See Edbury, *John of Ibelin*, 42, 56.

However, widows, like heiresses, were given in marriage as a form of feudal patronage, and this could stimulate resentment. Miles of Plancy gained considerable wealth by his marriage to widow Stephanie of Kerak and Montreal, which aroused jealousy, and he was eventually murdered.[143] Similarly Manasses of Hierges was rewarded for his services to Melisende in 1150 by marriage to Helvis, lady of Ramla and the widow of Barisan of Ibelin.[144] This marriage made Manasses particularly unpopular with Baldwin III's allies who, unsurprisingly, included the Ibelin sons, Hugh, Baldwin and Balian. It may have been a significant factor in the outbreak of the civil war, after which he was eventually forced to leave the kingdom.[145]

In some cases it was the widow herself who was criticised for entering into a remarriage, for avarice or lust. Alice of Antioch was perceived to have ultimately fallen victim to her own feminine desire for a new husband. One of her reputed reasons for taking control of the city was so that she could exercise choice over her new marriage partner. As a result, she supposedly fell for a ruse that Raymond of Poitiers intended to marry her, rather than her daughter Constance.[146] Ralph, who had become patriarch of Antioch in 1135 with Alice's help, persuaded her to believe the lie, and 'excessively credulous, she was fooled by that vain hope'.[147] Recent studies suggest that although he had initially supported Alice, Ralph was motivated to betray her by self-interest – he may have feared that diplomatic overtures to the Byzantine Empire in 1135 would result in the loss of his position to an orthodox patriarch.[148]

Alice's involvement in a proposed match between Constance and Manuel at this time cannot be proven,[149] but it seems unlikely that either Baldwin II or Fulk would have encouraged Byzantine overlordship of Antioch. Both kings had shown themselves willing to become involved in expeditions to the principality rather than allow this to happen, to the extent that they risked the support of their own nobles.[150] It is also unlikely that the Antiochene nobility would have made such an offer independently. Although some may have recognised the benefits of an alliance, the Latin Antiochene populace were vigorously opposed to Byzantine influence, as shown by their reaction to Emperor

---

[143] WT, 964.

[144] Ibid., 778. See Mayer, 'Queen Melisende', 115, for the date of the marriage; and idem, 'Carving up Crusaders: The Early Ibelins and Ramlas', 102–18, for an explanation of the complex genealogical problems surrounding Helvis of Ramla and the Ibelin family.

[145] WT, 779. See Mayer, 'Queen Melisende', 155–6.

[146] '... to enter into a second match through her own choice'. WT, 635–6.

[147] Ibid., 658.

[148] See Bernard Hamilton, 'Ralph of Domfront, Patriarch of Antioch (1135–40)', Nottingham Medieval Studies 28 (1984), 8–9. Phillips, Defenders, 61–2.

[149] See 83–4 above.

[150] Asbridge, 'Alice of Antioch', 45–6. Murray, 'Baldwin II and his Nobles', 66–8, 82–3.

John's attempt to establish his overlordship in 1138.[151] When Raymond finally arrived, he gave an oath of fealty to Patriarch Ralph for the hand of Constance and the principality.

Significantly, Ralph was supposed to secure a marriage between Alice and a brother of Raymond's named Henry as part of the deal, including her dower of Latakia and Jabala.[152] This part of the agreement has largely been dismissed by historians because no record of such a brother has been found, and there is no evidence that a remarriage consequently took place. That does not necessarily mean that Raymond had no plans for Alice's future, however: she could not have been much older than thirty in 1136, she was of royal blood, and her dowry was extremely lucrative. In fact, remarriage to a loyal dependant might have been the easiest way to neutralise her activities, so it is perhaps surprising that the kings of Jerusalem had not forced her into such a match earlier. This suggests that either the protection offered by her dower was too powerful, or they could not find a trustworthy husband of suitable rank whose loyalties would remain with the crown. Once Alice discovered Raymond's deception, we are told, she retired to her lands, 'afterwards pursuing the prince with relentless hatred'.[153] With these final remarks William consigned Alice to the role of the spurned woman, and while her date of death is uncertain, the marriage of her daughter unquestionably sounded the death knell for her political life in Antioch.

Later, as a widow herself, Constance came under criticism for her initial refusal to remarry. Baldwin III persistently asked her to do so, fearing that Antioch would suffer the same fate as Edessa because he was unable to provide personally for the protection of the principality. Amongst a list of possible suitors were: Ives, count of Soissons, who was desirable because of his French connections; Walter of Falkenburg, who was discreet, courteous, wise and valiant; and Ralph of Merle, a high-born nobleman with good sense and experience on the battlefield. These qualities were evidently desirable in a husband and in a future prince of Antioch, and the fact that William of Tyre lists these three candidates suggests that they may have been offered to Constance by Baldwin in accordance with the law. Her reason for rejecting these suitors was given as follows:

> She, however, fearing the shackles of wedlock and resolving to have a free and independent life, was largely ignoring that which the people wanted, being more concerned about pursuing matters of the flesh according to her own desires.[154]

---

[151] See WT, 678–9.

[152] Ibid., 658.

[153] Ibid., 659.

[154] Ibid., 786.

Constance was neglecting her duty as a female ruler to remarry. A general council to discuss the matter was called at Tripoli in 1152. Whether or not Queen Melisende attended the council under duress,[155] she and Hodierna, the countess of Tripoli, were drafted in to help persuade the reluctant widow to remarry. Despite this pressure, neither the king, nor the rest of her family were able to force Constance to marry against her will, possibly because she had a strong ally in the Church. Aimery of Limoges, the successor to Ralph as patriarch of Antioch, had aided her in government since the death of her husband in 1149. Aimery supported her refusal to remarry, following the ecclesiastical tradition of protecting the rights of widows, although William suggested that he was doing so to expand his own power.[156] In addition, Constance was the legitimate heir, and she had already produced four children, so there was no urgent dynastic vacuum – remarriage for military protection had to be the primary issue for the principality. It is notable that while there was considerable pressure on Constance to remarry, there never seems to have been a proposal that Queen Melisende should enter into a new union. Evidently her remarriage might have upset the delicate political balance in a kingdom where she was designated joint heir.

William's assertion that Constance did not want the 'shackles' of marriage was later proved wrong. He does not mention rumours that Constance sought a marriage alliance with Byzantium, although the candidate chosen by Emperor Manuel, Caesar John Roger, apparently proved unsatisfactory to her – John Kinnamos said she thought him too aged.[157] Instead, William played on perceptions of the inconstant nature of women to explain her behaviour: 'many illustrious and noble men were seeking her hand in marriage, [but] she refused in the manner of women'.[158] It is possible that Constance's experiences as a minor, eclipsed by a domineering mother and then married to an ambitious prince when still only a child, may have increased her determination to experience autonomy and choose her next partner when the chance arose. Eventually Constance found her match in Reynald of Châtillon, a knight of the king's retinue, but this decision was controversial because he was considered to be her social inferior. William wrote: 'Many were astonished that a woman so distinguished, powerful, and illustrious, and [once] the wife of such an excellent military man, would deign to marry a virtual commoner.'[159] He said that she chose Reynald secretly, because she wanted to get the consent of the king first. Reynald accordingly rushed to the king, Baldwin III, during the battle of Ascalon in 1153 to get his approval for the marriage.

[155] See 187 above.

[156] WT, 786.

[157] Kinnamos, *Deeds*, 97. See also 136 for a reference to the proposed marriage.

[158] WT, 795.

[159] *Ibid.*, 796.

The fact that Constance was perceived to have chosen her husband and married below her station might indicate that it was for reasons of love. Perhaps she admired Reynald's legendary ambition and pugnacious attitude towards the Muslims, and saw in him exactly what the harried principality of Antioch needed in a ruler. On the other hand, William's assessment of Aimery's ambition may have been correct, and Constance may have feared the encroaching power of the patriarch within her principality. Aimery was certainly unhappy about her new marriage, and subsequently he and the prince entered into a conflict that famously resulted in Reynald torturing the patriarch by smearing his head with honey and making him sit in the hot sun.[160] William of Tyre was shocked by this event, and criticised Reynald's character flaws. His censure might have stemmed from the prince's possible role in the election of Patriarch Eraclius: it has been argued that William went out of his way to obscure the important role that Reynald played in the politics of the kingdom, especially after his release from captivity in 1176.[161] In any case, his criticism reflected badly on Constance, as she had exhibited poor taste in her decision to marry a man William considered to be a liability.[162]

Did Constance change her mind about remarriage in order to keep control over her inheritance? Constance earned a similar reputation to her mother when she reputedly sought to maintain control of Antioch in 1163 even after her son Bohemond III had come of age.[163] She appealed to the Greek general Constantine Coloman for aid against her son when he rebelled, but this resulted in rioting from the people in Antioch. She was exiled, probably to the same dower lands her mother Alice had held, dying soon afterwards.[164] The parallels between their two careers are marked: both women displayed a tendency to appeal to Byzantium despite the empire's well-attested unpopularity amongst the Antiochene population. Perhaps as female regents they were in greater need of a powerful overlord to enforce their authority over unruly vassals. It was possible that by following her mother's example in turning to the

---

[160] Ibid., 809.

[161] See Hamilton, 'Elephant', 97–108.

[162] Baldwin III apparently considered Reynald's treatment of Aimery insane and foolish (WT, 809), and William was critical of his raids on Cyprus (WT, 823–5), and his dispute with Thierry of Flanders over Shaizar (WT, 837). In particular, he was disgusted by Reynald's obeisance to Emperor Manuel when attempting to restore relations between Byzantium and Antioch. WT, 844–5.

[163] There is some dispute over the exact chronology of events, but Lilie seems to favour the idea that Constance's appeal came after Manuel's marriage to Constance's daughter Maria in 1161, and that she took the opportunity provided by King Baldwin III's death to press her claim. Lilie, Byzantium, 187 n. 189.

[164] Michael the Syrian, Chronique de Michel le Syrien, patriarche jacobite d'Antioche (1166–1199), ed. and trans. Jean Chabot, 4 vols (Paris 1899–1924), 3.324.

Byzantines for aid, Constance fell into the same trap that had forced her into marriage with Raymond of Poitiers at such a young age. As well as mentioning her personal distaste for John Roger, John Kinnamos asserted that it was the Antiochene nobility who dissuaded Constance from the proposed marriage, and shortly afterwards she entered into an unexpected marriage with Reynald.[165] Perhaps the most persuasive interpretation is that her remarriage to Reynald was neither inspired by love nor a deliberate attempt by Constance to exercise choice, but was instead a necessary act of reassurance for disgruntled vassals who feared submission to a Byzantine overlord.

The match between Queen Sibylla of Jerusalem and Guy of Lusignan in 1180 also illustrates contemporary perceptions about a widow's decision to remarry. By that year, Sibylla had already fulfilled her dynastic duty and produced a male heir to the throne by her first husband, William of Montferrat. The marriage had been short-lived, but almost immediately after William's death, Philip of Flanders reputedly tried to use his connection of kinship with the two royal heiresses, Sibylla and Isabella, to further his own cause in the East. William of Tyre had a low opinion of Philip; he criticised his refusal to act as regent for the kingdom during the king's illness, and accused him of having ambitions of overlordship in Egypt. When the count complained that no one had approached him on the marriage of his kinswoman Sibylla, William saw this as proof that Philip's aim was to supplant the king.[166] He suggested that Philip wanted to marry off both princesses to the sons of Robert V, the advocate of Bethune, who had agreed to give up certain property claims to Philip's western lands in return for the marriages. There is also the possibility that Baldwin of Ibelin had strong objections to the idea, as Ernoul states that he intended to marry Sibylla himself.[167] The king, however, needed Philip's military aid and could not afford to offend the count openly. Baldwin IV's response was to play for time, and to do so he used the established customs relating to remarriage. To arrange a new marriage for a widow, especially a pregnant one, within a year of the death of her husband would not allow an honourable period for mourning.[168] He pointed out that Sibylla had been widowed scarcely three months, but they were prepared to listen to Philip's advice on the matter if he would put forward a candidate. The count, however, refused to do so unless all barons swore to abide by his decision, a situation which Baldwin IV and his nobles found untenable, and Philip harboured a grudge as a result.[169] Philip's crusade

---

[165] Kinnamos, *Deeds*, 97.

[166] WT, 979–80.

[167] Ernoul, 60.

[168] WT, 981. In fact, Hamilton argues that the links to Flanders and England resulting from such a match would have been beneficial to the Latin kingdom. Hamilton, *Leper King*, 126–7.

[169] WT, 981.

ended in substantial failure for a variety of reasons, but this particular attempt to assert his authority through matrimonial politics did little to improve relations between the crusaders and settlers.

By 1180, negotiations for Sibylla's remarriage were already underway. William of Tyre asserts that Baldwin was planning to marry her to the duke of Burgundy (Hugh III). However, threatened by the intimidating presence of Bohemond III of Antioch and Raymond III of Tripoli in his kingdom in 1180, he made a hasty decision to marry Sibylla to Guy of Lusignan. The marriage was also celebrated unexpectedly during Easter, which was against established custom. It has been thought that the king was experiencing worsening paranoia exacerbated by his medical condition, but William stated rather enigmatically that Baldwin chose Guy 'on account of various things that had occurred'.[170] Several contemporaries opined about what these 'reasons' may have been, and in order to explore them fully it is necessary to return to ideas about love within marriage.

Guy of Lusignan was a crusader from Poitou in Baldwin IV's royal entourage, and was evidently a capable soldier. Roger of Howden described Guy as 'handsome in appearance and proficient in arms', and believed that Sibylla chose him to be her husband because of his good looks. Afraid to tell her brother King Baldwin of her preference, 'she loved him secretly, and he himself slept with her'.[171] Baldwin responded violently in Roger's account, threatening to have them tortured or stoned, but finally responded to more lenient advice and allowed them to marry. If Sibylla had indeed indulged in an illicit relationship of this kind, it is possible that William may have wished to obscure it in his history. Sibylla was the mother of the future heir of the kingdom, Baldwin V, at the time when he was writing, and he would not have wanted to call into question the legitimacy of his succession. Ernoul was much more outspoken, suggesting that Guy had interfered with a prior arrangement, made by Sibylla herself, to marry Baldwin of Ibelin. Sibylla was then persuaded to change her mind by Guy's brother, Aimery of Lusignan, and her mother, Agnes, whom Ernoul accused of having a scandalous affair with each other.[172] In his account no mention is made of her mooted nuptials with Hugh of Burgundy, a fact that leads Hamilton to suggest that the tale was concocted by the pro-Ibelin author to provide 'an explanation of Baldwin's hatred of Guy which was acceptable within the terms of the chivalric code', or at least within the conventions of contemporary chivalric literature.[173]

Prejudice against Guy in narratives of the Latin East was evidently not

---

[170] WT, 1007.

[171] Roger of Howden, 'Gesta', 1.343.

[172] Ernoul, 56–60.

[173] Hamilton, *Leper King*, 154.

entirely based on his involvement in the disaster of Hattin in 1187.[174] William of Tyre, writing no later than 1184, was probably influenced by the breakdown of relations between Baldwin IV and his brother-in-law after the 1183 campaign against Saladin and his removal from regency.[175] Antipathy had existed between Guy and Raymond III of Tripoli since that date, and the latter was William of Tyre's preferred regent of the kingdom. William's history ends with the king's attempt to separate Guy and Sybilla. On hearing of Baldwin's plans to annul the marriage, Guy fled to Ascalon, sending word to Sibylla in Jerusalem to meet him there because he was afraid that the king would physically prevent her from returning to her husband.[176] His fear was not without justification, as the forced separation of Queen Isabella from Humphrey IV of Toron would later demonstrate.

After Baldwin V's death, Sibylla was pressured to divorce Guy in order to take the throne, in the same way that they had made her father Amalric divest himself of an unsuitable wife (Agnes) before his coronation. William of Newburgh wrote in the late 1190s that the Jerusalem nobility accepted her as queen, 'but objected to her unworthy marriage'.[177] Current scholarship interprets the rather bizarre coronation scene recounted by several historians as proof that Sibylla did in fact divorce Guy, but with the legitimacy conferred on her by coronation she immediately took back her repudiated husband, forcing the barons of Jerusalem to accept him as king.[178] *Eracles* described how she called her husband up to be crowned, saying 'Sire, come up and receive this crown, for I do not know where better I can bestow it.'[179] As a crowned heiress, the kingdom was hers to bestow, and her husband received the crown from her, but as a woman she was perceived to need a man to help her to govern.[180] She may have been convinced that Guy was the best hope for the kingdom. On the other hand, it seems likely that she had genuine feelings for him: had she been

[174] Smail has argued that Guy's reputation as an inept ruler and military leader is unjustified. Smail, 'Predicaments', 159–72.

[175] *Ibid.*, 168–72; Hamilton, *Leper King*, 189–92.

[176] WT, 1063. See also *Eracles*: 'He asked the patriarch to summon them, saying that he wanted to challenge the validity of the marriage and demonstrate that it was neither good nor legal.' *Eracles*, 17; trans. Edbury, 11.

[177] WN, 255.

[178] Sibylla's loyalty to her husband at her coronation was evidently a story that continued to catch the imagination of contemporaries; it was even retold in Robert of Clari's history of the Fourth Crusade. *Eracles*, 32–3; WN, 255; RC, 35. For the divorce, see Roger of Howden, *Chronica*, 315–16; *idem*, 'Gesta', 1.358–60; ATF, 859; and Roger of Wendover, *Flores Historiarum*, RS 84 (1886), 1.138–9. For a full discussion, see Kedar, 'The Patriarch Eraclius', 196–8. Hamilton adds the Latin continuation of William of Tyre to this list. See *Lateinische Forsetzung*, 64–5; and Hamilton, *Leper King*, 218–20. See also Gillingham, 'Love, Marriage and Politics', 244–8.

[179] *Eracles*, 33; trans. Edbury, 26.

[180] See 78–9 above.

at all dissatisfied with the marriage, she was given several good opportunities to escape it. After Jerusalem had fallen a year later, the *Itinerarium* described the tearful reunion of the couple at Tortosa after Guy's release from captivity: 'They exchanges kisses, they intertwined embraces, their joy elicited tears, and they rejoiced that they had escaped the disasters which had befallen them.'[181]

Sibylla's apparent devotion to Guy suggests that she did employ her own choice when accepting him as a husband, in accordance with the idea that widows had more freedom over their choice of second husband.[182] Perhaps she was influenced to take action by her first experiences of betrothal and marriage. For reasons unknown, her first suitor, Stephen of Sancerre, rejected her on his arrival in the East although he was 'obligated and already pledged', an embarrassing situation for both the young woman and her family.[183] William claimed that Stephen went on to indulge in licentious activities for the rest of his stay and earned the hatred of the settlers, but Phillips suggests that negotiations between Stephen and Amalric may have broken down over the exact terms of the marriage agreement.[184] The husband who was then chosen for her, William of Monferrat, was irascible and a heavy drinker according to William of Tyre. The marriage did not last long; after three months he succumbed to a mysterious illness, leaving Sibylla pregnant.[185] Gillingham concurs that the marriage between Guy and Sybilla was an example of a higher degree of free choice of partner, although he associates this with more general changes in attitudes towards marriage that were occurring in the twelfth century.[186]

Sibylla's sister Isabella was not so fortunate, however. Her political situation meant that she was subject to a succession of quick remarriages which elicited criticism from contemporary historians. Isabella married her third husband, Henry II of Champagne, a scant few days after the murder of Conrad of Monferrat by Assassins, although there was some question over her status as a widow because her first husband, Humphrey IV of Toron, was still alive. This third marriage drew much attention from contemporary chroniclers, not only because of the scandal involved, but because once more it exposed conflicts between the French and English contingents of the Third Crusade. According to *Eracles*, it was King Richard who wanted Isabella to marry Henry of Champagne, but the count was reluctant because she was pregnant, and Conrad's heir would be entitled to the kingdom. King Richard reputedly offered bribes of military aid and money, and with the provision that Henry's heirs would

---

181 *Itinerarium*, 25; trans. Nicholson, 42.

182 William of Newburgh wrote 'by her own choice she contracted a second marriage'. WN, 255.

183 *Ibid.*, 947.

184 *Ibid.* Phillips, *Defenders*, 205.

185 WT, 978.

186 Gillingham, 'Love, Marriage and Politics', 246.

take the crown after him, Henry agreed to the marriage. Despite criticising the speed of the marriage, *Eracles* admitted that there was political justification for moving so quickly: King Guy was involved in a plot against Richard with the Pisans of Tyre.[187]

Some pro-Angevin crusade narratives took yet another approach. Despite their avowed hatred for Conrad for not aiding the crusaders during the famine at Acre, both the *Itinerarium* and Ambroise provided a rather grand death scene for him. They described him receiving the sacraments, and instructing his wife to guard the city of Tyre and not give it up to anyone except King Richard or a lawful heir.[188] Whether Conrad did indeed survive long enough to give such instructions is open to question, but both texts wanted to assert that it was Richard's right to dispose of Tyre, bolstered by Conrad's dying wish. Later Isabella was seen to be defending King Richard's rights against the French.

> 'There is no one else,' she said, 'who has laboured so much to tear the country from the Turks' hands and restore it to its original liberty. He has the strongest right to dispose of the kingdom as seems best to him.'[189]

Isabella therefore became a mouthpiece for the author to justify Richard's superiority to the French monarch through his efforts of crusade. Apparently thwarted, the French asked Henry of Champagne to marry Isabella, but he refused to do so until he had consulted his uncle Richard, again asserting English dominance.[190] According to the *Itinerarium*, it was Richard who voiced doubts about the validity of the marriage because of Humphrey of Toron, but he agreed that Henry was the choice to rule the kingdom.[191] It was the French who encouraged Henry to pursue the marriage against Richard's advice, at which point Isabella offered him the keys to the city.[192] The author of the *Itinerarium* added: 'I don't think that those who persuaded the count to do this had much to do, for it is no effort to force the willing!'[193] He described the wedding as an attempt to bring peace to the English and French factions, although that aim was not ultimately achieved. The variations on Isabella's portrayal in opposing accounts demonstrate how the role of the widow-heiress and possession of her person and property through remarriage could become the focus of tensions between rival groups on crusade.

Isabella was fortunate enough to retain a degree of her original wealth and had royal blood, which was enough to make her a desirable match for a widow.

---

[187] *Eracles*, 143–4.

[188] *Itinerarium*, 340, Ambroise, 1.143, lns 8834–43.

[189] *Itinerarium*, 342; trans. Nicholson, 308.

[190] *Itinerarium*, 343.

[191] *Ibid.*, 347.

[192] *Ibid.*, 348.

[193] *Ibid.*, 348; trans. Nicholson, 313.

As with all prospective brides, lineage and character remained an important selling point. William of Tyre described Beatrice, the widow of William of Saône, as 'a woman of noble blood, but more noble in her actions', when she married Joscelin II of Edessa.[194] Her virtues may have been emphasised to contrast with William's criticism of Joscelin, whom he asserted was notorious for his licentiousness (and uncleanliness).[195] Others were not so lucky, and became recipients of charity. High death rates on the crusades meant that widows made up some of the legitimate poor in crusade armies, and were therefore eligible to receive charity from the nobility, at the instigation of the Church. Although women are not specifically mentioned, Ambroise and the *Itinerarium* tell how nobles at the siege of Acre were encouraged to give gifts to the needy by the bishop of Salisbury and celebrate those who were most generous in their charity.[196] After the account of the massacre of the garrison at Acre, Ambroise attempted to justify it as vengeance for the Christian martyrs of the siege of Acre, evoking pity for their widows and orphans left behind in the West.[197]

In accordance with ideas about royal protection, the kings of Jerusalem and crusader-kings took it upon themselves to provide for and arrange marriages for widows as an act of charity, but it could also be a useful means of patronage.[198] Fulcher of Chartres tells how Baldwin II involved himself in the succession to Antioch and then successfully defeated Il-Ghazi in 1120. He remained in the city until 'he had married widows, of which he found many there, to husbands in pious affection'.[199] William of Tyre emphasised his efforts to partner widows with men of suitable rank.[200] Widows of war sometimes had to marry below their station in order to support themselves and their families, allowing greater social mobility. Given the political situation in the aftermath of the Field of Blood in 1119, when a high percentage of the male aristocracy had lost their lives, it must have been difficult to find men of appropriate station. Immediately after the battle, Orderic Vitalis described Prince Roger's widow, Cecilia of le Bourcq, acting in an overtly military capacity as a feudal lord by knighting squires so that they could protect the city of Antioch.[201] Asbridge suggests that she herself may have married below her station after Roger's death, as she is later found to be 'Lady of Tarsus' holding lands in Cilicia. These may

---

[194] WT, 635; see above, 149–50.

[195] WT, 635.

[196] Ambroise, 1.71–2, lns 4407–56; *Itinerarium*, 135.

[197] Ambroise, 1.90, lns 5567–71.

[198] Guy of Lusignan gave land to widows as well as daughters in Cyprus; see 87 above.

[199] FC, 634.

[200] WT, 562.

[201] OV, 6.108. Cecilia was the sister of Baldwin II.

have been held in dower or given to her by her brother, Baldwin II, on her remarriage.[202]

Saladin, in 'a great act of courtesy', also supposedly provided for the ladies of Jerusalem whose fathers and husbands had been killed at Hattin. *Eracles* told how these daughters and widows apparently threw themselves upon his mercy, asking for 'counsel and aid' invoking the terminology of the feudal bond.[203] Saladin agreed to free those husbands who were alive, and provided for the women out of his own wealth, 'more to some and less to others according to who they were'.[204] However, Saladin was not entirely motivated by generosity if a widow could provide him with something he desired in return. He refused to release the son of widow, Stephanie of Milly, whose husband (Reynald of Châtillon) Saladin was said to have killed with his own hands, unless she nego-tiated the surrender of Kerak. She was unsuccessful, and although she was allowed to leave Jerusalem with all her wealth and retainers, her son remained in prison.[205]

GRIEF

Grief was an integral part of the imagery of widowhood which had strong feminine connotations, but it could be displayed by both men and women. It was used for a variety of purposes in crusade narratives. The *Itinerarium* described the crusaders' feelings of loss on the death of the Emperor Freder-ick I, as surpassing all tears and laments, even those of mothers for children and widows for husbands.[206] William of Tyre recounts how after the defeat of Louis VII's forces at Mount Cadmos during the Second Crusade women searched for their husbands and sons, mourning or waiting anxiously for news.[207] A particularly notable example of a grieving widow occurred in the narratives of both Robert of Rheims and Gilo of Paris, and may have been based on the source they shared, although there were variations in their accounts. Gualo II of Chaumont-Vexin was killed during the siege of Anti-och, and both Robert and Gilo gave detailed accounts of his wife's reaction to the news.[208] Although Robert asserted that she was of high nobility, he did not name her, whereas Gilo identified her as Humberga, the daughter of Hugh I of Le Puiset and Alice of Montlhéry.[209] He told how, already widowed

[202]   Asbridge, *Principality of Antioch*, 145–6, 159.

[203]   *Eracles*, 72.

[204]   'a l'une plus, et l'autre meins, selonc ce eles estoient'. *Eracles*, 72.

[205]   Ibn Al-Athīr, *Extrait du Kamel-Altevarykh*, 709. Imād al-Din, *Conquête de la Syrie*, 105.

[206]   *Itinerarium*, 56.

[207]   WT, 753.

[208]   Gilo of Paris, *Historia Vie Hierosolimitane*, lx.

[209]   She appears witnessing a charter in the *Cartulaire de l'abbaye de Saint Père de France*, ed. Morand F. Guérard (Paris, 1840), 240.

once,[210] she had embarked on crusade with her brother Everard III of Le Puiset, and her new husband Gualo, only for him to be slain by an act of treachery outside Antioch during a truce. Robert described her grief in the following terms:

> His wife stirred everyone to tears, as she tore at herself in a plaintive manner far beyond what was customary. It moved others with her to grief, and she could neither speak nor cry out because of her sobbing and rapid breath. She was descended from high nobility and, saving the frailty inherent to the flesh, her beauty outshone that of others. Now she was almost as still as a marble column, so that it might have been thought she was dead, had not some warmth of vitality been felt beating in the top of her breast; besides this sign, a vein could be observed pulsing hidden under the frail skin where downy hair separates the swelling eyelids. When she revived, forgetful of feminine modesty, she threw herself upon the ground and, tearing at her cheeks with her nails, pulled at her golden hair.[211]

Gilo also emphasised the physical manifestations of her grief, recounting the tearing of her cheeks and hair, as well as her initial inability to speak or move through sorrow.[212] These images were very stylised and owe much to Ovid's descriptions of mourning women in the *Heroides*, according to Grocock.[213] William of Tyre used similar conventions of grief to describe Queen Melisende's reaction to the death of her husband Fulk in a hunting accident:

> The queen, learning of her husband's death that was so unexpected and struck by the ill-omened event, tore at her clothes and hair, wailing and giving testament to the depth of her grief with sobs and laments, throwing herself onto the ground she embraced his lifeless corpse. The water in her eyes did not suffice for the welling of her continual tears and her

---

[210] Grocock and Siberry assert that her first husband, simply described as 'a count', was Robert, count of Meulan, although he was still alive until 1118. They do not provide a source for this assertion, and the marriage is not mentioned in the account of Robert's life given by Vaughn, who only refers to his marriage to Isabel/Elizabeth of Vermandois, as does Henry of Huntingdon. Orderic Vitalis, on the other hand, asserts that Robert was married first to Godvere of Tosny, before her marriage to Baldwin of Boulogne in 1096, which, as Mayer has shown, was probably an error for 1090; see III, n. 45 above. Chibnall considers this unlikely as Orderic gave no mention of an annulment between Godvere and Robert. See Gilo of Paris, *Historia Vie Hierosolimitane*, 127 n. 6: Sally Vaughn, 'Robert of Meulan and Raison d'État in the Anglo-Norman State, 1093–1118', *Albion* 10 (1978), 352–73; Henry of Huntingdon, *Historia Anglorum*, 598–9; and OV, 3.128–9, n. 1.

[211] RR, 795.

[212] Gilo of Paris, *Historia Vie Hierosolimitane*, 128–9.

[213] Christoper W. Grocock, 'Ovid the Crusader', in Charles Martindale ed. *Ovid Renewed* (Cambridge, 1988), 66–8.

voice, expressing her grief, was interrupted by frequent sobs. Nor could she satisfy her sorrow, though she cared for nothing else but to soothe her distress.[214]

Conversely, a lack of suitable grief could give rise to criticism. Amongst her other faults, Alice of Antioch was portrayed as a scheming and unnatural widow who demonstrated no grief at her husband's death, and began plotting her wicked plans as soon as she heard the news.[215]

Some of the more extreme expressions of sorrow were inappropriate for men, although they could weep and lament. For example, as the situation became more desperate around Antioch, Bohemond and Tancred led a raiding party into hostile territory and were ambushed by Turks. Albert of Aachen described how Bohemond wept and 'the people lamented violently' after his raiding party sustained heavy losses outside Antioch; the mourners included 'women, youths, boys, fathers, mothers, brothers and sisters, who had lost their very beloved friends, sons and relatives'.[216] On the death of his brother William, Tancred's grief '... turned the hearts of others and softened them into womanly tears. Their mouths took up womanly cries. Fingers tore hair from their beards, their cheeks and their heads.'[217] The marked similarity with the description of Gualo's widow may well be a result of Ralph of Caen's affection for Ovid, although he quotes both Virgil and Horace in the same passage. The story ends with the men tearing their armour to pieces – an interesting masculine twist on the expressions of sorrow. Ralph found some male tears inappropriate, however. He criticised Count Robert of Normandy for having an over-developed sense of mercy in the court of judgement: 'no one was brought to the count bound and in tears without an immediate order for the bound man to be released as tears poured from the ruler'.[218] According to Ralph, this 'softly-softly' approach to justice meant that Normandy was beset with unrestrained criminals.

It was acceptable for husbands to experience grief at the loss of a partner. At Dreux, while Philip II of France and Richard the Lionheart were finalising arrangements for the Third Crusade, a messenger arrived with the news that Philip's wife, Isabel of Hainault, had died. Despite the fact that he had tried to put her aside in 1184 for political reasons, this was described as a terrible blow to Philip; he was 'so completely devastated' that he considered backing out of the expedition.[219] Similarly, Villehardouin described Baldwin IX of Flanders'

[214] WT, 710–11.

[215] *Ibid.*, 623.

[216] AA, 218–19.

[217] GT, 624. See also GN 132–3 for Robert's proclivity for tears.

[218] *Ibid.*, 616; trans. Bachrach and Bachrach, 37.

[219] *Itinerarium*, 146; trans. Nicholson, 148. See also Ralph of Diceto, 'Ymagines Historiarum', 77. According to the *Itinerarium* the death of William of Apulia also affected the confidence of the general host.

mourning at the death of his wife, Marie, and how 'it gave great sorrow to all the Christians, for she was a very good and honourable lady', whom they had wanted to be empress.[220] In other cases the death of a spouse could inspire a man to take the cross. Count Fulk v of Anjou went to Jerusalem in 1120–1 after the death of his first wife, 'for the sake of prayer'.[221] Conversely, in some accounts grief went unremarked upon. Albert of Aachen described the death of Godvere of Tosny, whom Baldwin had entrusted to Duke Godfrey in her illness, and recounted that she was buried with Christian rites, but he did not mention Baldwin's reaction.[222]

These references were usually short and formulaic, which makes the account of Gualo's widow stand out in comparison. Robert of Rheims justified his inclusion of the story by asserting the political importance of the killing, as it signified the end of a truce. The story did emphasise Muslim treachery, but this could have been expressed without using a widow. Although Guibert of Nogent made no reference to Humberga, his *Dei Gesta Per Francos* was the only other narrative to record the truce and Gualo's death.[223] His source for this information was a letter from the knight Anselm of Ribemont, who asserted that an offer to surrender the city was made around 20 May and a truce followed with an exchange of envoys. As the constable of the king of France, Gualo was a member of Hugh of Vermandois' contingent, and therefore of considerable importance. Although Anselm described the surrender as a trap, Asbridge suggests that some of the Muslim garrison may have been attempting to organise an unsanctioned surrender at this point, prompting Yaghi Siyan to slaughter the crusaders on discovery of the plot.[224] A few days afterwards, according to Anselm, news came of Kerbogha's imminent arrival.[225]

Perhaps it is not so surprising that the crusaders, who had endured a dire siege and were teetering on the brink of success, lamented the death of Gualo: it signalled the end to a truce which might have offered them a resolution. Robert asserted that the impact of this death should not be under-estimated. On first mentioning the death, he told how 'There was great grief throughout the camp, since the death of Gualo was lamented by all the men and women with frequent sobbing'.[226] He later asserted: 'This incident cannot be passed over lightly, because the truce period had remained intact before the death of

---

[220] Villehardouin, 2.126; Gislebert of Mons emphasised their loving relationship in the early days of their marriage, and Ernoul also mentioned her death. Gislebert of Mons, *Chronique*, 192; Ernoul, 378.

[221] WT, 633.

[222] AA, 182–3.

[223] He identifies him as the constable of Philip I of France. GN, 332.

[224] Thomas S. Asbridge, *The First Crusade: A New History* (London, 2004), 199.

[225] 'Epistula 2 Anselmi', 159.

[226] RR, 795.

this man occurred.'[227] The likelihood of Asbridge's suggestion is borne out by Yaghi Siyan's brutal murder of Christian captives a short time before these events.[228] He did this to forestall the possibility of betrayal, and as Antioch ultimately fell through the treachery of an inhabitant, Firuz, his fears were evidently well-founded.

In Gilo's account, Humberga lamented that her husband's life 'which this treacherous race could not take away in war, has been taken ... by a trick'.[229] This was evidently a reference to breaking the truce, but it is possible that he also intended to reinforce the message that salvation was a reward for all who took the cross, whether or not they died in battle. Similarly, in Robert's version, the widow prayed to the Virgin for the soul of her husband, and to ensure his martyrdom:

> 'King in three persons, have pity on Gualo;
> And confer upon him the gift of life, as you are the one God.
> What had Gualo done wrong, that he should die outside of battle?
> Son of the Virgin Mother, wipe out Gualo's sin,
> A man you have saved from the events of so many battles,
> And whom you have now allowed to be martyred.'[230]

This demonstrated that a wife could have faith in the spiritual benefits of crusading and that her husband was a martyr to a just cause, even while bemoaning her fate. Apparently she regretted that she had not died with him, but this seems to have been more through devotion to her husband than to achieve martyrdom herself.[231] In Gilo's account Humberga also expressed fears for her own safety on crusade without a husband's protection:

> 'Am I to live without you, far away from the land of my father? Shall a woman live, following the camp without a husband ... death is a slight pain to me if I am joined with Gualo in death; if I am not to be enslaved by the savage Turks.'[232]

Gilo thus emphasised the dangers specific to women who took the cross, and seems to suggest that death was the preferable option to enslavement, or life as a camp follower, both of which held connotations of sexual defilement.[233] Similar fears were expressed by Queen Margaret in Damietta: she asserted that she would prefer to have her head cut off rather than be taken captive

---

[227] Ibid., 796.

[228] PT, 79–81.

[229] Gilo of Paris, Historia Vie Hierosolimitane, 128–9.

[230] RR, 795.

[231] Ibid.

[232] Gilo of Paris, Historia Vie Hierosolimitane, 129.

[233] Friedman, Encounters between Enemies, 169.

by the Saracens, presumably again to avoid the threat of sexual perfidy.[234] Humberga also lamented that she was unable to take part in burial rituals for her husband:

> 'Alas, poor me! I have performed no service of pity for you, husband … I have not wiped your mouth with my dress, nor closed your eyes with my hand, nor washed your wounds with my tears.'[235]

This demonstrates a close resemblance to aspects of the 'Widow of Ephesus' fable.[236] The beauty of the widow and her excessive grief, and the mistreatment and displacement of her husband's dead body were all key motifs. In Gilo's account, the fear of capture by the Turks also suggested her sexual availability. The story of Gualo's widow does not, however, mention a new love interest, or hold the traditional misogynistic hallmarks that characterised such tales, as they were customarily employed to caution men about the fickle nature of women.[237]

Although Humberga of Le Puiset has been identified as a real participant in the First Crusade, her appearance in the histories of Robert of Rhiems and Gilo of Paris demonstrates few of the practical issues associated with widows such as dower, remarriage or regency. Nor does she fit easily into the prevalent stereotypes of honourable matrons on crusade such as Margaret of Austria. Like Kerbogha's mother she is transformed into an invented character, and defined by love of her husband, and grief at his loss. The account of Humberga's sorrow provides a counterpoint to his heroism highly reminiscent of contemporary *chansons* and romances, and even if this stylised portrayal was influenced by a lost source, the fact that both Gilo and Robert considered it worthy of inclusion underlines its significance to their overall structure. Her status as a vehicle in the text, rather than an important individual, is borne out by the fact that Robert, unlike Gilo, did not even take the trouble to include her name.

---

[234] See 169–70 above.

[235] Gilo of Paris, *Historia Vie Hierosolimitane*, 129. Cf. 'Oh, I could be happy if I had been able to close his eyes at his last breath, wash his wounds with my tears, and brush off his hands and garments and put his dear body in the grave.' RR, 795–6.

[236] My thanks to Professor Brian J. Levy for bringing this to my attention.

[237] See Arden, 'Grief, Widowhood', 307–10.

Conclusion

THE sources which record the history of crusading and the Latin East during the twelfth and thirteenth centuries were subject to a wide variety of literary influences, both ecclesiastical and lay, and their perceptions of women varied accordingly. Preachers and canonists may have attempted to prevent women from taking the cross, and many authors of narratives agreed to this principle, but there was inherent disparity within both the theory of women's involvement in crusading and the practical reality of their presence on crusade expeditions – their role in 'historical' events. Women were not the only group treated in this manner – many criticisms applied to a range of anonymous non-combatants, including the sick, the young and the elderly. Such restrictions were seldom extended to individual noblewomen who took the cross, as long as they adhered to correct modes of behaviour. They usually accompanied their male kin who would take part in the fighting, and if they could provide financial support to the crusade army, rather than draining its resources, they were often welcomed.

However, high death rates on crusade through warfare, famine or disease could lead to rapid changes in the social arrangements between crusaders, both men and women. Whether they took part in an expedition or not, noblewomen and their families were identified with the aristocratic audience at whom the crusade message was aimed, and authors seemingly found no inherent contradiction in portraying women as a gender to be 'inhibitors', but recognising certain women to be 'enablers'. Even where official statutes or bishops successfully persuaded women to stay in the West, the spiritual and economic opportunities provided by a crusade army inevitably attracted camp followers, in a manner consistent with medieval warfare. Ultimately a combination of gender and social status, usually representing the polarised extremities of wealth and 'acceptable' behaviour, provided adequate reason for chroniclers to allow women onto the written page. Once there, authors saw those individuals who were sufficiently important to historical 'events' developing through their life-cycle stages at the points of marriage, motherhood and widowhood, further stratified criteria which choniclers could use to present their ideas to the audience in familiar terms.

Amongst medieval nobility, the most effective protection for daughters was the segregation of women from men in their childhood years. This made for strong gender identities, but because literate education was dominated by men, we are left with a very male-oriented view of female development which revolved around their entrance into married life. In crusade narratives, information about daughters is invariably scarce and linked to relationships with men, their portrayal often governed by traditional misogynistic ideas about the innate sinful and weak nature of young women. Chroniclers consistently reinforced the idea that 'maidens' were particularly vulnerable to the extreme conditions generated by the crusades and life in a hostile environment. They capitalised upon perceptions about their weakness to create a potent emotive tool for inciting hatred against the Muslims, as well as to chastise errant crusaders. They warned that concern should be taken not only to protect young women from men but also from themselves – those who did take the cross were often perceived to be irresponsible, and in some cases even deserved the unpleasant fate awaiting them. Where possible, crusaders were encouraged by example to make provision for the protection of their daughters at home, unless they were brought on crusade as dynastic 'coin' – with the hope of a prospective marriage. Accounts of noble daughters emphasise that lineage and wealth were both powerful negotiating tools, and perceived as fundamental to the success of international diplomacy and the provision of security in the Latin East. Such tools were usually wielded by heads of families to further their dynastic ambitions. It should not be forgotten, however, that youth was a criterion for withholding the exercise of power from both men and women.

As a daughter, an aristocratic woman may have lacked authority, but on entering married life she had a more visible public role. In the historical narratives of crusading and the Latin East, wives and prostitutes provided a discourse for the polarisation of views on sexual activity at a time when God was perceived to be intervening in human affairs and sex had tangible political and military consequences. Far from providing a uniform view, these histories drew from a variety of sources and reflect a range of attitudes towards wives and sexual relationships, from the wife as active patron and politician, to the victim of warfare and the lustful harlot. These distinctions were made in order to fulfil a didactic purpose. From an official standpoint, women who were not safely married or chaperoned were not of 'good character', and therefore endangered the crusade effort. For most authors this distinction hinged largely upon status rather than gender – the majority of women criticised for their sexual activities were unmarried and associated with the *pauperes* on crusade. Of course, the charge of unlawful sexual activity was levelled at certain noblewomen, but it is significant that those accused were usually involved in adultery and perceived to be acting beneath their station – *as if* they were prostitutes.

Attitudes were not uniformly fixed on these matters, as William of Tyre's failure to criticise Melisende's rumoured adultery suggests. Some authors, such as Fulcher of Chartres and Albert of Aachen, took a more critical view of the presence of wives regardless of status, and hence made clear the risks that awaited women on crusade even if they had the nominal protection of marriage or high birth. In doing so, however, they recognised that, after the success of the First Crusade, wives would continue to be attracted by the idea of crusading.

It appears that by the thirteenth century, when traditions of married couples taking the cross together were well established, most authors recognised that wives who accompanied their husbands on crusade might at least thwart the danger of adultery. In certain circumstances they could even defend their husbands. Many years after her crusade, a story circulated about Eleanor of Castille that she had saved her husband's life by sucking poison from a wound gained when Assassins attacked him, although there was no contemporary evidence of her involvement in the incident.[1]

Despite discouragement from some quarters, for at least a century wives had a legitimate right through their marital vows to accompany their husbands on crusade. Innocent III's decretal *Ex multa* (1201) opened the way for men to take the cross without their wives' consent, but in theory this also meant that wives could crusade without the permission of their husbands. Leaving aside wives who did not sympathise with the crusade idea, or took part at the will of their spouses, many may have taken the cross in fulfilment of vows that were equally as important to them as they were to their husbands. Perceptions of wives in historical narratives of the crusades do not simply reflect reformist views on restricting sexual licentiousness through the marital bond, they also reveal how men and women adapted to a new and certified way to salvation that did not rely on monastic celibacy.[2]

Motherhood was so closely identified with the female sex that its traits were often perceived to transcend the boundaries of status, wealth, and even religion. Whether they were applied to real mothers, men or inanimate subjects, maternal qualities were used to elicit sympathy in a variety of ways. Authors focused on the pain of childbirth, the physical vulnerability associated with it, and the combination of love and apprehension for the future that characterised a mother's relationship with her children. Crusaders' affection for parents was seen as an inhibiting factor, but some chroniclers explicitly recognised the contribution of mothers to the crusade effort, whether it took the form of educating pious sons, guarding their inheritances *in absentia*, providing funds or preserving aristocratic dynasties in the Latin East.

Perceptions about a woman's capacity for motherhood and maternal love were the crucial foundations supporting her authority to educate and act on behalf of her children. Parsons writes: 'As wives, queens were interlopers and potential adulteresses who inspired distrust and suspicion, but their maternal instinct to protect their children and their children's inheritance deserved sympathy and respect.'[3] Historical narratives of the crusades and the Latin East reflect these views to an extent, and chroniclers were also able to use the

---

[1]   Hamilton, 'Eleanor', 103.

[2]   Guibert of Nogent described crusade as 'a new means of attaining salvation'. GN, 87.

[3]   John Carmi Parsons, 'Family, Sex, and Power: The Rhythms of Medieval Queenship', in Parsons, *Medieval Queenship*, 6.

heightened idealisation of motherhood to highlight the shortcomings of certain female regents – a 'bad mother' was the worst of women. Individuals such as Eleanor of Aquitaine, Alice of Antioch, and Agnes of Courtenay were considered to have perverted their femininity in some measure by over-stretching the bounds of maternal authority. Conversely Melisende's conflict with her son was presented by William of Tyre almost as an extension of her maternal desire to protect him (and their inheritance) from the unruly influence of trouble-making cronies – a case of 'mother knows best'. Such an image is reflected in the example of Kerbogha's mother. Even as an isolated case study, the development of her conversation with Kerbogha through successive texts provides yet more new and relevant insights into the ideas of crusaders, the relationship between texts and authorship.

Although primarily defined by their marital status, perceptions about widows also rested on their age, status, wealth and individual actions. The widows of crusaders were often percieved as vulnerable, whether they faced threats to their position in the West, or went on crusade and ended up as captives, carried off to assuage the perceived insatiable carnality of the Muslims. In the history of the Latin East, the procession of widows and female regents indicated just how fragile the Christian presence in Holy Land was. Where widows held considerable power, respect was invariably drawn from their ability to manage their difficult circumstances and take on a masculine role 'beyond their sex'. They could be portrayed as honourable matrons, or as avaricious and selfish when occasion demanded: Adelaide of Sicily certainly seems to have polarised the views of historians. Queen Melisende, a legally sanctioned, efficient and capable ruler in William of Tyre's view, was endowed with manly qualities, while Alice of Antioch behaved in a manner unbecoming to her traditional female roles as a mother and widow, yet her devious actions were percieved as quintessentially feminine. With a few notable exceptions, it seems that authors of narratives of crusading, and particularly histories of the Latin East, were inclined to give widows a positive hearing. They seldom criticised those who ventured back into the cycle of marriage and motherhood in accordance with the law - as long as their choice of husband was approved.

By the time of the fall of Acre in 1291, economic expansion and population increases had coincided with developments in marriage law and inheritance that transformed the public role of women. After the loss of the Holy Land, the spiritual and earthly attractions of Jerusalem remained strongly entrenched in western medieval culture, however. Both historical narratives and fictional literature continued to eulogise crusaders and weave stories around the noble families of the Levant. A Latin presence persisted in the eastern Mediterranean through the remnants of Latin Greece, and the kingdom of Cyprus which resisted the Ottoman advance into the late sixteenth century. Expeditions such as the one which met defeat at Nicopolis in 1396 continued, but on a lesser scale than earlier crusades. In the first half of the fourteenth century a succession of

French kings made plans for crusading to the East, which never came to frui-tion because a variety of political and economic misfortunes conspired to thwart their ambitions. Menache asserts that the crusader vow of Philip the Fair and his sons in 1313, along with their accompanying knighthood, gave an impression of 'a more accessible monarch who personified the union between the dearest ideals of medieval society: knighthood and crusade'[4] The continuing *Recon-quista* in Iberia galvanised support for fighting against the infidel, reinforcing Islam as an ever-present threat to the borders of Christendom. Even after the Reformation, Philip II of Spain's struggle with the Ottomans in the Mediter-ranean in the late sixteenth century involved a Holy League that included the papacy, crusade preaching and indulgences.[5]

At the time when this study draws to a close, realistic prospects of re-estab-lishing a Latin presence in the East were failing. With hindsight, crusading to the Holy Land was effectively curtailed after 1291, and the possibility of mount-ing a successful expedition from the West grew increasingly distant. Nonethe-less, enthusiasm for crusading continued and some postulated theories on how to recapture the Holy Land which included roles for women. These usually revolved around marriage and procreation, but Dubois suggested that women could be educated in order to convert both husbands and Muslim women (through the practice of midwifery) to the ways of Christ.[6]

In the period 1344–8 Bridget of Sweden exhorted others, including Magnus II and VII, king of Sweden and Norway, to take part in a crusade against pagans and infidels. The mystic passed on advice given to her by Christ about how to ensure the success of an expedition.[7] Later in the fourteenth century Catherine of Siena wrote to kings, queens and other nobles in order to garner support for Gregory XI's crusading plans of the 1370s. Maier remarks on how her 'par-ticular brand of mysticism' seemed to bypass the traditional military aspects of crusading, interpreting the crusade as an opportunity for martyrdom which would enable the salvation of mankind, including non-Christians.[8] Lack of expeditions to the Holy Land did not prevent both male and female pilgrims

---

[4] Menache, *The Vox Dei*, 184. See Sylvia Schein, 'Philip IV and the Crusade: A Recon-sideration', in Edbury, *Crusade and Settlement*, 121–6. She asserts that crusade and its leadership were intrinsic to Philip's ideology of monarchy.

[5] See Norman Housley, *The Later Crusades 1274–1580: From Lyons to Alcazar* (Oxford, 1992), 136–50.

[6] See 65–6 above.

[7] Eric Christiansen, *The Northern Crusades and the Baltic Frontier*, 2nd edition (London, 1980), 183–5. See also Thomas Lindkvist, 'Crusades and Crusading Ideology in Sweden', in Alan V. Murray ed. *Crusade and Conversion on the Baltic Frontier 1150–1500* (Aldershot, 2001), 125–6.

[8] Maier, 'Roles of Women', 78–81.

making the journey to Jerusalem in the fourteenth and fifteenth centuries.[9] Other women donated money; in 1360 Elizabeth de Burgh, daughter of Joan of Acre, left 100 marks in her will to support five knights to fight in the Holy Land.[10] Why, therefore, did even the small references to the role played by women recede almost completely from crusade history?

Ultimately we must look to the stylistic developments of crusade histories, rather than ecclesiastical disapproval of women's participation in crusading, to explain the shortfall in historical writing about women on crusade. Despite embracing a wide variety of literary forms, from letters to monastic chronicles, narratives about crusading and the Latin East did have certain distinctive features. They reflected a spectrum of traditional views but combined new elements of literary style, lay influence and lay culture in their interpretation of a new historical phenomenon: crusading and the Latin presence in the Holy Land. It coincided with twelfth-century developments in historical writing by secular clerks or chaplains attached to households who were more interested in 'chivalrous topics'.[11] The lower ranks of the nobility also began to express more of an interest in cataloguing and celebrating their own deeds. By the thirteenth century, vernacular history was becoming the natural way for lay crusaders to record their experiences, and such works, according to Spiegel, 'perfectly suited the tastes and interests of the lay aristocracy' and were 'a new phenomenon in medieval historiography'.[12] The desire for details about the romantic as well as military exploits of heroes, to gain a deeper knowledge of their intimate lives, focused the attention of the historian on the individual. From the outset of the crusade movement, ecclesiastical authors had striven to appeal to the nobility, but the association of crusading with the chivalric and romantic ideals of the court, coupled with the physical loss of the Holy Land, meant that their exhortations for knights to crusade to Jerusalem itself lost impetus, and began to be interpreted as more of a literary *topos*.[13]

From the late twelfth century onwards, romances such as *Flore et Jehane*, or *La Fille du Comte de Pontieu*, had capitalised on the exotic elements of crusading to the East to provide a glittering backdrop to their stories.[14] The extreme hardship of crusading that had been firmly associated with penance came to serve as an example of adventurous and daring feats performed by knights to

---

[9] See Leigh Ann Craig, '"Stronger than Men and Braver than Knights": Women and the Pilgrimages to Jerusalem and Rome in the Later Middle Ages', *JMH* 29 (2003), 153–75.

[10] 'The Will of Elizabeth de Burgh', in *Testamenta Vetusta*, ed. H. Nicholas (London, 1836), 1.57.

[11] Keen, *Chivalry*, 32.

[12] Spiegel, *The Past as Text*, 180.

[13] Of course, crusades were still widely used by the Church and lay rulers to promote wars elsewhere in Europe and the Mediterranean. See Housley, *The Later Crusades*.

[14] See Trotter, *French Literature and the Crusades*, 127–69.

achieve honour. Crusading was appropriated into the family histories of the nobility in the West; nobles both male and female were proud to have ancestors who had taken part, and were concerned to honour them in the art and litera- ture that they patronised. Legends about the crusades continued to develop, as can be seen in the later Crusade Cycles or even in the Robin Hood stories. Crusading was increasingly associated with the knightly quest, whether a knight undertook brave deeds for a feudal lord, a lady-love, or the most ultimate of authorities, God. Such a development eventually affected the understanding of the term 'crusade' itself, with the religious basis of the concept subsumed into literary accounts of the military deeds of crusaders. Rather than promoting a doctrine of Holy War, the terminology of crusading has been absorbed into modern culture as a predominantly 'noble cause'; people often talk in terms of 'moral' or 'political' crusades, when in fact such expressions are still regarded by others as the worst form of injustice.

The decreasing need for religious propaganda in literature about crusading to the Holy Land combined with the effects of the Reformation and Enlight- enment to engender a 'secularisation' of attitudes towards crusading which is at least in part responsible for the limited historical studies on women in this field to date. Eighteenth- and nineteenth-century historians romanticised the military exploits of individual crusaders by emphasising their heroism and prowess, admiring their chivalric sensibilities while retaining mild condescen- sion for their credulous belief in the crusade ideal.[15] Following the lead of medi- eval writers, women were excised from their texts as historically unimportant unless they were transmitters of lineage or were perceived to be obstructing military activity. As Siberry's work on the image of crusading in the nineteenth and early twentieth centuries shows, women were usually relegated to the role of neglected bystander, even though contemporary sources explicitly state that women took part.[16]

A cursory overview of historical narratives does give the general impression that histories either criticised or at best were indifferent to the role of women on crusade, but this view is belied by the number of recent studies reconstruct- ing women's activities in relation to crusade and settlement. Even if women did not take the cross personally, by the fall of Acre in 1291 crusading had become an integral part of medieval society which had touched the lives of women all over Europe. Throughout the crusading era women committed themselves alongside their families to the Holy War, and without their support the bound- aries of Christendom could not have expanded, nor could a Latin society in the East have flourished for as long as it did. This study demonstrates that

[15] Many did question the motivation and practicality of the crusade movement, but the idea was still popular in literature and art, and crusading ancestors were celebrated. For more detail see Siberry, *The New Crusaders*.

[16] Siberry, 'The Crusader's Departure', 177–90.

there can be a *via media*, a way to account for the disparate opinions of women and crusading as they appear in crusade texts. It has been careful to avoid an approach that interprets language too literally, but has attempted to maintain a medieval perspective on the conventions surrounding the portrayal of women and to decipher the meanings that contemporaries intended to impart. Partner wrote of Guibert of Nogent's *Memoirs* that interpretation should be 'an activity of translation, not paraphrase'. She goes on to write:

> We need a new language, a non-twelfth century language, which respects the reality of the carnal letter but which opens onto a new realm of 'invisible things' ... The psychoanalytic premise which assumes the existence of layers of unseen, unseeable, permanently forgotten experience pressing on consciousness which can be recaptured only through translation, figuration, and allegory allows, as medieval exegesis allowed, things to be what they seem and what they do not seem to be, without contradiction.[17]

Despite the religious and military nature of crusade as subject matter, the histories pertaining to crusading themes can be adequately compared with the literature from ecclesiastical and chivalric origins; in fact, fundamental perceptions of women vary little beyond the choice of model to describe them. Narrative sources were carefully constructed either to justify the actions of crusaders and settlers or to promote concepts, including crusading itself. As a result, even brief mentions of women had significance because they were considered by the author to be part of his historical explanation, whether he was attempting to provide the 'truth', or edify his audience with didactic examples that were fundamental to the purpose of medieval history. Then, as now, it is the historian who makes the decision about which evidence to use, guided by the principal aims of his or her study. Whether they were 'real' women because they were involved in 'real' historical events, or invented female characters who acted as mirrors exposing the failings or superiority of men, perceptions of women in historical narratives were governed by the author and the sensibilities of his target audience.

This study has aimed to bring crusade narratives back into the wider sphere of medieval gender history as source-material for women, and it has proved that there is a wealth of information available to the historian who is prepared to ask the right questions: or, at least, a different combination of questions. The study of gender is only one of many tools available to assess the way that medieval authors perceived and described the world around them. Narratives must be read in their contemporary context, allowing for written and unwritten influences, and with recognition that the lives of both men and women

---

[17] Nancy F. Partner, 'The Family Romance of Guibert of Nogent', 362–3.

were restricted by social, political and economic factors as well as gender in the medieval period.

A comparison of life-cycle stages has demonstrated that models for women's behaviour varied with family role, but even these forms of social categorisation overlapped: wives, widows and virgins were subsumed into the wider debate about the relative virtues of chastity and marriage; mothers and wives vied for intercessory power with husbands and children; mothers, wives and widows often shared the role of regent. A further, most fundamental characteristic shaping perceptions of women in narratives of crusading and the Latin East was status. In narratives of crusading, individual noblewomen of sufficient means and status may not have enjoyed a high profile, but only Eleanor of Aquitaine seems to have been specifically targeted for causing the failure of an expedition, and unsurprisingly it was one which ended in a spectacular flop. Albert of Aachen's account is perhaps the only example where women both noble and poor regularly meet an unwelcome fate.[18]

The majority of narrative accounts of the 'inhibiting' influence of women usually focused on general subjects: with the exception of a few individuals, it was unnamed groups of wives, mothers or children who held crusaders back with their tears and imprecations. Fears about inappropriate sexual behaviour were also attached to anonymous groups of women, prostitutes or maidservants. The only individual to be explicitly accused of adultery while on crusade was Eleanor of Aquitaine, whose image looms disproportionately large, considering the number of noblewomen who took part in expeditions without censure in narratives.[19] The introduction of 'fictional' characters such as Melaz, Kerbogha's mother and Gualo's widow also allowed authors to present their own ideas about crusading to the audience in a format which would be readily received.

In comparison, histories of the settler society in the Latin East provide more scope for considering the activities of noblewomen outside the battlefield. To a certain extent this gave women a greater role in historical 'events' and provided authors with more subject matter to reveal their views on gender, but dependence of continuators on the tradition of William of Tyre, as well as the fragmentation of Frankish society in the Latin East during the later thirteenth century, also engendered limitations. The actual resources available to Levantine noblewomen of the thirteenth century were increasingly chipped away, and their legal right to regency gradually eroded. In these less beneficial circumstances, they lacked the political impact of their twelfth-century counterparts, and their role was often overshadowed by the import of calamitous military events to the Christians in the Holy Land.

By focusing on a specific group of narratives, this study has only dealt with

---

[18]   See 96–7, 99–100, 148–9, 151–2, 168, 211–12, 215, 233 above.

[19]   See 131–4, 140–1, 180–1 above.

a small portion of the available material for crusading. A comparison of women in the Latin East with those in other areas of medieval expansion such as Iberia and the Baltic could be particularly fruitful, considering the development of scholarship on medieval frontiers.[20] Perceptions of women and crusading could be extended into the centuries after a Latin kingdom existed in the East; Siberry has addressed the role of women in the popular image of crusading in the eighteenth and nineteenth centuries, but no specific study has addressed the role of women in the 'later crusades'.[21] A definitive history of women's roles in the settler society of the Latin East has yet to be produced, and there is certainly potential for more work on the effects of crusading on women who stayed in the West. At present, the field of medieval gender studies is expanding rapidly, both methodologically and theoretically, across the boundaries of different disciplines. A re-examination of crusade sources using modern critical techniques is only a small contribution in the growing collage of research in this field. However, the histories of crusading are ideally placed for such work: ensconced at the juncture of lay and ecclesiastical values that were the dominant force in shaping perceptions of the past, and future, of medieval women.

---

[20] See Robert Bartlett and Angus Mackay ed. *Medieval Frontier Societies* (Oxford, 1989); Daniel Power and Naomi Standen eds *Frontiers in Question, Eurasian Borderlands, 700–1700* (Basingstoke, 1999); Daniel Power, *The Norman Frontier in the Early Twelfth and Early Thirteenth Centuries* (Cambridge, 2004); and Nora Berend, 'Frontiers', in Nicholson, *Palgrave Advances in the Crusades*, 148–71.

[21] Siberry, 'The Crusader's Departure', in Edgington and Lambert, *Gendering the Crusades*, 177–90.

Bibliography

Primary Sources

Acta Sanctorum quotquot toto orbe coluntur, ed. Johannes Bollandus and G. Henschenius (Antwerp, 1643–); *Acta Sanctorum: Editio novissima*, ed. Joanne Carnandet *et al.* (Paris, 1863–).

Alberic of Trois Fontaines, *Chronicon*, ed. Paul Scheffer-Boichorst, MGH SS 23 (1874), 631–950.

Albert of Aachen, *Historia Ierosolymitana*, ed. and trans. Susan Edgington (Oxford, 2007).

Ambroise, *The History of the Holy War: Ambroise's Estoire de la Guerre Sainte*, ed. and trans. Marianne Ailes and Malcolm Barber, 2 vols (Woodbridge, 2003).

—— *L'Estoire de la Guerre Sainte par Ambroise*, ed. and trans. Gaston Paris (Paris, 1897).

St Ambrose, *De Viduis*, in Jacques-Paul Migne ed. *Patrologia Latina* 16 (Paris, 1880), cols 185–278.

—— trans. H. de Romestin, in *Some of the Principal Works of St. Ambrose* (Select Library of Nicene and Post-Nicene Fathers of the Christian Church) 10 (Michigan, 1955), 391–407.

Annales d'Aboulfeda, RHC Or. 1 (1872), 1–165.

Annales Marbacenses, ed. Hermann Bloch, MGH *Scr. Rer. Ger.* 9 (1907), 1–103.

Annales monasterii de Waverleia, in Henry Richards Luard ed. *Annales Monastici* (A.D. 1–1432), 5 vols, RS 36 (London, 1864–89), 2.129–411.

Annales ordinis S. Benedicti, ed. Jean Mabillon, 6 vols (Paris, 1703–39).

Anonymi Gesta Francorum, ed. Heinrich Hagenmeyer (Heidelberg, 1890).

—— *Gesta Francorum et aliorum Hierolsolimitanorum*, ed. and trans. Rosalind Hill, Nelson's Medieval Texts (London, 1962).

—— *Histoire Anonyme de la Première Croisade*, ed. Louis Bréhier (Paris, 1924).

Aristotle, 'Historia Animalium', trans. D'Arcy Wentworth Thompson, in *The Works of Aristotle* (Oxford, 1910).

St Augustine, 'De Nuptiis et Concupiscentia', *Patrologia Latina* 44 (Paris, 1865), cols 413–74.

Bahā' ad-Din, *The Rare and Excellent History of Saladin*, trans. Donald S. Richards (Aldershot, 2002).

Baudri of Bourgueil, *Historia Jerosolimitana*, in RHC Occ. 4 (1879), 1–111.

—— *Les oeuvres poétiques de Baudri de Bourgueil*, ed. Phyllis Abrahams (Paris, 1926).

St Bernard, *Sancti Bernardi Opera*, ed. Jean Leclercq and Henri Marie Rochais, 8 vols (Rome, 1955–77).

—— *The Letters of Saint Bernard of Clairvaux*, trans. Bruno Scott James, 2nd edition (Stroud, 1998).

——'Liber ad milites Templi de laude novae militiae', SBO 3.213–39.

Boccacio, Giovanni, *The Corbaccio*, trans. Anthony K. Cassell (Urbana, 1975).

The Canso d'Antioca: An Occitan Epic Chronicle of the First Crusade, ed. Linda M. Paterson and Caroline E. Sweetenham (Aldershot, 2003).

Cartulaire de l'abbaye de Saint Père de France, ed. Morand F. Guérard (Paris, 1840).

Cartulaire du Chapitre du St. Sépulchre du Jérusalem, ed. Geneviéve Bresc-Bautier (Paris, 1984).

Cartulaire générale de l'ordre du Temple 1119?–1150, ed. G. A. M. J. A. d'Albon (Paris, 1913–22).

La Chanson d'Antioche, ed. Suzanne DuParc Quioc, 2 vols (Paris, 1978).

La Chanson de Jérusalem, ed. Nigel Thorp (Tuscaloosa, 1992).

Chartes de l'abbaye de Saint Hubert-en-Ardenne, ed. Godefroid Kirth, 2 vols (Brussels, 1903).

Chaucer, Geoffrey, *The Wife of Bath*, ed. Peter G. Beidler (Boston, 1996).

Choniates, Niketas, *O City of Byzantium: The Annals of Niketas Choniates*, trans. Harry M. Magoulias (Detroit, 1984).

Christine de Pizan, *The Book of The City of Ladies* (Harmondsworth, 1999).

Chronica regia Coloniensis continuatio prima, 1175–1220, ed. Georg Waitz, MGH SS 24 (1879), 1–20.

Chronicon Ebersheimense, ed. Ludwig Weiland, MGH SS 23 (1874), 427–53.

La Chronique attribuée au connétable Smbat, ed. and trans. Gérard Dédéyan (Paris, 1980).

La Chronique d'Ernoul et de Bernard le Trésorier, ed. Louis de Mas Latrie (Paris, 1871).

Codagnelli, Johannes, *Annales Placentini Guelfi*, ed. Oswald Holder-Egger, MGH Scr. Rer. Ger. 23 (1901).

Contemporary Sources for the Fourth Crusade, trans. Alfred J. Andrea (Leiden, 2000).

Continuatio Annales Admuntenses 1140–1250, ed. Wilhelm Wattenbach, MGH SS 9 (1851), 579–93.

La Continuation de Guillaume de Tyr 1184–1197, ed. Margaret R. Morgan (Paris, 1982).

—— *The Conquest of Jerusalem and the Third Crusade*, trans. Peter W. Edbury (Aldershot, 1996).

Continuation de Guillaume de Tyr de 1229 à 1261, dite du manuscrit de Rothelin, in RHC Occ. 2 (1859), 489–639.

—— *Crusader Syria in the Thirteenth Century: The Rothelin Continuation of William of Tyre with Part of the Eracles or Acre Text*, trans. Janet Shirley (Aldershot, 1999).

Cronica Reinhardsbrunnensis, ed. Oswald Holder-Egger, 2 vols, MGH SS 30 (Hanover, 1896), 1.490–656.

Cynewulf, *Elene*, ed. Pamela O. E. Gradon (London, 1958).

De expugnatione Lyxbonensi, ed. and trans. Charles Wendell David (New York, 2001), with new foreword by Jonathan Phillips.

Documents Relatifs à la successibilité au trône et à la régence, in RHC Lois 2 (1843), 393–422.

—— *The Recovery of the Holy Land*, trans. Walther I. Brandt (New York, 1956).

Dubois, Pierre, *De Recuperatione Terre Sancte: Dalla 'Respublica Christiana' ai primi nazionalismi e alla politica antimediterrania*, ed. Angelo Diotti (Firenze, 1977), 117–211.

Ekkehard of Aura, *Hierosolymita, de oppressione, liberatione et restauratione Jerosolymitanae ecclesiae*, in RHC Occ. 5 (1895), 11–40.

—— *Hierosolymita*, ed. Heinrich Hagenmeyer (Tubingen, 1877).

L'Estoire de Eracles Empereur, in RHC Occ. 2 (1859), 1–481. See RHC Occ. 1 (1844) for translation of William of Tyre.

Estoires d'Outremer et de la Naissance Salehadin, ed. Margaret A. Jubb (London, 1990).

Eugenius III, *Quantum Praedecessores*, 90–2, in Rolf Grosse, 'Überlegungen zum Kreuzzugsaufruf Eugens III von 1145/6: Mit einer Neuedition von JL8876', *Francia* 18 (1991), 85–92.

—— *Divina Dispensatione 1*, ed. Paul Kehr, 'Papsturkunden in Malta', in *Papsturkunden in Italien: Reiserberichte zur Italia Pontificum*, 6 vols (Acta Romanorum Pontificum) (Rome, 1977), 2.108–10.

Fragmentum historicum vitam Ludovici VII, in RHGF 12 (Paris, 1877), 285–6.

Fulcher of Chartres, *Historia Hierosolymitana (1095–1127)*, ed. Heinrich Hagenmeyer (Heidelberg, 1913).

Geoffrey of Villehardouin, *La Conquête de Constantinople*, ed. and trans. Edmond Faral, 2 vols (Paris, 1938).

Gerald of Wales, 'De Principis Instructione Liber', in John S. Brewer, James F. Dimock George F. Warner eds *Giraldi Cambrensis Opera*, 8 vols, RS 21 (1861–91), 8.1–329.

—— 'Itinerarium Kambriae', in *Giraldi Cambrensis Opera*, 6.1–152.

Gervase of Canterbury, 'Chronica', in William Stubbs ed. *Gervasii Cantuariensis Opera Historica*, 2 vols, RS 73 (1879–80), vol. 1.

Gervase of Canterbury, 'Gesta Regum', in William Stubbs ed. *Gervasii Cantuariensis Opera Historica*, 2 vols, RS 73 (1879–80), vol. 2.

Les Gestes des Chiprois, in RHC Arm. 2 (1906), 653–1012.

—— part III (RHC Arm. 2.37–1012) translated in Paul Crawford, *The 'Templar of Tyre': Part III of the Deeds of the Cypriots* (Aldershot, 2003), 95–100.

Gilo of Paris, *The Historia Vie Hierosolimitane*, ed. and trans. Christoper W. Grocock and Elizabeth Siberry (Oxford, 1997).

Giselbert of Mons, *Chronique*, ed. Leon Vanderkindere (Brussels, 1904).

Guibert of Nogent, *Dei Gesta Per Francos et cinq autres textes*, ed. Robert B. C. Huygens, CCCM 127A (Turnhout, 1996).

—— *Autobiographie*, ed. Edmond-René Labande (Paris, 1981).

—— *A Monk's Confession: The Memoirs of Guibert of Nogent*, trans. Paul J. Archambault (University Park, PA, 1996).

—— *Self and Society in Medieval France*, ed. John F. Benton (New York, 1970).

Guillaume de Lorris and Jean de Meun, *The Romance of the Rose*, trans. Frances Horgan (Oxford, 1994).

Guillaume de Tyr et ses continuateurs: texte français du xiiie siècle, revu et annoté, ed. Paulin Paris (Paris, 1879–80).

Gunther of Pairis, *Hystoria Constantinopolitana*, ed. Peter Orth (Hildesheim, 1994).

—— *The Capture of Constantinople*, trans. Alfred J. Andrea (Philadelphia, 1997).

Henry of Huntingdon, *Historia Anglorum*, ed. and trans. Diana Greenaway (Oxford, 1996).

Histoire générale de Languedoc, ed. Joseph Vaissète, Claude Devic and Auguste Molinier, 16 vols (Toulouse, 1872–1904; reprinted Osnabrück, 1973).

Historia Diplomatica Friderici Secundi, ed. Jean L. A. Huillard-Bréhols, 6 vols (Paris, 1852–61).

Historia Gloriosi Regis Ludovici vii, in RHGF 12, 124–33.

Historia Welforum Weingartensis, in MGH SS 21 (1869), 454–72.

Hrotsvithae Opera, ed. Helene Homeyer (Paderborn, 1970).

Ibn Al-Athīr, *Extrait du Kamel-Altevarykh*, RHC Or. 1 (1872), 187–744.

—— *Histoire des Atabecs de Mosul* RHC Or. 2 (1876), 1–375.

'Imād al-Din al Isfahāni, *Conquête de la Syrie et de la Palestine par Saladin*, trans. Henri Massé (Paris, 1972).

Das Itinerarium peregrinorum: Eine zeitgenössische englische Chronik zum dritten Kreuzzug in ursprünglicher Gestalt, ed. Hans Eberhard Mayer, Schriften der MGH, 18 (Stuttgart, 1962).

'Itinerarium Peregrinorum et Gesta Regis Ricardi', in William Stubbs ed. *Chronicles and Memorials of the Reign of Richard 1*, 2 vols, RS 38 (London, 1864), vol. 1.

—— *Chronicle of the Third Crusade: A Translation of the Itinerarium Peregrinorum et Gesta Regis Ricardi*, ed. Helen Nicholson (Aldershot, 1997).

James of Vitry, 'Sermon 2', in Christoph T. Maier ed. and trans. *Crusade Propaganda and Ideology* (Cambridge, 2000), 100–27.

St Jerome, 'Letter to Eustochium', *Patrologia Latina* 22 (Paris, 1877), cols 394–425.

—— 'Letter to Furia', *Patrologia Latina* 22 (Paris, 1877), cols 550–60.

John of Ibelin, *Le Livre des Assises*, ed. Peter W. Edbury (Leiden, 2003).

John of Joinville, *Histoire de Saint Louis, Credo et lettre a Louis x*, ed. and trans. Natalis de Wailly (Paris, 1874).

John of Salisbury, *Memoirs of the Papal Court*, ed. and trans. Marjorie Chibnall (London, 1956).

Kinnamos, John, *The Deeds of John and Manuel Comnenus*, trans. Charles M. Brand (New York, 1976).

Die Konstitutionen Friedrichs II von Hohenstaufen für sein Köhngreich Sizilien, ed. and trans. Hermann Conrad, Thea von der Lieck-Bukyen und Wolfgang Wagner (Cologne, 1973).

Die Kreuzzugsbriefe aus den Jahren 1088–1100, ed. Heinrich Hagenmeyer (Innsbruck, 1901).

Lambert of Ardres, *Historia Comitum Ghisnensium*, MGH SS 24 (1879), 550–642.

Die Lateinische Forsetzung Wilhelms von Tyrus, ed. Marianne Salloch (Leipzig, 1934).

Liber miraculorum sancte Fidis, ed. Auguste Bouillet (Paris, 1997).

The Life of Christina of Markyate, a Twelfth Century Recluse, ed. and trans. Charles H. Talbot, 2nd edition (Oxford, 1987).

Lignages d'Outremer, ed. Marie Adélaide Nielen (Paris, 2003).

Le Livre au Roi, ed. and trans. Myriam Greilsammer (Paris, 1995).

Map, Walter, *De Nugis Curiailum*, ed. and trans Montague R. James, revised by Christopher N. L. Brooke and Roger A. B. Mynors (Oxford, 1983).

Marcabru: A Critical Edition, ed. Simon Gaunt, Ruth Harvey and Linda Patterson (Cambridge, 2000).

Marie de France, *Fables*, ed. and trans. Harriet Spiegel (Toronto, 1987).

—— *Lais*, ed. Alfred Ewert (Oxford, 1944).

Michael the Syrian, *Chronique de Michel le Syrien, patriarche jacobite d'Antioche (1166–1199)*, ed. and trans. Jean Chabot, 4 vols (Paris, 1899–1924).

The Miracles of Our Lady of Rocamadour, trans. Marcus Bull (Woodbridge, 1999).

Miracula Sancti Leonardi, in AA SS, Nov. 3, 160–8.

Monuments historiques, ed. Jules Tardif (Paris, 1866).

Niger, Ralph, *De Re Militari et triplici peregrinationis Ierosolimitanae*, ed. Ludwig Schmugge (Berlin, 1977).

Odo of Deuil, *De Profectione Ludovici VII in Orientem*, ed. and trans. Virginia Gingerick Berry (New York, 1948).

Ogerius Panis, 'Annales', in *Cafari et continuatio Annales Ianuensis (1198–1219)*, ed. Karolus Pertz MGH SS 18 (1863), 115–42.

Oliver of Paderborn, 'Historia Damiatina', ed. Hermann Hoogeweg, *Die Schriften des Kölner Domscholasters, späteren Bischofs von Paderborn und Kardinal Bischifs von S. Sabina* (Tübingen, 1894).

Ottonis et Rahewini Gesta Friderici Imperatoris, ed. Georg Waitz, 2 vols, MGH *Scr. Rer. Ger.* 46 (1912).

—— *The Deeds of Frederick Barbarossa – Otto of Freising*, trans. Charles Christopher Mierow (Toronto, 1994).

Paris, Matthew, *Chronica Majora*, ed. Henry Richard Luard, 7 vols, RS 57 (London, 1872–83).

Philip of Novara, *Livre*, RHC Lois 1 (1841), 469–571.

—— 'Les Gestes des Chiprois', in RHC *Arm.* 2 (1906), 670–736 (part II).

The Pilgrimage of Etheria, trans. M. L. McClure and Charles L. Feltoe (New York, 1919).

Ralph of Coggeshall, *Chronicon Anglorum*, ed. Joseph Stevenson, RS 66 (London, 1875).

Ralph of Diceto, 'Ymagines Historiarum', in William Stubbs ed. *The Historical Works of Master Ralph de Diceto*, 2 vols, RS 68 (London, 1876), 2.3–174.

Ranulf of Higden, *Polychronicon*, ed. Joseph R. Lumby, 9 vols, RS 41 (1882).

Ralph of Caen, *Gesta Tancredi*, in RHC *Occ.* 3 (1866), 603–716.

—— *The Gesta Tancredi of Ralph of Caen: A History of the Normans on the First Crusade*, ed. and trans. Bernard S. Bachrach and David S. Bachrach (Aldershot, 2005).

Raoul de Cambrai, ed. and trans. Sarah Kay (Oxford, 1992).

Raymond of Aguilers, *Le Liber de Raymond D'Aguilers*, ed. John Hugh and Laurita L. Hill (Paris, 1969).

Récits d'un ménéstrel de Rheims au treizième siècle, ed. Natalis de Wailly (Paris, 1876).

Recueil de chartes de l'abbaye de Cluny, ed. A. Bernard and A. Bruel, 6 vols (Paris, 1876–1903).

Regesta Regni Hierosolymitani (1097–1291), ed. Reinhold Röhricht, 2 vols (Innsbruck, 1893–1904).

Richard of Devizes, *Chronicon*, ed. and trans. John T. Appleby (London, 1963).

Rigord, 'Chronique', in Henri-Francois Delaborde ed. *Œuvres de Rigord et Guillaume le Breton*, 2 vols (Paris, 1882).

Robert of Clari, *La Conqête de Constantinople*, ed. Philippe Lauer (Paris, 1924).

—— *The Conquest of Constantinople*, trans. Edgar Holmes McNeal (Toronto, 1996).

Robert of Rheims, *Historia Hierosolymitana*, in RHC *Occ.* 3 (1864), 717–882.

—— *Robert the Monk's History of the First Crusade: Historia Iherosolimitana*, trans. Carol E. Sweetenham (Aldershot, 2005).

Roger of Howden, *Chronica*, ed. William Stubbs, 4 vols, RS 51 (London, 1868–71).

—— 'Gesta Henrici Secundis', in William Stubbs ed. *The Chronicle of the Reigns of Henry II and Richard I*, 2 vols, RS 49 (1867).

Roger of Wendover, *Flores Historiarum*, 3 vols, RS 84 (1886–9)

Rotuli de Oblatis et Finibus in Turri Londinensi asservati tempore regis Johannis, ed. Thomas Duffus Hardy (London, 1835).

Stephen of Bourbon, *Anecdotes Historiques, Légendes et Apologues*, ed. Albert Lecoy de La Marche (Paris, 1877).

Abbot Suger of Saint Denis, *Vita Ludovici Grossi Regis*, ed. and trans. Henri Waquet (Paris, 1964).

Testamenta Vetusta, ed. Nicholas H. Nicolas (London, 1826).

Thomas of Froidmont, *Hodoeporicon et pericula Margarite Iherosolimitane*, in Paul Gerhard Schmidt, "'Peregrinatio Periculosa." Thomas von Friedmont über die Jerusalemfahrten seiner Schwester Margareta', 472–85, in Justus Stache, Wolfgang Maaz, Fritz Wagner eds *Kontinuität und Wandel. Lateinische Poesie von Naevius bis Baudelaire. Franco Munari zum 65. Geburtstag* (Hildesheim, 1986), 461–85.

Tudebode, Peter, *Historia De Hierosolymitano Itinere*, ed. John Hugh and Laurita L. Hill (Paris, 1977).

Vitalis, Orderic, *The Ecclesiastical History of Orderic Vitalis*, ed. and trans. Marjorie Chibnall, 6 vols (Oxford, 1969–80).

Walter the Chancellor, *Bella Antiochena*, ed. Heinrich Hagenmeyer (Innsbruck, 1896).

—— *Walter the Chancellor's 'The Antiochene Wars'*, ed. Thomas S. Asbridge and Susan B. Edgington (Aldershot, 1999).

William of Jumiéges, Orderic Vitalis and Robert of Torigny, *Gesta Normannorum Ducum*, ed. and trans. Elisabeth van Houts, 2 vols (Oxford, 1995).

William of Malmesbury, *Gesta Regum Anglorum*, ed. and trans. Roger A. B. Mynors, completed by Rodney M. Thompson and Michael Winterbottom, 2 vols (Oxford, 1998–9).

William of Newburgh, 'Historia Rerum Anglicarum', in Richard Howlett ed. *Chronicles of the Reigns of Stephen, Henry II and Richard I*, 4 vols, RS 82 (London, 1884), vols 1–2.

William of St Pathus, 'Vie de Saint Louis par le Confesseur de la Reine Marguerite', in RHGF 20 (Paris, 1840), 58–120.

William of Tyre, *Chronicon*, ed. Robert B. C. Huygens, 2 vols (Turnhout, 1986).

—— *A History of Deeds Done Over the Sea*, ed. and trans. Emily A. Babcock and August C. Krey, 2 vols (Colombia University Press, 1943).

Secondary Sources

Adams, Jeremy duQuesnay, 'Modern Views of Medieval Chivalry, 1884–1984', in Howell Chickering and Thomas H. Seiler eds *The Study of Chivalry: Resources and Approaches* (Kalamazoo, 1988), 41–89.

Ainsworth, Peter, 'Legendary History: *Historia* and *Fabula*', in Deborah Mauskopf Deliyannis ed. *Historiography in the Middle Ages* (Leiden, 2003), 387–416.

Albu, Emily, *Norman Histories: Propaganda, Myth and Subversion* (Woodbridge, 2001).

Angold, Michael, *The Byzantine Empire 1025–1204*, 2nd edition (London, 1997).

Arden, Heather M., 'Grief, Widowhood and Women's Sexuality in Medieval French Literature', in Louise Mirrer ed. *Upon My Husband's Death: Widows in the Literature and Histories of Medieval Europe* (Ann Arbor, 1992), 305–19.

Ariès, Philip, *Centuries of Childhood*, trans. Robert Baldick (London, 1962).

Asbridge, Thomas S., *The First Crusade: A New History* (London, 2004).

——'Alice of Antioch: A Case Study of Female Power in the Twelfth Century', in Marcus Bull and Norman Housley eds *The Experience of Crusading: Western Approaches* (Cambridge, 2003), 1.29–47.

—— *The Creation of the Principality of Antioch, 1098–1130* (Woodbridge, 2000).

Badinter, Elisabeth, *The Myth of Motherhood: An Historical View of the Maternal Instinct* (London, 1981).

Barber, Malcolm, 'Women and Catharism', *Reading Medieval Studies* 3 (1977), 45–62.

Barber, Richard, *The Knight and Chivalry* (Ipswich, 1974).

Bartlett, Robert and Angus Mackay ed. *Medieval Frontier Societies* (Oxford, 1989).

Beer, Jeanette M. A., *Narrative Conventions of Truth in the Middle Ages* (Geneva, 1981).

Bell, Susan Groag, 'Medieval Women Book Owners: Arbiters of Lay Piety and Ambassadors of Culture', in Mary Erler and Maryanne Kowaleski eds *Women and Power in the Middle Ages* (Athens, GA, 1988), 149–87.

Bennet, Judith M., *Women in the Medieval Countryside: Gender and Household in Brigstock before the Plague* (Oxford, 1987).

Bennett, Matthew, 'Virile Latins, Effeminate Greeks and Strong Women: Gender Definitions on Crusade', in Susan Edgington and Sarah Lambert eds *Gendering the Crusades* (Cardiff, 2001), 16–30.

Berend, Nora, 'Frontiers' in Helen Nicholson ed. *Palgrave Advances in the Crusades*, (Basingstoke, 2005), 148–71.

Berkey, Jonathan, 'Women in Medieval Islamic Society', in Linda E. Mitchell ed. *Women in Medieval Western European Culture* (New York, 1999), 95–111.

Bidon, Danièle Alexandre and Didier Lett, *Children in the Middle Ages: Fifth–Fifteenth Centuries*, trans. Jody Gladding (Notre Dame, 1999).

Blamires, Alcuin, *The Case for Women in Medieval Culture* (Oxford, 1997).

—— with Karen Pratt and C. William Marx eds *Woman Defamed and Woman Defended: An Anthology of Medieval Texts* (Oxford, 1992).

Bloch, R. Howard, *Medieval Misogyny and the Invention of Western Romantic Love* (Chicago, 1991).

Bloss, Celestia Angenette, *Heroines of the Crusades* (Muscatine, IA, 1853; reprinted Ann Arbor, 2005).

Boase, Thomas R., *Kingdoms and Strongholds of the Crusaders* (London, 1971).

—— *Castles and Churches of the Crusading Kingdom* (London, 1967).

Bouchard, Constance Britain, 'Eleanor's Divorce from Louis VII: The Uses of Consangunity', in Bonnie Wheeler and John Carmi Parsons eds *Eleanor of Aquitaine, Lord and Lady* (Basingstoke, 2002), 223–35.

——'Family Structure and Family Consciousness among the French Aristocracy in the Ninth to Eleventh Centuries', *Francia* 14 (1986), 639–58.

Bradbury, James, *The Medieval Siege* (Woodbridge, 1992).

Brand, Charles M., *Byzantium Confronts the West 1180–1204* (Cambridge, MA, 1968).

Broadhurst, Karen, 'Henry II of England and Eleanor of Aquitaine: Patrons of Literature in French?', *Viator* 27 (1996), 53–84.

Brooke, Christopher N. L., *The Medieval Idea of Marriage* (Oxford, 1989).

—— 'John of Salisbury and his World', in Michael Wilks ed. *The World of John of Salisbury* (London, 1984), 1–20.

Brown, Elizabeth A. R., 'Eleanor of Aquitaine Reconsidered: The Woman and Her Seasons', in Bonnie Wheeler and John Carmi Parsons eds *Eleanor of Aquitaine, Lord and Lady* (Basingstoke, 2002), 1–54.

—— 'Eleanor of Aquitaine: Parent, Queen and Duchess', in William W. Kibler ed. *Eleanor of Aquitaine, Patron and Politician* (Austin, 1977), 9–23.

Brundage, James A., 'The Canon Law of Divorce in the Mid-Twelfth Century: Louis VII and Eleanor of Aquitaine', in Bonnie Wheeler and John Carmi Parsons eds *Eleanor of Aquitaine, Lord and Lady* (Basingstoke, 2002), 213–21.

—— 'Widows as Disadvantaged Persons in Medieval Canon Law', in Louise Mirrer ed. *Upon My Husband's Death: Widows in the Literature and Histories of Medieval Europe* (Ann Arbor, 1992), 193–206.

—— *Law, Sex and Christian Society in Medieval Europe* (Chicago, 1987).

—— 'Prostitution, Miscegenation and Sexual Purity in the First Crusade', in Peter Edbury ed. *Crusade and Settlement* (Cardiff, 1985), 57–65.

—— Marriage Law in the Latin Kingdom of Jerusalem', in Benjamin Z. Kedar, Hans E. Mayer and Raymond C. Smail eds *Outremer: Studies in the History of the Crusading Kingdom of Jerusalem Presented to Joshua Prawer* (Jerusalem, 1982), 258–71.

—— *Medieval Canon Law and the Crusader* (Madison, 1969).

—— 'The Crusader's Wife; a Canonistic Quandary', *Studia Gratiana* 12 (1967), 425–41.

—— 'The Crusader's Wife Revisited', *Studia Gratiana* 14 (1967), 243–51.

—— 'An Errant Crusader: Stephen of Blois', *Traditio* 16 (1960), 380–94.

Bull, Marcus and Catherine Léglu eds *The World of Eleanor of Aquitaine: Literature and Society in Southern France between the Eleventh and Thirteenth Centuries* (Woodbridge, 2005).

—— *Knightly Piety and the Lay Response to the First Crusade: The Limousin and Gascony c. 970–c. 1130* (Oxford, 1993).

Cahen, Claude, *La Syrie du Nord à l'époque des croisades et la principauté d'Antioche* (Paris, 1940).

Carlson, David, 'Religious Writers and Church Councils', in Howell Chickering and Thomas H. Seiler eds *The Study of Chivalry: Resources and Approaches* (Kalamazoo, 1988), 141–71.

Carr, David, 'Narrative and the Real World: An Argument for Continuity', *History and Theory* 25 (1986), 117–31.

Chibnall, Marjorie, 'Women in Orderic Vitalis', *Haskins Society Journal* 2 (1990), 105–21.

Chickering, Howell, 'Introduction', in Howell Chickering and Thomas H. Seiler eds *The Study of Chivalry: Resources and Approaches* (Kalamazoo, 1988), 1–38.

Christiansen, Eric, *The Northern Crusades and the Baltic Frontier*, 2nd edition (London, 1980).

Clanchy, Michael T., *From Memory to Written Record*, 2nd edition (Oxford, 1993).

Classen, Peter, 'Res Gestae, Universal History, Apocalypse; Visions of Past and Future', in Robert L. Benson and Giles Constable eds *Renaissance and Renewal in the Twelfth Century* (Oxford, 1982), 387–417.

Cole, Penny, "O God, the Heathen have come into Thy Inheritance" (Ps. 78.1): The Theme of Religious Pollution in Crusade Documents, 1095–1188', in Maya Shatzmiller ed. *Crusaders and Muslims in Twelfth Century Syria* (Leiden, 1993), 84–111.

—— *The Preaching of the Crusades to the Holy Land, 1095–1270* (Cambridge, MA, 1991).

Constable, Giles, 'The Historiography of the Crusades', in Angeliki E. Laiou and Roy Parvitz Mottahedeh eds *The Crusades from the Perspective of Byzantium and the Muslim World* (Washington DC, 2001), 1–22.

——'Medieval Charters as a Source for the History of the Crusades', in Peter Edbury ed. *Crusade and Settlement* (Cardiff, 1985), 73–89.

——'The Financing of the Crusades in the Twelfth Century', in Benjamin Z. Kedar, Hans E. Mayer and Raymond C. Smail eds *Outremer: Studies in the History of the Crusading Kingdom of Jerusalem Presented to Joshua Prawer* (Jerusalem, 1982), 64–88.

——'The Second Crusade as Seen by Contemporaries', *Traditio* 9 (1953), 213–79.

Cowdrey, Herbert E. J., 'Pope Gregory VII's "Crusading" Plans of 1074', in Benjamin Z. Kedar ed. *The Horns of Hattin* (Jerusalem, 1992), 27–40.

Craig, Leigh Ann, "Stronger than Men and Braver than Knights": Women and the Pilgrimages to Jerusalem and Rome in the Later Middle Ages', *JMH* 29 (2003), 153–75.

Crouch, David, *The Birth of Nobility: Constructing the Aristocracy in England and France, 900–1300* (Harlow, 2005).

—— *The Image of the Aristocracy in Britain 1000–1300* (London, 1992).

Damien-Grint, Peter, *The New Historians of the Twelfth Century Renaissance* (Woodbridge, 1999).

Daniel, Norman, *The Arabs and Medieval Europe* (London and Beirut, 1975).

Davies, Ralph H. C., 'William of Tyre', in Derek Baker ed. *Relations between East and West in the Middle Ages* (Edinburgh, 1973), 64–76.

DeAragon, RáGena C., 'Wife, Widow, and Mother: Some Comparisons between Eleanor of Aquitaine and Noblewomen of the Anglo-Norman and Angevin World', in Bonnie Wheeler and John Carmi Parsons eds *Eleanor of Aquitaine, Lord and Lady* (Basingstoke, 2002), 97–113.

Derbes, Anne and Mark Sandona, 'Amazons and Crusaders: The *Histoire Universelle* in Flanders and the Holy Land', in Daniel H. Weiss and Lisa Mahoney eds *France and the Holy Land: Frankish Culture at the End of the Crusades* (Baltimore, 2004), 187–229.

Dernbecher, Christine, '*Deus et virum suum diligens.*' *Zur rolle und Bedeutung der Frau im Umfeld der Kreuzzüge* (St Ingbert, 2003).

Dickson, Gary, 'The Genesis of the Children's Crusade (1212)', in his *Religious Enthusiasm in the Medieval West: Revivals, Crusades, Saints* (Aldershot, 2000), 1–52. First published as 'La genèse de la croisade des enfants (1212)', *Bibliothèque de l'École des chartes* 153 (1995).

——'Stephen of Cloyes, Philip Augustus and the Children's Crusade', in Barbara N. Sargent-Baur ed. *Journeys Toward God: Pilgrimage and Crusade* (Kalamazoo, 1992), 83–105.

Dillard, Heath, *Daughters of the Reconquest* (Cambridge, 1989).

Dronke, Peter, *Medieval Latin and the Rise of the European Love Lyric*, 2 vols (Oxford, 1968).

Duby, Georges, *Women of the Twelfth Century: Eleanor of Aquitaine and Six Others*, trans. Jean Birrel (Oxford, 1997).

—— 'Women and Power', in Thomas N. Bisson ed. *Cultures of Power: Lordship, Status and Process in Twelfth Century Europe* (Philadelphia, 1995), 69–85.

—— *Love in Twelfth Century France*, trans. Jane Dunnett (Oxford, 1994).

—— *Love and Marriage in the Middle Ages*, trans. Jane Dunnett (Oxford, 1994).

—— *The Knight, the Lady and the Priest*, trans. Barbara Bray (New York, 1983).

——'The Culture of the Knightly Class: Audience and Patronage', in Robert L. Benson and Giles Constable eds *Renaissance and Renewal in the Twelfth Century* (Oxford, 1982), 248–62.

—— *Medieval Marriage* (Baltimore, 1978).

——'Dans la France du Nord-Ouest au xiie siècle: les "jeunes" de la société aristocratique', *Annales ESC* 19 (1964), 839–43; trans. Cynthia Postan in *The Chivalrous Society* (Berkeley, 1977), 112–22.

Dunbabin, Jean, 'Discovering a Past for the French Aristocracy', in Paul Magdalino ed. *The Perception of the Past in Twelfth Century Europe* (London, 1992), 1–14.

Eckenstein, Lina, *Women under Monasticism: Chapters on Saint-Lore and Convent Life Between A.D. 500 and A.D. 1500* (New York, 1963).

Edbury, Peter W., 'Women and the High Court of Jerusalem according to John of Ibelin', in Damien Coulon, Catherine Otten-Froux, Paul Pagès and Dominique Valérian eds *Chemins d'outremer: Études sur la Méditerranée médiévale offertes à Michel Balard*, 2 vols (Paris, 2004), 1.285–92.

—— *John of Ibelin and the Kingdom of Jerusalem* (Woodbridge, 1997), 88.

—— 'The Lyon *Eracles* and the Old French continuations of William of Tyre', in Benjamin Z. Kedar, Jonathan Riley-Smith and Rudolph Hiestand eds *Montjoie: Studies in Crusade History in Honour of Hans Eberhard Mayer* (Aldershot, 1997), 139–53.

—— 'Preaching the Crusade in Wales', in Alfred Haverkamp and Hanna Vollrath eds *England and Germany in the High Middle Ages* (Oxford, 1996), 221–33.

—— *The Kingdom of Cyprus and the Crusades, 1191–1374* (Cambridge, 1991).

—— with John Gordon Rowe, *William of Tyre, Historian of the Latin East* (Cambridge, 1988).

—— ed. *Crusade and Settlement* (Cardiff, 1985).

Edgington, Susan B., 'Romance and Reality in the Sources for the Sieges of Antioch, 1097–8', in Charalambos Dendrinos, Jonathan Harris, Eirene Harvalia-Crook and Judith Herrin eds *Porphyrogenita. Essays on the History and Literature of Byzantium and the Latin East in Honour of Julian Chrysostomides* (Aldershot, 2003), 33–45.

—— with Sarah Lambert eds *Gendering the Crusades* (Cardiff, 2001).

—— '"Sont çou ore les fems que jo voi la venir?" Women in the *Chanson d'Antioche*', in Susan Edgington and Sarah Lambert eds *Gendering the Crusades* (Cardiff, 2001), 154–62.

—— 'Albert of Aachen, St. Bernard and the Second Crusade', in Jonathan Phillips and Martin Hoch eds *The Second Crusade: Scope and Consequences* (Manchester, 2001), 54–70.

—— 'Albert of Aachen and the Chansons de Geste', in John France and William G. Zajac eds *The Crusades and their Sources: Essays Presented to Bernard Hamilton* (Aldershot, 1998), 23–37.

—— 'The First Crusade: Reviewing the Evidence', in Jonathan Phillips ed. *The First Crusade: Origins and Impact* (Manchester, 1997), 55–77.

Epstein, Steven A., *Genoa and the Genoese 958–1528* (Chapel Hill, 1996).

Evans, Michael R., '"Unfit to Bear Arms": The Gendering of Arms and Armour in Accounts of Women on Crusade', in Susan Edgington and Sarah Lambert eds *Gendering the Crusades* (Cardiff, 2001), 44–58.

Evergates, Theodore, 'Aristocratic Women in the County of Champagne', in Theodore Evergates ed. *Aristocratic Women in Medieval France* (Philadelphia, 1999), 74–110.

—— 'Nobles and Knights in Twelfth Century France', in Thomas N. Bisson ed. *Cultures of Power: Lordship, Status and Process in Twelfth Century Europe* (Philadelphia, 1995), 11–35.

Farmer, Sharon, 'Persuasive Voices: Clerical Images of Medieval wives', *Speculum* 61 (1986), 517–43.

Ferrante, Joan M., *To the Glory of Her Sex: Women's Roles in the Composition of Medieval Texts* (Indianapolis, 1997).

Flori, Jean, *Aliénor d'Aquitaine: La Reine Insoumise* (Paris, 2004).

Folda, Jaroslav, *The Art of the Crusaders in the Holy Land 1098–1197* (Cambridge, 1995).

——'Manuscripts of the *History of Outremer* by William of Tyre: A Handlist', *Scriptorium* 27 (1973), 90–5.

Forey, Alan J., 'Women and the Military Orders in the Twelfth and Thirteenth Centuries', *Studia Monastica* 29 (1987), 63–92.

Foulet, Alfred, 'The Epic Cycle of the Crusades', in Kenneth M. Setton ed. *A History of the Crusades*, 6 vols (Madison, 1969–89), 6.98–115.

France, John, 'Two Types of Vision on the First Crusade: Stephen of Valences and Peter Bartholomew', *Crusades* 5 (2006), 1–20.

——'The Anonymous *Gesta Francorum* and the *Historia Francorum qui ceperunt Iherusalem* of Raymond of Aguilers and the *Historia de Hierosolymitano itinere* of Peter Tudebode: An Analysis of the Textual Relationship between Primary Sources for the First Crusade', in John France and William G. Zajac eds *The Crusades and their Sources: Essays Presented to Bernard Hamilton* (Aldershot, 1998), 39–67.

——'The Use of the Anonymous *Gesta Francorum* in the Early Twelfth Century Sources for the First Crusade', in Alan V. Murray ed. *From Clermont to Jerusalem: The Crusades and Crusader Societies 1095–1500* (Turnhout, 1998), 29–39.

——'Patronage and the Appeal of the First Crusade', in Jonathan Phillips ed. *The First Crusade: Origins and Impact* (Manchester, 1997), 5–20.

Friedman, Yvonne, *Encounter Between Enemies: Captivity and Ransom in the Latin Kingdom of Jerusalem* (Leiden, 2002).

——'Women in Captivity and their Ransom during the Crusader Period', in Michael Goodrich, Sophia Menache and Sylvia Schein eds *Cross-cultural Convergences in the Crusader Period: Essays Presented to Aryeh Grabois on his 65th Birthday* (New York, 1995), 75–87.

Geldsetzer, Sabine, *Frauen auf Kreuzzügen* (Darmstadt, 2003).

Gerish, Deborah, 'Gender Theory', in Helen Nicholson ed. *Palgrave Advances in the Crusades* (Basingstoke, 2005), 130–47.

Gillingham, John, *Richard I* (London, 1999).

——'Roger of Howden on Crusade', in his *Richard Cœur de Lion: Kingship, Chivalry and War in the Twelfth Century* (London, 1994), 141–53.

——'Richard I and Berengaria of Navarre', in his *Richard Cœur de Lion: Kingship, Chivalry and War in the Twelfth Century* (London, 1994), 119–39.

——'Love, Marriage and Politics in the Twelfth Century', in his *Richard Cœur de Lion: Kingship, Chivalry and War in the Twelfth Century* (London, 1994), 243–55.

——'Some Legends of Richard the Lionheart: Their Development and their Influence', in Janet L. Nelson ed. *Richard Cœur de Lion in History and Myth* (Exeter, 1992), 61–6.

Gold, Penny Schine, *The Lady and the Virgin: Image, Attitude and Experience in Twelfth Century France* (Chicago, 1985).

Goodich, Michael E., *From Birth to Old Age: The Human Life-Cycle in Medieval Thought 1250–1350* (London, 1989).

Grant, Lindy, *Abbot Suger of Saint Denis: Church and State in Twelfth-Century France* (London, 1998).

Grocock, Christopher W., 'Ovid the Crusader', in Charles Martindale ed. *Ovid Renewed* (Cambridge, 1988), 55–69.

Guth, Klaus, 'Patronage of Elizabeth in the High Middle Ages in Hospitals of the Teutonic Order in the Bailiwick of Franconia', in Malcolm Barber ed. *The Military Orders: Fighting for the Faith and Caring for the Sick* (Aldershot, 1994), 245–52.

Hamilton, Bernard, 'The Old French Translation of William of Tyre as an Historical Source', in Peter Edbury and Jonathan Phillips eds *The Experience of Crusading: Defining the Crusader Kingdom* (Cambridge, 2003), 2.93–112.

—— *The Leper King and his Heirs: Baldwin IV and the Crusader Kingdom of Jerusalem* (Cambridge, 2000).

—— 'Our Lady of Saidnaiya: An Orthodox Shrine Revered by Muslims and Knights Templar at the Time of the Crusades', in Robert N. Swanson ed. *The Holy Land, Holy Lands, and Christian History* (Woodbridge, 2000), 207–15.

—— 'King Consorts of Jerusalem and their Entourages from the West from 1186 to 1250', in Hans E. Mayer ed. *Die Kreuzfahrerstaaten als multikulturel Gesellschaft* (Munich, 1997), 13–24. Reprinted in Bernard Hamilton, *Crusaders, Cathars and the Holy Places* (Aldershot, 1999).

—— 'Eleanor of Castile and the Crusading Movement', in B. Arbel ed. *Intercultural Contacts in the Medieval Mediterranean* (London, 1996), 92–103. Reprinted in Bernard Hamilton, *Crusaders, Cathars and the Holy Places* (Aldershot, 1999).

—— 'Miles of Plancy and the Fief of Beirut', in Benjamin Z. Kedar ed. *The Horns of Hattin* (Jerusalem, 1992), 136–46. Reprinted in Bernard Hamilton, *Crusaders, Cathars and the Holy Places* (Aldershot, 1999).

—— 'The Titular Nobility of the Latin East: the Case of Agnes of Courtenay', in Peter Edbury ed. *Crusade and Settlement* (Cardiff, 1985), 197–203. Reprinted in Bernard Hamilton, *Crusaders, Cathars and the Holy Places* (Aldershot, 1999).

—— 'Ralph of Domfront, Patriarch of Antioch (1135–40)', *Nottingham Medieval Studies* 28 (1984). Reprinted in Bernard Hamilton, *Crusaders, Cathars and the Holy Places* (Aldershot, 1999).

—— 'The Elephant of Christ: Reynald of Châtillon', in Derek Baker ed. *Religious Motivation: Biographical and Sociological Problems for the Church Historian* (Oxford, 1978), 97–108.

—— 'Women in the Crusader States: The Queens of Jerusalem (1100–1190)', in Derek Baker ed. *Medieval Women* (Oxford, 1978), 143–74. Reprinted in Bernard Hamilton, *Crusaders, Cathars and the Holy Places* (Aldershot, 1999).

Harari, Yuval Noah, 'Eyewitnessing in Accounts of the First Crusade: The Gesta Francorum and Other Contemporary Narratives', *Crusades* 3 (2004), 77–99.

Harris, Jonathan, *Byzantium and the Crusades* (London, 2003).

Hay, David, 'Gender Bias and Religious Intolerance in Accounts of the "Massacres" of the First Crusade', in Michael Gervers and James M. Powell eds *Tolerance and Intolerance: Social Conflict in the Age of the Crusades* (New York, 2001), 3–10.

de Hemptinne, Thérèse, 'Les épouses de croisés et pèlerins flamands aux xɪᵉ et xɪɪᵉ siècles: l'exemple des comtesses de Flandre Clémence et Sibylle', in Michel Balard ed. *Autour de la Première Croisade* (Paris, 1996), 83–95.

Herlihy, David, *Medieval Households* (Cambridge, MA, 1985).

Hiestand, Rudolph, 'Die Herren von Sidon und die Thronfolgekrise des Jahres 1163 im Köngreich Jerusalem', in Benjamin Z. Kedar, Jonathan Riley-Smith and Rudolph Hiestand eds *Montjoie: Studies in Crusade History in Honour of Hans Eberhard Mayer* (Aldershot, 1997), 77–90.

——'Il Cronista Medievale e il suo pubblico: Alcune osservazione in margine alla storiographia delle crociate', *Annali della Facoltà di lettere e filosophia dell'università di Napoli* 27 (1984–5), 207–27.

Hill, Barbara, *Imperial Woman in Byzantium 1025–1204: Patronage, Power and Ideology* (Edinburgh, 1999).

Hoch, Martin, 'The Price of Failure: The Second Crusade as a Turning Point in the History of the Latin East', in Jonathan Phillips and Martin Hoch eds *The Second Crusade: Scope and Consequences* (Manchester, 2001), 180–200.

Hodgson, Natasha, 'Women and Crusade', in Alan V. Murray ed. *The Crusades: An Encylopaedia*, 4 vols (Santa Barbara, 2006), vol. 4, 1285–1290.

——'Nobility, Women and Historical Narratives of the Crusades and the Latin East', *Al-Masaq: Islam and the Medieval Mediterranean* 17 (2005), 61–85.

——'The Role of Kerbogha's Mother in the *Gesta Francorum* and Selected Chronicles of the First Crusade', in Susan Edgington and Sarah Lambert eds *Gendering the Crusades* (Cardiff, 2001), 163–76.

Hoff, Joan, 'Gender as a Postmodern Category of Paralysis', *Women's Historical Review* 3 (1994), 149–68.

Hollingsworth, Thomas H., 'A Demographic Study of the British Ducal Families', *Population Studies* 11 (1957), 4–26.

Hollister, Charles Warren, 'Anglo-Norman Political Culture and the Twelfth Century Renaissance', in Charles Warren Hollister ed. *Anglo-Norman Political Culture and the Twelfth Century Renaissance: Proceedings of the Borchard Conference on Anglo-Norman History, 1995* (Woodbridge, 1997), 1–16.

Holt, Peter M., 'Baybars' Treaty with the Lady of Beirut in 667/1269', in Peter Edbury ed. *Crusade and Settlement* (Cardiff, 1985), 242–5.

Housley, Norman, *The Later Crusades 1274–1580: From Lyons to Alcazar* (Oxford, 1992).

van Houts, Elisabeth, *Memory and Gender in Medieval Europe 900–1200* (London, 1999).

Hughes, Diane Owen, 'From Brideprice to Dowry in Mediterranean Europe', *Journal of Family History* 3 (1978), 262–96.

Huneycutt, Lois L., '"Proclaiming her dignity abroad": The Literary and Artistic Network of Mathilda of Scotland, Queen of England, 1100–1118', in June Hall McCash ed. *The Cultural Patronage of Medieval Women* (Athens, GA, 1996), 155–74.

Jackson, William E., 'Poet, Woman and Crusade in Songs of Marcabru, Guiot de Dijon, and Albrecht von Johansdorf', *Medievalia* 22 (1999), 265–89.

Jacoby, David, 'Society, Culture, and the Arts in Crusader Acre', in Daniel H. Weiss and Lisa Mahoney eds *France and the Holy Land: Frankish Culture at the End of the Crusades* (Baltimore, 2004), 97–137.

Jewell, Helen, *Women in Medieval England* (Manchester, 1996).

Johansson, Warren and William A. Percy, 'Homosexuality', in Vern L. Bullough and James A. Brundage eds *Handbook of Medieval Sexuality* (London, 1996), 155–89.

Johns, Susan M., *Noblewomen, Aristocracy and Power in the Twelfth Century Anglo-Norman Realm* (Manchester, 2003).

Jordan, William C., 'The Representation of the Crusades in the Songs Attributed to Thibaud, Count Palatine of Champagne', *JMH* 25 (1999), 27–34.

—— *Louis IX and the Challenge of the Crusade* (Princeton, 1979).

Kaeuper, Richard, *Chivalry and Violence in Medieval Europe* (Oxford, 1999).

Kantor, Jonathan, 'A Psychological Source: The *Memoirs* of Abbot Guibert of Nogent', *JMH* 2 (1976), 281–303.

Kay, Sarah, *The Chansons de geste in the Age of Romance: Political Fictions* (Oxford, 1995).

Kedar, Benjamin Z., 'The Jerusalem Massacre of July 1099 in the Western Historiography of the Crusades', *Crusades* 3 (2004), 15–75.

—— ed. *The Horns of Hattin* (Jerusalem, 1992).

—— 'The Patriarch Eraclius', in Benjamin Z. Kedar, Hans E. Mayer and Raymond C. Smail eds *Outremer: Studies in the History of the Crusading Kingdom of Jerusalem Presented to Joshua Prawer* (Jerusalem, 1982), 177–204.

—— 'The Passenger List of a Crusader Ship, 1250: Towards the Popular Element on the Seventh Crusade', *Studi Medievali*, Series 3 (1972), 269–79.

Keen, Maurice, *Chivalry* (New Haven, 1984).

Kostick, Conor, 'Women and the First Crusade', in C. Meek and C. Lawless eds *Studies on Medieval and Early Modern Women*, vol. 3 (Dublin, 2005), 57–68.

Krey, August C., 'A Neglected Passage in the *Gesta* and its Bearing on the Literature of the First Crusade', in Louis J. Paetow ed. *The Crusades and Other Historical Essays Presented to Dana C. Munro* (New York, 1928), 68–76.

Labarge, Margaret Wade, *Women in Medieval Life: A Small Sound of the Trumpet* (London, 1986).

Lambert, Sarah, 'Crusading or Spinning', in Susan Edgington and Sarah Lambert eds *Gendering the Crusades* (Cardiff, 2001), 1–15.

—— 'Queen or Consort: Rulership and Politics in the Latin East 1118–1228', in Anne Duggan ed. *Queens and Queenship in Medieval Europe* (Woodbridge, 1997), 153–69.

LaMonte, John L., 'The Lords of Sidon in the Twelfth and Thirteenth Centuries', *Byzantion* 17 (1944–5), 183–211.

—— 'The Lords of le Puiset on Crusade', *Speculum* 17 (1942), 100–18.

Leclercq, Jean, *Monks on Marriage: A Twelfth Century View* (New York, 1982).

Lee, Becky R., 'A Company of Women and Men: Men's Recollections of Childbirth in Medieval England', *Journal of Family History* 27 (2002), 92–100.

Lewis, Katherine J., Noel James Menuge and Kim Phillips eds *Young Medieval Women* (Stroud, 1999).

Leyser, Conrad, 'Custom, Truth and Gender in Eleventh Century Reform', in Robert N. Swanson ed. *Gender and the Christian Religion* (Woodbridge, 1998), 75–91.

Leyser, Henrietta, *Medieval Women: A Social History of Women in England 450–1500* (London, 1995).

Lilie, Ralph-Johannes, *Byzantium and the Crusader States, 1096–1204*, trans. J. C. Morris and Jean E. Ridings (Oxford, 1993).

Lindkvist, Thomas, 'Crusades and Crusading Ideology in Sweden', in Alan V. Murray ed. *Crusade and Conversion on the Baltic Frontier 1150–1500* (Aldershot, 2001), 119–30.

Lindsay, Jack, *The Troubadours and their World of the Twelfth and Thirteenth Centuries* (London, 1976).

Livermore, Harold, 'The Conquest of Lisbon and its Author', *Portuguese Studies* 6 (1990), 1–16.

Livingstone, Amy, 'Powerful Allies and Dangerous Adversaries; Noblewomen in Medieval Society', in Linda E. Mitchell ed. *Women in Medieval Western European Culture* (New York, 1999), 7–30.

——'Aristocratic Women in the Chartrain', in Theodore Evergates ed. *Aristocratic Women in Medieval France* (Philadelphia, 1999), 44–73.

Lloyd, Simon, *English Society and the Crusade 1216–1307* (Oxford, 1988).

Lock, Peter, *The Franks in the Aegean, 1204–1500* (London, 1995).

LoPrete, Kimberley A., 'Adela of Blois: Familial Alliances and Female Lordship', in Theodore Evergates ed. *Aristocratic Women in Medieval France* (Philadelphia, 1999), 7–43.

Lower, Michael, *The Baron's Crusade: A Call to Arms and its Consequences* (Philadelphia, 2005).

Lusse, Jackie, 'D'Étienne à Jean de Joinville: L'ascension d'une famille seigneuriale champenoise', in Dominique Guénot ed. *Jean de Joinville: De la Champagne aux Royaumes d'Outremer* (Paris, 1998), 1–47.

Magdalino, Paul, *The Empire of Manuel I Komnenos 1143–1180* (Cambridge, 1993).

Maier, Christoph T., 'The Roles of Women in the Crusade Movement: A Survey', in *JMH* 30 (2004), 61–82.

——'The *Bible moralisée* and the Crusades', in Marcus Bull and Norman Housley eds *The Experience of Crusading: Western Approaches* (Cambridge, 2003), I.209–22.

Marshall, Christopher, *Warfare in the Latin East, 1192–1291* (Cambridge, 1992).

Matthews, Donald, *The Norman Kingdom of Sicily* (Cambridge, 1992).

Mayer, Hans E., 'The Beginnings of King Amalric of Jerusalem', in Benjamin Z. Kedar ed. *The Horns of Hattin* (Jerusalem, 1992), 121–35.

——'Angevins *versus* Normans: The New Men of King Fulk of Jerusalem', *American Philosophical Society* 133 (1989), 1–25.

——'Guillaume de Tyr à l'École', *Mémoires de l'Académie des sciences arts et belles lettres de Dijon* 127 (1988), 257–65.

——'Die Legitimität Balduins iv von Jerusalem und das testament der Agnes von Courtenay', *Historisches Jahrbuch* 108 (1988), 63–89.

——'The Succession to Baldwin ii of Jerusalem', *Dumbarton Oaks Papers* 39 (1985), 139–47.

——'Études sur l'histoire de Baudouin i^{er} Roi de Jérusalem', in his *Melanges sur L'Histoire du Royaume Latin de Jérusalem* (Paris, 1984), 10–91.

——'Carving up Crusaders: The Early Ibelins and Ramlas', in Benjamin Z. Kedar, Hans E. Mayer and Raymond C. Smail eds *Outremer: Studies in the History of the Crusading Kingdom of Jerusalem Presented to Joshua Prawer* (Jerusalem, 1982), 102–18.

——'Studies in the History of Queen Melisende of Jerusalem', *Dumbarton Oaks Papers* 26 (1972), 93–182.

Mazeika, Rasa, "Nowhere was the Fragility of their Sex Apparent": Women Warriors in the Baltic Crusade Chronicles', in Alan V. Murray ed. *From Clermont to Jerusalem: The Crusades and Crusader Societies 1095–1500* (Turnhout, 1998), 229–48.

McCannon, Afrodesia E., 'Two Capetian Queens as the Foreground for an Aristocrat's Anxiety in the Vie de Saint Louis', in Kathleen Nolan ed. *Capetian Women* (London, 2003), 163–75.

McCracken, Peggy, 'Scandalizing Desire: Eleanor of Aquitaine and the Chroniclers', in Bonnie Wheeler and John Carmi Parsons eds *Eleanor of Aquitaine, Lord and Lady* (Basingstoke, 2002), 247–63.

McLaughlin, Megan, 'The Woman Warrior; Gender, Warfare and Society in Medieval Europe', *Women's Studies* 17 (1990), 193–209.

McNamara, Jo Ann, 'Women and Power through the Family Revisited', in Mary Erler and Maryanne Kowaleski eds *Gendering the Master Narrative: Women and Power in the Middle Ages* (London, 2003), 17–30.

——'The *Herrenfrage*: The Restructuring of the Gender System, 1050–1150', in Clare A. Lees, with Thelma Fenster and Jo Ann McNamara eds *Medieval Masculinities: Regarding Men in the Middle Ages* (Minneapolis, 1994), 3–29.

——and Suzanne Wemple, 'The Power of Women through the Family in Medieval Europe, 500–1100', *Feminist Studies* 1 (1973), 126–41. Reprinted in Mary Erler and Maryanne Kowaleski eds *Women and Power in the Middle Ages* (Athens, GA, 1988), 83–101.

Menache, Sophia, *The Vox Dei: Communication in the Middle Ages* (Oxford, 1990).

Morgan, Margaret R., 'The Rothelin Continuation of William of Tyre', in Benjamin Z. Kedar, Hans E. Mayer and Raymond C. Smail eds *Outremer: Studies in the History of the Crusading Kingdom of Jerusalem Presented to Joshua Prawer* (Jerusalem, 1982), 244–57.

——*The Chronicle of Ernoul and the Continuations of William of Tyre* (Oxford, 1973).

Morris, Colin, 'Picturing the Crusades: The Uses of Visual Propaganda, c. 1095–1250', in John France and William G. Zajac eds *The Crusades and their Sources: Essays Presented to Bernard Hamilton* (Aldershot, 1998), 195–216.

——'The *Gesta Francorum* as Narrative History', *Reading Medieval Studies* 19 (1993), 55–71.

——'Policy and Visions. The Case of the Holy Lance at Antioch', in John Gillingham and James C. Holt eds *War and Government in the Middle Ages: Essays in honour of J. O. Prestwich* (Cambridge, 1984), 33–45.

Mosher Stuard, Susan, 'The Chase after Theory: Considering Medieval Women', *Gender and History* 4 (1992), 135–46.

Murray, Alan V., *The Crusader Kingdom of Jerusalem: A Dynastic History 1099–1125* (Oxford, 2000).

——'Daimbert of Pisa, the *Domus Godefridi* and the Accession of Baldwin I of Jerusalem', in Alan V. Murray ed. *From Clermont to Jerusalem: The Crusades and Crusader Societies 1095–1500* (Turnhout, 1998), 81–102.

——'Baldwin II and his Nobles: Baronial Factionalism and Dissent in the Kingdom of Jerusalem', *Nottingham Medieval Studies* 38 (1994), 60–85.

Nelson, Janet L., 'Gender, Memory and Social Power', in Pauline Stafford and Anneke B. Mulder-Bakker eds *Gendering the Middle Ages* (Oxford, 2001), 192–204.

Nicholas, David, *Medieval Flanders* (Harlow, 1992).

Nicholas, Karen S., 'Countesses as Rulers in Flanders', in Theodore Evergates ed. *Aristocratic Women in Medieval France* (Philadelphia, 1999), 111–37.

Nicholson, Helen, 'Women on the Third Crusade', *JMH* 23 (1997), 335–49.

Noble, Peter, 'Villehardouin, Robert de Clari and Henri de Valenciennes: Their Different Approaches to the Fourth Crusade', in Erik Kooper ed. *The Medieval Chronicle: Proceedings of the 1st International Conference on the Medieval Chronicle* (Amsterdam, 1999), 202–11.

Orme, Nicholas, *Medieval Children* (New Haven, 2001).

—— *From Childhood to Chivalry: The Education of the English Kings and Aristocracy 1066–1530* (London, 1984).

Owen, Douglas D. R., *Eleanor of Aquitaine, Queen and Legend* (Oxford, 1993).

Parsons, John Carmi and Bonnie Wheeler, 'Medieval Mothering, Medieval Motherers', in John Carmi Parsons and Bonnie Wheeler eds *Medieval Mothering* (New York, 1996), ix–xvii.

——'The Pregnant Queen as Counsellor and the Medieval Construction of Motherhood', in John Carmi Parsons and Bonnie Wheeler eds *Medieval Mothering* (New York, 1996), 39–61.

——'Family, Sex, and Power: The Rhythms of Medieval Queenship', in John Carmi Parsons ed. *Medieval Queenship* (Stroud, 1994), 1–11.

——'Mothers, Daughters Marriage, Power: Some Plantagenet Evidence 1150–1500', in John Carmi Parsons ed. *Medieval Queenship* (Stroud, 1994), 63–78.

Partner, Nancy F., 'The Family Romance of Guibert of Nogent: His Story/Her Story', in John Carmi Parsons and Bonnie Wheeler eds *Medieval Mothering* (New York, 1996), 359–79.

Partner, P., *The Lands of St. Peter* (London, 1972).

Paterson, Linda M., 'Occitan Literature and the Holy Land', in Marcus Bull and Catherine Léglu eds *The World of Eleanor of Aquitaine: Literature and Society in Southern France between the Eleventh and Thirteenth Centuries* (Woodbridge, 2005), 83–99.

Phillips, Jonathan, *The Second Crusade: Extending the Frontiers of Christendom* (New Haven, 2007).

——'Odo of Deuil's *De Profectione Ludovici VII in Orientem* as a source for the Second Crusade', in Marcus Bull and Norman Housley eds *The Experience of Crusading: Western Approaches* (Cambridge, 2003), 1.80–95.

——'Ideas of Crusade and Holy War in the Conquest of Lisbon', in Robert N. Swanson ed. *The Holy Land, Holy Lands, and Christian History* (Woodbridge, 2000), 23–141.

——'The Murder of Charles the Good and the Second Crusade: Household, Nobility, and Traditions of Crusading in Medieval Flanders', *Medieval Prosopography* 19 (1998), 55–76.

—— *Defenders of the Holy Land: Relations between the Latin East and the West 1119–1187* (Oxford, 1996).

Phillips, Kim M., *Medieval Maidens: Young Women and Gender in England c. 1270– c. 1540* (Manchester, 2003).

Porges, Walter, 'The Clergy, the Poor and the Non-combatants on the First Crusade', *Speculum* 21 (1946), 1–23.

Poulet, André, 'Capetian Women and the Regency: The Genesis of a Vocation', in John Carmi Parsons ed. *Medieval Queenship* (Stroud, 1994), 93–116.

Powell, James M., 'Myth, Legend, Propaganda, History: The First Crusade, 1140– ca.1300', in Michel Balard ed. *Autour de la Première Croisade* (Paris, 1996), 127–41.

——'The Role of Women on the Fifth Crusade', in Benjamin Z. Kedar ed. *The Horns of Hattin* (Jerusalem, 1992), 294–301.

—— *Anatomy of a Crusade, 1213–1221* (Philadelphia, 1986).

Power, Daniel, *The Norman Frontier in the Early Twelfth and Early Thirteenth Centuries* (Cambridge, 2004).

——with Naomi Standen eds *Frontiers in Question, Eurasian Borderlands, 700–1700* (Basingstoke, 1999).

Power, Eileen, *Medieval Women*, ed. Michael M. Postan (Cambridge, 1975).

Prawer, Joshua, *Crusader Institutions* (Oxford, 1980).

Pringle, Denys, *The Churches of the Crusader Kingdom of Jerusalem*, 3 vols (Cambridge, 1993–2007).

Prutz, Hans, 'Studien über Wilhelm von Tyrus', *Neues Archiv der Gesellachft für ältere deutsche Geschichtskunde* 8 (1883), 91–132.

Pryor, John, 'The Eracles and William of Tyre: An Interim Report', in Benjamin Z. Kedar ed. *The Horns of Hattin* (Jerusalem, 1992), 270–93.

—— *Geography, Technology and War: Studies in the Maritime History of the Mediterranean 649–1571* (Cambridge, 1992).

Purcell, Maureen, 'Women Crusaders, a Temporary Canonical Aberration?', in Leighton O Frappell ed. *Principalities, Power and Estates: Studies in Medieval and Early Modern Government and Society* (Adelaide, 1979), 57–67.

Raedts, Peter, 'The Children's Crusade of 1212', *JMH* 3 (1977), 279–323.

Richard, Jean, *Louis IX, Crusader King of France*, trans. Jean Birrell (Cambridge, 1992).

Riley-Smith, Jonathan, 'Casualties and the Number of Knights on the First Crusade', *Crusades* 1 (2002), 13–28.

—— *The First Crusaders 1095–1131* (Cambridge, 1997).

—— 'Families, Crusades and Settlemant in the Latin East 1102–1131', in Hans E. Mayer ed. *Die Kreuzfahrerstaaten als multikulturel Gesellschaft* (Munich, 1997), 1–12.

—— 'The Crusading Movement and Historians', in Jonathan Riley-Smith ed. *The Oxford Illustrated History of the Crusades* (Oxford, 1995), 1–12.

—— 'Family Traditions and Participation in the Second Crusade', in Michael Gervers ed. *The Second Crusade and the Cistercians* (New York, 1992), 101–8.

—— 'Crusading as an Act of Love', *History* 65 (1980), 177–92.

—— *The Feudal Nobility and the Kingdom of Jerusalem, 1174–1277* (London, 1973).

Robinson, Ian S., *The Papacy 1073–1198: Continuity and Innovation* (Cambridge, 1990).

Rosenthal, Joel T., 'Medieval Longevity and the Secular Peerage, 1350–1500', *Population Studies* 11 (1973), 287–93.

Rousseau, Constance M., 'Home Front and Battlefield: The Gendering of Papal Crusading Policy (1095–1221)', in Susan Edgington and Sarah Lambert eds *Gendering the Crusades* (Cardiff, 2001), 31–44.

Michael Routledge, 'Songs', in Jonathan Riley-Smith ed. *The Oxford Illustrated History of the Crusades* (Oxford, 1995), 91–111.

Rubenstein, Jay, 'What is the Gesta Francorum, and Who was Peter Tudebode?', *Revue Mabillon* 16 (2005), 179–204.

Runciman, Steven, *A History of the Crusades*, 3 vols (Cambridge, 1951–4).

Sassier, Yves, *Louis VII* (Paris, 1991).

Schein, Sylvia, 'Philip IV and the Crusade: A Reconsideration', in Peter Edbury ed. *Crusade and Settlement* (Cardiff, 1985), 121–6.

Schulz, James A., *The Knowledge of Childhood in the German Middle Ages 1100–1350* (Philadelphia, 1995).

Shadis, Miriam, 'Blanche of Castile and Facinger's "Medieval Queenship"', in Kathleen Nolan ed. *Capetian Women* (London, 2003), 137–61.

Shahar, Shulamith, *The Fourth Estate: A History hhhhhhhof Women in the Middle Ages*, 2nd edition (London, 1991).

—— *Childhood in the Middle Ages*, trans. Chaya Galai (London, 1990).

Sheehan, Michael M., 'The Influence of Canon Law on the Property Rights of Married Women in England', in James K. Farge ed. *Marriage, Family and Law in Medieval Europe: Collected Studies* (Cardiff, 1996), 16–30.

Shopkow, Leah, *History and Community: Norman Historical Writing in the Eleventh and Twelfth Centuries* (Washington DC, 1997).

Siberry, Elizabeth, 'The Crusader's Departure and Return: A Much Later Perspective', in Susan Edgington and Sarah Lambert eds *Gendering the Crusades* (Cardiff, 2001), 177–90.

—— *The New Crusaders: Images of the Crusades in the Nineteenth and Early Twentieth Centuries* (Aldershot, 2000).

—— *Criticism of Crusading 1095–1274* (Oxford, 1985).

Sivery, Gérard, *Blanche de Castille* (Paris, 1990).

Skinner, Patricia, *Women in Medieval Italian Society 500–1200* (Harlow, 2001).

Slack, Corliss Konwiser, *Crusade Charters 1138–1270* (Tempe, 2001).

Smail, Raymond C., 'The Predicaments of Guy of Lusignan 1183–1187', in Benjamin Z. Kedar, Hans E. Mayer and Raymond C. Smail eds *Outremer: Studies in the History of the Crusading Kingdom of Jerusalem Presented to Joshua Prawer* (Jerusalem, 1982), 159–72.

Spiegel, Gabrielle M., 'Theory into Practice: Reading Medieval Chronicles', in Erik Kooper ed. *The Medieval Chronicle: Proceedings of the 1st International Conference on the Medieval Chronicle* (Amsterdam, 1999), 1–12.

—— *The Past as Text* (London, 1997).

—— *Romancing the Past: The Rise of Vernacular Prose Historiography in Thirteenth Century France* (Berkeley, 1993).

Spreadbury, Jo, 'The Gender of the Church: The Female Image of *Ecclesia* in the Middle Ages', *Studies in Church History* 34 (1998), 93–103.

Stafford, Pauline, 'The Portrayal of Royal Women in England, Mid-Tenth to Mid-Twelfth Centuries', in John Carmi Parsons ed. *Medieval Queenship* (Stroud, 1994), 143–67.

Stevenson, William B. *The Crusaders in the East* (Cambridge, 1907).

Strickland, Matthew, *War and Chivalry* (Cambridge, 1996).

Stroll, Mary, 'Maria Regina: Papal Symbol', in Anne Duggan ed. *Queens and Queenship in Medieval Europe* (Woodbridge, 1997), 173–203.

Swanson, Robert N. L., *The Twelfth Century Renaissance* (Manchester, 1999).

Tessera, Miriam Rita, 'Philip Count of Flanders and Hildegard of Bingen: Crusading against the Saracens or Crusading against Deadly Sin', in Susan Edgington and Sarah Lambert eds *Gendering the Crusades* (Cardiff, 2001), 77–93.

Thomas, Hugh M., *Vassals, Heiresses, Crusaders and Thugs: The Gentry of Angevin Yorkshire 1154–1216* (Philadelphia, 1993).

Thompson, Rodney. M., *William of Malmesbury*, 2nd edition (Woodbridge, 2003).

Throop, Susanna, 'Vengeance and the Crusades', *Crusades* 5 (2006), 21–38.

Tibble, Steven, *Monarchy and Lordships in the Latin Kingdom of Jerusalem 1099–1291* (Oxford, 1989).

Treadgold, Warren, *A History of the Byzantine State and Society* (Stanford, 1997).

Trindade, Ann, *Berengaria: In Search of Richard the Lionheart's Queen* (Dublin, 1999).

Trotter, David A., *Medieval French Literature and the Crusades, 1100–1300* (Geneva, 1988).

Tyerman, Christopher, *The Invention of the Crusades* (London, 1998).

—— *England and the Crusades, 1095–1588* (London, 1988).

Vaughan, Richard, *Matthew Paris* (Cambridge, 1958).

Vaughn, Sally, 'Robert of Meulan and Raison d'État in the Anglo-Norman State', 1093–1118', *Albion* 10 (1978), 352–73.

Walker, Curtis H., 'Eleanor of Aquitaine and the Disaster at Cadmos Mountain on the Second Crusade', *American Historical Review* 55 (1950), 857–61.

Ward, Jennifer, *Women of the English Nobility and Gentry 1066–1500* (Manchester, 1995).

Warren, Frederick M., 'The Enamoured Moslem Princess in Orderic Vitalis and the French Epic', *Publications of the Modern Language Association of America* 29 (1914), 341–58.

Webb, Diana, *Medieval European Pilgrimage 700–1500* (Basingstoke, 2002).

de Weever, Jacqueline, *Sheba's Daughters: Whitening and Demonising the Saracen Woman in Medieval French Epic* (London, 1998).

White, Hayden, *The Content of the Form: Narrative Discourse and Historical Representation* (Baltimore, 1987).

Wogan-Browne, Jocelyn, *Saints' Lives and Women's Literary Culture: Virginity and its Authorisations* (Oxford, 2001).

Wolf, Kenneth Baxter, 'Crusade and Narrative: Bohemond and the *Gesta Francorum*', *JMH* 17 (1991), 207–16.

Wolff, Robert Lee, 'Baldwin of Flanders and Hainault, First Latin Emperor of Constantinople: His Life, Death and Resurrection, 1172–1225', *Speculum* 27 (1952), 281–322.

Index

Warfare in History

The Battle of Hastings: Sources and Interpretations, *edited and introduced by Stephen Morillo*

Infantry Warfare in the Early Fourteenth Century: Discipline, Tactics, and Technology, *Kelly DeVries*

The Art of Warfare in Western Europe during the Middle Ages, from the Eighth Century to 1340 (second edition), *J.F. Verbruggen*

Knights and Peasants: The Hundred Years War in the French Countryside, *Nicholas Wright*

Society at War: The Experience of England and France during the Hundred Years War, *edited by Christopher Allmand*

The Circle of War in the Middle Ages: Essays on Medieval Military and Naval History, *edited by Donald J. Kagay and L.J. Andrew Villalon*

The Anglo-Scots Wars, 1513–1550: A Military History, *Gervase Phillips*

The Norwegian Invasion of England in 1066, *Kelly DeVries*

The Wars of Edward III: Sources and Interpretations, *edited by Clifford J. Rogers*

The Battle of Agincourt: Sources and Interpretations, *Anne Curry*

War Cruel and Sharp: English Strategy under Edward III, 1327–1360, *Clifford J. Rogers*

The Normans and their Adversaries at War: Essays in Memory of C. Warren Hollister, *edited by Richard P. Abels and Bernard S. Bachrach*

The Battle of the Golden Spurs (Courtrai, 11 July 1302): A Contribution to the History of Flanders' War of Liberation, 1297–1305, *J.F. Verbruggen*

War at Sea in the Middle Ages and the Renaissance, *edited by John B. Hattendorf and Richard W. Unger*

Swein Forkbeard's Invasions and the Danish Conquest of England, 991–1017, *Ian Howard*

Religion and the conduct of war, c.300–1215, *David S. Bachrach*

Warfare in Medieval Brabant, 1356–1406, *Sergio Boffa*

Renaissance Military Memoirs: War, History and Identity, 1450–1600, *Yuval Harari*

The Place of War in English History, 1066–1214, *J.O. Prestwich, edited by Michael Prestwich*

War and the Soldier in the Fourteenth Century, *Adrian R. Bell*

German War Planning, 1891–1914: Sources and Interpretations, *Terence Zuber*

The Battle of Crécy, 1346, *Andrew Ayton and Sir Philip Preston*